Computer Fundamentals and Programming

Computer Fundamentals and Programming

Ashok N. Kamthane
Associate Professor,
Department of Electronics and Telecommunication Engineering
S.G.G.S. Institute of Engineering and Technology,
Nanded, Maharashtra

and

ITL Education Solutions Limited
Research and Development Wing
New Delhi

ISBN 9788131794791
First Impression, 2013
Second Impression, 2021
Third Impression, 2024

Published by Pearson India Education Services Pvt. Ltd, CIN: U72200TN2005PTC057128.

Head Office: 1st Floor, Berger Tower, Plot No. C-001A/2, Sector 16B, Noida - 201 301, Uttar Pradesh, India.
Registered Office: Featherlite, 'The Address' 5th Floor, Survey No 203/10B, 200 Ft MMRD Road, Zamin Pallavaram, Chennai – 600 044.
Website: in.pearson.com; Email: companysecretary.india@pearson.com

Printed in India at: Manipal Technologies Limited, Manipal

To my beloved parents
Late Sumanbai and Namdev Kamthane

Ashok N. Kamthane

I would like to dedicate this book to my uncle,
Shri G.K. Jaju,
for his understanding, constant support and trust in me.
He has always inspired me to aim higher and achieve bigger.
He has been a great friend, philosopher and guide.

Rohit Khurana

Contents

Preface

The world today is witnessing a new kind of revolution—the *Information Revolution*—ushered in by technology. This revolution is far more sweeping than any other revolution in history in its reach and influence, bringing fundamental changes in all aspects of our life. Information technology (IT) is the engine used to drive useful information systems. This includes computers, software, and the Internet/intranet and telecommunication systems. IT provides the means for collecting, storing, encoding, processing, analyzing, transmitting, receiving and printing text, audio or video information.

C is one of the famous and important programming languages because of its qualities. Its syntax looks like general English language, and hence, it is simple and easy to learn. Besides, it is built with abundant features by the developer, which is presented in the book. In India and worldwide, most of the skilled people use C as a programming language.

Almost all boards of examinations, universities and Government of India have recognized the importance of software and its impact on economy. Most of universities, boards, and training institutes have included C language in the curricula. It is expected to learn the basics of a language, develop programming skills and acquire expertise to develop software packages and applications.

Keeping pace with these trends and to meet the requirements of modern curricula, all universities have integrated the study of computer fundamentals and C programming in B.Tech., MCA, MBA, BCA and B.Sc. courses. The book in your hand, *Computer Fundamentals and Programming*, in its unique easy-to-understand question-and-answer format directly addresses the need of students enrolled in these courses.

The questions and corresponding answers in this book have been designed and selected to cover all the fundamentals that one must learn in order to pursue virtually any endeavour in the IT field.

Numerous multiple-choice questions, programs and their outputs, and questions to identify the bugs in the C programs, etc., have been designed and selected that cater [illegible] need of students to solve the examination papers and face the C aptitude test in campus interviews. The reader/programmer may lead a successful career in the development of application software packages after thoroughly reading the book and implementing the programs.

The organized and accessible format allows the students to quickly find the questions on specific topics. In simple words, reading this book will benefit an[illegible] who wishes to arm themselves with substantive computer and programming skills.

Computer Fundamentals and Programming is a par[illegible] series named *Express Learning Series*, which has a number of books designed as quick re[illegible] guides to important undergraduate and postgraduate courses.

Unique Features

1. Designed as a student-friendly, self-learning guide, the book is written in a clear, concise and lucid manner.
2. Easy-to-understand question-and-answer format.
3. Includes questions that have appeared in previous years' question papers as well as new questions, which have been organized in the relevant chapters.
4. All types of questions, including MCQs and brief and detailed questions, are covered.
5. Solutions to numerical questions and questions involving programming that have appeared in previous examinations are provided.
6. All ideas and concepts are presented with clear examples.
7. Text is well structured and well supported with suitable diagrams.
8. Inter-chapter dependencies are kept to a minimum.
9. A comprehensive index is given at the end of the book for quick access to desired topics.

Chapter Organization

The book is divided into two parts, with Part I titled *Computer Fundamentals* and Part II titled as *Programming Concepts*.

Part I: Computer Fundamentals

All the questions–answers are organized into six chapters. A brief discussion of these chapters is as follows:

- *Chapter 1* provides an overview of the history of computers and the basic digital computer concepts. It describes how computations are carried out using arithmetic and logic units, registers and the control unit. In addition, it introduces the reader to the various types of memory devices and the input and output devices.
- *Chapter 2* discusses about number systems and conversion between different number systems.
- *Chapter 3* provides an outlook on operating systems along with their types and functions.
- *Chapter 4* describes the fundamentals of computer software and its relationship with the hardware in building up a fully functional computer system. It also deals with programming and various programming tools such as algorithm, flowchart and pseudocode.
- *Chapter 5* provides a foundation to harness the power of word processing, spreadsheet programs and creating presentations using Microsoft Office Word, Excel and PowerPoint 2003, respectively.
- *Chapter 6* deals with data communication and computer network along with important concepts like transmission modes, network topology and the OSI and the TCP/IP reference models. It also introduces the reader to the different Internet services such as browsing, searching and sending and receiving e-mails.

Part II: Programming Concepts

All the questions–answers are organized [illegible] chapters. A brief discussion of these chapters is as follows:

- *Chapter 1* unfolds the basics of computer and introduction to C. This chapter introduces the reader to the fundamentals of a computer and [illegible]ory information on C language is provided. The topics covered are parts of a computer system, features of C language, rules for writing a program, methods to edit and run the programs with Turbo C compiler, etc.

- *Chapter 2* deals with C declaration. It focuses on C data types, differences between signed and unsigned data types, variables, constants, C keywords, type conversion, dynamic initialization, etc.
- *Chapter 3* explains various C operators and their priorities. This chapter presents arithmetic, relational, and logical operators. It also embodies increment, decrement (unary operators) and assignment operators. Other operators such as comma, conditional operators and bitwise operators are presented in this chapter. Precedence of operators and associativity rule are also explained.
- *Chapter 4* enlightens the readers with formatted input and output functions such as `scanf()` and `printf()` functions. The unformatted functions such as `putchar()`, `getche()`, `gets()`, etc., are described in this chapter. The special symbols such as escape sequences together with their applications have also been discussed.
- *Chapter 5* covers the decision-making statements supported by C language. This chapter details how the control can be transferred from one part of the program to other part. The programmer can make the program powerful by using control statements such as `if`, `if-else`, nested `if-else` statements and `switch case`. To change the flow of the program, the programmer can use keywords such as `break`, `continue` and `goto`.
- *Chupter 6* discusses control loop structures that explain 'how' statements are executed several times until a condition is satisfied. In this chapter, the reader follows program loop structures, which is also known as iterative or repetitive structure. Three types of loop control statements are illustrated, with programming examples. They are `for`, `while` and `do-while` loop statements. Syntaxes of these control statements are briefed.
- *Chapter 7* covers one-dimensional, two-dimensional and multidimensional arrays. It deals with both integer and character arrays. A description on accessing and displaying array elements on the screen is presented in this chapter. Various operations on an array that can be performed are described in this chapter.
- *Chapter 8* focusses on strings. This chapter teaches the reader how to declare and initialize a string. The various formats for displaying the strings are described through numerous examples. String handling has a strong impact in real-life string problems such as conversion of lower to upper case, reversing, concatenation, comparing, searching and replacing of string elements. Methods of performing these operations with and without standard library functions are also explained.
- *Chapter 9* deals with the most important feature of the C language, i.e. pointers. This chapter is important but is difficult to understand easily. Through examples, the reader is made familiar with pointers. The reader is enlightened about declaration and initialization of pointers. The learner studies how to access variables using pointers. How pointers are used to allocate memory dynamically at run time is illustrated using memory allocation functions such as `malloc()` and `calloc()` functions. How memory is handled efficiently with pointers is explained in this chapter. This chapter consists of arithmetic operations on pointers, pointers and arrays, pointers to pointers, etc.
- *Chapter 10* is one of the important chapters on functions. After reading this chapter, a reader will learn how a large-sized program is divided into smaller ones and how a modular program should be developed. A programmer learns the definition and declaration of a function. In this chapter, topics such as return statements, types of functions, functions with passing arguments, etc., are described in detail. "Call by value" and "call by reference" and the answers are given with many programming examples. The recursive nature of function is also described. Direct and indirect recursive functions have been explained clearly.

- *Chapter 11* enlightens the reader on the variables used in C in different situations. It covers topics such as types of variables, local variables and global variables. The various storage classes of a variable are included in this chapter. Also, explanation on `auto`, `extern`, `static`, and `register` variables are presented in this chapter.
- *Chapter 12* describes how to make use of preprocessor directives. This chapter also discusses how various macros are to be used. This chapter enlightens preprocessor directives such as `#define`, `#undef`, `#include`, `#line`, `token pasting` and `stringizing` operations, conditional compilation, etc., through C and illustrations are provided for the ease of the reader. By reading this chapter, the reader learns how to display a programmer's own error messages using `#error` directive, and by making various warnings, on/off is displayed by the compiler using the `#pragma` directive. The reader is also exposed to predefined `macros` in `ctype.h` in this chapter.
- *Chapter 13* discusses structures and unions. This is another powerful chapter of C language. One can get derived data type using structures and unions. The user can decide the heterogeneous data types to be included in the body of a structure. Use of dot operator (.) and pointer (->) are explained in this chapter for accessing members of structure. Declaration and initialization of structure and union can be learnt from this chapter. The `typedef` facility can be used for creating user-defined data types and this is illustrated with many examples. Enumerated data type, union, etc., are the important subtitles of this chapter. Enumerated data type provides user-defined data types. Union is a principal method by which the programmer can derive dissimilar data types. Last but not the least, the DOS and ROM-BIOS functions and their applications are explained.
- *Chapter 14* is on files. This chapter explains the procedure for opening a file, storing information in it and reading it. How to read a file, how to append information in it, etc., are explained in this chapter. Many file-handling commands are discussed in this chapter. Text and binary files are discussed in this chapter. Command line arguments to accept arguments from command prompt are described. Simulation of various DOS commands with examples is also provided. The reader is also made familiar with I/O redirections in which MSDOS redirects to send the result to the disk instead of seeing information on the monitor.
- *Chapter 15* deals with graphics. How to draw various figures/images using C library graphics functions can be studied from graphics chapter. This chapter enlightens the reader about the initialization of graphics with library graphics functions and a number of programming examples.

Ashok N. Kamthane
Rohit Khurana

Acknowledgements

I would like to thank all those who have encouraged me to write technical books, especially Prof. B. M. Naik, former Principal of S.G.G.S. College of Engineering and Technology, Nanded, who has been a driving force for the publication of books and who acted as a source of inspiration throughout my life. His dynamism and leadership led me to write this book. I will never forget his instinct, support, and words of wisdom.

Special thanks are due to the members of the Board of Governors of S.G.G.S. Institute of Engineering and Technology, who motivated me to write this book. They are Shri Baba Kalyani, Chairman and Managing Director of Bharat Forge Ltd, Pune, Mr Kamlesh Pande, and Dr L. M. Waghmare, Director of our institute. I am thankful to the director for extending his help in writing the book.

My sincere thanks go to Prof. S. D. Mahajan, Director of Technical Education, Maharashtra State, and Ex-Board of Governors of this college, Dr M. B. Kinhalkar, Former Home Minister, and Dr T. R. Sontakke, Ex-Principal, for inspiring me to write this book.

I am grateful to all my colleagues, friends, and students who extended moral support. Among them are Dr S. V. Bonde, Dr R. R. Manthalkar, Dr S. S. Gajre, Prof. R. K. Chavan, Dr J. V. L. Venkatesh, Dr Y. V. Joshi, Dr M. B. Kokre, Dr Lenina Birgale, Dr P. Kar, Dr P. D. Jadhav, Prof. P. G. Jadhav, Dr P. Pramanik, Dr P. G. Solankar, Dr V. K. Joshi, Dr S. G. Kahalekar, Dr A. Chakraborty, Dr B. M. Dabde, Dr U. V. Kulkarni, Dr V. M. Nandedkar, Dr M. L. Waikar, Dr R. S. Holambe, Dr B. M. Patre, Dr. V. R. Thool, Dr V. G. Asutkar, Dr D. D. Doye, Prof. P. S. Nalawade, Prof. S. S. Hatkar, Dr R. C. Thool, Dr A. V. Nandedkar, Dr P. D. Dahe, Dr P. D. Ullagadi, Dr A. B. Gonde, Dr P. B. Londhe, Prof. N. G. Megde, Dr A. S. Sontakke, Prof. A. M. Bainwad, Prof. Deepak Bacchewar, Prof. R. P. Parvekar, Prof. N. M. Khandare, Dr V. B. Tungikar, Dr R. N. Joshi, Dr P. T. Patil, Dr L. G. Patil, and Prof. A. I. Tamboli. I am also thankful to my friends Prof. S. L. Kotgire, Mr Balaji Bacchewar, Mr M. M. Jahagirdar, Mr L. M. Buddhewar, Mr K. M. Buddhewar, Mr D. V. Deshpande, Mr S. R. Kokane, Mr Ganpat Shinde, Mr M. G. Damkondawar, Mr R. D. Yeramwar, Mr S. R. Tumma, Mr R. Somajwar, Mr Yennawar O. N., Mr S. R. Mana, and Mr Annes for their help.

I take this opportunity to thank the production editorial teams at Pearson Education, especially Mr M. E. Sethurajan, Ms V. Pavithra and Ms Neha Goomer for their painstaking work in bringing out this book in a record time.

Also, I express my thanks to Prof. Barulkar Jeetendrasinh, who reviewed the manuscript and suggested improvements.

Last, but not the least, my thanks are due to my wife Surekha for her patience and support while writing this book. My sons Amol and Amit, daughter Sangita, and daughter-in-law Swaroopa were also a great help and extended their support to me at all the times.

Ashok N. Kamthane

I would like to thank the following people for their help in bringing out this book.

- Our publisher Pearson Education, their editorial team and panel reviewers for their valuable contribution towards content enrichment.
- Our technical and editorial consultants for devoting their precious time to improve the quality of the book.
- Our entire research and development team who have put in their sincere efforts to bring out a high-quality book.

Rohit Khurana
Founder and CEO
ITL ESL

Feedback

For any suggestions and comments about this book, please free to send an e-mail to ankamthane@gmail.com or itlesl@rediffmail.com.

Hope you enjoy reading this book as much as we have enjoyed writing it.

PART I

Computer Fundamentals

1

Fundamentals of Computers

1. Define computer.

Ans: A 'computer' is an electronic machine used for performing calculations and controlling operations that can be expressed either in logical or numerical terms. In simple words, it is an electronic device that performs diverse operations with the help of instructions needed to process the information in order to achieve desired results. Using this versatile machine, millions of complex calculations can be done in a mere fraction of time and difficult decisions can be made with more accuracy at low cost. Although the application domain of a computer depends totally on human creativity and imagination, it covers a huge area of applications including education, industries, government, medicine, scientific research, law and music and arts.

2. State the characteristics of a computer in detail.

(or)

Explain the features of computer available for individuals and organizations.

Ans: Today, much of the world's infrastructure depends on computers and it has profoundly changed our lives, mostly for better. Some of the characteristics of the computers that make them an essential part of every emerging technology and a desirable tool in the human development are as follows:

- **Speed:** Computers process data at an extremely fast rate – millions of instructions per second. In few seconds, a computer can perform a huge task that a normal human being may take days or even years to complete. The speed of a computer is calculated in MHz (Megahertz), that is, one million instructions per second. At present, a powerful computer can perform billions of operations in just one second.
- **Accuracy:** Besides efficiency, computers are accurate as well. The level of accuracy depends on the instructions and the type of machine being used. Since computer is capable of doing only what it is instructed to do, faulty instructions for data processing may lead to faulty results. This is known as *GIGO (Garbage In Garbage Out)*.

- **Diligence:** Computer, being a machine, does not suffer from the human traits of tiredness and lack of concentration. If four million calculations have to be performed, then the computer will perform the last four-millionth calculation with the same accuracy and speed as the first calculation.
- **Reliability:** Generally, reliability is the measurement of performance of a computer, which is measured against some predetermined standard for operation without any failure. The major reason behind the reliability of the computers is that, at hardware level, it does not require any human intervention between its processing operations. Moreover, computers have built-in diagnostic capabilities, which help in continuous monitoring of the system.
- **Storage capability:** Computers can store large amounts of data and can recall the required information almost instantaneously. The main memory of the computer is relatively small and it can hold only a certain amount of information, therefore, the data is stored on secondary storage devices such as magnetic tape or disks. Small sections of the data can be accessed very quickly and brought into the storage devices, as and when required, for processing.
- **Versatility:** Computers are quite versatile in nature. They can perform multiple tasks simultaneously with great ease. For example, at one moment it can be used to draft a letter, another moment it can be used to play music and in between, one can print a document as well. All this work is possible by changing the program (computer instructions).
- **Resource sharing:** In the initial stages of development, computers used to be isolated machines. With the tremendous growth in computer technologies, computers today have the capability to connect with each other. This has made the sharing of costly resources such as printers possible. Apart from device sharing, data and information can also be shared among groups of computers, thus creating a large information and knowledge base.

3. Explain in detail about the evolution of computers.

Ans: The need for a device to do calculations along with the growth in commerce and other human activities explain the evolution of computers. Computers were preceded by many devices which mankind developed for their computing requirements. However, many centuries elapsed before technology was adequately advanced to develop computers. Some of the ancient time devices which led to evolution of computers are as follows:

Sand Tables

In ancient times, people used fingers to perform the calculations such as addition and subtraction. Even today, simple calculations are done on fingers. Soon, mankind realized that it would be easier to do calculations with pebbles as compared to fingers. Consequently, pebbles were used to represent numbers, which led to the development of sand tables. They are known to be the earliest device for computation. A sand table consists of three grooves in the sand with a maximum of 10 pebbles in each groove. To increase the count by one, a pebble has to be added in the right-hand groove. When 10 pebbles were collected in the right groove, they were removed and one pebble was added to the adjacent left groove.

Abacus

Abacus is a counting device devised by the people in Asia Minor to simplify the process of counting. The word 'abacus' was derived from Arabic word 'abaq' which means 'dust'. An abacus consists of sliding beads arranges on a rack, which has two parts, namely, *upper* and *lower*. The upper part contains two beads and the lower part contains five beads per wire. The numbers are represented by the position of the beads on the rack. For example, in the upper part of the rack, a raised bead denotes 0 whereas a lowered bead denotes digit 5. In the lower part, a raised bead stands for 1 and a lowered bead for 0. The arithmetic operations such as addition and subtraction can be performed by positioning the beads appropriately.

Napier Bones

In 1614, a Scottish mathematician, John Napier made a more sophisticated computing machine called 'Napier bones'. This was a small instrument made up of 10 rods, on which the multiplication table was engraved. It was made up of the strips of ivory bones, and so the name Napier bones. This device enabled the multiplication in a fast manner, if one of the numbers was of one digit only (e.g., $6 \times 6{,}745$). Incidentally, Napier also played a key role in the development of logarithms, which stimulated the invention of slide rule, which substituted the addition of logarithms for multiplication. This was a remarkable invention as it enabled to perform the multiplication and division operations by converting them into simple addition and subtraction.

Slide Rule

The invention of logarithms influenced the development of another famous invention known as 'slide rule'. In AD 1620, the first slide rule came into existence. It was jointly devised by two British mathematicians, Edmund Gunter and William Oughtred. It was based on the principle that the actual distances from the starting point of the rule are directly proportional to the logarithm of the numbers printed on the rule. The slide rule is embodied by two sets of scales that are joined together, with a marginal space between them. This space is enough for the free movement of the slide in the groove of the rule. The suitable alliance of two scales enabled the slide rule to perform multiplication and division by a method of addition and subtraction.

Pascaline

In 1623, Wilhelm Schickard invented the calculating clock, which could add and subtract, and indicated the overflow by ringing a bell. Subsequently, it helped in the evolution of Pascaline. In AD 1642, French mathematician, scientist and philosopher, Blaise Pascal invented the first functional automatic calculator. It had a complex arrangement of wheels, gears and windows for displaying numbers. It was operated by a series of dials attached to wheels with each wheel having ten segments (numbered from zero to nine) on its circumference. When a wheel made a complete turn, the wheel on its left advanced by one segment. Indicators above the dial displayed the correct answer. However, usage of this device was limited to addition and subtraction only.

Analytical Engine

Analytical engine is considered to be the first general purpose programmable computer. Babbage's innovation in the design of the analytical engine made it possible to test the sign of a computed number and take one course of action if the sign was positive and another if the sign was negative. Babbage also designed this device to advance or reverse the flow of punched cards to permit branching to any desired instruction within a program. Lady Ada Lovelace helped Babbage in the development of the analytical engine. She wrote articles and programs for the proposed machine. Due to her contributions, she is known as the first programmer. However, Babbage never completed the analytical engine, but his proposal for this device reviewed the basic elements of modern computer such as input/output, storage, processor and control unit.

Hollerith's Tabulator

Herman Hollerith invented the punched-card tabulating machine to process the data collected in the United States' census. This electronic machine was able to read the information on the cards and process it electronically. It consisted of a tabulator, a sorter with compartments electronically controlled by the tabulator's counter and the device used to punch data onto cards. This tabulator could read the presence or absence of holes in the cards by using spring-mounted nails that passed through the holes to make electrical connections. In 1896, Hollerith founded the Tabulating Machine Company, which was later named as International Business Machines (IBM).

4. Explain about the generations of computers.

Ans: The history of computer development is often discussed with reference to the different generations of computing devices. In computer terminology, the word 'generation' is described as a stage of technological development or innovation. A major technological development that fundamentally changed the way the computers operate, resulting in increasingly smaller, cheaper and more powerful and more efficient and reliable devices characterize each generation of computer. According to the type of processor installed in a machine, there are five generations of computers which are as follows:

First Generation (1940–1956): Vacuum Tubes

First generation computers were vacuum tubes/thermionic valves-based machines. These computers used vacuum tubes for circuitry and magnetic drums for memory. A 'magnetic drum' is a metal cylinder coated with magnetic iron-oxide material on which data and programs can be stored. The input was based on punched cards and paper tape and the output was in the form of printouts.

First generation computers relied on binary-coded language also called 'machine language' (language of 0s and 1s) to perform operations and were able to solve only one problem at a time. These were the fastest computing devices of their times (computation time was in milliseconds). However, each machine was fed with different binary codes and were difficult to program. This resulted in lack of versatility and speed. Moreover, since thousands of vacuum tubes were used, they generated a large amount of heat. Therefore, air conditioning was essential. In addition, to run on different types of computers, instructions must be rewritten or recompiled. Some examples of first generation computers are ENIAC, EDVAC and UNIVAC.

Second Generation (1956–1963): Transistors

Second generation computers used transistors, which were superior to vacuum tubes. A 'transistor' is made up of semiconductor material such as germanium and silicon. It usually has three leads and performs electrical functions such as voltage, current or power amplification with low power requirements. Since transistor is a small device, the physical size of computers was greatly reduced. Computers became smaller, faster, cheaper, energy-efficient and more reliable than their predecessors. In second generation computers, magnetic cores were used as primary memory and magnetic disks as secondary storage devices. However, they still relied on punched cards for input and printouts for output.

One of the major developments of this generation includes the progress from machine language to assembly language. Assembly language uses mnemonics (abbreviations) for instructions rather than numbers, for example, ADD for addition and MULT for multiplication. As a result, programming became less cumbersome. These computers were more reliable and less prone to hardware failure, hence, they required less frequent maintenance. Moreover, these were more portable and generated less amount of heat. However, the second generation computers still required air conditioning and manual assembly of individual components into a functioning unit. Some examples of second generation computers are PDP-8, IBM 1401 and IBM 7090.

Third Generation (1964–early 1970s): Integrated Circuits

The development of the integrated circuit was the trait of the third generation computers. An 'integrated circuit' (also called an 'IC') consists of a single chip (usually silicon) with many components such as transistors and resistors fabricated on it. Integrated circuits replaced several individually wired transistors. This development made computers smaller in size, reliable and efficient.

Instead of punched cards and printouts, users interacted with third generation computers through keyboards and monitors and interfaced with operating system. This allowed the device to run many different applications simultaneously with a central program that monitored the memory. For the first time, computers became accessible to mass audience because they were smaller and cheaper than their predecessors. The main advantage of these computers was that manual assembling of individual components was not required, so it reduced the large requirement of labour and cost. However, highly sophisticated technologies were required for the manufacturing of IC chips. Some examples of third generation computers are NCR 395 and B6500.

Fourth Generation (Early 1970s–till date): Microprocessors

The fourth generation is an extension of third generation technology. Although, the technology of this generation is still based on the integrated circuit, these have been made readily available to us because of the development of the microprocessor (circuits containing millions of transistors). The Intel 4004 chip, which was developed in 1971, took the IC one step further by locating all the components of a computer (central processing unit, memory and input and output controls) on a miniscule chip. A microprocessor is built onto a single piece of silicon, known as 'chip'. It is about 0.5 cm along one side and no more than 0.05 cm thick.

The fourth generation computers led to an era of Large-Scale Integration (LSI) and Very-Large-Scale Integration (VLSI) technology. LSI technology allowed thousands of transistors to be constructed on one small slice of silicon material, whereas VLSI squeezed hundreds of thousands of components on to a single chip. Ultra-large-scale integration (ULSI) increased that number into millions. This way, computers became smaller and cheaper than even before.

The fourth generation computers became more powerful, compact, reliable and affordable. As a result, it gave rise to the personal computer (PC) revolution. During this period, magnetic core memories were substituted by semiconductor memories that resulted in faster random access main memories. Moreover, secondary memories such as hard disks became economical, smaller and bigger in capacity. The other significant development of this era was that these computers could be linked together to form networks, which eventually led to the development of the Internet. This generation also saw the development of the 'Graphical User Interfaces (GUIs)', mouse and hand-held devices. Despite many advantages, this generation required complex and sophisticated technology for the manufacturing of CPU and the other components. Some examples of fourth generation computers are Apple II, Altair 8800 and CRAY-1.

Fifth Generation (Present and beyond): Artificial Intelligence

The dream of creating a human-like computer that would be capable of reasoning and reaching at a decision through a series of 'what-if-then' analyses have existed since the beginning of computer technology. Such a computer would learn from its mistakes and possess the skill of experts. These are the objectives for creating the fifth generation of computers. The starting point for the fifth generation of computers had been set in the early 1990s. The process of developing fifth generation computers is still in the development stage and will use the concept of expert system. The 'expert system' is defined as a computer information system that attempts to mimic the thought process and reasoning of experts in specific areas.

5. Write down the generation-wise development of the computer hardware.

Ans: The hardware used in five generations is listed in Table 1.1.

Table 1.1 Hardware Used in Various Generations

Generations	Hardware Used
First	Vacuum tubes
Second	Transistor
Third	Integrated circuits
Fourth	Very-large-scale integration
Fifth	Ultra-large-scale integration

6. Write the classification of computers according to purpose and data handling.

Ans: These days, computers are available in many sizes and types. One can have a computer that can fit in the palm of the hand to those that can occupy the entire room. Some computers are designed to be used by a single user only, whereas some computers can handle the needs of many users simultaneously. Computers also differ based on their data processing abilities. In general, they can be classified according to purpose, data handling and functionality. The classification of computers according to purpose and data handling only are discussed as follows:

Classification According to Purpose

Computers are designed for different purposes. According to the need, they can be classified into two categories, which are described as follows:

- **General purpose computers:** As the name suggests, they are designed to perform a range of tasks. These computers have the ability to store numerous programs. These machines can be used for various applications, ranging from scientific as well as business purpose applications. Even though such computers are versatile, they generally lack in speed and efficiency. The computers that are used in schools and homes are general purpose computers.
- **Specific purpose computers:** They are designed to handle a specific problem or to perform a single specific task. A set of instructions for the specific task is built into the machine. Hence, they cannot be used for other applications unless their circuits are redesigned, that is, they lack versatility. However, being designed for specific tasks, they can provide the result very quickly and efficiently. These computers are used for airline reservations, satellite tracking and air traffic control.

Classification According to Type of Data Handling Techniques

Different types of computers process the data in a different manner. According to the basic data handling techniques, computers can be classified into the following three categories:

- **Analog computers:** A computing machine that operates on data in the form of continuously variable physical quantities is known as 'analog computer'. These computers do not deal directly with the numbers. They measure continuous physical magnitudes (such as temperature, pressure and voltage), which are analogous to the numbers under consideration. For example, the petrol pump may have an analog computer that converts the flow of pumped petrol into two measurements – the quantity of petrol and the price for that quantity. Analog computers are used for scientific and engineering purposes. One of the characteristics of these computers is that they give approximate results since they deal with quantities that vary continuously. The main feature of analog computers is that they are very fast in operation as all the calculations are done in parallel mode. It is very easy to get graphical results directly using analog computer. However, the accuracy of analog computers is less.
- **Digital computers:** A computer that operates with information, numerical or otherwise, represented in a digital form is known as 'digital computer'. Such computers process data (including text, sound, graphics and video) into a digital value (in 0s and 1s). In digital computers, analog quantities must be converted into digital quantity before processing. In this case, the output will also be digital. If analog output is desired, the digital output has to be converted into analog quantity. The components, which perform these conversions, are the essential parts or peripherals of the digital computer. Digital computers can give the results with more accuracy and at a faster rate. The accuracy of such computers is limited only by the size of their registers and memory. The desktop PC at the home is a classic example of digital computer.
- **Hybrid computers:** They incorporated the measuring feature of an analog computer and counting feature of a digital computer. For computational purposes, these computers use the analog components and for the storage of intermediate results, digital memories are used. In order to bind the powers of analog and digital techniques, analog to digital and digital to analog, the hybrid computers comprehensively use converters. Such computers are broadly used for scientific applications, various fields of engineering and in industrial control processes.

7. Write the classification of computers according to functionality.

Ans: Based on physical size, performance and application areas, computers can be generally divided into four major categories, namely, *micro*, *mini*, *mainframe* and *super* computers. All of these are described as follows:

Micro Computers

A micro computer is a small, low-cost digital computer, which usually consists of a microprocessor, a storage unit, an input channel and an output channel, all of which may be on one chip inserted into one or several PC boards. The addition of a power supply and connecting cables, appropriate peripherals (keyboard, monitor, printer, disk drives and others), an operating system and other software programs can provide a complete micro computer system. The micro computer is generally the smallest of the computer family. Originally, these were designed for individual users only, but nowadays they have become powerful tools for many businesses that, when networked together, can serve more than one user. IBM-PC Pentium 100, IBM-PC Pentium 200 and Apple Macintosh are some of the examples of micro computers. Micro computers include desktop, laptop and hand-held models, such as personal digital assistants (PDAs).

Mini Computers

A mini computer is a small digital computer that normally able to process and store less data than a mainframe but more than a micro computer, while doing task less rapidly than a mainframe but more rapidly than a micro computer. These computers are about the size of a two-drawer filing cabinet. Generally, they are used as desktop devices that are often connected to a mainframe in order to perform the auxiliary operations.

Mini computer (sometimes called a 'mid-range computer') is designed to meet the computing needs of several people simultaneously in a small to medium-sized business environment. It is capable of supporting from 4 to about 200 simultaneous users. It serves as a centralized storehouse for a cluster of workstations or as a network server. Mini computers are usually multi-user systems so these are used in interactive applications in industries, research organizations, colleges and universities. They are also used for real-time controls and engineering design work. Some of the widely used mini computers are PDP 11, IBM (8000 series) and VAX 7500.

Mainframes

A mainframe is an ultra-high performance computer made for high-volume, processor-intensive computing. It consists of a high-end computer processor, with related peripheral devices, capable of supporting large volumes of data processing, high performance online transaction processing and extensive data storage and retrieval. Normally, it is able to process and store more data than a mini computer and far more than a micro computer. Moreover, it is designed to perform at a faster rate than a mini computer and at even more faster rate than a micro computer. Mainframes are the second largest (in capability and size) of the computer family, the largest being the super computers. However, they can usually execute many programs simultaneously at a high speed, whereas super computers are designed for a single process.

Mainframes allow its user to maintain a large amount of data storage at a centralized location and to access and process this data from different computers located at different locations. They are typically used by large businesses and for scientific purposes. Some examples of mainframe are IBM's ES000, VAX 8000 and CDC 6600.

Super Computers

Super computers are the special purpose machines that are specially designed to maximize the numbers of FLOPS (Floating Point Operation per Second). Any computer below one gigaflop/sec is not considered a super computer. It has the highest processing speed at a given time for solving scientific and engineering problems. Essentially, it contains a number of CPUs that operate in parallel to make it faster. Its processing speed lies in the range of 400–10,000 MFLOPS (Millions of Floating Point Operation per Second). Due to this feature, super computers help in many applications including information retrieval and computer-aided design.

A super computer can process a great deal of data and make extensive calculations very quickly. It can resolve complex mathematical equations in a few hours, which would have taken many years when performed using a paper and pencil or using a hand calculator. It is the fastest, costliest and most powerful computer available today. Typically, super computers are used to solve multi-variant mathematical problems of existent physical processes, such as aerodynamics, metrology and plasma physics. They are also required by the military strategists to simulate defense scenarios. Cinema technicians use them to produce sophisticated movie animations. Scientists build complex models and simulate them in a super computer. However, super computer has a limited broad-spectrum use because of its price and limited market. The largest commercial uses of super computers are in the entertainment/advertising industry. CRAY-3, Cyber 205 and PARAM are some well-known super computers.

8. Write a short note on the following:
(a) Desktop computer
(b) Laptop
(c) Hand-held computers

Ans:

(a) **Desktop computer:** A desktop computer, also known as 'personal computer' ('PC'), is principally intended for stand-alone use by an individual. These are the most common type of micro computers. These micro computers typically consist of a system unit, a display monitor, a keyboard, internal hard disk storage and other peripheral devices. It is to be noted that they are not very expensive for the individuals or the small businesses. Some of the major personal computer manufacturers are APPLE, IBM, Dell and Hewlett-Packard.

(b) **Laptop:** It is a portable computer that a user can carry around. Since the laptop resembles a notebook, it is also known as a 'notebook'. Laptops are small computers enclosing all the basic features of a normal desktop computer. The biggest advantage of laptops is that they are lightweight and one can use them anywhere and at anytime, especially when one is travelling. Moreover, they need not any external power supply as a rechargeable battery is completely self-contained. However, they are expensive as compared to desktop computers.

(c) **A hand-held computer:** A hand-held computer, also called 'personal digital assistant' ('PDA'), is a portable computer that can conveniently be stored in a pocket (of sufficient size) and used while the user is holding it. PDAs are essentially small portable computers and are slightly bigger than the common calculators. A PDA user generally uses a pen or electronic stylus, instead of a keyboard for input. The monitor is very small and is the only apparent form of output. Since these computers can be easily fitted on the top of the palm, they are also known as 'palmtop' computers. Hand-held computers usually have no disk drive rather they use small cards to store programs and data. However, they can be connected to a printer or a disk drive to generate output or store data. They have limited memory and are less powerful as compared to desktop computers. Some examples of hand-held computers are Apple Newton, Casio Cassiopeia and Franklin eBook Man.

9. What are the various applications of computer?

Ans: In the last few decades, computer technology has revolutionized the businesses and other aspects of human life all over the world. Practically, every company, large or small, is now directly or indirectly dependent on computers for data processing. Computers not only save time, but also save paper work. Some of the areas where computers are being used are listed as follows:

- **Science:** Scientists have been using computers to develop theories, to analyze and test the data. The fast speed and the accuracy of the computer allow different scientific analyses to be carried out. They can be used to generate detailed studies of how earthquakes affect buildings or pollution affects weather pattern. Satellite-based applications could not have been possible without the use of computers. It would not be possible to get the information of our solar system and the cosmos without computers.
- **Education:** Computers have also revolutionized the whole process of education. Currently, the classrooms, libraries and museums are utilizing computers to make the education much more interesting. Unlike recorded television shows, computer-aided education (CAE) and computer-based training (CBT) packages are making learning much more interactive.

- **Medicine and health care:** There has been an increasing use of computers in the field of medicine. Now, doctors are using computers right from diagnosing the illness to monitoring a patient's status during complex surgery. By using automated imaging techniques, doctors are able to look inside a person's body and can study each organ in detail (such as CAT scans or MRI scans), which was not possible few years ago. There are several examples of special purpose computers that can operate within the human body such as a cochlear implant, a special kind of hearing aid that makes it possible for deaf people to hear.
- **Engineering/Architecture/Manufacturing:** The architects and engineers extensively use computers in designing and drawings. Using computers, a three-dimensional view of an object can be simulated. By using techniques such as virtual reality, architects can explore houses that have been designed but not built. The manufacturing factories are using computerized robotic arms in order to perform hazardous jobs. Besides, computer aided manufacturing (CAM) can be used in designing the product, ordering the parts and planning production.
- **Entertainment:** Computers are finding greater use in entertainment industry. They are used to control the images and sounds. The special effects, which mesmerize the audience, would not have been possible without the computers. In addition, computerized animation and colourful graphics have modernized the film industry.
- **Communication:** E-mail (or electronic mail) is one of the communication media in which computer is used. Through e-mail, messages and reports are passed from one person to one or more persons. The advantage of e-mail service is that while transferring the messages it saves time, avoids wastage of paper and is instantly delivered to the recipient. Moreover, the person who is receiving the messages can read the messages whenever he/she is free and can save it, reply it, forward it or delete it from the computer.
- **Business application:** This is one of the important uses of the computer. Initially, computers were used for batch processing jobs, where one does not require the immediate response from the computer. Currently, computers are mainly used for real-time applications (for example, at the sales counter) that require immediate response from the computer. There are various concerns for which computers are used, such as in business forecasting, to prepare pay bills and personal records, in banking operations and data storage, in various types of life insurance business, and as an aid to management. Businesses are also using the networking of computers, where a number of computers are connected together to share the data and the information. The use of e-mail and Internet has changed the ways of doing business.
- **Publishing:** Computers have created a field known as 'desktop publishing' ('DTP'). In DTP, with the help of computer and a laser printer one can perform the publishing job all by oneself. Many of the tasks requiring long manual hours, such as making table of contents and index, can be automatically performed using the computers and DTP software.
- **Banking:** In the field of banking and finance, computers are extensively used. People can use the automated teller machine (ATM) services 24 hours of the day to deposit and withdraw cash. When different branches of a bank are connected through computer networks, inert-branch transactions can be performed by the computers without any delay.

10. Draw the block diagram of a digital computer and explain its various components.

Ans: A computer can be viewed as a system, which consists of a number of interrelated components that work together with the aim of converting data into information. There are several computer systems in the market with a wide variety of makes, models and peripherals. In general, a computer system comprises four components, namely, *central processing unit* (*CPU*), *input unit*, *output unit* and *storage* (or *memory*) *unit*. The block diagram of a digital computer is shown in Figure 1.1.

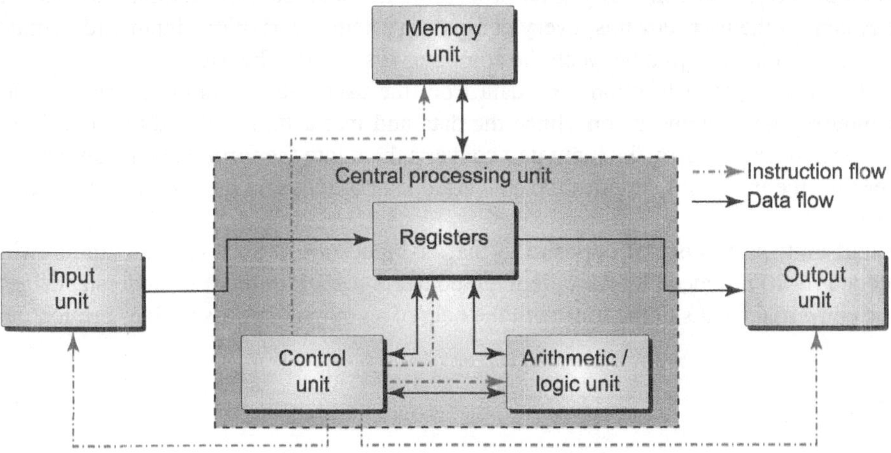

Figure 1.1 Block Diagram of Digital Computer

CPU

CPU, also known as 'processor', is the brain of the computer system that processes data (input) and converts it into meaningful information (output). It is a highly complex, extensive set of electronic circuitry, which executes stored program instructions. A CPU controls all internal and external devices, performs arithmetic and logic operations, and operates only on binary data, that is, data composed of 1s and 0s. In addition, it also controls the usage of main memory to store data and instructions and controls the sequence of operations. The CPU consists of three main subsystems, which are described as follows:

- **Arithmetic logic unit (ALU):** This unit performs the arithmetic (add, subtract) and logical operations (and, or) on the data made available to it. Whenever an arithmetic or logical operation is to be performed, the required data is transferred from the memory unit to ALU, the operation is performed and the result is returned to memory unit. Before the completion of the processing, data may need to be transferred back and forth several times between these two sections. Subsequently, the results are transferred from internal storage to an output device.
- **Control unit (CU):** This unit checks the correctness of the sequence of operations. It fetches the program instructions from the memory unit, interprets them and ensures correct execution of the program. It also controls the input/output devices and directs the overall functioning of the other units of the computer.
- **Registers:** These are the special-purpose; high-speed temporary memory units that can hold varied information such as data, instructions, addresses and intermediate results of calculations. Essentially, they hold the information that the CPU is currently working on. Registers can be considered as the CPU's working memory, a special additional storage location that provides the advantage of speed.

Input and Output Unit

The user must enter instructions and data into the computer system before any operation can be performed on the given data. Similarly, after processing the data, the information must go out from the computer system to the user. For this, every computer system incorporates input and output units that serve as a communication media between the computer system and the user.

An 'input unit' accepts instructions and data from the user with the help of input devices such as keyboard, mouse, light pen and so on. Since the data and instructions entered through different input devices will be in different form, the input unit converts them into the form that the computer can understand. After this, the input unit supplies the converted instructions and data to the computer for further processing.

The 'output unit' performs just opposite to that of input unit. It accepts the outputs (which are in machine-coded form) produced by the computer, converts them into the user understandable form and supplies the converted results to the user with the help of an output devices such as printer, monitor and plotter.

Storage Unit

A computer system incorporates 'storage unit' to store the input entered through input unit before processing starts and to store the results produced by the computer before supplying them to the output unit. The storage unit of a computer comprises two types of memory/storage, namely, 'primary' and 'secondary'.

The primary memory (also called 'main memory') is the part of a computer that holds the instructions and data currently being processed by the CPU, the intermediate results produced during the course of calculations and the recently processed data. While the instructions and data remain in main memory, the CPU can access them directly and quickly. However, primary memory is quite expensive and has a limited storage capacity. Due to limited size of primary memory, a computer employs 'secondary memory', which is extensively used for storing data and instructions. It supplies the stored information to the other units of computer as and when required. It is less expensive and has higher storage capacity than the primary memory. Some commonly used secondary storage devices are floppy disks, hard disks and tape drives.

11. Explain Von Neumann architecture.

Ans: The earliest computers such as ENIAC and Colossus were program-controlled machines in which writing a new program or changing some existing program required re-wiring, restructuring or redesigning the machines. Thus, programming in these computers was a quite tedious task. To ease the programming process, an idea known as 'stored program concept' was proposed by a mathematician and an early computer scientist named John Von Neumann. According to this concept, both data and instructions are kept in the main memory. Thus, a computer could get its instructions from the memory and the programs could be setup or changed from within the memory as well, without having to redesign the computer. All the computers based on stored program concept are known as Von Neumann systems employing the 'Von Neumann architecture'.

Most of the conventional and today's modern computers that are based on Von Neumann architecture consists of four hardware components: a CPU with control unit, ALU, main memory and an I/O system (see Figure 1.2). In addition, these computers can process the instructions in a sequential manner. The architecture shown in Figure 1.2 depicts the working of a Von Neumann computer. Here, the I/O instructions are passed through ALU to the control unit. All the programs are executed by following the

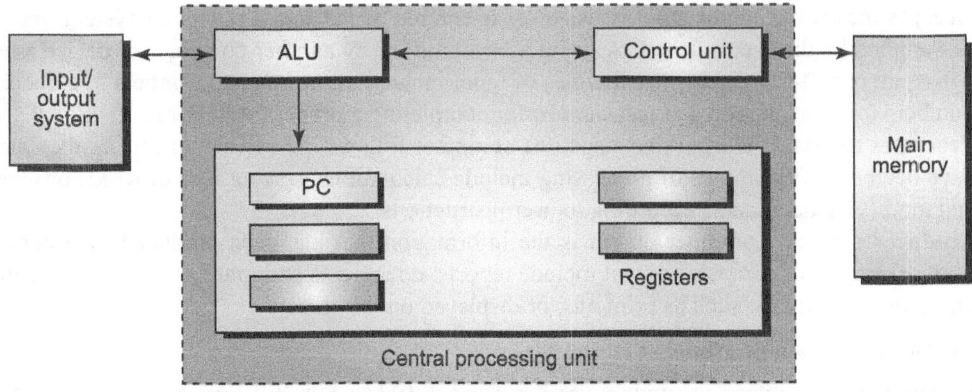

Figure 1.2 Von Neumann Architecture

'Von Neumann execution cycle' or 'fetch-decode-execute cycle', which describes the working of the machine. One iteration of this cycle involves the following steps:

1. The control unit determines the location of the next program instruction to be executed using the program counter and fetches it from the main memory.
2. The instruction is then decoded into the language understandable by the ALU.
3. The required data operands for executing the instructions are fetched from main memory and stored into the CPU registers.
4. The instructions are executed by ALU and the results are placed in registers or memory.

12. What are the phases of information processing cycle? Explain briefly.

Ans: A task is assigned to computer in a set of step-by-step instructions, which is known as 'program'. These instructions tell the computer what to do with input in order to produce the required output. To complete any task, a computer performs three basic steps which are as follows (see Figure 1.3):

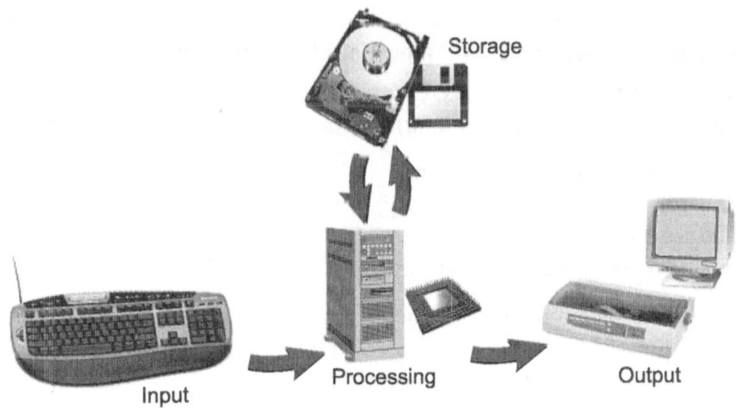

Figure 1.3 Basic Computer Operations

1. **Accepts input:** Computer input is whatever is entered or fed into a computer system. Input can be supplied by the user (such as by using a keyboard) or by another computer or device (such as a diskette or CD-ROM). Some examples of input include the words and symbols in a document, numbers for a calculation and instructions for completing a process, and so on.
2. **Processes the data:** During this stage, the computer follows the instructions using the data that have been input. Examples of processing include calculations, sorting lists of words or numbers and modifying documents according to user instructions.
3. **Produces output:** Computer output is the information that has been produced by a computer. Some examples of computer output include reports, documents and graphs. Output can be in several different formats, such as printouts, or displayed on the screen.

13. Discuss some limitations of computers.

Ans: Although computers are widely used in various fields, but still they have some limitations which are as follows:

- The computers are faster, more diligent, accurate and versatile than human beings but they cannot replace them. Thus, one can say that they do not have any intelligence.
- They can only perform what they are programmed to do. They work only on stored procedures and cannot think for themselves. Thus, they cannot make any decisions of their own.
- They need well-defined instructions to perform any operation. Therefore, they are unable to give any conclusion without going through intermediate steps and thus, cannot generate information on their own.
- Their use is limited in areas where qualitative considerations are important. For instance, they can make plans based on situations and information but they cannot foresee whether they will succeed or not.
- They cannot correct wrong instructions. If the instructions are not accurate then the working of the computer will not be accurate. Therefore, computer will give wrong information if feed with wrong data.
- They need to be installed in a dust-free place. As some parts of computers get heated up due to heavy processing, therefore, the ambient temperature of system should be maintained.
- Computer parts require regular checking and maintenance in order to give correct result. This is because sometimes a program which was running correctly for some period of time might produce an error when re-run later.

14. What are the functions of a CPU? How does the CPU perform them?

Ans: The central processing unit (CPU) is referred to as the brain of a computer system as it converts data (input) into meaningful information (output). Its functions can be summed up as follows:

- Carrying out arithmetic and logic functions.
- Controlling the use of main storage (memory) to store data and instructions.
- Controlling the sequence of operations.
- Controlling all the parts of the computer system

The CPU accomplishes its functions with the help of its three main subsystems (see Figure 1.4): the *arithmetic and logic unit* (*ALU*), the *control unit* (*CU*) and the *registers*, which help the processor in performing its functions correctly. These are described as follows:

- **ALU:** It contains the electronic circuitry that executes all arithmetic and logical operations on the data made available to it. The data required to perform the arithmetic and logical functions are input from the designated registers. ALU comprises two units which are as follows:

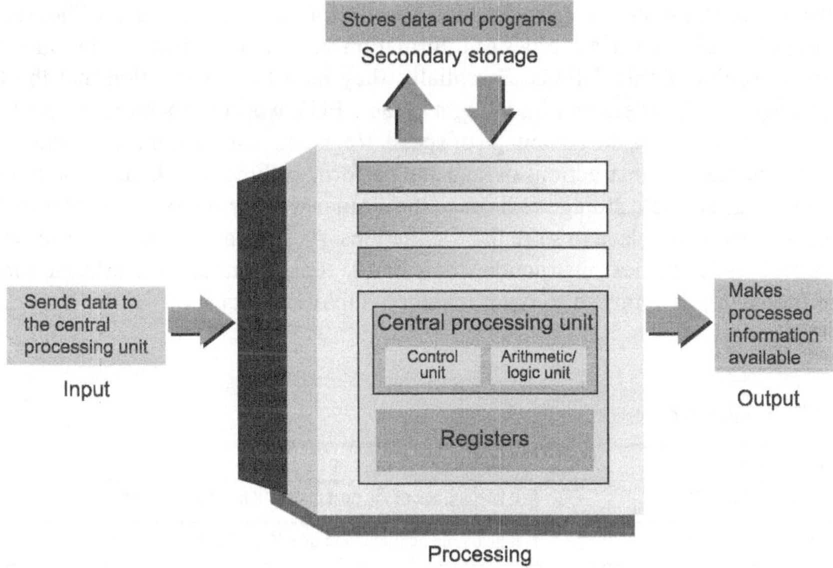

Figure 1.4 CPU

- **Arithmetic unit (AU):** It contains the circuitry that is responsible for performing the actual computing and carrying out the arithmetic calculations, such as addition, subtraction, multiplication and division. It can perform these operations at a very high speed.
- **Logic unit (LU):** It enables the CPU to make logical operations based on the instructions provided to it. These operations are logical comparison between data items. The LU can compare numbers, letters or special characters and can then take action based on the result of the comparison. Logical operations of the LU test for three conditions: *equal-to condition*, *less-than condition* and *greater-than condition*. In a test for 'equal-to condition', the ALU compares two values to determine if they are equal. For example, if the number of tickets sold equals the number of seats in a cinema hall, then houseful is declared. To test 'less-than condition', the ALU compares values to determine if one is less than another. For example, if a person purchases less than two tickets, then no discount rate is given. In a test for 'greater-than condition', the ALU determines if one value is greater than another. For example, if a person purchases greater than two tickets, then discount rate is 5%.

- **CU:** It contains circuitry that uses electrical signals to direct the entire computer system to carry out, or execute, stored program instructions. This resembles orchestra leader who himself does not play a musical instrument but directs other people to play the musical instrument in a harmonized manner. It also does not execute program instructions; rather, it directs other parts of the system to do so by communicating with both ALU and memory. It controls the I/O devices and transfer of data to and from the primary storage. An analogy can be considered between the CU and the traffic police. The CU decides which action will occur just as the traffic police takes decisions on which lanes traffic will move or stop. It also determines what data are needed, where they are stored and where to store the results of the operation as well as sends the control signals to the devices involved in the execution of the instructions. It administers the movement of large amount of instructions and data used by the computer. In order to maintain the proper sequence of events required for any processing task, the CU uses clock inputs.

- **Registers:** These are the special-purpose, high-speed temporary memory units. These are temporary storage areas for holding various types of information such as data, instructions, addresses and the intermediate results of calculations. Essentially, they hold the information that the CPU is currently working on. Registers can be thought of as CPU's working memory, a special additional storage location that offers the advantage of speed. Registers work under the direction of the CU to accept, hold and transfer instructions or data and perform arithmetic or logical comparisons at high speed. The CU uses a data storage register in the similar way a store owner uses a cash register as a temporary, convenient place to store the transactions. As soon as a particular instruction or piece of data is processed, the next instruction immediately replaces it, and the information that results from the processing is returned to main memory. Table 1.2 lists some of the important registers used in CPU.

Table 1.2 Registers and Functions

Register Name	Function
Program counter (PC)	It keeps track of the next instruction to be executed.
Instruction register (IR)	It holds the instruction to be decoded by the control unit.
Memory address register (MAR)	It holds the address of the next location in memory to be accessed.
Memory buffer register (MBR)	It is used for storing data either coming to the CPU or data being transferred by the CPU.
Accumulator (ACC)	It is a general-purpose register used for storing temporary results and results produced by ALU.
Data register (DR)	It is used for storing the operands and other data.

15. Explain the concept of main memory and its types.

Ans: The 'memory' is the part of the computer that holds data and instructions for processing. Logically it is an integral component of the CPU but physically it is a separate part placed on the computer's motherboard. It stores program instructions or data for only as long as they pertain the program to be in operation. The CPU accesses the main memory in random manner, that is, the CPU can access any location of this memory to either read information from it or store information in it.

The memory in a computer system is of three fundamental types which are as follows:

- **Internal processor memory:** This memory is placed within the CPU (processor) or is attached to a special fast bus. Internal memory usually includes cache memory and special registers, both of which can be directly accessed by the processor. This memory is used for temporary storage of data and instructions on which the CPU is currently working. It is the fastest among all the memories but is the most expensive also. Therefore, a very diminutive part of internal processor memory is used in the computer system. It is generally used to compensate for the speed gap between the primary memory and the processor.
- **Primary memory:** Random Access Memory (RAM) and Read Only Memory (ROM) fall under the category of the primary memory. This memory is also known as 'main memory'. Every computer comes with a small amount of ROM that contains the boot firmware (called 'BIOS'). This holds enough information to enable the computer to check its hardware and load its operating system into RAM at the time of system booting. RAM is the place where the computer temporarily

stores its operating system, application programs and current data so that the computer's processor can reach them quickly and easily. It is volatile in nature, that is, when the power is switched off; the data in this memory are lost. Unlike RAM, ROM is non-volatile. Even when the computer is switched off, the contents of the ROM remain available.

- **Secondary memory:** This memory (also known as 'auxiliary memory') provides backup storage for instructions (computer programs) and data. The most commonly used secondary storage devices are magnetic disk and magnetic tapes. These are the least expensive as well as have much larger storage capacity than primary memory. The instructions and data stored on secondary storage devices are permanent in nature. They can only be removed if the user wants it so or the device is destroyed. Secondary memory can also be used as 'overflow memory' (also known as 'virtual memory'), when the capacity of main memory is surpassed. It is to be noted that that unlike processor memory and main memory, secondary memory is not directly accessible to the processor. Firstly, the data and instructions from secondary memory have to be shifted to main memory and then to the processor.

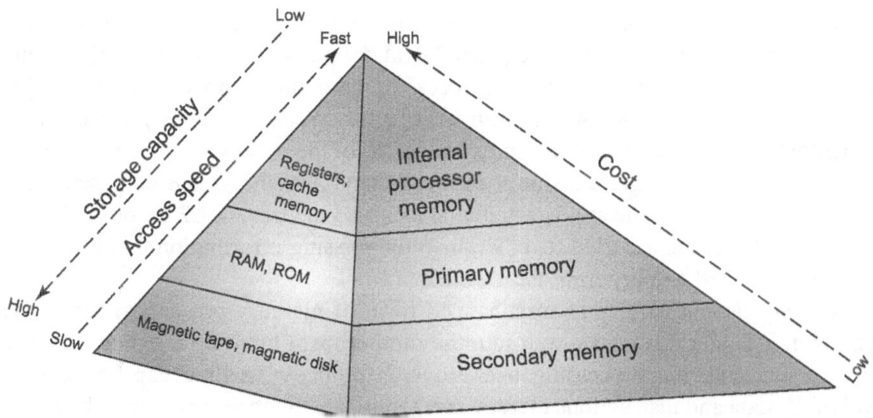

Figure 1.5 Memory Hierarchy

Figure 1.5 illustrates the memory hierarchy. The CPU accesses memory according to a distinct hierarchy. When the data come from permanent storage (for example, hard disk), firstly they go in RAM. The reason behind it is that if the CPU has to access the hard disk constantly to retrieve every piece of required data, it would operate very slowly. When the data are kept in primary memory, the CPU can access them more quickly. Subsequently, the CPU stores the required pieces of data and instructions in processor memory (cache and registers) to process the data.

16. What is cache? What are the uses or advantages of cache memory? Explain with the help of an example.

Ans: The 'cache' is a very high speed, expensive piece of memory, which is used to speed up the memory retrieval process. Without the cache memory, every request from CPU to access data would be sent to the main memory, which in response sends the data back to CPU through the system bus. This is a slow process in computing terms, so to overcome this problem cache memory has been introduced.

This extremely fast memory would store data that are frequently accessed. This achieves the quickest possible response time to the CPU. However, it is very expensive.

Consider an example of library system. When a person comes into the library and asks for a book, the librarian searches for the requested book in the bookshelves, retrieves the book and delivers it to the person. After the person reads the book, it is returned to the library. At the same time, if any other person comes in requesting the same book, which is still placed on the librarian's desk, the librarian does not have to go through the process of searching the book in the bookshelves. This results in saving of precious time in retrieving the requested book, and thus improving the efficiency of the work. This analogy can be related to computer's cache system. The computer uses logic to determine which data are the most frequently accessed and keeps them in the cache.

17. Discuss different types of cache.

Ans: A cache is a piece of very fast memory, made from high-speed static RAM that reduces the access time of the data. It is generally incorporated in the processor, where valuable data and program segments are kept. Cache memory can be categorized into three levels, which are described as follows:

- **L1 cache:** This cache is closest to the processor and hence is termed as 'primary' or L1 'cache'. Each time the processor requests information from memory, the cache controller on the chip uses special circuitry to first check if the requested data are already in the cache. If it is present, then the system is spared from time-consuming access to the main memory. In a typical CPU, primary cache ranges in size from 8 to 64 KB, with larger amounts on the newer processors. This type of cache memory is very fast because it runs at the speed of the processor since it is integrated into it.
- **L2 cache:** This cache is larger but slower in speed than L1 cache. It is used to see recent accesses that is not picked by L1 cache and is usually 64 to 2 MB in size. An L2 cache is also found on the CPU. If L1 and L2 cache are used together, then the missing information that is not present in L1 cache can be retrieved quickly from the L2 cache.
- **L3 cache:** This cache memory is an enhanced form of memory present on the motherboard of the computer. It is an extra cache built into the motherboard between the processor and the main memory to speed up the processing operations. It reduces the time gap between request and retrieval of the data and instructions thereby accessing data much more quickly than main memory. L3 cache is being used with processors nowadays having more than 3 MB of storage in it.

18. Distinguish between primary memory and secondary memory.

Ans: The two basic types of memories are primary memory and secondary memory. Some of the differences between these two memories are listed in Table 1.3.

Table 1.3 Differences between Primary Memory and Secondary Memory

Primary Memory	Secondary Memory
• It is directly accessed by the CPU for the purpose of storing and retrieving information. • It is accessed with the help of address bus and data bus. • It does not hold the data when the power is turned off, that is, it is volatile in nature. • It is much faster than secondary memory. • It is more costly as compared to secondary memory. Therefore, a computer system usually comprises a small primary memory.	• It is not directly accessible by the CPU. • It is accessed by using input/output channels. • It holds the data even when the power is turned off, that is, it is non-volatile in nature. • It is comparatively slower. • Secondary memory devices are less costly. Therefore, a computer system usually comprises much larger secondary memory.

19. How can data be accessed from secondary storage devices?

Ans: Secondary storage devices facilitate storing of data and instructions permanently. The data stored on a secondary storage device can be accessed, depending upon how they stored on the device. Primarily, there are two methods of accessing data from the secondary storage devices which are as follows:

- **Sequential access:** It means the computer system must search the storage device from the beginning until the desired data are found. The most common sequential access storage device is magnetic tape where data are stored and processed sequentially. Suppose, a tape contains information regarding employees of an organization. Now, to look for employee number 100's information, the computer will have to start with employee number 1 and then go past 2, 3 and so on, until it finally comes to 100. The sequential access method is quite simple than other methods but searching for data is slow.
- **Direct access:** It means that the computer can go directly to the location, where the data that the user wants, is stored. The direct access method is also called 'random access'. The most common direct access storage devices are magnetic disk and optical disk. In these devices, the data is stored as a numbered sequence of blocks. Thus, one can access block 12, then access block 78 and then block 2. The direct access method is ideal for applications such as airline reservation systems or computer-based directory assistance operations. In these cases, there is no fixed pattern of the requests for data.

20. Differentiate between RAM and ROM.

Ans: Both RAM and ROM fall under primary memory. But, still there exits some differences between them, which is listed in Table 1.4.

Table 1.4 Differences between RAM and ROM

RAM	ROM
• RAM is a form of memory in which one can both read and write the required data. • It is a volatile memory, that is, it stores the data temporarily. The information gets erased when the power is switched off. • It is used where the data changes on frequent basis. • It is also known as 'direct access memory', since it can be directly accessed by the user.	• As it is a read only memory, so it can only be read by the CPU. Hence, users cannot write anything into it. • It is a non-volatile memory, that is, it stores the data permanently. Its contents are not lost even when the power is switched off. • Its contents are written at the time of its IC fabrication, thus its data is not changed. • It is not accessible to user.

21. Explain in brief various types of RAM.

Ans: 'RAM' is like the computer's scratch card. It allows the computer to store data for immediate manipulation and to keep track of what is currently being processed. It is the place in a computer where the operating system, application programs and data in current use are kept so that they can be accessed quickly by the computer's processor. It is much faster to read from and write to than the other kinds of storage in a computer such as the hard disk or floppy disk. RAM is of two types which are as follows:

- **Static RAM (SRAM):** The word static indicates that the memory retains its contents as long as power is being supplied. However, as soon as the power goes down, the data is lost. This makes SRAM a volatile memory as opposed to read only memory (ROM). SRAM need not be refreshed (pulse of current through all the memory cells) periodically. It is very fast but much more expensive than DRAM. SRAM is often used as cache memory due to its high speed.

- **Dynamic RAM (DRAM):** It is named so because it is very unstable. The data continues to move in and out of the memory as long as power is available. Unlike SRAM, DRAM must be continually refreshed in order to maintain the data. This is done by placing the memory on a refresh circuit that rewrites the data several hundred times per second. DRAM is used for most system memory because it is cheap and small.

22. What is the difference between SRAM and DRAM?

Ans: The primary difference between SRAM and DRAM is the life of the data they store. SRAM retains its contents as long as electrical power is supplied to the chip. If the power is turned off, its contents are lost. On the other hand, DRAM must be continuously refreshed after about every 15 microseconds. This is true even when power is supplied constantly. SRAM chips are not as dense as DRAM chips, that is, the total number of cells in the SRAM chip is less than that on DRAM chip. SRAM is beneficial because it is fast, has low latency (the time lag between a request and the action being performed), and need not be refreshed. However, it is large and expensive, requires more power to operate and produces a lot of heat. In contrast, DRAM is simple, small and space efficient. It may be slower and may have a longer latency than SRAM, but it is still very useful. Typical access time of SRAM is 25 nanoseconds, whereas of DRAM 60 nanoseconds. SRAM is useful for low amount of memory. Anything over 4 MB is very bulky. SRAM is good for internal memory in processors, and cache, but DRAM is best for system's main memory. DRAM is used where its small size and power efficiency outweigh its slowness as compared to SRAM.

23. Explain in brief various types of ROM.

Ans: Memories in the ROM family are distinguished by the methods used to write data on them and the number of times they can be rewritten. This classification reflects the evolution of ROM devices from hard-wired to programmable to erasable-and-programmable. One common feature of all these devices is their ability to retain data and programs even during a power failure. ROMs are of different types which are as follows:

- **Masked ROM:** The very first ROMs, known as masked ROMs, were hard-wired devices that contained a pre-programmed set of data or instructions. The contents of such ROMs had to be specified before chip production so the actual data could be used to arrange the transistors inside the chip.
- **Programmable ROM (PROM):** Creating a ROM chip from scratch is a time-consuming and an expensive process. For this reason, developers created a type of ROM known as Programmable Read-only Memory (PROM), which can be programmed. Blank PROM chips can be bought economically and coded by the users with the help of a special device known as 'PROM-programmer'. However, once a PROM has been programmed, its contents can never be changed. As a result, PROM is also known as 'one-time programmable' ('OTP') device. Like other ROMs, PROM is also non-volatile. However, it is more fragile than other ROMs as a jolt of static electricity can easily cause fuses in the PROM to burn out, thus changing the bit pattern from 1 to 0. Nevertheless, blank PROMs are economical and are great for prototyping the data for a ROM before committing to the costly ROM fabrication process.
- **Erasable programmable ROM (EPROM):** This type of ROM is programmed in exactly the same manner as a PROM. However, unlike PROM, an EPROM can be erased and reprogrammed repeatedly. It can be erased by simply exposing the device to a strong source of ultraviolet light for a certain

amount of time. Note that an EPROM eraser is not selective; it will erase the entire EPROM. Although EPROM is more expensive than PROM, its ability to be reprogrammed makes it more useful.

- **Electrically erasable programmable ROM (EEPROM):** This type of ROM can be erased by an electrical charge and then written to by using slightly higher-than-normal voltage. EEPROM can be erased one byte at a time, rather than erasing the entire chip with ultraviolet light. Hence, the process of re-programming is flexible, but slow. Also, changing the contents does not require any additional committed equipment. As these chips can be changed without opening a casing, they are often used to store programmable instructions in devices such as printers.
- **Flash ROM:** This type of ROM is also called 'flash BIOS' or 'flash memory'. It is a type of constantly powered non-volatile memory that can be erased and re-programmed in blocks. It is a variation of EEPROM, which, unlike flash memory, is erased and rewritten at the byte level. Flash memory is often used to hold the control code such as the BIOS in a personal computer. When BIOS needs to be changed or rewritten, the flash memory can be written in block (rather than byte) sizes, thus making it easier to update. Flash memory gets its name because the microchip is organized so that a section of memory cells are erased in a single action or 'flash'. Flash memory is used in digital cellular phones, digital cameras and other devices.

24. List various units which help in measuring the computer memory.

Ans: All the quantities, physical or otherwise, are measured in some units. For example, length is measured in meters and mass in grams. Likewise, for measuring computer memory, a standard unit is required. Various units which are used to measure computer memory are as follows:

- **Bit:** It is the smallest unit of data on a machine and a single bit can hold only one of two values: 0 or 1. Bit is represented as b.
- **Byte:** A unit of eight bits is known as a byte. Hence, a byte is able to contain any binary number between 00000000 and 11111111. It is represented as B.
- **Kilobyte:** In a decimal system, kilo stands for 1000, but in a binary system, kilo refers to 1024. Therefore, a kilobyte is equal to 1024 bytes. It is usually represented as KB.
- **Megabyte:** It comprises 1024 kilobytes, or 1,048,576 bytes. However, since this number is hard to remember, a megabyte can be thought of as a million bytes. Megabyte is the standard unit of measurement for RAM and is represented as MB.
- **Gigabyte:** It consists of 1024 megabytes (1,073,741,824 bytes). It is the standard unit of measurement for hard disks and is often represented as GB.
- **Terabyte:** It refers to 1024 gigabytes and is often represented as TB. Terabyte memory is usually associated with super computers only.

25. What are the different types of ports and interfaces associated with computer?

(or)

Mention the standard I/O ports available in a computer.

Ans: Ports and interfaces are a generic name for the various holes (and their associated electronics), found at the back of the computer, using which external devices are connected to the computer's motherboard. Different interfaces and ports run at varying speeds and work best with specific types of devices. The different types of ports used in computers are as follows:

- **PS/2 port:** It is a standard serial port connector used to plug computer mouse and keyboards into personal computer. It consists of 6 pins in small, round shape socket.

- **Serial port:** It is a general-purpose communications port, through which data is passed serially, that is, one bit at a time. These ports are used for transmitting data over long distances. In the past, most digital cameras were connected to a computer's serial port in order to transfer images to the computer.
- **Parallel port:** It is an interface on a computer that supports transmission of multiple bits of data (usually 8 bits) at the same time. This port transmits data faster than a serial port and is exclusively used for connecting peripherals such as printers and CD-ROM drives.
- **SCSI port:** These ports are used in transmitting data up to seven devices in a daisy chain fashion and at a speed faster than serial and parallel ports (usually 32 bits at a time). These ports are hardware interface, which includes an expansion board that plugs into the computer called a 'SCSI host adapter' or 'SCSI controller'. Device which can be connected to SCSI ports are hard-disk drives and network adapters.
- **Universal serial bus (USB) port:** It is a plug-and-play hardware interface for connecting peripherals such as the keyboard, mouse, joystick, scanner, printer and modem. It supports a maximum bandwidth of 12 MB/sec and has the capability to connect up to 127 devices. With USB port, a new device can be added to the computer without adding an adapter card. These ports are replacement for parallel and serial ports.

26. What are the factors that affect the processing speed of a computer?

Ans: There are several factors that contribute to or affect the performance and processing speed of a computer. These are described as follows:

- **Processor speed:** CPU carries out all major functions required for computer processing. Thus, its speed (measured in megahertz) is one of the most important factors that affect the performance of a computer. More the speed of the processor, faster the computer will perform.
- **CPU registers:** The size of a CPU register indicates the word size of a computer, which means the amount of data a computer can work with at a given time. The bigger the word size of computer, more quickly the computer will process the data.
- **RAM:** The amount of RAM in a computer plays a major contribution to the performance of a computer. More is the amount of RAM in a computer, more and bigger programs can remain active in memory and executed at a faster speed. This ultimately makes the computer run faster.
- **Computer bus:** A 'bus' is a set of connections between two or more components of a computer, which are designed to transfer several/all bits of a word from source to destination. It is a shared media of information transfer. There are two types of buses which are mainly used in a computer, namely, *data bus* and *address bus*. The 'data bus' is a group of parallel lines that connects the CPU, memory and other hardware devices on the motherboard. Depending on the number of wires in it, one can measure the speed at which data travels between hardware components. For example, if there is an eight-wire bus, then it is capable of transmitting eight bits at a given time. On the other hand, the 'address bus' is an electric path that connects the CPU and RAM and carries the memory addresses. The number of wires in it determines the amount of RAM that a CPU can address at a time. For example, if the address bus contains eight wires then it means, the CPU can address 2^8, i.e., 256 bytes of RAM at a time. Hence, greater the width of data and address bus, faster will be the computer.
- **Viruses:** Viruses when enter in a computer run silently in the background, utilizing system resources. They also start corrupting the data and programs, due to which the systems get slower or even may crash.

27. Explain the specifications of CPU on which its performance can be compared.

Ans: There are several specifications on the basis of which processors' performance can be compared. Some of these specifications are as follows:

- **Series:** Today, there are several processor series available in the market which has a great impact on processors' performance. Few examples of processor series include Core 2 Duo, Core i7, Athlon 64 × 2 and Phenom II × 4. Each of these series has different size of cache, number of cores, price and other features. The processor series help us to determine if the processor is a low-end, mainstream or high-end one.
- **Multi-core (Dual, triple or quad core):** Today, multi-core processors are available in the market in which more than CPU core are put on a single chip. If the two CPU cores are put on a single chip then the processor is called 'dual-core processor'. Similarly when three cores are placed on a single chip, then it is called 'triple-core processor' and so on. More the number of cores present in the processor, the faster the CPU will perform. However, more number of cores results into increased power consumption.
- **Frequency:** It refers to the speed at which the processor runs. It is one of the most important factors in measuring the performance of CPU.
- **Cache:** Cache is the fastest piece of memory used by the processor to store data that are to be processed or the recently accessed data. The size of cache memory greatly affects the performance of processor. This is because more the cache we have, more data can be stored by a processor and more quickly data can be accessed too.
- **64-bit support:** In earlier times, computer users switched from 16-bit processor to 32-bit processor so that a larger amount of computer memory could be addressed by the CPU at a time. Nowadays, users are switching to 64-bit processors in order to improve the performance of processor.

28. How does one specify the configuration of a computer system?

Ans: The way a system is setup, or the assortment of components that makes up the system, is termed as the 'configuration of a PC'. The configuration can refer to either hardware or software, or both. The typical computer configuration includes RAM (latest 3GB and minimal-512MB), hard disk (latest-500GB and minimal-160GB), modem, DVD-writer, LCD monitor, Windows operating system (latest versions are 7, vista), processor (earlier-Intel dual core and latest-Intel core 2 Quad), motherboard, keyboard and optical mouse.

29. With a neat sketch, explain the working of magnetic disk.

Ans: Magnetic disks are the widely used and popular medium for direct access secondary storage. They offer high storage capacity and reliability and have capability to access the stored data directly. A magnetic disk consists of a plastic/metal circular plate/platter, which is coated with magnetic oxide layer. Data are represented as magnetized spots on a disk. A magnetized spot represents 1 and the absence of a magnetized spot represents 0. To read the data, the magnetized spots on the disk are converted into electrical impulses, which are then transferred to the processor. To write the data onto disk, the electrical impulses received from the processor are converted into magnetized spots on the disk. The data in a magnetic disk can be erased and reused virtually infinitely. The disk is designed to reside in a protective case or cartridge to shield it from the dust and other external interference.

Data in a magnetic disk are recorded on the surface of the circular tracks with the help of read/write head, which is mounted on the access arm assembly. These heads can be in multiple numbers to access the adjacent tracks simultaneously and making a disk faster. The access arm assembly can be positioned in both inward and outward direction so that the read/write head can move on the horizontal surfaces of the disk. In case of multiple disk packs, each disk surface has its own read/write head, which works in harmony with other heads to record the data. Therefore, information is stored on the tracks, constituting a cylindrical shape through a disk pack (see Figure 1.6). The process of accessing data from magnetic disk comprises three steps which are as follows:

1. **Seek:** As soon as the disk unit receives the read/write command, the read/write heads are positioned on the specific track on the disk platter. The time taken in doing so is known as 'seek time'. It is the average time required to move the heads to the desired track on the disk. Seek times of modern disks may range between 2–15 milliseconds but the seek time of most common disks is 9 milliseconds.
2. **Rotate:** Once the heads are positioned on the desired track, the head of the specific platter is activated. Since the disk is rotated constantly, the head has to wait for the required sector or cluster (desired data) to come under it. This waiting time is known as 'rotational delay time' or 'latency' of the disk. The rotational latency of a disk with 7200 rpm is 4.17 milliseconds.
3. **Data transfer:** Once the read/write head is positioned over the desired sector, the data can be transferred to or from the disk to primary memory. The rate at which the data is read from or written to the disk is known as 'data transfer rate'. It is measured in kilobits per second (kbps). The data transfer rate depends upon the rotational speed of the disk. If the disk has a rotational speed of 6,000 rpm (rotations per minute), having 125 sectors and 512 bytes/sector, the data transfer rate per rotation will be $125 \times 512 = 64{,}000$ bytes. Hence, the total transfer rate per second will be $64{,}000 \times 6{,}000/60 = 6{,}400{,}000$ bytes/second or 6.4 MB/second.

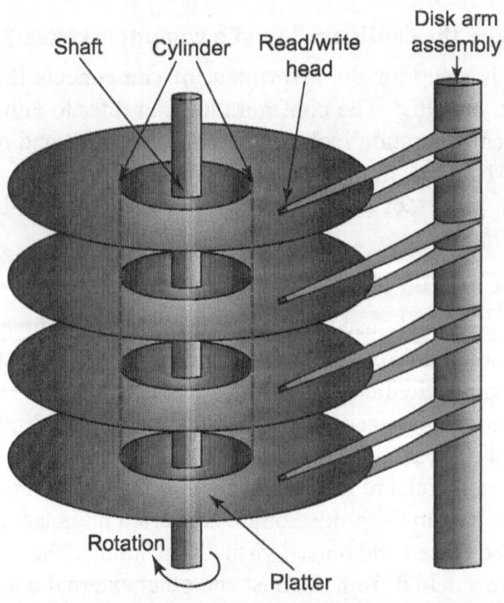

Figure 1.6 Disk pack and cylinder

30. What do you mean by optical disk?

Ans: An 'optical disk' is a flat, circular, plastic disk coated with material on which bits may be stored in the form of highly reflective areas and significantly less reflective areas, from which the stored data may be read when illuminated with a narrow-beam source, such as a laser diode. These disks are capable of storing enormously high amount of data in a limited amount of space. The optical disk storage system consists of a rotating disk coated with a thin layer of metal (aluminium, gold or silver) that acts as a reflective surface and a laser beam, which is used as a read/write head for recording data onto the disk. Optical disk comes in various sizes and capacities which are made in somewhat different ways for different purposes. 'Compact disk' ('CD'), 'digital versatile disk' ('DVD'), and 'blu-ray disk' ('BD') are the three forms of optical disks. Each requires a different type of disk drive for being accessed.

31. Explain the following storage devices:

(a) Floppy disk
(b) Hard disk
(c) CD
(d) DVD

Ans:

(a) A 'floppy disk' is a round, flat piece of Mylar plastic coated with ferric oxide (a rust-like substance containing tiny particles capable of holding a magnetic field) and encased in a protective plastic cover (disk jacket). It is a removable disk and is read and written by a floppy disk drive (FDD), which is a device that performs the basic operation on a disk, including rotating the disk and reading and writing data onto it. The data on the floppy disk can easily be accessed randomly. The disk drive's read/write head alters the magnetic orientation of the particles, where orientation in one-direction represents '1' and orientation in the other represents '0'.

Traditionally, floppy disks were used on personal computers to distribute software, transfer data between computers and create small backups. Earlier, 5¼-inch floppy disks were used. Later, a new format of 3½-inch floppy disk came into existence, which has larger storage capacity and supports faster data transfer as compared to 5¼-inch floppy disks. Floppy diskettes are small, inexpensive, readily available, easy to store and have a good shelf life if stored properly. They also possess the write-protect feature, which allows the users to protect a diskette from being written on. To write-protect a diskette, the user has to shift a slide lever towards the edge of the disk, uncovering a hole. The key advantage of floppy disk is that it is portable.

(b) The 'hard disk', also called the 'hard drive', is the major storage unit of the computer. It consists of a stack of disk platters that are made up of aluminium alloy or glass substrate coated with a magnetic material and protective layers. They are tightly sealed to prevent any dust particle, which causes head crash, from getting inside. Hard disk can be external (removable) or internal (fixed) and can hold a large amount of data. The capacity that is the amount of information that a hard disk can store is measured in bytes. A typical computer today comes with 80–320 GB of hard disk. The storage capacity of hard disk has increased dramatically since the day it was introduced. The hard disk speed is measured in terms of access time (typically in milliseconds). A hard disk with lower access time is faster than a hard disk with higher access time; the lower the access time, the faster the hard disk.

(c) CD ('Compact Disk') is the most popular and the least expensive type of optical disk. It was originally intended only for storing music (in the form of digital audio) and can record about 80 minutes of uninterrupted playing time. A CD is capable of being used as a data storage device along with storing of digital audio.

A CD is a shiny, silver colour metal disk of 12 cm in diameter. A typical optical disk is made up of three layers: a *polycarbonate base* through which light can pass, a *layer of aluminium* and a protective *layer of acrylic* on top of that. The pits of CD are typically 0.5 microns wide, 0.83–3 microns long and 0.15 microns deep. A CD has one track that spirals from the centre to the outside edge. If one could remove the track from a standard 12 cm CD, it would stretch for three and a half miles. The single track is divided into sectors of equal length and density. Files are stored on these particular contiguous sectors. CDs are available in various formats, namely, *CD-ROM* (*compact disk-read only memory*), *CD-R* (*compact disk-recordable*) and *CD-RW* (*compact disk-rewritable*) disks.

(d) 'DVD' ('Digital Versatile Disk'), initially called 'Digital Video Disk', is a high-capacity data storage medium. At first glance, a DVD can easily be mistaken for a CD as both are plastic disks 120 mm in diameter and 1.2 mm thick and both rely on lasers to read data. However, the DVD's seven-fold increase in data capacity over the CD has been largely achieved by tightening up the tolerances throughout the predecessor system. In DVD, the tracks are placed closer together, thereby allowing more tracks per disk. The DVD's *track pitch* (the distance between each) is reduced to 0.74 micron, less than half of CD's 1.6 micron. The pits, in which the data is stored, are also a lot smaller, thus allowing more pits per track. The minimum pit length of a single layer DVD is 0.4 micron as compared to 0.834 micron for a CD. With the number of pits having a direct bearing on capacity levels, DVD's reduced track pitch and pit size alone give DVDs four times the storage capacity of CDs.

32. What do you mean by CD-ROM, CD-R and CD-RW?

Ans: A 'CD-ROM' disk comes with pre-recorded data by the manufactures and can be read but cannot be altered. 'CD-R' is a type of 'WORM' ('write once-read many') disk that allows you to record your own data. Once written, the data on the CD-R can be read but cannot be altered. A 'CD-RW' disk is rewritable version of CD-R that means, it allows writing, erasing and rewriting of data several times.

The data recorded on all CD formats can be read using the CD-ROM drive; however, to write data on CD-R and CD-RW disks, one needs a special peripheral device known as 'CD-writer' (or 'CD-burner').

33. Differentiate between magnetic storage and optical storage.

Ans: Though both magnetic and optical storage are the secondary memories, there is a huge difference in their storage techniques, storage capacities, etc. Some differences between the two are listed in Table 1.5.

Table 1.5 Differences between Magnetic Storage and Optical Storage

Magnetic storage	Optical storage
• Magnetic storage devices store the data in magnetic form. • They tend to have large storage capacity as compared to optical media. For example, hard disks. • They are optimized for high speed. • Magnetic storage technology has been used for computers since 1950. Thus, they are used to store important files and software. • They are affected by magnetic field. • These storage devices are not as portable as optical devices as they are mostly placed inside the computer. Moreover, if magnetic devices are kept near to a strong magnetic field area (such as loudspeaker), then the device is more likely to get damaged.	• Optical storage devices store the data optically, that is, use a laser beam to read/write. • They have limited storage capacity as compared to magnetic media. • They are much slower as compared to the magnetic media. For example, CDs and DVDs can access the data at a faster rate to play music and movies, but are slower than hard disks. • This technology is used for keeping portable data such as movies and music. • They are not affected by magnetic field. • These storage devices are portable as they are smaller in size, light weight and removable.

34. A magnetic disk pack has 12 surfaces out of which 10 are readable. Each surface has 50 tracks and each track is divided into a number of sectors. If the total capacity of the disk pack is 5,000 KB and the capacity of each sector is 512 bytes then:

(a) How many cylinders are present in the disk pack?

(b) How many sectors are present on each track?

Ans:

(a) Number of cylinders $= 12 \times 50$
$= 600$

(b) Number of sectors $= \dfrac{5{,}000 \times 1{,}024}{512} = 10{,}000$

35. What are input devices and output devices?

Ans: An 'input device' is an electromechanical device that allows the user to feed information into the computer for analysis, storage and to give commands to the computer. Data and instructions are entered into the computer's memory through an input device. It captures information and translates it into a form that can be processed and used by the other parts of the computer.

After processing the input data, the computer provides the results with the help of output devices. An 'output device' converts machine-readable information into human-readable form. The basic functioning of output device is just the opposite of the input device, that is, the data is fed into the computer system through the input device while the output is taken out from the computer through the output device. However, the output, which comes out from CPU, is in the form of digital signals. The output devices display the processed information by converting them into graphical, alphanumeric or audio-visual form.

36. List various input, output and input-output devices.

Ans: Some of the basic input, output and input-output devices are listed as follows:

- **Input devices**
  - Keyboard
  - Graphics tablet
  - Trackball
  - Barcode reader
  - Gamepad
  - Joystick
  - Microphone
  - Mouse (pointing device)
  - Scanner
  - Webcam
  - Touchpad
  - Light pen
  - Microphone
  - Electronic whiteboard
- **Output devices**
  - Monitor
  - Printer
  - Plotter

- Projector
- Computer output microfilm (COM)
- Speakers

- **Input-output devices**
  - Modems
  - Network cards
  - Touch screen
  - Headsets
  - Audio card/sound card
  - CD
  - Hard drive
  - Digital camera

37. Discuss the operations of the following devices:

(a) Light pen

(b) Touch screen

(c) Game controller

Ans:

(a) A 'light pen' (sometimes called a 'mouse pen') is a hand-held electro-optical pointing device which when touched to or aimed closely at a connected computer monitor, will allow the computer to determine where on that screen the pen is aimed. It facilitates drawing images and selects objects on the display screen by directly pointing to the objects. It is a pen-like device that can be used directly on the monitor screen without requiring any special hand/eye coordinating skills. As the light pen moves over the screen, the lines or images are drawn. The working of light pen is as follows:

The light pen contains a lens and a photo detector located in its tip. When the electron beam that sweeps the monitor strikes the phosphor within the light pen's field of view, the light emitted by the phosphor is focused through the lens and onto the photo detector. Due to this, the signal current is increased and is transmitted to the computer. The position of the beam is tracked by the horizontal and vertical counters, which relay this information to a register. This cycle is repeated for every frame produced by the electron beam. By noting when a scan goes by and measuring the interval between scan lines or entire screen refreshes, an accurate position of the photo detector on the screen is determined. The light pen software generates x-y vectors corresponding to a point on the screen, which may be used to make a selection by activating a switch on the light pen.

(b) A 'touch screen' is a special kind of input device that allows the direct selection of a menu item or the desired icon with the touch of finger. Essentially, it registers the input when a finger or other object is touched to the screen. Typically, it is used in information-providing systems such as hospitals, airlines and railway reservation counters, amusement parks, etc. The working of touch screen is described as follows:

A basic touch screen has three main components; namely, a *touch sensor*, *a controller* and a *software driver*. The 'touch sensor' or panel is a clear glass panel with a touch responsive surface. It is placed over a display screen so that the responsive area of the panel covers the viewable area of the video screen. There are several different touch sensor technologies in the market today, each using a different method to detect touch input. These methods are optical, acoustical and electrical methods. In optical method, the infrared beams interlace the surface of the screen and when a light beam is broken, that particular location is recorded. In acoustical method, the ultrasonic acoustic waves pass over the surface of the screen and when the wave signals are interrupted by some contact with the screen, the location is recorded. In electrical method, the panel has an electrical current going through it and touching the screen causes a voltage change, which is used to determine the location of the touch to the screen. The controller connects the touch sensor and the computer. It takes information from the touch sensor and translates it into information that a computer can understand. The driver is a software update for the computer system that allows the touch screen and computer to work together. It tells the operating system how to interpret the touch event information that is sent from the controller.

(c) A 'game controller' (also known as 'joystick') is a pointing device that moves in all directions and controls the movement of the cursor. The basic design of a joystick consists of a stick that is attached to a plastic base with a flexible rubber sheath. This plastic base houses a circuit board that sits beneath the stick. The electronic circuitry measures the movement of the stick from its central position and sends the information for processing. Joystick also consists of buttons which can be programmed to indicate certain actions once a position on the screen has been selected using stick. It offers three types of control, namely, *digital*, *glide* and *direct*. Digital control allows movement in a limited number of directions such as up, down, left and right. Glide and direct control allow movements in all directions (360 degrees). Direct control joysticks have the added ability to respond to the distance and speed with which the user moves the stick. The various applications in which joystick is used are flight simulators, playing computer games, training simulators, CAD/CAM systems and for controlling industrial robots. The working of joystick is as follows:

A joystick is designed to inform the computer about the positioning of the stick at any given time. This is done by providing the x-y coordinates of the stick. The x-axis represents the side-to-side position and the y-axis represents the forward block position. The circuit board that sits directly underneath the stick carries electricity from one contact point to another. When the joystick is in neutral position, all but one of the individual circuits is broken. Each broken section is covered with a simple plastic button containing a tiny metal disc. When the stick is moved in any direction, it pushes down on one of these buttons, pressing the conductive metal disc against the circuit board. This closes the circuit, that is, it completes the connection between the two wire sections. When the circuit is closed, electricity can flow down a wire from the computer and to another wire leading back to the computer. When the computer picks up a charge on a particular wire, it knows that the joystick is in the right position to complete that particular circuit. The joystick buttons work exactly the same way. When a button is pressed down, it completes a circuit and the computer recognises a command.

38. Explain in brief about OCR.

Ans: 'OCR' ('optical character recognition') is a software that scans the text document. This means that OCR software translates the bitmap image of text to the ASCII codes that the computer can interpret as letters, numbers and special characters. Because of OCR, data entry becomes easier, error-free and less time consuming. However, it is very expensive and if the document is not typed properly, it will become difficult for the OCR to recognize the characters. Furthermore, except for tab stops and paragraph marks, most documents formatting are lost during text scanning. The output from a finished text scan will be a single column editable text file. This text file will always require spell checking and proof reading as well as re-formatting to get the desired final layout.

39. Differentiate between hard copy and soft copy output.

Ans: The outputs, which can be easily understood and used by human beings, are of the two forms, namely, *hard copy* and *soft copy*. These two are discussed as follows:

- **Hard copy:** The physical form of output is known as hard copy. In general, it refers to the recorded information copied from a computer onto paper or some other durable surface such as microfilm. Hard copy output is permanent and a relatively stable form of output. This type of output is also highly portable. Paper is one of the most widely used hard copy output media. The principal examples are printouts, whether text or graphics from printers.
- **Soft copy:** The electronic version of an output, which usually resides in computer memory and/or on disk, is known as soft copy. Unlike hard copy, soft copy is not a permanent form of output. It is transient and is usually displayed on the screen. This kind of output is not tangible, that is, it cannot be touched. Soft copy output includes audio and visual form of output, which is generated using a computer. In addition, textual or graphical information displayed on a computer monitor is also soft copy form of output.

40. What is the usage of printer? Write some characteristics of impact and non-impact printers. Give examples of each.

Ans: A printer prints information and data from the computer onto a paper. Generally, the printer prints 80 or 132 columns of characters in each line, and prints either on single sheets, or on a continuous roll of paper, depending upon the printer itself. The printers are divided into two categories which are as follows:

Impact printers

An impact printer uses pins or hammers that press an inked ribbon against the paper to make a mark on the paper. Each hammer is embossed with a specific shape which is transferred onto the paper through the inked ribbon thereby producing a printed character. Some impact printers can print only one character at a time, whereas others can print an entire line. The three most commonly used impact printers are dot matrix printers, daisy wheel printers and drum printers. Some characteristics of impact printers are as follows:

- There is physical contact with the paper to produce an image.
- They are relatively cheap. The primary recurring costs for these printers are the ink ribbons and paper.
- Due to being robust and low cost, they are useful for bulk printing.
- They can withstand dusty environment, vibrations and extreme temperature.
- They are ideal for printing multiple copies (that is, carbon copies) because they can easily print through many layers of paper.
- Due to its striking activity, impact printers are very noisy.
- Since they are mechanical in nature, they tend to be slow.

Non-impact printers

Unlike impact printers, a non-impact printer forms characters and images without making direct physical contact between printing mechanism and paper. In this printer, the print head does not make contact with the paper, and no inked ribbon is required. Ink can be sprayed against the paper and then heat and pressure are used to fuse a fine black powder into the shape of a character. The major technologies competing in the market of non-impact printers are ink-jet and laser. Some characteristics of non-impact printers are as follows:

- They are faster because they have fewer moving parts.
- They are quieter because there is no striking mechanism involved and only few moving parts are used.
- They possess the ability to change typefaces automatically.
- They produce high-quality graphics.
- They cannot print carbon copies.

41. Explain laser printer and its working concept in detail.

Ans: A laser printer provides the highest quality text and images for personal computers today. It is a very fast printer, which operates on the same principle as that of a photocopy machine. Most laser printers can print text and graphics with a very high quality resolution. They are also known as 'page printers' because they process and store the entire page before they actually print it. They produce sharp, crisp images of both text and graphics, providing resolutions from 300 to 2,400 dpi. Today, the resolution of most printers is 600 dpi. They are quiet and fast, able to print 4–32 text-only pages per minute for individual microcomputers and up to 200 pages per minute for mainframes. Laser printers can print in excess of 2000 lines per minute. Furthermore, they can print in different fonts, that is, type styles and sizes. Laser printers are often faster than ink-jet printers but are more expensive to buy and maintain than the other printers. The cost of these printers depends on a combination of costs of paper, toner replacement and drum replacement. These printers are useful for volume printing because of their speed. The working of laser printer is described as follows:

Working of a Laser Printer

The core component of laser printing system is the photoconductive drum. A rotating mirror inside the printer causes the beam of a laser to sweep across the photoconductive drum. Initially, the beam of laser charges the photoconductive drum positively. When the charged photoconductor is exposed to an optical image through a beam of light to discharge, a latent or invisible image is formed. At the point where the laser strikes the surface of drum, it creates a dot of positive charge. These points are represented by a black dot, which will be printed on the paper. After this, the printer coats the drum with a container, which contains a black powder called 'toner'. This toner is negatively charged, and so it clings to the positive areas of the drum surface. When the powder pattern gets fixed, the drum is rotated and the paper is fed into the drum surface via a pressure roller. This pressure roller transfers the black toner onto the paper. Since the paper is moving at the same speed as the drum, the paper picks up the image pattern precisely. Finally, the printer passes the paper through the fuser, a pair of heated rollers. As the paper passes through these rollers, the loose toner powder gets melted and fuses with the fibres in the paper. The paper is then brought out of the printer. Figure 1.7 illustrates the working of laser printer.

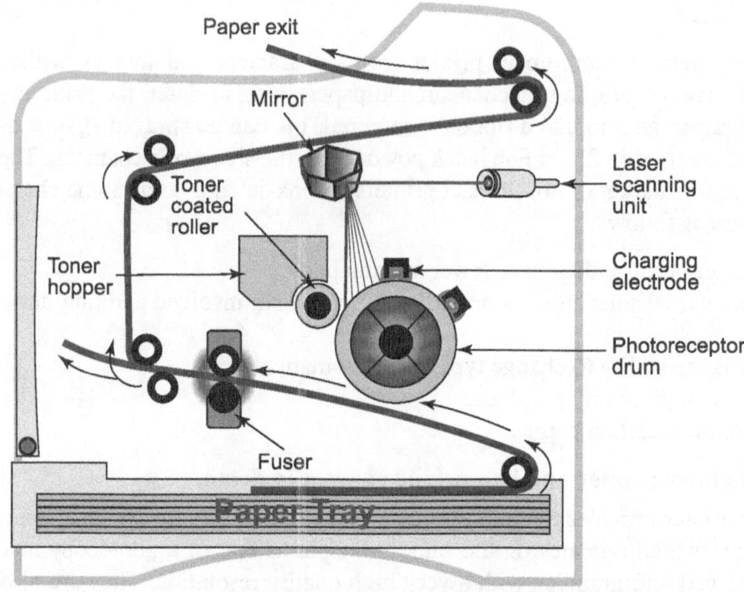

Figure 1.7 Working of a Laser Printer

42. What is the role of visual display unit? Also discuss the types of monitors.

Ans: The monitor, also known as 'visual display unit' ('VDU'), is the most frequently used output device for producing soft-copy output. A computer monitor is a TV-like display attached to the computer on which the output can be displayed and viewed. The computer monitor can either be a monochrome display or a colour display. A monochrome screen uses only one colour (usually white, green, amber or black) to display text on contrasting background. Colour screens commonly display 256 colors at one time from a selection of over 2,56,000 choices. Monitors are available in various sizes like 14, 15, 17, 19 and 21 inches. The size of the display is described based on two parameters, namely, *aspect ratio* and *screen size*. 'Aspect ratio' is the ratio of the width of the display screen to the height, that is, the ratio of vertical points to the horizontal points necessary to produce equal-length lines in both directions on the screen. Generally, computer displays have an aspect ratio of 4:3. Like televisions, 'screen sizes' are normally measured diagonally (in inches), the distance from one corner to the opposite corner. The description of various types of monitors is as follows:

- **Cathode ray tube (CRT):** Nowadays, most computer monitors are based on cathode ray tube (CRT) technology. The basic operation of these tubes is similar to that in television sets. The primary components in a CRT are the heated metal cathode and a control grid. Heat is supplied to the cathode by directing a current through a coil of wire, called the 'filament', inside the cylindrical cathode structure. This causes electrons to be boiled off the hot cathode surface. In the vacuum inside the CRT envelope, the free, negatively charged electrons are then accelerated toward the phosphor coating by a highly positive voltage. The accelerating voltage can be generated with a positively charged metal coating on the inside of the CRT envelope near the phosphor screen, or an accelerating anode can be used.

- **Liquid crystal display (LCD):** With the widespread use of smaller computers like PDAs and laptops, a new type of display liquid crystal display (LCD) has made a big impact on computer market. LCD screens have been used since long on notebook computers but are also becoming popular as a desktop monitor. The term liquid crystal sounds like a contradiction. We generally conceive a crystal as a solid material such as quartz and a liquid as water-like fluid. However, some substances can exist in an odd state that is semi-liquid and semi-solid. When they are in this state, their molecules tend to maintain their orientation like the molecules in a solid, but also move around to different positions like the molecules in a liquid. Thus, liquid crystals are neither a solid nor a liquid. Manufacturers use this amazing ability of liquid crystals to display images.
- **Plasma display:** A plasma display (also known as 'thin-panel') is constructed by filling a gas (Neon or Xenon) between the two glass plates. One glass plate consists of vertical conductors and the other consists of horizontal conductors. When the voltage is applied to the pair of horizontal and vertical conductors, the gas at the intersection of two conductors glows. The advantage of plasma display is that it has the capability of producing more than 16 million colours and is lighter and less bulky than CRT. However, it is heavier than LCD display and requires more power.
- **Thin-film electroluminescent display:** This display is similar to the plasma display except the fact that the space between the glass plates is filled with phosphorescent substance (usually zinc sulphide doped with manganese) instead of gas. When the high voltage is applied to the crossing conductors, the phosphoric substance at the intersection of two conductors becomes conductor and generates the electrical energy. This energy is absorbed by the manganese atoms and then released as a spot of light. The main problem with thin-film electroluminescent displays is that they require more power.

Multiple-choice Questions

1. GIGO stands for ________.

   (a) Garbage in garbage out (b) Gigabyte in gigabyte out
   (c) Get in get out (d) None of the above

2. Modifications in sand tables resulted in a device known as ________.

   (a) Computer (b) Pascaline (c) Abacus (d) All of the above

3. Which computers are based on vacuum tube technology?

   (a) First generation (b) Second generation
   (c) Third generation (d) Fourth generation

4. Which type of computer you will most likely to encounter at the department of motor vehicles?

   (a) Smart phone (b) Mainframe
   (c) Super computer (d) Mini computer

5. Which of these is an example of hand-held computer?

   (a) RAM (b) PDA (c) BUS (d) CMOS

6. Stylus is used to input data in

   (a) Laptop (b) Desktop (c) PDA (d) None of these

7. Which of the following acts as the primary controlling mechanism for the computer's hardware?
   (a) RAM (b) CPU (c) Operating system (d) CD ROM
8. Which of these is not a part of CPU?
   (a) CU (b) ALU (c) L2 cache (d) L3 cache
9. ALU is a part of ________.
   (a) Memory (b) CPU (c) Input device (d) Output device
10. Which of the following caches holds the most recently used data or instructions?
    (a) L1 (b) L2 (c) L3 (d) L4
11. The register which contains the instructions that are to be executed is known as ________.
    (a) Index register (b) MAR (c) Instruction register (d) MBR
12. Which one of the following units represents the largest amount of data?
    (a) KB (b) GB (c) TB (d) MB
13. Which of the following devices stores the instructions that help the computer start up?
    (a) RAM (b) ROM (c) Monitor (d) CD ROM
14. Memory that loses data when the power is turned off is considered as ________.
    (a) Volatile memory (b) Static memory
    (c) Dynamic memory (d) Refreshed memory
15. Which of the following is not used as secondary storage?
    (a) Semiconductor memory (b) Magnetic drum
    (c) Magnetic disk (d) Magnetic tape
16. An example for magnetic storage device is ________.
    (a) CD ROM (b) Hard disk (c) Flash memory (d) DVD
17. A laser printer's speed is measured in ________.
    (a) cps (b) ppm (c) dpi (d) lpm
18. A computer resolution is determined by ________.
    (a) Monitor (b) Video controller (c) CPU (d) System unit
19. ________ is also known as thin-panel.
    (a) Plasma display (b) LCD (c) CRT (d) None of the above

Answers

1. (a) 2. (c) 3. (a) 4. (b) 5. (b) 6. (c) 7. (c) 8. (d) 9. (b) 10. (a)
11. (c) 12. (c) 13. (b) 14. (a) 15. (a) 16. (b) 17. (c) 18. (b) 19. (a)

2

Number Systems

1. Define number system. Write in brief about positional and non-positional number system.

Ans: A number system defines a set of values used to represent 'quantity'. In ancient times, people used to count on their fingers. When the fingers became insufficient for counting, stones, pebbles or sticks were used to indicate the values. This method of counting is called the 'non-positional number system'. It was very difficult to perform arithmetic with such a number system, as it had no symbol for zero. The most common non-positional number system is the Roman number system, in which only a few characters such as I, V, X, L, C, D and M are used to represent the numbers. These systems are often clumsy and it is very difficult to perform calculations for large numbers.

On the other hand, a 'positional number system' requires a finite number of symbols/digits of the system to represent arbitrarily large numbers. When using these systems, the execution of numerical calculations becomes simplified because a finite set of digits are used. The value of each digit in a number is defined not only by the symbol, but also by the symbol's position. The most popular positional number system being used today is the decimal number system. Some other commonly used positional number systems include binary, octal and hexadecimal number systems.

2. What information is conveyed by radix in the number system? Tabulate the types of number systems used by the computers.

Ans: In the number system, the 'radix' (also called 'base') tells the number of symbols used in the system. In the earlier days, different civilizations were using different radixes. The Egyptians used the radix 2, the Babylonians used the radix 60 and Mayans used the radixes 18 and 20. In contrast, modern computers use the radix 2 because they recognize only two symbols, which are represented in digital circuits as 0s and 1s. The radix of the system is always expressed in decimal numbers. The base or radix of the decimal system is 10. This implies that there are 10 symbols: 0, 1, 2, 3, 4, 5, 6, 7, 8 and 9. Similarly, the system using three symbols 0, 1 and 2 will be of base 3; four symbols will be of base 4 and so forth.

The base of a number system is indicated by a subscript (decimal number) and this will be followed by the value of the number.

For example,

$(7592)_{10}$ is of base 10 number system.

$(214)_8$ is of base 8 number system.

$(123)_{16}$ is of base 16 number system.

The types of number system used by the computers are listed in Table 2.1.

Table 2.1 Types of Number System

Number System	Radix Value	Set of Digits	Example
Decimal	$r = 10$	(0, 1, 2, 3, 4, 5, 6, 7, 8, 9)	$(25)_{10}$
Binary	$r = 2$	(0, 1)	$(11001)_2$
Octal	$r = 8$	(0, 1, 2, 3, 4, 5, 6, 7)	$(31)_8$
Hexadecimal	$r = 16$	(0, 1, 2, 3, 4, 5, 6, 7, 8, 9, A, B, C, D, E, F)	$(19)_{16}$

3. Discuss binary number system.

Ans: A 'binary number system' is a base 2 number system, that is, it uses only two symbols 0 and 1 to represent each quantity. The two symbols of the binary number are also known as 'bits'. The binary number system is the computer's native number system. This is because the computers do not use the 10 digits of the decimal system for counting and arithmetic. Their CPU and memory are made up of millions of tiny switches that can be either in the ON or OFF states. The symbols 0 and 1 of the binary number system are used to refer for the two states OFF and ON of these switches, respectively.

Like decimal system, in binary number system also, the position of a digit in a number indicates its value. Instead of ones, tens, hundreds, thousands, etc., as in the decimal system, the columns in the binary system contains ones, twos, fours, eights, etc. Each column represents a number in powers of 2; starting with 2^0 for the left most column, power is incremented by 1 for each additional column to the right.

4. List the different symbols of hexadecimal number system.

Ans: Hexadecimal number system uses 0 to 9 and A to F to represent a number, where A is equivalent to decimal 10 and the largest hexadecimal digit F is equivalent to decimal 15. The base for hexadecimal number is 16. The different symbols used in hexadecimal number system are described in Table 2.2.

Table 2.2 Symbols Used in Hexadecimal Number System

Decimal	Hexadecimal
0	0
1	1
2	2
3	3
4	4
5	5
6	6
7	7
8	8
9	9
10	A
11	B
12	C
13	D
14	E
15	F

5. What are signed and unsigned numbers?

Ans: The binary numbers are represented as either *signed* or *unsigned* numbers. An 'n-bit signed' binary number consists of two parts: one part denotes the sign of the number and the other part denotes the magnitude of the number. The MSB (most significant bit) is always a 'sign' bit, which denotes the sign of the number and the convention is that 0 and 1 denote '+' and '−', respectively. The remaining (n−1) bits denote the magnitude of the number as shown in Figure 2.1.

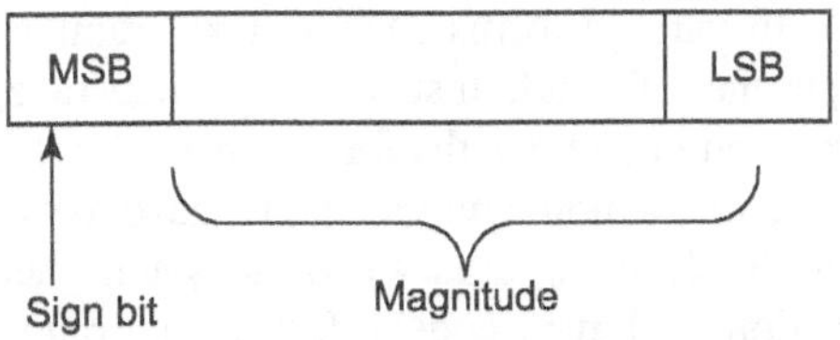

Figure 2.1 Representation of Signed Binary Number

In some applications, there is no need to include the sign along with the number while representing the numbers into the computers. The numbers that have no sign associated with them are called 'unsigned' numbers. All the bits in unsigned binary number represent the magnitude of the number as shown in Figure 2.2.

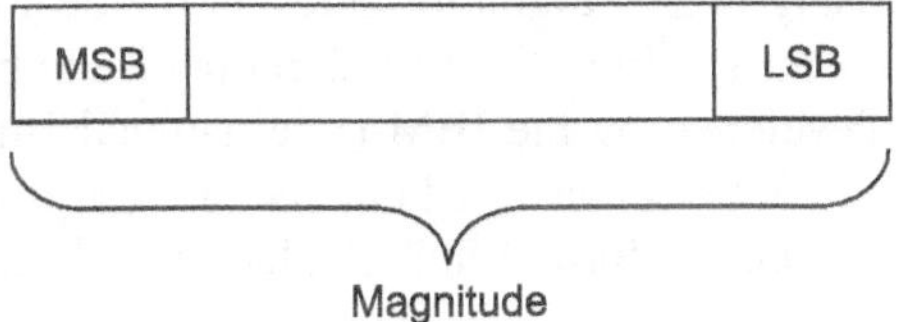

Figure 2.2 Representation of Unsigned Binary Number

The rules for signed and unsigned binary numbers are as follows:

- In an unsigned number, the MSB is a weighted position bit.
- In a signed number, the MSB (the sign bit) is 0 for a positive number.
- In a signed number, the MSB (the sign bit) is 1 for a negative number.

6. Write a short note on complement.

Ans: The complement of a number is the number which when added to the original will make it equal to a multiple of the base number system. The complement of a number can be used as a representation of that number as a negative and as a positive number that represents a negative. Consequently, complements are used in the digital computers for simplifying the subtraction operation and for the logical operation.

For every base r system, there are two types of complements: r's complement and (r−1)'s complement. That is,
For decimal r = 10, we have 9s and 10s complement.
For binary r = 2, we have 1s and 2s complement.
For octal r = 8, we have 7s and 8s complement.
For hexadecimal r = 16, we have 15s and 16s complement.

7. How are characters represented in computers?

Ans: There are a lot of ways to represent numeric, alphabetic and special characters in computer's internal storage area. In computers, the code is made up of fixed size groups of binary positions. Each binary position in a group is assigned a specific value; for example, 8, 4, 2 or 1. In this way, every character can be represented by a combination of bits that is unique. There are many coding schemes available for representing characters. The most commonly used coding systems are American Standard Code for Information Interchange (ASCII) and Unicode.

8. What is the purpose of the binary coding system? Briefly explain the terms: BCD, ASCII and EBCDIC.

Ans: Data can be available in various forms such as text, numbers, images, audio and video. To represent such data in computer, the information such as alphabets (a–z, A–Z), numbers (0, 1, 2, …, 9), special symbols (!, @, #, $, etc.) and images (in the form of pixels/picture elements) has to be converted into sequences of bits, that is, 0 and 1. Audio and video data have to be converted from analogue signal to digital signal. This is accomplished using binary coding system that uses specialized codes (binary codes) to represent the information. A 'binary code' refers to an arrangement of bits (combination of 0s and 1s) representing the specific information, such as letters, symbols and digits. An n-bit binary code represents 2^n distinct combination of 1s and 0s, where each combination represents one element of the set being coded. There are various binary coding schemes including Binary Coded Decimal (BCD), ASCII and Extended Binary Coded Decimal Interchange Code (EBCDIC), which are used these days to represent the data. These coding systems are described as follows:

- BCD: It is a method of using binary digits to represent the decimal digits 0 to 9. Each decimal digit is represented by four binary digits. The BCD coding is the binary equivalent of the decimal digit. BCD system was developed by the IBM (International Business Machines) Corporation. With BCD, each digit of a number is converted into its binary equivalent rather than converting the entire decimal number to its binary form. Similarly, letters and special characters can be coded in the binary form.

  Let us determine the BCD value for the decimal number 5319. Since there are four digits in our decimal number, there are four bytes in our BCD number. They are:

Thousands—Hundreds	Tens—Units
53	19
0 1 0 1 0 0 1 1	0 0 0 1 1 0 0 1

Binary code decimal digits (0–9) are represented using four bits. The valid combinations of bits and their respective values are shown in Table 2.3.

Table 2.3 Binary Coded Decimal

Decimal Code	BCD Digit
0	0000
1	0001
2	0010
3	0011
4	0100
5	0101
6	0110
7	0111
8	1000
9	1001

The latest version of BCD used a 6-bit code. These BCD codes defined 6-bit words, which allowed representing a maximum of 64, that is, 2^6 symbols.

- ASCII: It is a standardized alphanumeric code used for representing alphabets (A–Z and a–z), digits (0–9) and other symbols. This code is developed by IBM and has been universally accepted for being used in most computers and other electronic equipments. It was originally designed as a 7-bit code and, thus, it can represent 128 characters and symbols. Later on, IBM developed a new version of ASCII, called as ASCII-8, which is an 8-bit code with MSB always 0.

  ASCII is commonly used in the transmission of data through data communication and is used almost exclusively to represent the data internally in the microcomputers. In ASCII, rather than breaking letters into three groups, upper case letters are assigned codes beginning with hexadecimal value 41 and continuing sequentially through hexadecimal value 5A. Similarly, lower case letters are assigned hexadecimal values of 61 through 7A. The standard ASCII code defines 128 character codes (from 0 to 127), of which, the first 32 are control codes (non-printable) and the other 96 are representable characters.
- EBCDIC: It uses 8 bits for each character, it is possible to represent 256 different characters or bit combinations. This provides a unique code for each decimal value 0 to 9 (for a total of 10), each upper case letter and lower case letter (for a total of 52), and for a variety of special characters. Since, it is an 8-bit code, each group of the eight bits makes up one alphabetic, numeric or special character and is called a 'byte'. The bit pattern 1100 is the zone combination (zone and digit) used for the alphabetic characters A through I, 1101 is used for the characters J through R and 1110 is the zone combination used for characters S through Z. The bit pattern 1111 is the zone combination used when representing decimal digits.

9. How are signed numbers represented using 2s complement?

Ans: A signed number is represented by a sign bit and the magnitude bits. For a positive signed number, the sign bit is 0, while for a negative signed number, the sign bit is 1. The representation of signed number using 2s complement method differs for positive and negative signed numbers. In case of positive signed number, the binary equivalent of the number is determined and a '0' bit is placed in front of the MSB. For example, the 2s complement representation of $+(12)_{10}$ is shown in Table 2.4.

Table 2.4 2s Complement Representation of $+(12)_{10}$

Binary Form		1	1	0	0
With Sign Bit	0	1	1	0	0

On the other hand, if the number is negative, the magnitude is represented in 2s complement form and a sign bit 1 is placed in front of the MSB. For example, the 2s complement representation of $-(12)_{10}$ is shown in Table 2.5.

Table 2.5 2s Complement Representation of $-(12)_{10}$

Binary Number		1	1	0	0
1s Complement		0	0	1	1
2s Complement		0	1	0	0
With Sign Bit	1	0	1	0	0

10. What are the disadvantages of using BCD code? How do we remove this problem? Is BCD code weighted code? If yes, then explain.

Ans: The disadvantages of using BCD code are as follows:

- This coding is not sufficient for business purposes, as a 4-bit BCD code can represent only 16 (that is, 2^4) symbols, even a 6-bit BCD code can also represent only 64 (that is, 2^6) symbols.
- The BCD representation of a decimal number requires more bits than its equivalent binary representation. For example, the BCD code of decimal number 215 is 0010 0001 0101 (requires12 bits), while its binary equivalent is 1101 0111 (requires 8 bits). In general, a decimal number with k digits requires 4k bits in BCD.
- Computers using BCD codes could work only with upper case letters and 0 to 9 numbers and a few characters. This is not sufficient for providing decimal numbers (10), lowercase letters (26), uppercase letters (26) and a large number of other special characters (28+).

To remove above problems, the BCD code was extended from a 6-bit code to an 8-bit code, which comes to known as Extended Binary Coded Decimal Interchange Code (EBCDIC). The added 2 bits are used as additional zone bits, expanding the zone to 4 bits. Thus, it is possible to represent 256 (2^8) different characters instead of 64 (2^6) by making use of EBCDIC.

Yes, BCD code is a weighted code, as it is possible to assign weights to the binary bits according to their positions. The weights in the 4-bit BCD code are 8(2^3), 4(2^2), 2(2^1) and 1(2^0).

11. How do we convert binary numbers into gray codes?

Ans: A binary number is converted to its equivalent gray code by performing the following steps.

1. Take the MSB of the binary code as the MSB of the gray code word.
2. Starting from left to right, add each adjacent pair of bits in the binary code to get the next gray code bit, while ignoring the carries.

For example, consider a binary number 10100111 that is to be converted to its equivalent gray code. The required conversion is illustrated as follows.

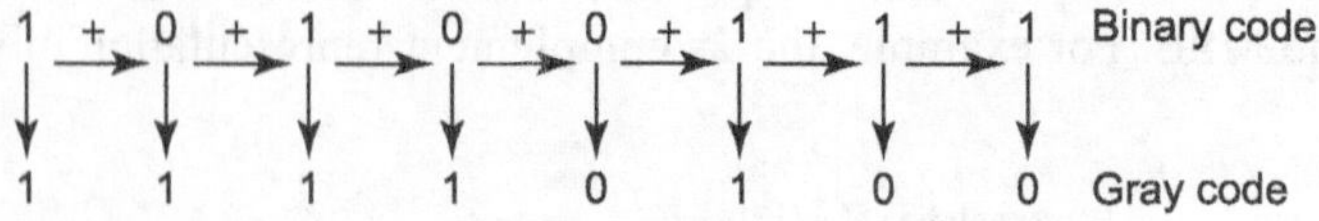

Thus, the required gray code is 11110100.

12. Convert the following:

(a) $(0.4375)_{10}$ to $()_2$
(b) $(2AD)_{16}$ to $()_2$
(c) $(11100111101)_2$ to $()_{16}$
(d) $(1110101101)_2$ to $()_{10}$
(e) $(A2B.D8)_{16}$ to $()_{10}$

Ans: (a) To convert $(0.4375)_{10}$ into binary form, multiply the fraction part (0.4375) by 2. Then, separate the integer and fraction parts of the result. Repeat the above steps until the fraction part becomes zero. Finally, write the integer parts (in downward direction) to form the binary equivalent of given number. The conversion of $(0.4375)_{10}$ to binary is shown here.

	Integer part
$.4375 \times 2 = 0.875$	0
$.875 \times 2 = 1.75$ 1	1
$.75 \times 2 = 1.5$ 1	1
$.5 \times 2 = 1.0$ 1	1

Thus, $(0.4375)_{10} = (0.0111)_2$.

(b) To convert $(2AD)_{16}$ to binary form, first replace each hexadecimal digit by its 4-bit binary equivalent and then combine all the groups as shown in Table 2.6.

Table 2.6 Conversion of $(2AD)_{16}$ into Its Binary Form

Hexadecimal number	2	A	D
Binary coded value	0010	1010	1101

Thus, $(2AD)_{16} = (001010101101)_2$.

(c) To convert $(11100111101)_2$ to its hexadecimal form, first divide it into 4-bit groups starting from right to left and then replace each group by its hexadecimal equivalent as shown in Table 2.7.

Table 2.7 Conversion of $(11100111101)_2$ into Its Hexadecimal Form

Binary value	0111	0011	1101
Hexadecimal number	7	3	D

Thus, $(11100111101)_2 = (73D)_{16}$.

(d) To convert $(1110101101)_2$ into its decimal equivalent, multiply each bit by its corresponding binary weight and then add all the products as shown here.

$$(1110101101)_2 = 1 \times 2^9 + 1 \times 2^8 + 1 \times 2^7 + 0 \times 2^6 + 1 \times 2^5 + 0 \times 2^4 + 1 \times 2^3 + 1 \times 2^2 + 0 \times 2^1 + 1 \times 2^0$$

$$= 512 + 256 + 128 + 0 + 32 + 0 + 8 + 4 + 0 + 1$$

$$= 941$$

Thus, $(1110101101)_2 = (941)_{10}$

(e) To convert $(ABD.D8)_{16}$ into its decimal equivalent, multiply each hexadecimal digit by its corresponding weight and then add all the products as shown here.

$$(A2B.D8)_{16} - A \times 16^2 + 2 \times 16^1 + B \times 16^0 + D \times 16^{-1} + 8 \times 16^{-2}$$

$$= 10 \times 16^2 + 2 \times 16^1 + 11 \times 16^0 + 13 \times 16^{-1} + 8 \times 16^{-2}$$

$$= 2560 + 32 + 11 + 0.8125 + 0.03125$$

$$= 2603.84375$$

Thus, $(A2B.D8)_{16} = (2603.84375)_{10}$

13. Convert the decimal number 59.8125 into binary and octal.

Conversion to Binary

The integer part of given decimal number (that is, 59) is converted to its binary equivalent as shown here.

Divisor	Dividend	Remainder	
2	59		
2	29	1	LSB ↑
2	14	1	
2	7	0	
2	3	1	
2	1	1	
	0	1	MSB

Thus, $(59)_{10} = (111011)_2$.

The fraction part of given decimal number (that is, .8125) is converted to its binary equivalent as shown here.

	Integer part
$0.8125 \times 2 = 1.6250$	1 ↓
$0.625 \times 2 = 1.250$	1
$0.25 \times 2 = 0.50$	0
$0.5 \times 2 = 1.0$	1

Thus, $(.8125)_{10} = (.1101)_2$.

On combining the integer and fraction parts, we get $(59.8125)_{10} = (111011.1101)_2$.

Conversion to Octal

The integer part of given decimal number (that is, 59) is converted to its octal equivalent as shown here.

Divisor	Dividend	Remainder	
8	59		
8	7	3	LSB
	0	7	MSB

Thus, $(59)_{10} = (73)_8$.

The fraction part of given decimal number (that is, .8125) is converted to its octal equivalent as shown here.

	Integer part
$0.8125 \times 8 = 6.5$	6 ↓
$0.5 \times 8 = 4.0$	4

Thus, $(0.8125)_{10} = (0.64)_2$.

On combining the integer and fraction parts, we get $(59.8125)_{10} = (73.64)_8$.

14. Using 2s complement system perform $(51)_{10} - (27)_{10}$ in binary.

Ans: First, convert $(51)_{10}$ into its binary equivalent as shown here.

		Remainder	
2	51		
2	25	1	LSB ↑
2	12	1	
2	6	0	
2	3	0	
2	1	1	
	0	1	MSB

Thus, $(51)_{10} = (110011)_2$.
Similarly, we can convert $(27)_{10}$ into binary form as shown here.

		Remainder	
2	27		
2	13	1	LSB ↑
2	6	1	
2	3	0	
2	1	1	
	0	1	MSB

After taking remainder bits from MSB to LSB, we have $(11011)_2$.
Thus, $(27)_{10} = (11011)_2$.
Now, we have to perform $(110011)_2 - (11011)_2$ using 2s complement. This operation is equivalent to $(110011)_2$ + 2s complement of $(011011)_2$. The 2s complement of $(011011)_2$ is $(100101)_2$. Thus, the addition operation is performed as follows:

```
      1   1 1 1 ← Carry
      1 1 0 0 1 1
 +    1 0 0 1 0 1
 ----------------
 1    0 1 1 0 0 0
 ↑
Discard carry bit
```

Thus, the result is $(11000)_2$.

15. Convert $(A5B)_{16}$ into octal.

Ans: To convert $(A5B)_{16}$ into its octal equivalent, first replace each hexadecimal digit by its 4-bit binary equivalent, divide the number into 3-bit groups starting from right to left (add additional zeros to the left if required) and then replace each 3-bit group by its octal equivalent.

$(A5B)_{16}$ = 1010 0101 1011

= 101 001 011 011

= 5133

Thus, $(A5B)_{16} = (5133)_8$.

Multiple-choice Questions

1. The most popular positional number system being used today is the ________.
   (a) Decimal number system
   (b) Digital number system
   (c) Binary number system
   (d) None of the above

2. The base for hexadecimal number is ________.
   (a) 8
   (b) 6
   (c) 16
   (d) 4
3. In an 8-bit unsigned binary number, each number added or subtracted must be between ________.
   (a) 0 and 255
   (b) 0 and 225
   (c) 1 and 255
   (d) 50 and 250
4. Which of the following is not a standard text code system?
   (a) ASCII
   (b) UNICODE
   (c) EBCDIC
   (d) LCD
5. EBCDIC stands for ________.
   (a) Extended Binary Coded Decimal Internal Code
   (b) Extended Binary Coded Decimal Interchange Code
   (c) Extensive Binary Coded Decimal Internal Code
   (d) Extended Binary Coded Decimal Interchange Calculation

Answers

1. (a) 2. (c) 3. (a) 4. (d) 5. (b)

3

Operating Systems

1. What is an operating system? Explain the six types of operating systems.

Ans: An 'operating system' (OS) is a collection of system programs that together control the operation of a computer system. The OS along with hardware, application and other system softwares and users constitute a computer system. It is the most important part of any computer system. It acts as an intermediary between a user and the computer hardware. The OS has evolved immensely from its primitive days to the present digital era. From batch processing systems to the latest embedded systems, the OS can be classified into six broad categories that are described as follows:

- **Batch processing OS:** This type of OS was one of the first to evolve. It allowed only one program to run at a time. These kinds of OS can still be found on some mainframe computers running batches of jobs. It works on a series of programs that are held in a queue. The OS is responsible for scheduling the jobs according to priority and the resources required. These are good at churning through large numbers of repetitive jobs on large computers. For example, this OS would be best suited for a company wishing to automate their payrolls. A list of employees will be entered, their monthly salaries will be calculated, and corresponding pay slips would be printed. Batch processing is useful for this purpose, since these procedures are to be repeated for every employee and each month.
- **Multi-user or time-sharing OS:** This system is used in computer networks that allow different users to access the same data and application programs on the same network. It builds a user database account, which defines the rights that users can have on a particular resource of the system. Some of the common examples of multi-user OS include Windows XP and Linux.
- **Multi-programming or multi-tasking OS:** In this system, more than one process can be executed concurrently. The processor is switched rapidly between the processes. Hence, a user can have more than one process running at a time. For example, a user on his/her computer can have a word processor and an audio CD player running at the same time. It allows the user to switch between the running applications and even transfer data between them. That is, a user can copy a picture from an Internet opened in the browser application and paste it into an image editing application.
- **Real-time OS (RTOS):** This system is designed to respond to an event within a pre-determined time. This kind of OS is primarily used in process control, telecommunications, and so on. The OS monitors various inputs that affect the execution of processes, changing the computers model

of the environment, thus affecting the output, within a guaranteed time period (usually less than 1 second). As this OS responds quickly, it is often used in applications such as flight reservation system, railway reservation system and military applications. Two common examples of RTOS are Windows CE and Lynx OS.

- **Multi-processor OS:** This system can incorporate more than one processor dedicated to the running processes. This technique of using more than one processor is often called 'parallel processing'. The main advantage of this OS is that it increases the system throughput by getting more work done in less time.
- **Embedded OS:** It refers to the OS that is self-contained in the device and resident in ROM. Since embedded systems are usually not the general-purpose systems, they are lighter or less resource intensive as compared to general-purpose OS. Most of these OSs also offer real-time OS qualities. Typical systems that use embedded OS are household appliances, car management systems, traffic control systems, and energy management systems.

2. Give the functions of OS.

Ans: The OS is the main aspect of a device and is very important to its overall function. Without it, the computer will not be able to work. Thus, the main functions of OS are as follows:

- **Process management:** As a process manager, the OS handles the creation and deletion of processes, suspension and resumption of processes and scheduling and synchronization of processes.
- **Memory management:** As a memory manager, the OS handles the allocation and de-allocation of memory space as required by various programs.
- **File management:** The OS is responsible for creation and deletion of files and directories. It also takes care of other file-related activities such as organizing, storing, retrieving, naming and protecting the files.
- **Device management:** OS provides input/output sub-system between process and device driver. It handles the device caches, buffers and interrupts. It also detects the device failures and notifies the same to the user.
- **Security management:** The OS protects system resources and information against destruction and unauthorized use.
- **User interface:** OS provides the interface between the user and the hardware. The user interface is the layer that actually interacts with the computer operator. The interface consists of a set of commands or menus through which a user communicates with a program.

3. Define the terms uniprogramming and multi-programming.

Ans: 'Uniprogramming' means performing only one program at a time. In a uniprogrammed system, the users can perform only one task at a time. On the other hand, in 'multi-programming', multiple programs can reside in main memory at the same time and these programs can be executed concurrently thereby requiring the system resources to be shared among them.

4. What is a deadlock? How this situation arises? What are the two schemes which ensure that deadlock never occurs?

Ans: In a multi-programming environment, several processes may compete for a limited number of resources. A process requests for the required resource and if it is not available, then the process enters in the waiting state and remains in that state until it acquires the resource. There might be a situation when the process has to wait endlessly because the requested resource may be held by other waiting processes. This type of situation is known as 'deadlock'. A deadlock situation arises if the following four conditions hold simultaneously on the system:

- **Mutual exclusion:** Only one process can use a resource at a time. If another process requests for the resource, the requesting process has to wait until the requested resource is released.
- **Hold and wait:** In this situation, a process might be holding some resource while waiting for additional resource, which is currently being held by the other process.
- **No preemption:** Resources cannot be preempted, that is, resources cannot be forcibly removed from a process. A resource can only be released voluntarily by the holding process, after that process has completed its task.
- **Circular wait:** This situation may arise when a set of processes waiting for allocation of resources held by other processes forms a circular chain in which each process is waiting for the resource held by its successor process in the chain.

  The two schemes that ensure that deadlock never occurs are as follows:
- **Deadlock prevention:** The system should ensure that at least one of the four deadlock-causing conditions would not hold true, so that deadlock can be prevented.
- **Deadlock avoidance:** Additional information concerning which resources a process will require and use during its lifetime should be provided to the OS beforehand. For example, in a system with one CD drive and a printer, process P might request first for the CD drive and later for the printer, before releasing both resources. On the other hand, process Q might request first for the printer and the CD drive later. With this knowledge in advance, the OS will never allow allocation of a resource to a process if it leads to a deadlock thereby avoiding the deadlock.

5. Write in brief on the following terms.

(a) Buffer
(b) CLI
(c) GUI

(a) A 'buffer' is a temporary storage area that takes a stream of bits from a device such as keyboard to a serial communication port. Buffers hold the bits and then release them to the CPU at a convenient rate, so that the CPU can act on it. This task is important when a number of processes are running and taking up the processor's time. The operating system instructs a buffer to continue taking the input from the device. In addition, it also instructs the buffer to stop sending data back to the CPU if the process, using the input, is suspended. When the process, requiring input, is made active once again, the operating system will command the buffer to send data again. This process allows a keyboard to deal with external users at a higher speed.

(b) 'CLI' (stands for 'command line interface') is an interface provided by OS, which facilitates the user to enter commands via an interactive terminal. This interface was used in early days of computing where commands were only means to initiate programs, applications etc. To use CLI, a user had to learn many commands for proper operation of the system.

(c) 'GUI' (stands for 'graphical user interface') is an interface, which provides user with pictures rather than just characters to interact with the machine. These OSs display icons, buttons, dialog boxes, etc., on the screen. The user sends instructions by moving a pointer on the screen (generally mouse) and selecting certain objects by pressing buttons on the mouse while the mouse pointer is pointing at them.

6. List some popular OSs.

Ans: Some examples of popular OSs are UNIX, Linux, MS-DOS, Mac and Microsoft Windows (Windows 95, Windows 98, Windows 2000, Windows XP and Windows 2007).

7. Write a short note on DOS.

Ans: The 'Disk Operating System' (DOS) is a single user operating system released by Microsoft in the early 1980s. DOS, also known as 'MS-DOS', is a CLI that enables users to organize data files, load and execute (run) program files and control the input and output devices attached to the computer. Every operation that can be performed with a GUI can also be performed with DOS. The MS-DOS environment gives the user a quick and direct access to the basic utilities of a computer. All tasks are accomplished by typing commands at a command prompt (at the cursor location). A 'prompt' is defined as a character or string of characters used in the command line interface to indicate that a computer is ready to accept commands from users. In DOS, '>' is used as a prompt, which is preceded by other information such as current drive and path of the current working directory.

A file is a primary unit of storage in computers. DOS uses a unique filename to describe the content of a file and keep track of the file, so that one can use it later. In DOS, the name of a file is divided into two parts: the *filename* itself and an *extension*. For example, the filename `Stu.doc` has two parts, namely, `Stu` (filename) and `.doc` (extension). Some of the different file extensions used by DOS are `.com, .exe, .bat, .txt` etc. Moreover, files are organized under different directories. A 'directory' allows users to group files under one category. Every disk has one basic directory called the 'root' directory, which is created automatically when the disk is formatted. In addition to files, a directory can contain other directories also in itself known as 'subdirectories'. Each subdirectory can hold files and further subdirectories. Furthermore to access a file, a user may have to traverse through different directories. Thus, a 'pathname' is used to instruct the computer where to look for any particular file. A pathname is a sequence of directories separated by a backslash ('\') followed by a filename. For example, the pathname for a file named `STU` can be `C:\Student\Details\Stu.doc.` In this pathname, C drive contains a directory `Student` in which `Details` is a subdirectory where the file `Stu.doc` is stored.

8. Give the syntax of the following DOS commands:

(a) DIR
(b) DISKCOPY
(c) FORMAT
(d) TIME

Ans: The given commands are described as follows:

(a) DIR: It is used to display the list of files or subdirectories present in a directory. The syntax of this command is:

```
DIR [Drive:] [Path] [Filename] [/A [[:] Attributes] [/B] [/C] [/D]
[/L] [/N] [/O [[:] Sortorder]] [/P] [/Q] [/S] [/T [[:] Timefield]]
[/W] [/X] [/4]
```

where,

[*Drive:*] specifies the drive.
[*Path*] specifies the pathname.
[*Filename*] specifies the filename.

[/*A*] displays files with the specified attributes. Different attributes are *D* (directory), *H* (hidden files), *S* (system files), *R* (read-only files), *A* (files ready for archiving), - (prefix meaning not).
[/*B*] uses bare format with no heading information or summary.
[/*C*] displays thousand separators in the file size.
[/*W*] uses the wide list format.
[/*D*] same as /W, the only difference is files are sorted by column.
[/*L*] uses lowercase.
[/*N*] displays a new long list format, where filenames are displayed on the far right.
[/*O*] lists files in sorted order. The sort order is specified by *N* (name), *E* (extension), *G* (group directory first), *S* (size), *D* (date) or - (prefix to reverse order).
[/*P*] pauses after each screen full of information.
[/*Q*] displays the owner of the file.
[/*S*] displays files in a specified directory and all subdirectory.
[/*T*] determines which time field is used for sorting. Time field options are *C* (creation), *A* (last access) or *W* (last written).
[/*X*] displays short names, inserted before the long name.
[/*4*] displays years in four digits.

(b) DISKCOPY: It is used to copy the contents of one disk drive to another provided the two disks are of the same type. The syntax of this command is:

```
DISKCOPY [drive 1: [drive 2 : ] ] [/V]
```

where,

[*drive 1*] specifies the source disk.
[*drive 2*] specifies the target disk.
[/*V*] verifies the information once it is copied.

(c) FORMAT: It is used to format a disk. The syntax of this command is:

```
FORMAT     Volume     [/FS:filesystem][/V:label][/Q][/X][/A:size]
[/F:size][/T:tracks][/N:sectors]
```

where,

Volume specifies the drive.
[/*FS:filesystem*] specifies the file system.
[/*V:label*] specifies the volume label.
[/*Q*] performs a quick format.
[/*X*] forces the volume to dismount first, if necessary.
[/*A:size*] overrides the default allocation unit size.
[/*F:size*] specifies the floppy disk size.
[/*T:tracks*] specifies the number of tracks each side.
[/*N:sectors*] specifies the number of sectors per track.

(d) TIME: It is used to display or set the system time. The syntax of this command is:

```
TIME [/T]
```

where,
[/T] displays *only* the current time.

For example, to display the current time, use the following command.

```
C:\>TIME /T
03:59 PM.
```

9. List and give the usage of any five UNIX commands.

Ans: Five UNIX commands are discussed as follows:

- **pwd:** It is used to know the present working directory. To know in which directory you are currently working, type pwd and press 'Enter' as shown below.

  ```
  $ pwd      # present working directory
  /usr1/dept3/dir5
  ```

  It says that the `usr1` is currently logged in and is currently present at directory `dir5` of parent directory `dept3`.

- **cat:** It is used to display the contents of a file. Suppose that we have a file named `file1` and we want to display its contents on screen. We can do this by executing the `cat` command as follows:

  ```
  $ cat file1
  Book
  Pen
  Eraser
  Handbook
  Chalk
  Duster
  Blackboard
  Diary
  ```

- **ls:** It is used to list all the files in the current directory. The usage of this command is shown as follows:

  ```
  $ ls
  hello.c
  palindrome.c
  prime.pas
  prog1.cpp
  dir2
  ```

- **cd:** It is used to change to a new directory. For example, the following command changes the current directory to `mydir`.

  ```
  $ cd mydir
  ```

  When `cd` is executed without any argument, it will take you back to your home directory.

- **wc:** It is used to count the number of lines, words and characters in the specified file(s). For example, the following command counts and displays the number of lines, words and characters, respectively, in the `file1`.

  ```
  $ wc file1
  8 8 47 file1
  ```

In the above output, first number 8 is representing the number of lines, the next number 8 is representing the number of words and the last number 47 is representing the number of characters in `file1`. Notice that the name of the file is also displayed in the output. To count the number of lines, words and characters individually, we can use `–w`, `–c` and `–l` options with the `wc` command.

10. Explain the features of Linux OS.

Ans: Linux provides a complete system with built-in multi-user and multi-tasking capabilities that take advantage of the entire processing power of the computer system. Some of its features are as follows:

- **Full multi-tasking and 32-bit support:** Linux, like all other versions of UNIX, is a real multi-tasking system, which allows multiple users to run many programs on the same system at once. Linux is also a full 32-bit operating system utilizing the special protected-mode feature of Intel 80386 and 80486 processors.
- **Virtual memory:** Linux can use a portion of your hard drive as virtual memory, which increases the efficiency of your system by keeping active processes in RAM and places less frequently used or inactive portions of memory on disk.
- **The X window system:** The X Window System is a graphics system for UNIX machines. This powerful interface supports many applications and is the standard interface for the industry. Linux comes with complete Xfree86 graphical user interface (GUI) that is based on X Window System.
- **Built-in networking support:** Linux uses standard TCP/IP protocols including Network File System (NFS) and Network Information Service (NIS, formerly known as YP). You can access the Internet by connecting your system with an Ethernet card or over a modem to another system.
- **Shared libraries:** Each application instead of keeping its own copy of software shares a common library of subroutines it can call at run time. This saves a lot of hard drive space on your system.
- **Compatibility with the IEEE POSIX.1 standard:** Because of this compatibility, Linux supports many of the standards set forth for all UNIX systems.
- **Non-proprietary source code:** The Linux Kernel uses no code from AT&T (original developers of UNIX) or any other proprietary source. Other organizations such as commercial companies and programmers from all over the world have developed software for Linux and the source of Linux is freely available.

11. List some features of Windows OS.

Ans: Windows OS is developed by Microsoft to overcome the limitations of DOS OS. The main features of Microsoft Windows are as follows:

- The interface used in Windows OSs is GUI. Therefore, it is more convenient for a new user to learn and work on it.
- File naming can contain up to 255 characters as well as some punctuation marks, such as commas, semi-colons.
- It has built-in communications and networking features, so that a system can act as a network client or server.
- It is multi-user OS where a user can run more than one program at a time. This means that a user at the same time can have a word processor and an audio CD player running on their computer.
- It provides a rich set of system administration and software development tools.

12. Discuss in brief on any four versions of Windows OS.

Ans: MS-Windows is the most popular series of operating systems. Windows 95 revolutionized the personal computer system market and then came Windows NT, Windows 98, Windows ME, Windows 2000, Windows XP, Windows Vista and Windows 7. Here, we describe Windows 2000, Windows XP, Windows Vista and Windows 7 operating systems.

Windows 2000

Windows 2000 OS is a 32-bit preemptive multi-tasking operating system. It is the successor to the Windows NT operating system. It introduces new concepts such as X.500-based directory service, support for plug-and-play devices, a new file system, which supports distributed file system, and support for more processors and memory. Microsoft introduced four versions of Windows 2000 including *Windows 2000 Professional, Windows 2000 Server, Windows 2000 Advanced Server* and *Windows 2000 Datacenter Server*.

Windows 2000 'process manager' provides basic services for creating, scheduling and deleting processes. It differentiates processes based on priorities. Every process is created as a single executing thread; the process can create additional threads. The highest priority ready process is moved to standby state, so it will be the first process to run among the pool of other ready processes. The scheduler operates over all threads. The 'memory manager' in Windows 2000 primarily acts as a virtual memory (VM) manager. The VM manager in Windows 2000 uses the paging management scheme with page size of 4 KB. The memory architecture of Windows 2000 is based on a flat, linear address space accessed via 32-bit addresses. Windows 2000 supports multiple paging files. Performance can be greatly enhanced if multiple paging files are created on different disks. The 'device manager' in Windows 2000 provides a description about the drivers and equipment that are installed on a computer and how they are functioning. Windows 2000 Server incorporates the plug-and-play (PnP) manager to recognize and adjust to the changes in the hardware configuration. Compatible devices can now be installed and Windows 2000 will automatically configure the device. The resources used by different devices, or the resources, which could be used by devices, and loading of appropriate drives for devices is being looked after by the PnP manager.

Windows XP

Windows XP OS was introduced in 2001 by Microsoft and is a part of the Windows family of OS. Along with a redesigned look and feel to the user interface, this new OS uses a more stable and reliable environment than previous versions of Windows. The OS provides a new interface that uses graphics to simplify navigation and completing common tasks, thus, making learning and working easier. Microsoft released Windows XP in two versions, namely, *Windows XP Home* and *Windows XP Professional*. 'Windows XP Home Edition' is designed for home use and small businesses, while 'Windows XP Professional' is specifically designed for advanced home computing, businesses and larger organizations.

Windows XP provides a new interface to simplify navigation and perform common tasks (such as creating and opening of a file) easily. The various features that make Windows XP a powerful, fast, efficient and stable OS are as follows:

- **Improved interface:** Windows XP provides a completely redesigned interface that lets one access programs more quickly. In addition, Windows XP keeps a record of the programs and files one uses more often. In addition, Windows XP displays the most used items in the Start Menu while it hides the least used items.

- **More reliable:** Windows XP is based on the same technology that is used in Microsoft Windows NT and Windows 2000. This makes Windows XP much more stable than Windows 95, Windows 98 and Windows ME and greatly reduces the number of system crashes and system restarts.
- **Better file and folder management:** Windows XP makes it easier to view and work with files and folders. For example, Thumbnails view lets one to preview photos and images and the new File and Folder tasks pane lets one to easily copy, move, rename or delete any file or folder.
- **Remote desktop:** Windows XP includes a feature known as 'Remote Desktop' that allows one to access the Windows session from another computer just as if one was in front of the computer. For example, one can connect to the office computer from home and have access to all of the files and network resources as though one was in front of computer at office. One can leave programs running at work and on reaching home he/she can see the desktop at work displayed on the home computer with the same programs running.

Windows Vista

Windows Vista, the successor to Windows XP, was released in 2008 by Microsoft. Since its release, it has revolutionized the market of desktop operating systems. It includes a wide variety of features that tend to increase the efficiency and productivity of users. By keeping in mind the needs of both home and business users, Microsoft has released five editions of Windows Vista, which are: *Windows Vista Home Basic*, *Windows Vista Home Premium*, *Windows Vista Ultimate*, *Windows Vista Business* and *Windows Vista Enterprise*. Out of these editions, the 'Home Basic' and 'Home Premium' editions are specifically designed for home users depending on their levels of personal computing, while the 'Business' and 'Enterprise' editions best suit to the needs of business users. The 'Ultimate' edition combines the best features of home and business editions and, thus, is well suited for both home and business users.

Windows Vista includes many features, some of which are entirely new while others have been improved as compared to earlier versions of Windows. Some of these features are as follows:

- **Windows aero:** All the basic elements of Windows such as icons, menus, dialog windows, etc., have been redesigned to provide better visuals. The Aero interface takes advantage of latest graphics hardware and provides smoother window handling, enhanced animations and glass visual effects (transparencies).
- **Windows sidebar:** It is a transparent panel on which you can place 'gadgets', which are small applications providing specific information such as weather, time and calendar. The Sidebar can be placed at any side of the screen (left or right). Though Vista comes with some gadgets, you can also download different types of gadgets from the Internet as per your choice and add them to the Sidebar.
- **Instant search:** Windows Vista includes an Instant Search feature that lets you search files, folders or whatever you want from almost every system window including Explorer and Start Menu. In addition, as you type in the search box, Windows searches instantly and provides you the search results. This makes the searching easier and faster.
- **Windows ready boost:** This is the new surprising feature in Windows Vista that enables you to use USB flash memory as main memory thereby improving system performance. Hence, you need not purchase a RAM chip and insert it into motherboard slot; rather you can just plug a USB flash memory. As you plug a flash memory, Vista determines whether using flash memory as RAM can increase the system performance and if it is, you will be asked whether to use flash as RAM.

Windows 7

Windows 7 is the latest version of Windows operating system that has been released by Microsoft in 2009 to be used on home and business desktops, laptops, Tablet PCs, netbooks and Media Center PCs. It provides enhanced user interface making it more user-friendly, improved performance to get the tasks done efficiently, new level of security to protect precious data from unauthorized access, and so on. Advancements in handwriting and speech recognition, support for virtual hard disk and multi-touch and redesigned taskbar are some of the new features in Windows 7. One more noticeable change is that some of the applications that have been included with prior releases of Windows including Windows Movie Maker, Windows Mail, Windows Calendar and Windows Photo Gallery are not included in Windows 7. The reason for removal is that these applications demand frequent updates than the operating system itself. These applications are now freely available from Microsoft website as a separate package called 'Windows Live Essential'.

Microsoft has released Windows 7 in six different editions, namely, *Windows 7 Starter, Windows 7 Home Basic, Windows 7 Home Premium, Windows 7 Professional, Windows 7 Enterprise* and *Windows 7 Ultimate*. The 'Windows 7 Starter' is the most basic edition of Windows 7 and contains the fewest features of all the Windows 7 editions. The 'Windows 7 Home Basic' edition contains features that make them suitable for home users. Like Home Basic edition, 'Windows 7 Home Premium' edition is also intended for home users; however, it contains some new features such as touch-screen support and Aero effects that have been excluded from the Home Basic edition. The 'Windows 7 Professional' edition is suited for small business users, as it provides support for being used as Remote Desktop Server, location aware printing, Encrypting File System and so on. The 'Windows 7 Enterprise' edition targets the enterprise segment with features including Multi-lingual User Interface, UNIX application support and BitLocker Drive Encryption. The 'Windows 7 Ultimate' edition contains exactly the same features as Windows 7 Enterprise edition. The only difference is that Ultimate edition is available on individual license basis. Hence, individuals can purchase Windows 7 Ultimate edition.

Like Windows Vista, Windows 7 is also greeted with a new look and style of desktop including Aero themes and gadgets. In addition, the Windows 7 is equipped with some more Aero features, redesigned taskbar and Start menu, Jump lists and many more new features. The new Aero features of Windows 7 include Aero peek, Aero shake and Aero snap. Gadgets can be placed anywhere on the desktop as per your convenient instead of being fixed on Window side bar in Windows Vista. Taskbar has undergone the major modifications in Windows 7. You may immediately notice that it is taller than the taskbar in the previous versions of Windows. One main reason for making it taller is to enable it to accommodate the touch screen input. Moreover, Windows 7 includes a wide variety of accessories/programs such as Calculator, Command Prompt, Connect to a Network Projector, Math Input Panel, Snipping Tool, Sound Recorder, Sticky Notes, etc. All these programs are grouped under the 'Accessories' folder available in 'All Programs' on the 'Start' menu.

Multiple-choice Questions

1. Which of the following OSs allows only one program to run at a time?

   (a) Real-time (b) Batch processing
   (c) Multi-processor (d) Embedded

2. Which of the following is/are function(s) of OS?

   (a) Device management (b) File management
   (c) Memory management (d) All of these

3. _________ ensure(s) that deadlock will never occur.
   (a) Deadlock avoidance
   (b) Deadlock prevention
   (c) Both (a) and (b)
   (d) Circular wait
4. DOS stands for _________.
   (a) Distributed operating system
   (b) Disk operating system
   (c) Driver operating system
   (d) Diskless operating system
5. Which of the following command copies the contents of one disk to another?
   (a) DISKCOPY
   (b) PATH
   (c) wc
   (d) md
6. Which of the following is a freeware OS?
   (a) MS-DOS
   (b) WIN-XP
   (c) Linux
   (d) WIN-95
7. Math input panel is present in which of the following OS?
   (a) Windows 2000
   (b) Windows XP
   (c) Windows Vista
   (d) Windows 7

Answers

1. (b) 2. (d) 3. (c) 4. (b) 5. (a) 6. (c) 7. (a)

4

Computer Software and Programming

1. What do you understand by software and software package?

Ans: Software is a generic term for organized collection of computer data and instructions. It is responsible for controlling, integrating and managing the hardware components of a computer and to accomplish specific tasks. In other words, software tells the computer what to do and how to do it. For example, software instructs the hardware what to display on the user's screen, what kinds of input to take from the user and what kinds of output to generate. Thus, software communicates with the hardware by organizing the control sequences and the hardware carries out the instructions defined by the software. As we know, a computer needs to be instructed to perform any task. Therefore, the user issues instructions and the CPU acts in accordance with the instructions. Thus, these set of instructions, which control the sequence of operations, are known as 'programs', and collectively programs are called 'software'. It is an intangible commodity, that is, the part of a computer system that users cannot touch.

A set of programs that are specifically written to provide the user a precise functionality such as solving a specific problem is termed as a 'software package'. For example, word-processing software package provides functionality to the user to create text documents such as letters and mailing lists. Similarly, an image-processing software package assists a user in drawing and manipulating graphics.

2. Differentiate between software and hardware.

Ans: 'Software' refers to the computer programs that are loaded into a computer system, whereas 'hardware' refers to all the visible devices, which are assembled together to build a computer system. Therefore, one can say that the software is a set of instructions that tells the hardware what to do and how to perform the requested actions. There are some differences between software and hardware, which are listed in Table 4.1.

Table 4.1 Differences Between Software and Hardware

Basis of Difference	Software	Hardware
Types	Some software types are system software, programming software and application software.	Some hardware types are motherboard, CPU, RAM, BIOS, power supply, CD-ROM drive, video display controller, computer bus and floppy disk.
Interdependency	To deliver its set of instructions, software is installed on hardware.	It starts functioning once software is loaded.
Function	It controls, integrates and manages the hardware components of a computer to accomplish specific tasks.	It serves as the delivery system for software solutions.
Failure	Software failure is systematic. It does not have an increasing failure rate.	Its failure is random. It does have increasing failure rate.
Reliability	It needs constant testing after upgrades.	It stays at steady reliability level in useful life.
Examples	Quickbooks, Adobe Acrobat, Winoms-Cs, Internet Explorer, Microsoft Word and Microsoft Excel are some examples of software.	CD-ROM, monitors, scanners, printers, video cards, routers, modems and label makers are some examples of hardware.

3. Describe the different types of software with examples.

Ans: Software can be classified into two categories, namely, *system software* and *application software*. 'System software' is a generic term for referring to any computer program whose purpose is to help the user to run the computer system, whereas 'application software' employs the capabilities of a computer directly to a task that the user wishes to perform. As an analogy, one can equate an electric bulb to an application and the electric power generation plant with system. The power plant merely generates electricity. It is not really of any use until harnessed to an application such as the electric bulb, which performs a service that the user desires. Figure 4.1 illustrates the different categories of software.

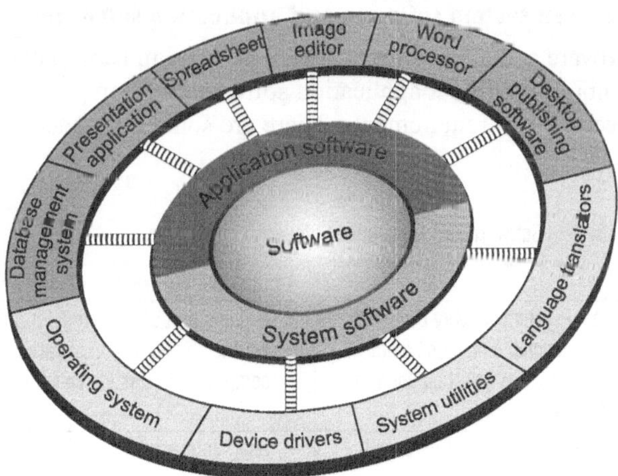

Figure 4.1 Software Categories

System Software

It consists of several programs, which are directly responsible for controlling, integrating and managing the individual hardware components of a computer system. A new computer system is always accompanied with some software either stored in a CD or DVD, which is supplied by the manufacturer. This software manages and supports the computer system and its information processing activities. System software is more transparent and less noticed by the users, as it usually interacts with the hardware or the applications. This software provides a programming environment in which programmers can create applications to accommodate their needs. This environment provides functions that are not available at the hardware level and performs the tasks related to the execution of an application program. Hence, system software acts as an interface between the hardware of the computer and the software applications. In simple terms, system software makes the computer functional. It provides basic functionality such as file management, visual display and keyboard input and it is used by application software to accomplish these functions. Some examples of system software are operating system (OS), device drivers, language translators and system utilities.

Application Software

It is used to accomplish specific tasks rather than just managing a computer system. For a user, the computer system has no specific use without the application software. It may consist of a single program, such as Microsoft's Notepad (for writing and editing simple text) or a collection of programs, which work together to accomplish a task such as database management software. Application software may also include a larger collection of related but independent programs and packages (a software suite), which have a common user interface or shared data format, such as Microsoft Office Suite. However, application software is dependent on system software. Thus, system software (such as operating system) acts as an interface between the user and the computer hardware, while application software performs specific tasks. Application software ranges from games, calculators and word processors (document-creating programs), to programs that paint images on screen (image editors). Some examples of application software are word processors, spreadsheets, image editor, database management system, presentation applications and desktop publishing software.

4. Differentiate between system software and application software.

Ans: Both system software and application software go hand in hand. That is, without system software, the computer will not run; without application software, the computer, no matter how powerful, will not be helpful in meeting user requirements. There are some differences between them which are listed in Table 4.2.

Table 4.2 Differences Between System Software and Application Software

System Software	Application Software
• It is basically the main functional system of every computer program. It contains the basic functional units such as the program files, system services, basic configuration units, system back-ups and main drivers.	• It is one part of the computer program that permits the access and utilization of various available applications made compatible to existing computer units and programs.
• Generally, users do not interact with system software, as it works in the background.	• Users interact with application software while doing different activities.

(Continued)

• It gets installed when the operating system is installed on the computer.	• It is installed according to the requirements of the user.
• A computer may not require more than one type of system software.	• There may be a number of application software programs installed on the computer at the same time.
• It includes programs such as compilers, debuggers, drivers and assemblers.	• It includes media players, word processors and spreadsheet programs.
• It can run independently of the application software.	• It cannot run without the presence of the system software.

5. Explain various application software packages.

Ans: Application software is regarded as important software, as it helps the user to do specific task rather than just managing a computer system. It continuously interacts with the real world and helps to solve related problems. It serves a great deal of importance in the areas such as entertainment, education, communication, business, health and government. Some of the commonly used application software packages and their uses are given as follows:

- **Word processor:** It is used to compose, format, edit and print electronic documents. Word processing is one of the earliest applications for office productivity and the personal computer. It involves not only typing, but also checking the spelling and grammar of the text and arranging it correctly on the page. A variety of different typefaces are available for a variety of effects. It is possible to include pictures, graphs, charts and many other things within the text of the document. It also allows for changes in margins, fonts and colour. Nowadays, virtually, all personal computers are equipped with a word-processing program, which has functions for writing letters, reports or other documents and printing. Examples of some well-known word processors are Microsoft Word and WordPerfect.
- **Spreadsheet:** It is used by bookkeepers and accountants mainly for financial purposes. This application is in the form of a rectangular grid, which allows text, numbers and complex functions to be entered into a matrix of thousands of individual cells. The spreadsheet provides sheets containing cells, each of which may contain text and/or numbers. Cells may also contain equations that calculate results from data placed in other cells or series of cells. For example, a column of numbers totalled in a single cell containing an equation relating to that column. It is used predominantly for accounting and other numerically based tasks, because financial and mathematical data and analyses are often managed in a tabular style, with columns of financial figures being manipulated and then influencing other data computations. Examples of spreadsheet applications are Microsoft Excel and Lotus 1-2-3.
- **Image editor:** It is designed specifically for capturing, creating, editing and manipulating images. It also provides a variety of special features for creating and altering images. In addition to offering a host of filters and image transformation algorithms, some image editors also enable the user to create and superimpose layers. With image editing software, one can darken or lighten an image, rotate it, adjust its contrast, crop out extraneous detail and much more. Some examples of these programs are Adobe Photoshop, Adobe Illustrator and CorelDraw.
- **Database management system:** It is a collection of programs that allow storage, modification and extraction of information from a database (which is a collection of interrelated records) in an efficient manner. It supports the structuring of the database in a standard format and provides tools for data input, verification, storage, retrieval, query and manipulation. When such software is used, information systems can be changed much more easily as the organization's information requirements change. New categories of data can be added to the database without disrupting

the existing system. It also controls the security and integrity of the database from unauthorized access. Some examples of database management systems are FoxPro and Oracle.

- **Presentation application:** A presentation is a means of expressing ideas in form of visual images, audio and animation. To prepare presentations, presentation software is used. It allows the users to create presentation by producing slides or handouts for presentation of projects. Essentially, such computer programs allow users to create a variety of visually appealing electronic slides for presentations. Microsoft PowerPoint is one of the most famous presentation applications.
- **Desktop publishing software:** Desktop publishing is a technique of using a personal computer to design images and pages, assemble type and graphics and then using a laser printer or image-setter to output the assembled pages onto paper, film or printing plate. Thus, to create magazines, books, etc., desktop publishing software is used. Such software assists in creating sophisticated documents including complicated page designs, detailed illustrations and camera-ready typefaces. Quark Express and Adobe PageMaker are examples of desktop publishing software.

6. Explain the steps involved in software development.

Ans: Before starting the development of software, the problem that needs to be solved has to be determined. There are different approaches to problem solving. Most require breaking the problem into a series of smaller steps. One common technique is to use the 'software development steps' (Figure 4.2), with the number of steps that may vary according to the person who has formalized the development. Often the process runs in a loop, for example, as the current process is completed, new demands appear and the development process commences again. Software development steps include the following phases:

1. **Analyse/define the problem:** The problem is analysed precisely and completely. Based on understanding, the developer knows about the scope within which the problem needs to be analysed.
2. **Task analysis:** After analysing the problem, the developer needs to develop various solutions to solve the given problem. From these solutions, the optimum solution (by experimenting with all the solutions) is chosen, which can solve the problem comfortably and economically.
3. **Designing phase:** After selecting the appropriate solution, algorithm is developed to depict the basic logic of the selected solution. An algorithm depicts the solution in logical steps (sequence of

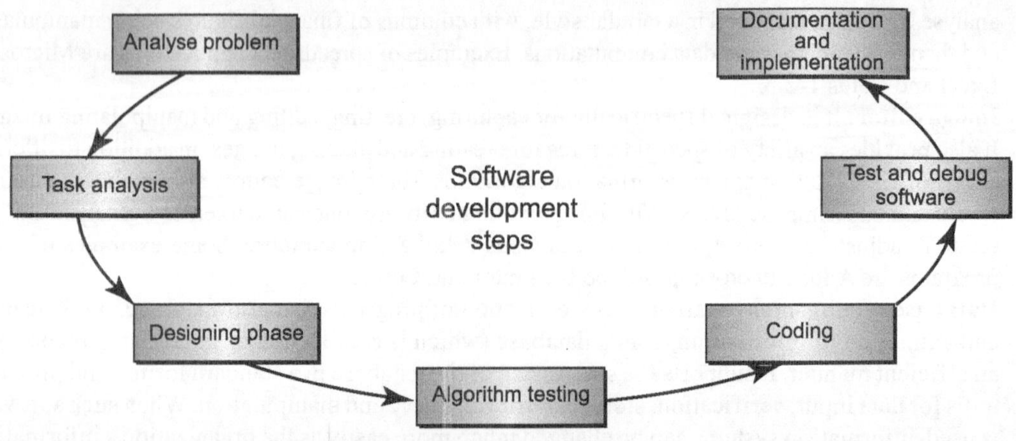

Figure 4.2 Software Development Steps

instructions). Further, algorithm is represented by flowcharts and pseudo codes. These tools make program logic clear and they eventually help in coding.

4. **Testing the algorithm for accuracy:** Before converting the algorithms into actual code, it should be checked for accuracy. The main purpose of checking an algorithm is to identify major logical errors at an early stage, because logical errors are often difficult to detect and correct at later stages. The testing also ensures that the algorithm is a 'true' one and it should work for both normal and unusual data.
5. **Coding:** After meeting all the design considerations, the actual coding of the software takes place in the chosen programming language. Depending upon application domain and available resources, a program can be written by using computer languages of different levels such as machine, assembly or high-level languages (HLLs).
6. **Test and debug the software:** It is common for the initial software code to contain errors. A program compiler and programmer-designed test data machine tests the code for syntax errors. The results obtained are compared with results calculated manually from this test data. Depending upon the complexity of the software, several rounds of testing may be required.
7. **Documentation and implementation:** Once the software is free from all the errors, it is the duty of the software developers to ensure that the software is supported by suitable documentation. After documentation, the software is installed on the end user's machine.

7. Briefly describe computer program. Also discuss its characteristics.

Ans: A computer can perform a variety of tasks such as receiving data, processing it and producing useful results. However, it cannot perform on its own and needs to be instructed to perform even a simple task. It works on a set of instructions called 'computer program', which clearly specifies the ways to carry out a task.

A program consists of a series of instructions that a computer processes to perform the required operation. In addition, it also includes some fixed data, required to perform the instructions and the process of defining those instructions and data. Thus, in order to design a program, a programmer must determine three basic rudiments which are as follows:

1. The instructions to be performed.
2. The order in which those instructions are to be performed.
3. The data required to perform those instructions.

To perform a task using a program, a programmer has to consider various inputs of the program along with the process, which is required to convert the input into desired output. Suppose that we want to calculate the sum of two numbers, A and B, and store the sum in C. Here, A and B are the inputs, addition is the process and C is the output of the program (Figure 4.3).

Characteristics of a Program

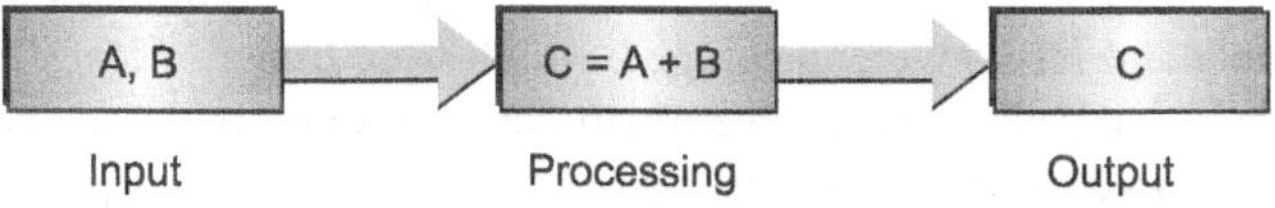

Figure 4.3 Program Performing a Task

A program should be written in such a manner that it is easier to understand the underlying logic. A few important characteristics that a computer program should possess are as follows:

- **Portability:** It refers to the ability of a program to run on different platforms (operating systems) with or without minimal changes. Due to rapid development in hardware and the software, nowadays platform change is a common phenomenon. Hence, if a program is developed for a particular platform, then the life span of the program is severely affected.
- **Readability:** The program should be written in such a way that it makes other programmers or users to follow the logic of the program without much effort. If a program is written structurally, it helps the programmers to understand their own program in a better way. Even if some computational efficiency needs to be sacrificed for better readability, it is advisable to use a more user-friendly approach, unless the application's processing is of utmost importance.
- **Efficiency:** Every program requires certain processing time and memory to process the instructions and data. As you must have realized, processing power and memory are the most precious resources of a computer, a program should be laid out in such a manner that it utilizes the least amount of memory and processing time.
- **Structural:** To develop a program, the task must be broken down into a number of subtasks. These subtasks are developed independently and each subtask is able to perform the assigned job without the help of any other subtask. If a program is developed structurally, the program not only becomes more readable, but also easier for testing and documenting processes.
- **Flexibility:** A program should be flexible enough to handle most of the changes without having to rewrite the entire program. Most of the programs are developed for a certain period and they require modifications from time to time. For example, in case of payroll management, as the time progresses, some employees may leave the company while some others may join. Hence, the payroll application should be flexible enough to incorporate all the changes without having to reconstruct the entire application.
- **Generality:** Apart from flexibility, the program should also be general. By generality, we mean that if a program is developed for a particular task, then it should be able to be used for all similar tasks of the same domain. For example, if a program is developed for a particular organization, then it should also suit other similar organizations.
- **Documentation:** It is one of the most important components of an application development. Even if a program is developed following the best programming practices, it will be rendered useless if the end user is not able to fully utilize the functionality of the application. A well-documented application is also useful for other programmers because even in the absence of the author, they can understand it.

8. What are the different types/levels of programming languages?

Ans: Computers understand only one language and that is binary language or the language of 0s and 1s. Binary language is also known as 'machine language'. In the initial years of computer programming, all the instructions were given in binary form only. Although these programs were easily understood by the computer, it proved too difficult for a normal human being to remember all the instructions in the form of 0s and 1s. Therefore, the computer remained a mystery to a common person until other languages, such as assembly and HLLs were developed, which were easier to learn and understand. These languages use commands that have some degree of similarity with English (such as 'if else' and 'exit'). Programming languages can be divided into three major categories:

- **Machine language:** It is the native language of computers. It uses only 0s and 1s to represent data and the instructions.
- **Assembly language:** It corresponds to symbolic instructions and executable machine codes and was created to use letters instead of 0s and 1s to run a machine.
- **High-level language:** These languages are written using a set of words and symbols following some rules similar to a natural language such as English. The programs written in HLLs are known as 'source programs' and these programs are converted into machine-readable form by using compilers or interpreters.

9. What is the significance or advantages of different levels of computer languages?

Ans: Every language has its own advantages.

Advantages of machine language

Even though machine language is not a human-friendly language, it offers the following advantages:

- **Translation free:** Machine language is the only language that computers understand. Thus, the programs written in machine language can be directly executed without the need for conversion.
- **High speed:** Since no conversion is needed, the applications developed using machine language is extremely fast. It is usually used for complex applications such as space control system, nuclear reactors and chemical processing.

Advantages of assembly language

Assembly language allows better human-readable method of writing programs as compared to writing in binary bit patterns. The advantages of using assembly language to develop a program are as follows:

- **Easy to understand and use:** Assembly language uses mnemonics instead of using numerical opcodes and memory locations as used in machine language. Hence, the programs written in assembly language are much easier to understand and use as compared to its machine language counterpart. Being a more user-friendly language as compared to machine language, assembly programs are easier to modify.
- **Less error prone:** Since mnemonic codes and symbolic addresses are used, the programmer does not have to keep track of the storage locations of the data and instructions. Hence, there are fewer errors while writing an assembly language program. Even in case of errors, assembly programs provide better facility to locate and correct them as compared to machine language programs. Moreover, assemblers also provide various mechanisms to locate the errors. For example, in case of adding two variables such as ADD `A`, `B`, if the variables (`A` and `B`) are not defined in the program, the assembler will give an error indicating the same, so that the programmer can easily correct the mistake.
- **Efficiency:** Assembly programs can run much faster and use less memory and other resources than a similar program written in HLL. The speed increment of 2–20 times faster is common, and occasionally, an increase of hundreds of times faster is also possible.
- **More control on hardware:** Assembly language also gives direct access to key machine features essential for implementing certain kinds of low-level routines such as an operating system kernel or micro-kernel, device drivers and machine control.

Advantages of HLLs

HLLs are useful in developing complex software. Unlike assembly language, the programmer need not learn the instruction set of each computer being worked with. The various advantages of using HLLs are as follows:

- **Readability:** Since HLLs are closer to natural languages, they are easier to learn and understand. In addition, a programmer need not be aware of computer architecture; even a common person can use it without much difficulty. This is the main reason of HLL's popularity.
- **Machine independent:** HLLs are machine independent in the sense that a program created using HLL can be used on different platforms with very little or no change at all.
- **Easy debugging:** HLLs include the support for ideas of abstraction, so that programmers can concentrate on finding the solution to the problem rapidly, rather than on low-level details of data representation, which results in fewer errors. Moreover, the compilers and interpreters are designed in such a way that they detect and point out the errors instantaneously.
- **Easier to maintain:** As compared to low-level languages, the programs written in HLL are easier to modify and maintain.
- **Easy documentation:** Since the statements written in HLL are similar to natural languages, they are easier to be documented as compared to low-level languages.

10. What is an algorithm? State its characteristics.

Ans: An 'algorithm' is defined as a finite sequence of explicit instructions that when provided with a set of input values produces an output and then terminates. To be an algorithm, the steps must be unambiguous and after a finite number of steps, the solution of the problem should be achieved. However, algorithms can have steps that repeat (iterate) or require decisions (logic and comparison) until the task is completed.

Different algorithms may accomplish the same task, with a different set of instructions, in more or less the same time, space and effort. For example, two different recipes for preparing tea, one 'add the sugar' while 'boiling the water' and the other add the sugar 'after boiling the water' produce the same result. However, performing an algorithm correctly does not guarantee a solution, if the algorithm is flawed or not appropriate to the context. For example, preparing the tea algorithm will fail if there are no tea leaves present; even if all the motions of preparing the tea are performed as if the tea leaves were there. Once an algorithm has been designed, it can be represented as flowchart, pseudocode or decision table, which is further expressed in programming language to develop computer programs. Some desirable characteristics of algorithm are:

- There must be no ambiguity in any instruction.
- There should not be any uncertainty about which instruction is to be executed next.
- The algorithm should terminate after a finite number of steps. An algorithm cannot be open-ended.
- The algorithm must be general enough to deal with any contingency.

11. Define a flowchart. Give some advantages and disadvantages of using it.

Ans: A 'flowchart' is a pictorial representation of an algorithm in which the steps are drawn in the form of different shapes of boxes and the logical flow is indicated by interconnecting arrows. The 'boxes' represent operations and the 'arrows' represent the sequence in which the operations are implemented. The primary purpose of the flowchart is to help the programmer in understanding the logic of the program. Therefore, it is always not necessary to include all the required steps in detail. Flowcharts outline the general procedure. Since they provide an alternative and visual way of representing the information flow in a program, program developers often find them very valuable.

The advantages (or the reasons) of using flowcharts as a problem-solving tool are given as follows:

- **Makes logic clear:** The main advantage of using a flowchart to plan a task is that it provides a pictorial representation of the task, which makes the logic easier to follow. The symbols are connected in such a way that they show the movement (flow) of information through the system visibly. The steps and how each step is connected to the next can be clearly seen. Even less experienced personnel can trace the actions represented by a flowchart, that is, flowcharts are ideal for visualizing fundamental control structures employed in computer programming.
- **Communication:** Being a graphical representation of a problem-solving logic, flowcharts are better way of communicating the logic of a system to all concerned. The diagrammatical representation of logic is easier to communicate to all the interested parties as compared to actual program code, as the users may not be aware of all the programming techniques and jargons.
- **Effective analysis:** With the help of a flowchart, the problem can be analysed in an effective way. This is because the analyzing duties of the programmers can be delegated to other persons, who may or may not know the programming techniques, as they have a broad idea about the logic. Being outsiders, they often tend to test and analyse the logic in an unbiased manner.
- **Useful in coding:** The flowcharts act as a guide or blueprint during the analysis and program development phases. Once the flowcharts are ready, the programmers can plan the coding process effectively, as they know where to begin and where to end, making sure that no steps are omitted. As a result, error-free programs are developed in HLLs and that too at a faster rate.
- **Proper testing and debugging:** By nature, a flowchart helps in detecting the errors in a program, as the developers know exactly what the logic should do. Developers can test various data for a process, so that the program can handle every contingency.
- **Appropriate documentation:** Flowcharts serve as a good program documentation tool. Since normally the programs are developed for novice users, they can take the help of the program documentation to know what the program actually does and how to use the program.

Flowcharts can be used for designing the basic concept of the program in pictorial form but cannot be used for programming purposes. Some of the limitations of the flowchart are given as follows:

- **Complex:** The major disadvantage in using flowcharts is that when a program is very large, the flowcharts may continue for many pages, making them hard to follow. Flowcharts tend to get large very quickly and it is difficult to follow the represented process. It is also very laborious to draw a flowchart for a large program. You can very well imagine the nightmare when a flowchart is to be developed for a program, consisting of thousands of statements.
- **Costly:** Drawing flowcharts are viable only if the problem-solving logic is straightforward and not very lengthy. However, if flowcharts are to be drawn for a huge application, the time and the cost factors of program development may get out of proportion, making it a costly affair.
- **Difficult to modify:** Due to its symbolic nature, any changes or modification to a flowchart usually requires redrawing the entire logic again, and redrawing a complex flowchart is not a simple task. It is not easy to draw thousands of flow lines and symbols along with proper spacing, especially for a large complex program.

12. List some standard symbols used in flowchart with their description.

Ans: A flowchart is drawn according to the defined rules and using standard flowchart symbols prescribed by American National Standard Institute (ANSI). Some standard symbols that are frequently used for drawing flowcharts are shown in Table 4.3.

Table 4.3 Flowchart Symbols

Symbol	Symbol Name	Description
	Flow lines	Flow lines are used to connect symbols. These lines indicate the sequence of steps and the direction of flow of control.
	Terminal	This symbol is used to represent the beginning (start), the termination (end) or halt (pause) in the program logic.
	Input/Output	This symbol represents information entering or leaving the system such as customer order (input) and servicing (output).
	Processing	This symbol is used for representing arithmetic and data movement instructions. It can represent a single step ('add two cups of flour') or an entire sub-process ('make bread') within a larger process.
	Decision	This symbol denotes a decision (or branch) to be made. The program should continue along one of the two routes (IF/ELSE). This symbol has one entry and two exit paths. The path chosen depends on whether the answer to a question is yes or no.
	Connector	This symbol is used to join different flow lines.
	Off-page connector	This symbol is used to indicate that the flowchart continues on the next page.
	Document	This symbol is used to represent a paper document produced during the flowchart process.
	Annotation	This symbol is used to provide additional information about another flowchart symbol. The content may be in the form of descriptive comments, remarks or explanatory notes.
	Manual input	This symbol represents input to be given by a developer/programmer.
	Manual operation	This symbol shows that the process has to be done by a developer/programmer.
	Online storage	This symbol represents the online data storage such as hard disks, magnetic drums or other storage devices.
	Offline storage	This symbol represents the offline data storage such as sales on OCR and data on punched cards.
	Communication link	This symbol is used to represent data received or to be transmitted from an external system.
	Magnetic disk	This symbol is used to represent read from or write to a magnetic disk.

13. Explain the guidelines for preparing flowcharts.

Ans: The following guidelines should be used for creating a flowchart:

- The flowchart should be clear, neat and easy to follow.
- The flowchart must have a logical start and finish.
- In drawing a proper flowchart, all necessary requirements should be listed in logical order.

- Only one flow line should come out from a process symbol.

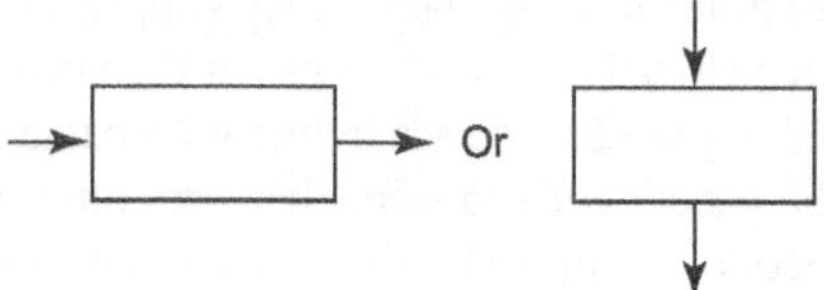

- Only one flow line should enter a decision symbol. However, two or three flow lines (one for each possible answer) may leave the decision symbol.

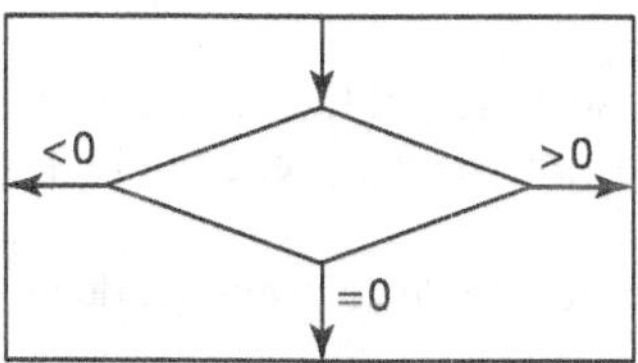

- Only one flow line is used with a terminal symbol.

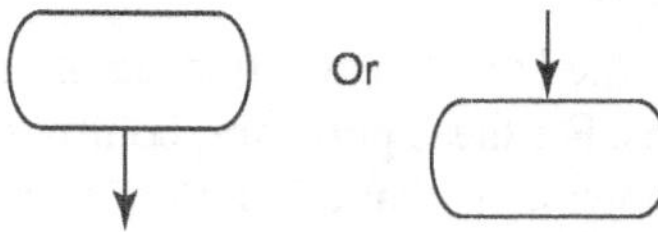

- Within standard symbols, write briefly. If necessary, use the annotation symbol to describe data or process more clearly.

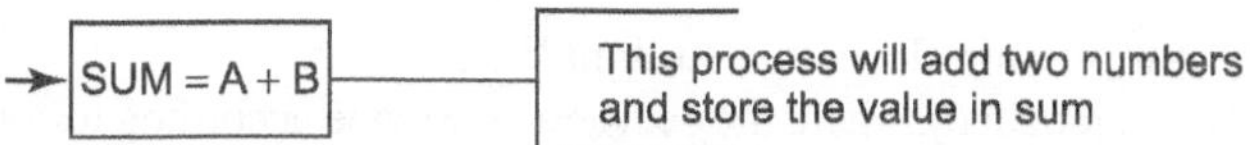

- In case of complex flowcharts, connector symbols are used to reduce the number of flow lines.
- Intersection of flow lines should be avoided to make it a more effective and better way of representing communication.
- It is useful to test the validity of the flowchart with normal/unusual test data.

14. What is pseudocode? Give some advantages and disadvantages of using it.

Ans: *Pseudocode* is made up of two words, namely *pseudo* and *code*. 'Pseudo' means imitation and 'code' refers to instructions, written in a programming language. As the name suggests, pseudocode is not a real programming code, but it models and may even look like programming code. It is a generic way of describing an algorithm without using any specific programming language-related notations.

In simple terms, pseudocode is an outline of a program, written in a form that can be easily converted into actual programming statements. It uses plain English statements rather than symbols, to represent the processes in a computer program. It is also known as 'PDL' (program design language), as it emphasizes more on the design aspect of a computer program and 'structured English', because usually pseudocode instructions are written in normal English, but in a structured way.

Pseudocode allows the programmer to focus on the steps required to solve a program rather than on how to use the computer language. Some of the most significant benefits of using pseudocode are as follows:

- Since it is language independent, it can be used by most programmers. It allows the developer to express the problem logic in plain natural language.

- It is easier to develop a program from a pseudocode rather than from a flowchart or decision table. Programmers do not have to think about syntaxes; they simply have to concentrate on the underlying logic. The focus is on the steps to solve a problem rather than on how to use the computer language.
- The words and phrases used in pseudocode are in line with basic computer operations. This simplifies the translation from the pseudocode to a specific programming language.
- Unlike flowcharts, pseudocode is compact and does not tend to run over many pages. Its simple structure and readability make it easier to modify.

Although pseudocode is a very simple mechanism to simplify problem-solving logic, it has some limitations that are as follows:

- It does not provide visual representation of the program's logic.
- There are no accepted standards for writing pseudocode. Programmers use their own style of writing pseudocode.
- It is quite difficult for the beginners to write pseudocode as compared to draw flowchart.

15. Explain sequence logic, selection logic and iteration logic design structure in the pseudocode and flowchart.

Ans: A program is usually not limited to a linear sequence of instructions. During its process, it may diverge, repeat code or take decisions. For these purposes, control structures specify what has to be done to perform the program. Program statements that affect the order in which statements are executed, or that affect whether statements are executed, are called 'control structures'. They affect the flow of simulation code since a control structure evaluates statements and then executes code according to the result. Essentially, there are three control structures:

(i) **Sequence**, where information flows in a straight line.
(ii) **Selection** (decision or branched), where the decisions are made according to some predefined condition.
(iii) **Iteration/Repetition** (looping), where the logic (sequence of steps) is repeated in a loop until the desired output is obtained.

Sequence Control Structure

As the name implies, in a sequence structure, the instructions to be computed simply follow one another in a logical progression. This structure is denoted by writing one action after another, each action on a line by itself, and all actions aligned with the logical indent. The actions are performed in the same sequence (top to bottom) in which they are written.

Typical sequence operations consist of process and I/O steps. Figure 4.4 depicts the flowchart and pseudocode for sequence construct.

Selection Control Structure

A selection structure allows the program to make a choice between two alternate paths, whether it is *true* or *false*. The first statement of a selection structure is a conditional statement. Once the sequence of steps in the selected path has been carried out, the paths are rejoined and then the next instruction is carried out. Thus, the selection structure has only a single entry and a single exit. Figure 4.5 depicts the flowchart and pseudocode for selection construct. From this figure, it is clear that if the condition is true, Action 1 will be performed otherwise Action 2 will be performed. After performing the list of actions, the control of the program moves on to the other actions in the process flow.

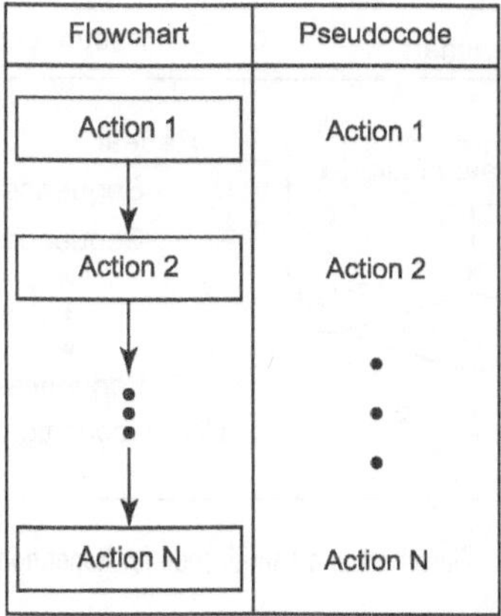

Figure 4.4 Flowchart and Pseudocode for Sequence Construct

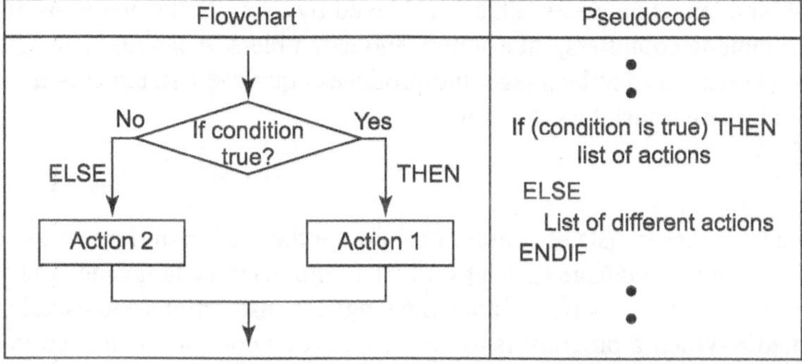

Figure 4.5 Flowchart and Pseudocode for Selection Construct

Iteration/Repetition Control Structure

Iteration or loop pattern causes an interruption in the normal sequence of processing. It directs the system to loop back to a previous statement in the program, repeating the same sequence over and again, usually with new data. When a sequence of statements is repeated against a condition, it is said to be in a *loop*. Using looping, the programmer avoids writing the same set of instructions again. The looping process can either be one time or multiple times until the desired output is obtained within a single program. Figure 4.6 depicts the flowchart and pseudocode for repetition construct.

16. What is the difference between a program and algorithm?

Ans: An algorithm is a finite sequence of steps that guides to the solution of a problem it and is written in a simple language such as 'English', so that it can be easily understand by any user. On the other hand, a computer program is also a set of instructions to solve a specific problem but written in any of the programming languages such as C++, JAVA and VB.

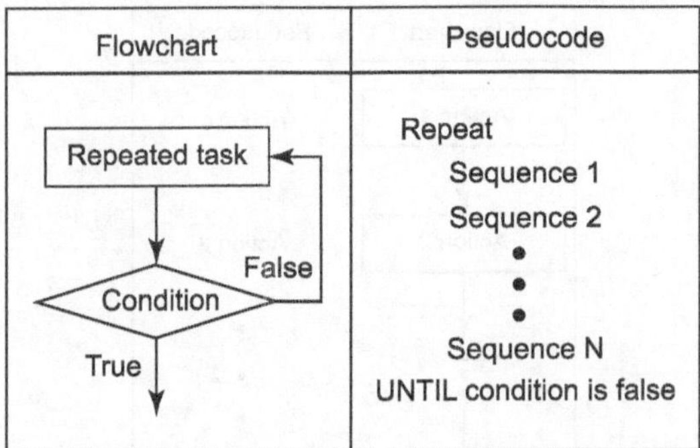

Figure 4.6 Flowchart and Pseudocode for Repetition Construct

17. Explain in detail the working of three types of language translators.

Ans: Since computers understand only machine language, it is necessary to convert the HLL programs into machine language codes. This is achieved by using 'language translators' or 'language processors', which include compilers, interpreters and assemblers. A language translator, as the name implies, accepts statements in one language and produces equivalent statements in another language. The description of all these translators is as follows:

Compiler

It is a kind of translator that translates a program into another program, known as 'target language'. Usually, compiler is used for language translator of HLL into machine language. The compiler replaces single high-level statement with a series of machine language instructions and usually resides on a disk or other storage media. When a program is to be compiled, its compiler is loaded into main memory. The compiler stores the entire high-level program, scans it and translates the whole program into an equivalent machine language program. During the translation process, the compiler reads the source program and checks the syntax (grammatical) errors. If there is any error, the compiler generates an error message, which is usually displayed on the screen. In case of errors, the compiler will not create the object code until all the errors are rectified.

Once the program has been compiled, the resulting machine code is saved in an executable file, which can be run on its own at any time. To be precise, once the executable is generated, there is no need for the actual source code file. Anyway, it is worthwhile to keep the source file(s) because if the source code is modified, it is necessary to recompile the program again to regenerate the executable file containing amendments. Figure 4.7 illustrates the working of a compiler.

Interpreter

It is also a language translator and translates HLL into machine language. However, unlike compilers, it translates a statement in a program and executes the statement immediately before translating the next source language statement (Figure 4.8). When an error is encountered in the program, the execution of the program is halted and an error message is displayed. An interpreted language such as BASIC and LISP has its own interpreters.

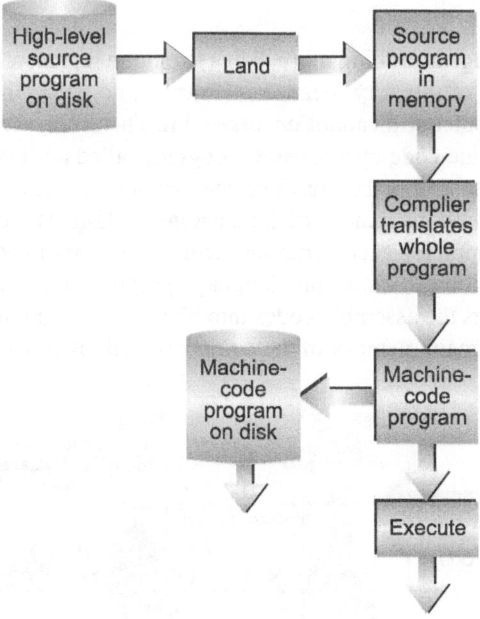

Figure 4.7 Working of a Compiler

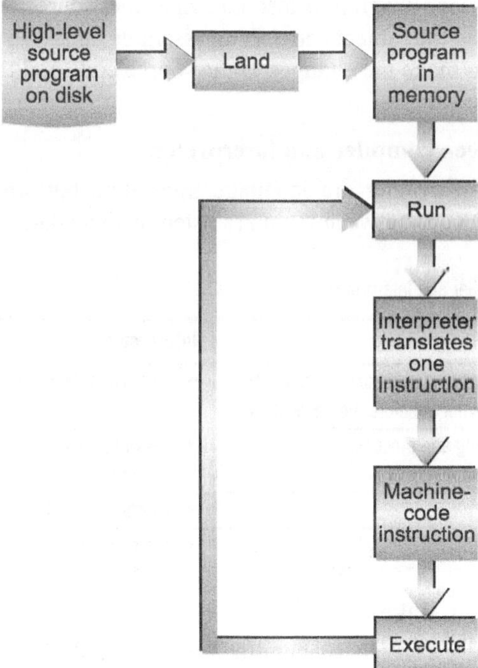

Figure 4.8 Working of an Interpreter

Assembler

As we know, assembly language is nothing more than a symbolic representation of machine code, which allows symbolic designation of memory locations. However, no matter how close assembly language is to machine code, the computer still cannot understand it. Therefore, the assembly language program must be translated into machine code by a separate program called an 'assembler'. The assembler program recognizes the character strings that make up the symbolic names of the various machine operations and substitutes the required machine code for each instruction. At the same time, it also calculates the required address in memory for each symbolic name of a memory location and substitutes those addresses for the names resulting in a machine language program that can run on its own at any time. In short, an assembler converts the assembly codes into binary codes and then it assembles the machine-understandable code into the main memory of the computer, making it ready for execution (Figure 4.9).

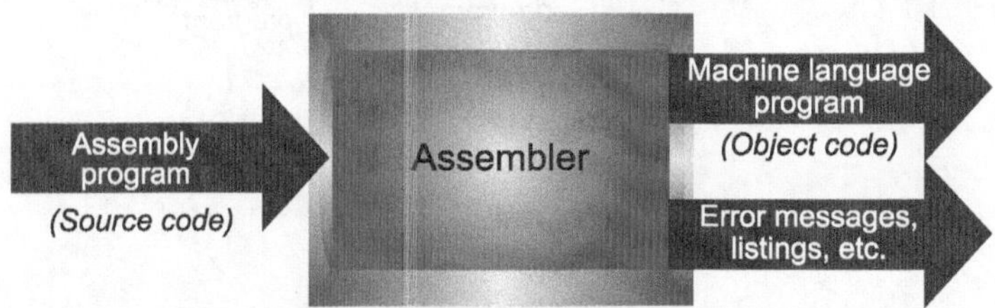

Figure 4.9 Working of an Assembler

The original assembly language program is also known as the 'source code', while the final machine language program is designated the 'object code'. If an assembly language program needs to be changed or corrected, it is necessary to make the changes to the source code and then re-assemble it to create a new object program.

18. Differentiate between compiler and interpreter.

Ans: Both compiler and interpreter are language translators but still there is a huge difference between the two. Some differences between them are listed in Table 4.4.

Table 4.4 Differences Between Compiler and Interpreter

Compiler	Interpreter
• It converts the entire program or set of instructions written in HLL into executable code (machine language) before their execution.	• It converts the code during the run time one line at a time.
• A lot of time is required for analysing and processing the program.	• Less time is spent for analysing and processing the program.
• Program execution is faster.	• Program execution is relatively slow.
• The resulting code is in machine-specific binary form.	• The resulting code is intermediate code.

19. Write a short note on linker.

Ans: An application usually consists of hundreds or thousands of lines of codes. The codes are divided into logical groups and stored in different modules, so that the debugging and maintenance of the codes become easier. Hence, for an application, it is always advisable to adhere to structural (modular) programming practices. When a program is broken into several modules, each module can be modified and compiled independently. In such a case, these modules have to be linked together to create a complete application. This job is done by a tool known as 'linker'. A linker is a program that links several object modules and libraries to form a single, coherent program (executable). Object modules are the machine code output from an assembler or compiler and contain executable machine code and data, together with information that allows the linker to combine the modules together to form a program.

Generally, all HLLs use some in-built functions such as calculating square roots and finding logarithm values. These functions are usually provided by the language itself; the programmer need not code them separately. During the program execution process, when a program invokes any in-built function, the linker transfers the control to that program where the function is defined, by making the addresses of these functions known to the calling program.

20. What do you mean by text editor? Discuss their features.

Ans: A 'text editor' is a utility program used for editing plain text files. A plain text file consists of a collection of numbers, letters, symbols etc. Text editor is usually used for changing configuration files and programming language source code. Some of the basic features of a text editor are as follows:

- **Cut, copy and paste:** Text editors provide the method of moving, deleting and duplicating text within a file or between multiples files.
- **Undo and redo:** Text editors offer the way to undo and redo the last edit. Undo, as the name suggests, allows you to unwrap the last changes made to the document, whereas redo lets you reverse the last undo. Modern editors usually provide a multiple level history such that issuing the undo command repeatedly will turn back the document to successively older edits, while redo command will cycle the edits forward toward the most recent changes. However, the number of changes remembered by editor depends on its type.
- **String searching algorithm:** By using this feature, the user can find any string from the file and then can replace it with the desired string. Moreover, in advanced text editors, conditional and unconditional searches and replace options are also available.
- **Data transformation:** This feature allows the user to merge the content of desired file into the currently working file.
- **Syntax highlighting:** This feature highlights the software code and other text that appears in an organized or predictable format.

21. State the basic features of any good programming language.

Ans: The features of one programming language may differ from the other. One can be easy and simple while another can be difficult and complex. We judge the success and strength of a programming language with respect to standard features. To begin the language selection process, it is important to establish some criteria for what makes a language good. The basic features that should be there in every programming language are as follows:

- **Ease of use:** The language should be easy in writing codes for the programs and executing them. The ease and clarity of a language depend upon its syntax. It should be capable enough to provide clear, simple and unified set of concepts. The vocabulary of the language should resemble English (or some other natural language). Symbols, abbreviations and jargon should be avoided unless they are already known to most people. Simplicity helps in the readability of the language. A simple language is easier to grasp and code.

- **Portability:** The language should support the construction of code in a way that it could be distributed across multiple platforms (operating systems). Computer languages should be independent of any particular hardware or operating system, that is, programs written on one platform should be able to be transferred to any other computer or platform and there it should perform accurately.
- **Naturalness for the application:** The language should have a syntax that allows the program structure to show the underlying logical structure of an algorithm. A programming language should provide a conceptual framework for thinking through algorithms and means of expressing those algorithms through flowcharts. The advantage of displaying a program in algorithms and flowcharts is that even a novice can understand them easily without learning any programming language.
- **Reliability:** The language should support construction of components that perform their intended functions in a satisfactory manner throughout its lifetime. Reliability is concerned with making a system failure free, and thus, is concerned with all possible errors. The language should have the support of error detection as well as prevention. It should detect some kinds of specific errors. For example, some errors can be prevented by a strict syntax checking. Moreover, the language should also be able to detect and report errors in the program. For example, arithmetic overflow and assertions should be detected properly and reported to the programmers immediately, so that the error can be rectified. The language should provide reliability by supporting explicit mechanisms for dealing with problems that are detected when the system is in operation (exception handling).
- **Performance:** By performance, we mean that the language should be capable of interacting not only with the end users, but also with the hardware. The language should also support software engineering mechanism, discouraging or prohibiting poor practices and supporting maintenance activities. Nowadays, the hardware has become very sophisticated and quite fast. Hence, the application developed using a good language should tap the maximum resources of the available hardware power in terms of speed and memory efficiency.
- **Cost:** Cost component is a primary concern before deploying a language at a commercial level. It includes several costs such as:
  - Program execution and translation cost.
  - Program creation, testing and use cost.
  - Program maintenance cost.
- **Promote structural programming:** We know that structural programming is the best way to create an application. Hence, a good language should be capable of supporting structural programming. Since, by nature, structural programming facilitates ease in understanding the code, a program is easier to create, debug and maintain. A structured program also helps programmers to visualize the problem in a logical way, thereby reducing the possibility of errors in the code.
- **Reusability:** The language should facilitate the adaptation of code for use in other applications. Code is reusable when it is independent of other codes. It is very common, for example, to reuse common data structures, such as stacks, queues and trees. When these have been defined with common operations on the structures, these abstract data types become easy to reuse.

22. Write an algorithm to find the sum of the first *n* even numbers, where *n* should be read from the user.

Ans:

```
Step 1: Start
Step 2: Initialize variables i, j and sum
              i=1, j=2 and sum=0
Step 3: Read n
Step 4: While i <= n then
             Add j to sum
             Increment i by 1 and j by 2
           End while
Step 5: Display sum
Step 6: Stop
```

23. Write an algorithm to find the factorial of a given number.

Ans:

```
Step 1: Start
Step 2: Read num
Step 3: Initialize variable fact with 1
Step 4: If num > 0 then
           Multiply fact by num and store value in fact
           Decrement value of num by 1
           go to Step 4
        Else
           Display fact
        End if
Step 5: Stop
```

24. Write an algorithm to find the largest number among three given numbers and outline the steps in the algorithm with the input 5, 17 and 3.

Ans:

```
Step 1: Start
Step 2: Read three numbers A, B, C
Step 3: Find the larger number between A and B and store it
        in MAX_AB
Step 4: Find the larger number between MAX_AB and C and store
        it in MAX
Step 5: Display MAX
Step 6: Stop
```

Given three numbers are 5, 17 and 3. Since out of 5 and 17, 17 is larger, we store 17 in MAX_AB. Now, from MAX_AB (that is, 17) and 3, 17 is larger, we store 17 in MAX. Thus, the maximum of given numbers is 17.

25. Write an algorithm to find the average of *n* numbers.

Ans:

```
Step 1: Start
Step 2: Initialize variables i, Sum
             i = 1 and sum = 0
```

```
Step 3: Read n
Step 4: While i <= n
              Read num
              Add num to sum
              Increment i by 1
           End while
Step 5: Calculate Average = Sum / n
Step 6: Display Average
Step 7: Stop
```

26. Write an algorithm to generate a Fibonacci series.

Ans:

```
Step 1: Start
Step 2: Initialize sum=0, A=0, B=1, i=3
Step 3: Read the number of terms you want in the Fibonacci
        series, say n
Step 4: Display A, B
Step 5: While i <= n
         Add A and B and store value in sum
         Display sum
         Assign the value of B to A, that is, A=B
         Assign the value of sum to B, that is, B=sum
         Increment i by 1
          End while
Step 6: Stop
```

27. Write an algorithm to test whether the given number is prime or not.

Ans:

```
Step 1: Start
Step 2: Read num
Step 3: Initialize div = 2
Step 4: Calculate half = num/2
Step 5: While (div <= half)
              Divide num by div and store remainder in rem
              If rem = 0 then
            Display given number is not prime
            Go to Step 7
              End if
              Increment div by 1
           End while
Step 6: Display given number is prime
Step 7: Stop
```

28. Draw a flowchart to check whether a given number is odd or even.

Ans: The flowchart to check whether a number is even or odd is shown here.

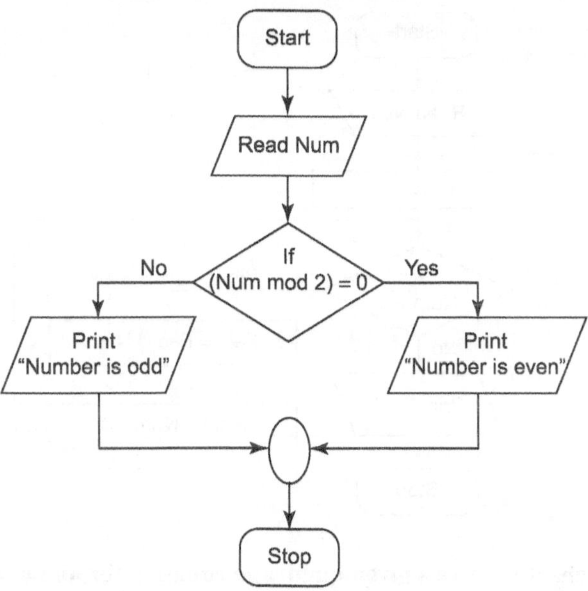

29. Draw a flowchart to compute sum of *n* natural numbers.

Ans: The flowchart to compute the sum of *n* natural numbers is shown here.

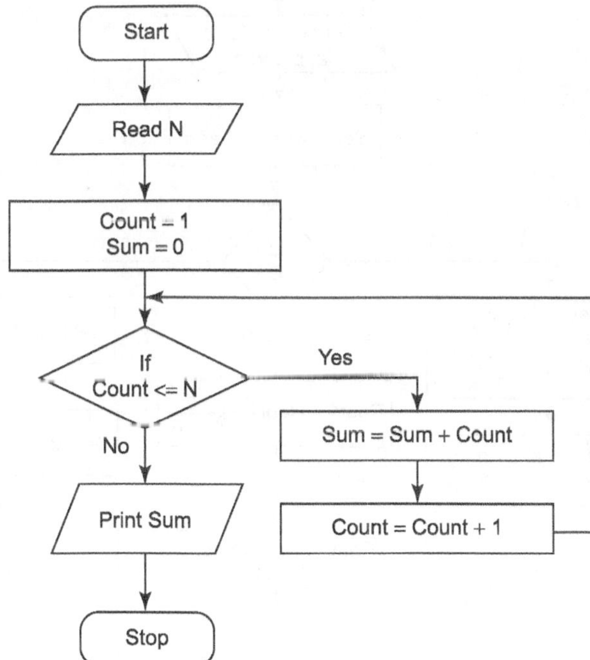

30. Draw a flowchart to compute the factorial of a number.

Ans: The flowchart to compute the factorial of a number is shown here.

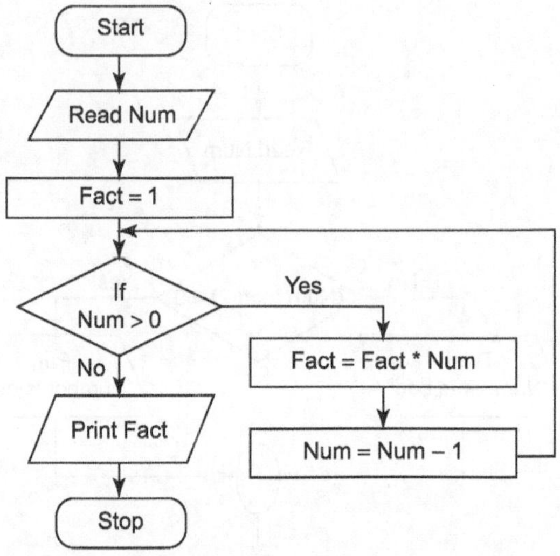

31. Draw a flowchart to solve a given quadratic equation for all possible cases.

Ans: The flowchart to find the roots of a quadratic equation is shown here.

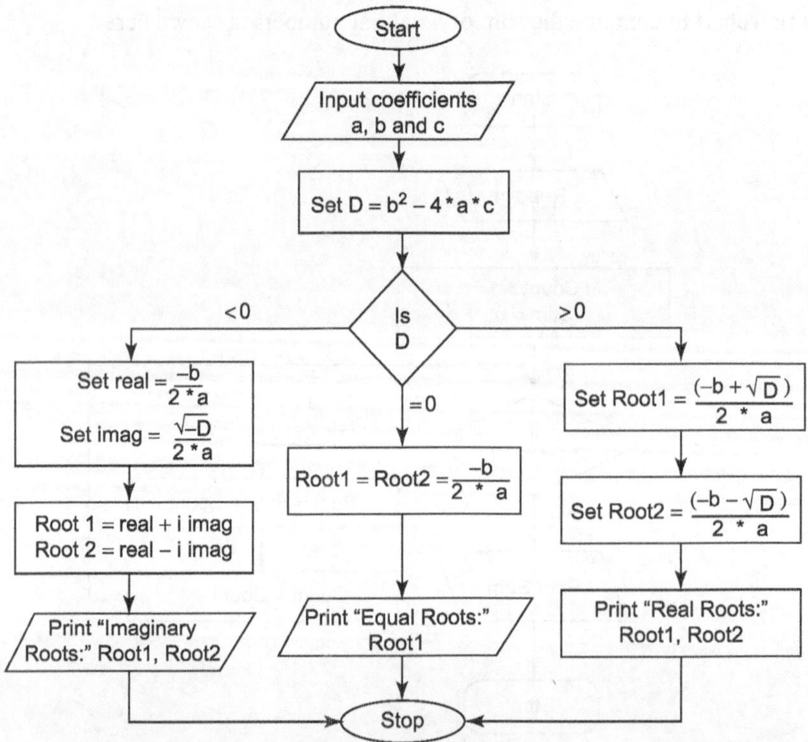

32. Draw a flowchart to test whether a given number is prime or not.

Ans: The flowchart to check whether a number is prime or not is shown here.

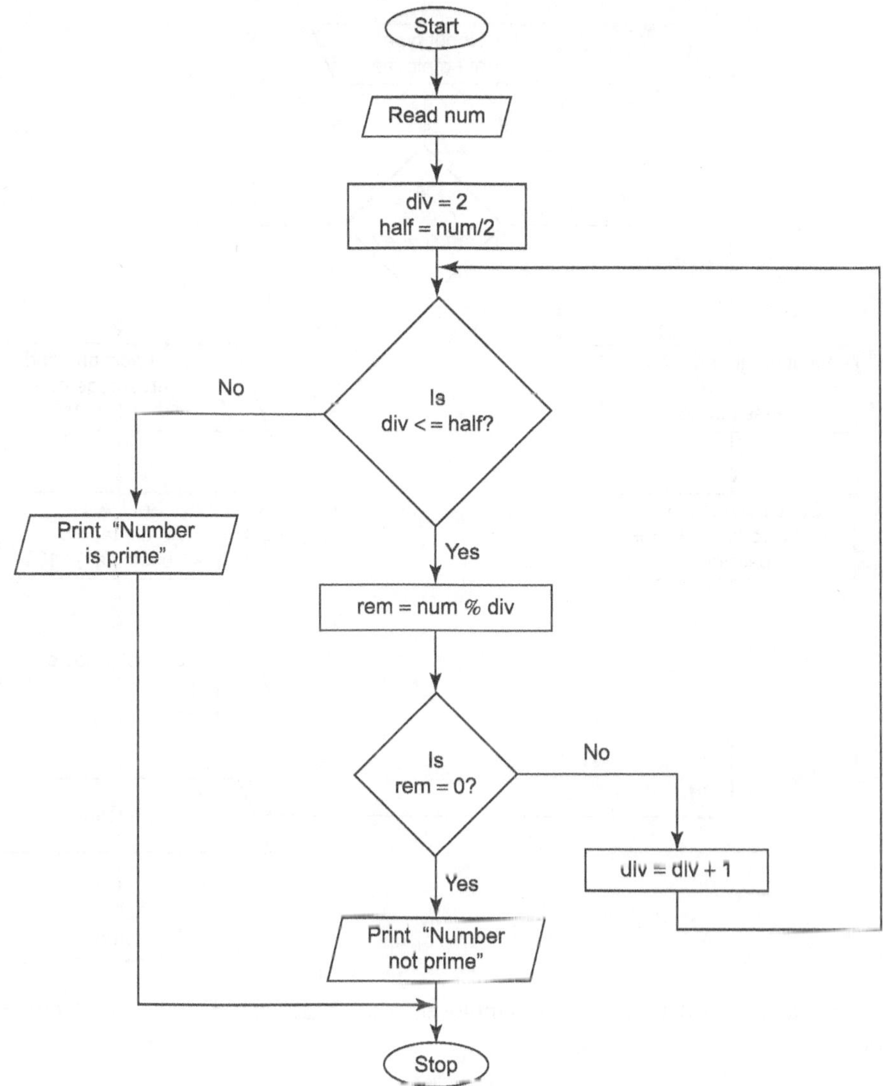

33. Draw a flowchart to compute the salary of an employee in a company. Assume that there are two types of employees in the company: daily wages and regular. Salary is calculated as number of hours worked * wages/hour for daily wages and basic pay + (% of DA * basic pay)/100 + HRA + MA for a regular employee. Sketch the flow of your design for regular employee with basic pay = 5000, % of DA = 75% and HRA = 500.

Ans: The flowchart to compute the salary of an employee in a company is shown here.

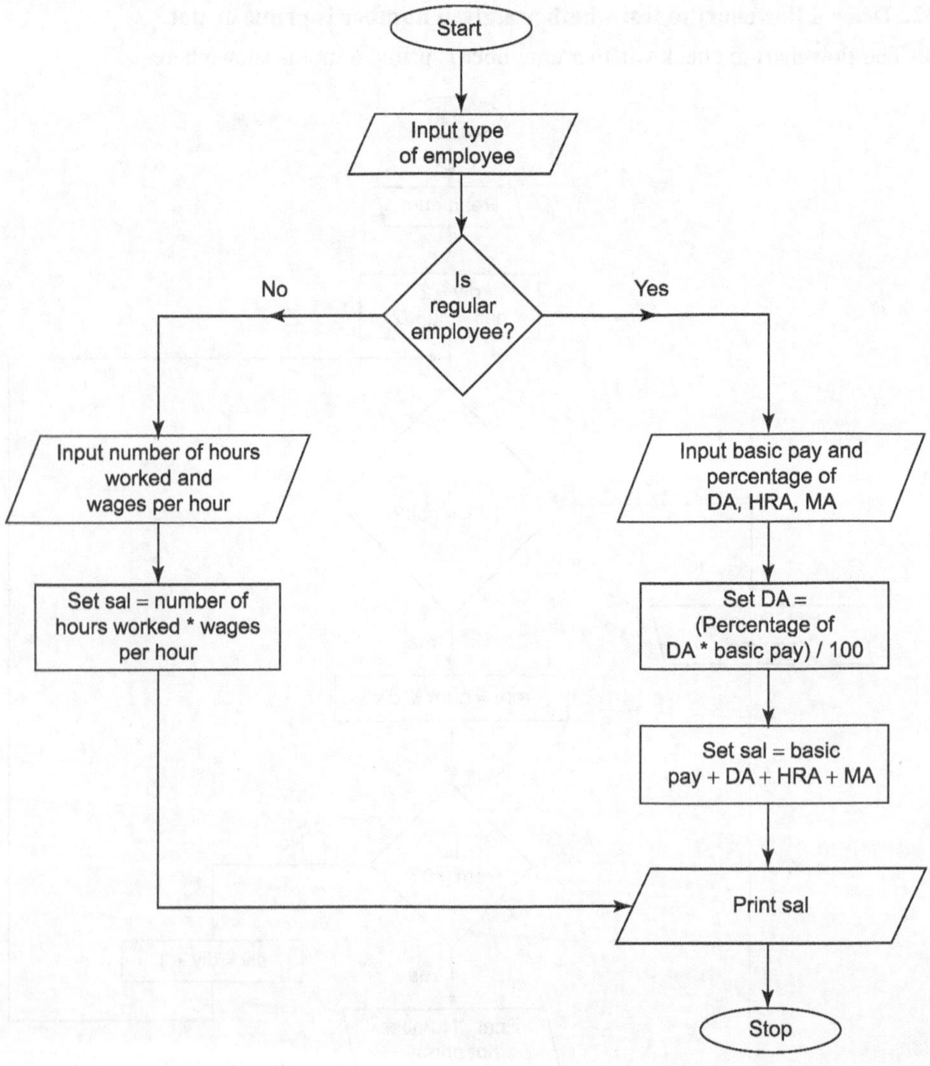

Steps to calculate the salary of regular employee when basic pay = 5000, % of DA = 75% and HRA = 500:

1. Start
2. The regular employee is input.
3. Its basic pay (5000), percentage of DA (75%), HRA (500) and MA (0) is input.
4. Then DA is calculated in the following manner:
   DA = (75 * 5000) / 100
   = 3750
5. Sal = 5000 + 3750 + 500 + 0
   = 9250

34. Draw a flowchart to add two matrices.

Ans: The flowchart to add two matrices is shown here.

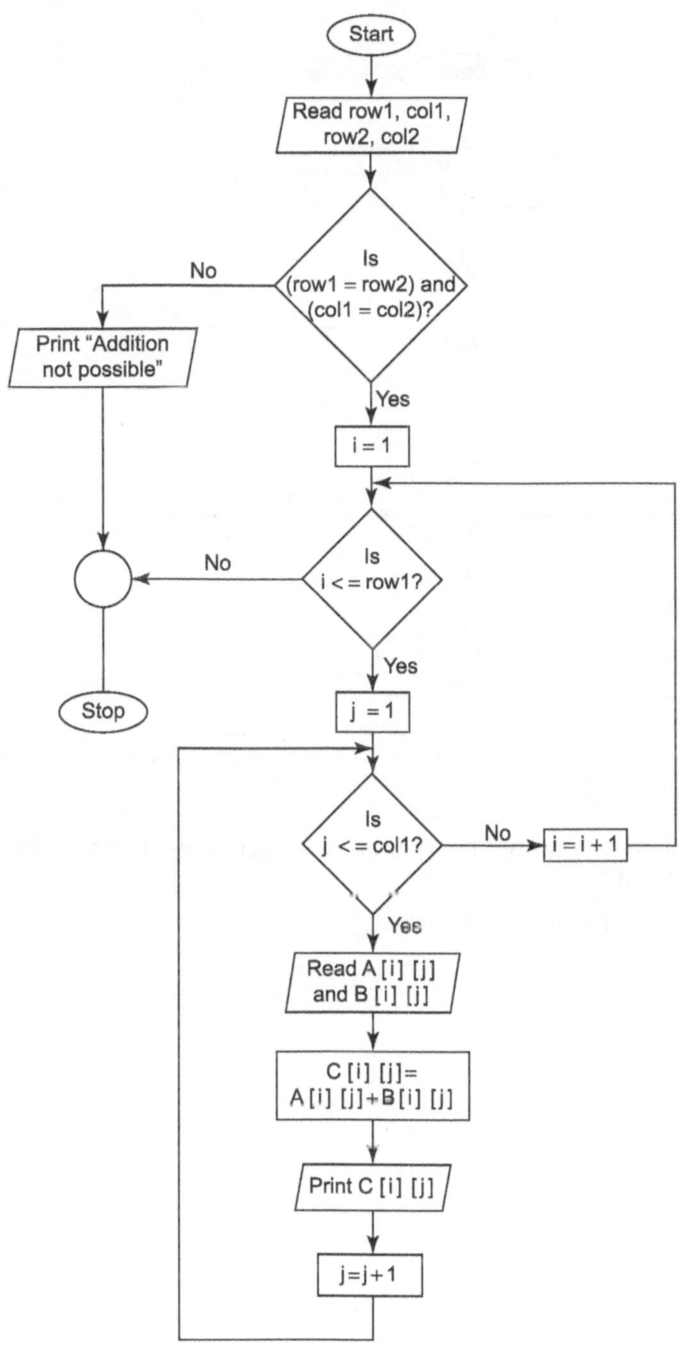

35. Draw a flowchart to find the smallest of three numbers.

Ans: The flowchart to find the smallest of three numbers is shown here.

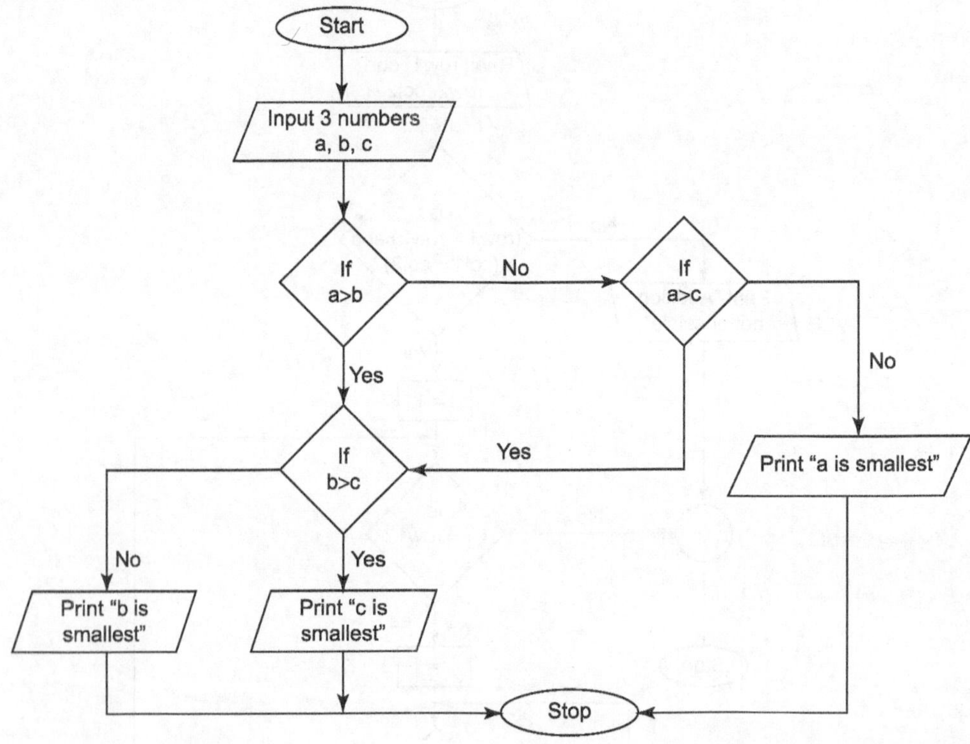

36. Draw a flowchart to find the sum of all integers ranging from 100 to 200 and divisible by both 2 and 3.

Ans: The required flowchart is shown here.

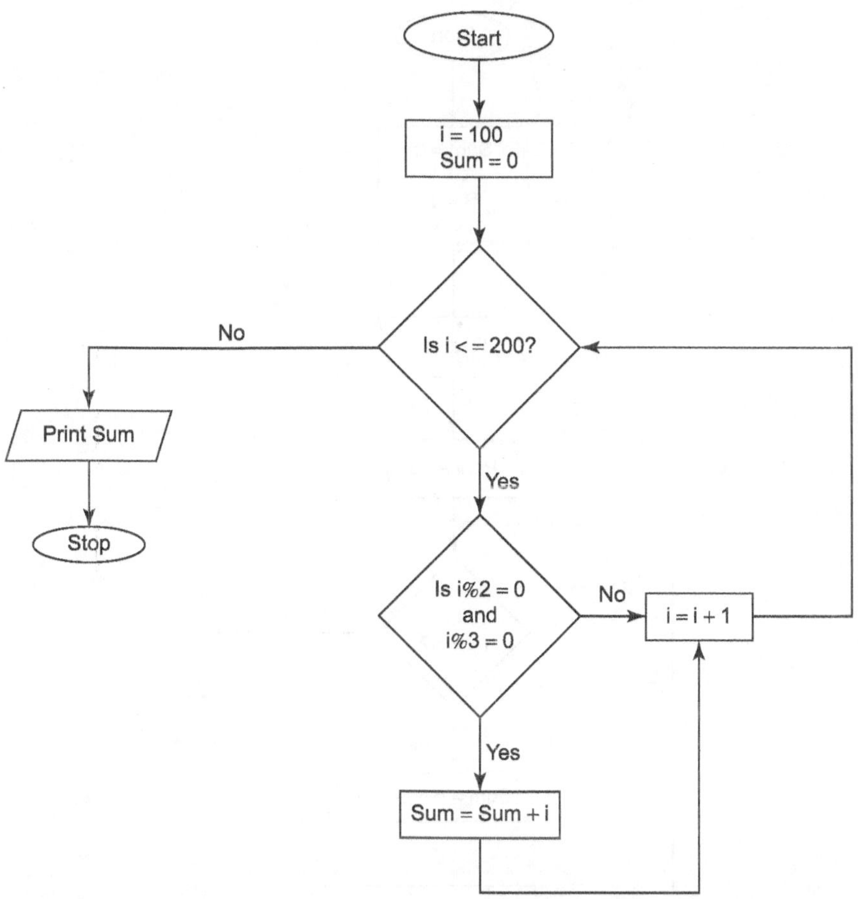

37. Draw a flowchart to display the first *n* terms of the Fibonacci series. The first two terms of the series are 1 and 1, respectively. The *n*th term of the series F is defined as $F_n = F_{n-1} + F_{n-2}$.

Ans: The flowchart to display the first *n* terms of the Fibonacci series is shown here.

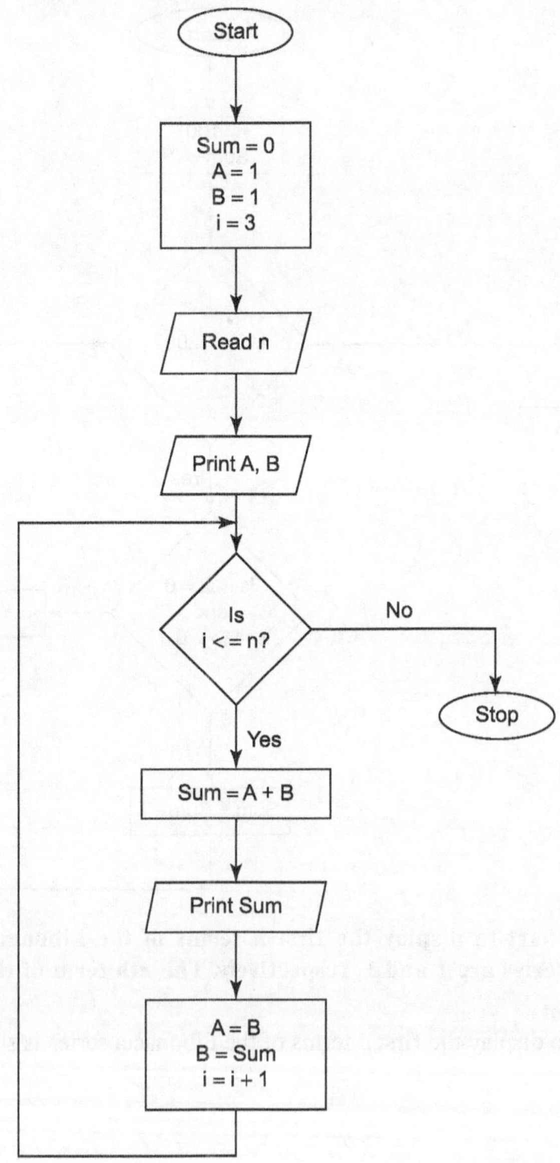

38. Write a pseudocode using while statement to print numbers from 10 down to 1.

Ans:

```
SET num = 10
DO WHILE num >= 1
  DISPLAY num
  SET num = num - 1
ENDDO
STOP
```

39. Write a pseudocode for calculating the compound interest.

Ans:

```
PROMPT user to enter Principle
PROMPT user to enter Rate
PROMPT user to enter Time
COMPUTE CI = Principle * (1 + Rate/100)^Time
DISPLAY CI
STOP
```

Multiple-choice Questions

1. Software is a (an) _________ in a computer system.
   (a) Intangible commodity (b) CD-ROM
   (c) Scanner (d) BIOS
2. Which of the following is not hardware?
   (a) Keyboard (b) Modem (c) MS Word (d) Monitor
3. Microsoft's Notepad is an example of _________.
   (a) Application software (b) Programming software
   (c) System software (d) All of these
4. Which of the following is not a phase of software development process?
   (a) Task analysis (b) Analyse the problem
   (c) Designing (d) Translation
5. Binary language is also known as _________.
   (a) Machine language (b) Assembly language
   (c) System language (d) Programming language
6. The step-by-step procedure to solve a particular problem is called _________.
   (a) Flowchart (b) Program (c) Instruction (d) Algorithm
7. Processing and flow lines are parts of a _________.
   (a) Algorithm (b) Flowchart (c) Pseudocode (d) Program
8. Which translator converts the entire HLL program into an equivalent machine language at once?
   (a) Assembler (b) Computer (c) Compiler (d) Interpreter
9. The original assembly language program is also known as _________.
   (a) Object code (b) Source code (c) Basic code (d) None of these
10. Which of these application software packages is used to create magazines or books?
    (a) Word processors (b) Spreadsheets
    (c) Presentation software (d) Desktop publishing

Answers

1. (a) 2. (c) 3. (a) 4. (d) 5. (a) 6. (d) 7. (b) 8. (c) 9. (b) 10. (d)

5

Introduction to Office Packages

1. What is an office package? List any four office packages.

Ans: An 'office package' (also called 'office suite') is a collection of productivity software or programs where each software is intended to perform some specialized operations. A number office software packages are available in the market for different operating systems. Some examples of such packages are as follows:

- **Office package for Microsoft Windows:** MS Office, WordPerfect Office and MS Works.
- **Office package for DOS:** Breadbox office and Corel WordPerfect for DOS.
- **Office package for Mac:** NeoOffice, MarinerPak and Microsoft Office for Mac.
- **Office package for UNIX:** AUIS and Siag Office.

2. What do you know about MS Office? What are the various components of MS Office?

Ans: 'Microsoft Office' (MS Office) is a commercial office suite of related applications, services and servers for the Microsoft Windows and Mac OS X operating systems. It was first launched by Microsoft in 1989, and afterwards, several versions have been released. The current versions of MS Office are Office 2010 for Microsoft Windows and Office 2011 for Mac OS X. However, MS Office 2003 is one of the commonly used productivity suites, which was released by Microsoft on 21 October 2003.

Components of MS Office

The first version of MS Office contained only three components including Microsoft Word, Microsoft Excel and Microsoft PowerPoint. However, over the years, a number of new components have been added to the suite. For example, the components of MS Office 2003 include Word 2003, Excel 2003, PowerPoint 2003, Outlook 2003, Access 2003, Publisher 2003, InfoPath 2003, Project 2003, Visio 2003, FrontPage 2003 and OneNote 2003.

3. Define word processor and explain its features.

Ans: A 'word processor' is an application program used to create, format, edit and print electronic documents. It enables to develop and modify documents such as letters, reports and memos, store them electronically on a disk, display them on the screen and print them on a printer. The use of a word-processing program results in reduced retyping time for error-free hard copy, facilitation of document revision, change before committing to paper, faster output speed, reduced proofreading and elimination of stationary wastage.

Features of Word Processor

Using the built-in features of a word processor, you can create letters, tables, newsletters and academic papers that are easier to revise and much more aesthetically pleasing than the documents created using a typewriter. Some of the other features that make the word processors a powerful tool to create documents are as follows:

- **Extensive built-in features:** Word processors can be used to make mail merge documents, envelopes, labels etc.
- **Easy to learn:** To operate word processors, no special skills are required. Most of the word processors are easy to learn and use.
- **Foreign language features:** Word processors allow documents to be created in languages other than English. This is helpful for users who do not know English or require work to be done in some other 'specified' language.
- **Table and graphics:** The use of tables, charts and graphics is also supported by the word processors. All these elements increase the visual clarity of the text.
- **Linking and embedding:** Word processors allow linking and embedding of objects such as a chart, a video clip, a picture etc. in a document. This is possible by using Object Linking and Embedding (OLE) technology that can be used to share information between programs.
- **Easy formatting:** Word processors help in formatting style, font and paragraph to increase the readability of the text and to enhance the visual appearance.
- **Extensive help:** Word processors include an extensive built-in help feature that can be used to ask queries. The users can easily utilize this built-in feature to know how to perform an action or set of actions etc.
- **Spelling and grammar check:** Word processors help to check and remove spelling and grammatical mistakes. They also help in knowing synonym(s) or the meaning of a particular word.

4. What is MS Word? What are its advantages?

Ans: 'Microsoft Word' (MS Word), sold as a part of the MS Office Suite is one of the most popular and widely used word processors that can be effectively used to produce professional documents quickly and efficiently. The first version of MS Word was introduced in 1989 that included only some basic features. Since then, a number of versions have been released (the latest being Word 2010) and with each version, MS Word has grown substantially with many features such as common spell checker and data integration. MS Word 2003 is one of the most widely used versions. It is highly versatile tool, ideal for creating short documents such as letters and memos with enough layout and graphics-handling capabilities for a sophisticated publishing.

Advantages of MS Word

MS Word is a word processor that enables you more than creating and editing a document. It offers a wide variety of other functions and tools that allow you to format the document. Some of the advantages of MS Word are as follows:

- You can make changes to a document without retyping the entire document unlike conventional typewriter.
- Selected text or paragraphs can be moved or copied throughout the document.
- You can arrange the text in columnar style as we see in the newspaper. Textboxes can be added to the document.
- Page layout and margins can be adjusted as per the requirement.
- Word can provide the statistics of your document such as total number of characters, words or lines in the document.
- Page numbers and header and footer can be included.
- You can merge multiple files or documents.

5. Write a short note on Format Painter.

Ans: 'Format Painter' is a handy feature for formatting text. It provides a quick way of copying formatting from one piece of text to another. For example, if you are formatting a paragraph heading with a certain font face, size and style and you want to format another heading the same way, you need not manually add each attribute to the new heading. Instead, you can use the Format Painter, which is a time-saving feature for quickly copying the format of a block of text. This can be done by following the steps:

1. Select the text containing the formatting you wish to copy.
2. To copy formatting to a single location, click once on the Format Painter button ( ) on the Standard Toolbar. To copy it to multiple locations, double-click on the Format Painter button. Notice that the mouse pointer changes to resemble a paintbrush ( ).
3. Now, click and drag the mouse to select the text you wish to format and then release the mouse.
4. If the format painter is copied by double-clicking, press the Esc key to come out of painter mode.

6. What do you mean by headers and footers? Write the steps to insert headers and footers in a document.

Ans: 'Headers' are text that appears at the top of every page, and 'footers' contain text that appears at the bottom of each page. Every Word document contains header and footer areas where you can put a document title, author name, page number, graphics and any other essentials that you want to repeat over several (or all) pages in the document. If nothing is inserted in the headers and footers, they still exist, but are left blank and take up no space on the page. What you put in the header or footer appears on every page of the document.

To insert header and footer in a document, follow the steps given below:

1. Select **Header and Footer** option from the **View** menu. This displays the Header and Footer toolbar with a dotted box for header at the top of the page and a dotted box for footer at the bottom of the page (Figure 5.1).

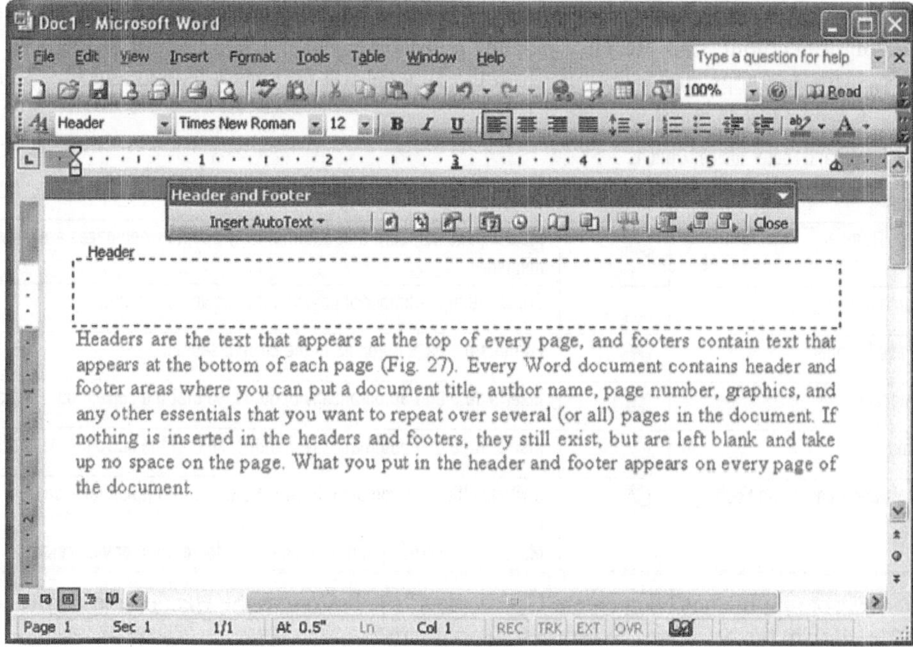

(a) Header

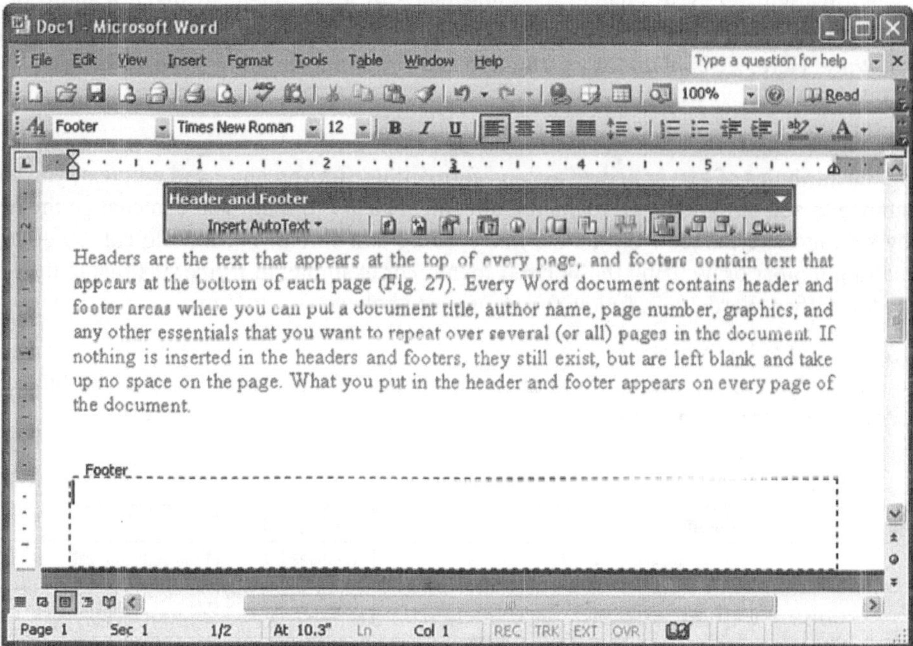

(b) Footer

Figure 5.1 Header and Footer

2. Type the text in header and/or footer box. Note that headers and footers can be formatted (like changing font colour, size, etc.) just like any other text.
3. If necessary, use appropriate options from the Header and Footer toolbar to add time, insert page number, date, etc., as listed in Table 5.1.

Table 5.1 Header and Footer Toolbar Options

Command	Button	Description
Insert Page Number		Inserts page numbers that automatically update when pages are added or deleted.
Insert Number of Pages		Prints the total number of pages in the active document.
Format Page Number		Formats the page numbers in the current section.
Insert Date		Inserts date that automatically updates, so that the current date is displayed.
Insert Time		Inserts time that automatically updates, so that the current time is displayed.
Switch Between Header and Footer		Switches the insertion point between the header and footer areas. Or Moves the insertion point from header to footer area or vice versa.

4. After text or graphic has been entered, click the **Close** button on the Header and Footer toolbar or double-click in the work area to return to work there.

7. Explain any three formatting features in MS Word.

Ans: 'Formatting' refers to change the appearance of a document to make it more presentable. Formatting features of MS Word include *text formatting*, *paragraph formatting*, *column formatting* and *page formatting*. Here, we explain text, paragraph and column formatting.

Text Formatting

Changing the attributes of text is known as 'text formatting'. As you enter and edit text, you can change its appearance to add emphasis and make the document easier to read. You can change the appearance of text by setting the typeface (font), size, line spacing and colour. Formatting can be done by using the Formatting toolbar or by using the **Format** menu. For example, to format text using the Formatting toolbar in MS Office Word 2003, follow the steps given below:

1. Select the text to be formatted.
2. Use buttons on the Formatting toolbar to format the selected text. Some of the buttons used in formatting text are given in Table 5.2.

Table 5.2 Formatting Text

Command	Button	Description
Font	Times New Roman	Changes the font of the selected text.
Font Size	12	Changes the font size of the selected text.
Bold	B	Bolds the selected text.

(Continued)

Table 5.2 (Continued)

Command	Button	Description
Italic	*I*	Italicizes the selected text.
Underline	U	Underlines the selected text.
Highlight	ab	Highlights the selected text.
Font Color	A	Changes font colour of the selected text.

Paragraph Formatting

In addition to desired portions of text, you can also format the entire paragraph at once. Paragraph formatting includes 'alignment' and 'indentation' operations. These operations are performed to give a well-defined 'structure' to the document. This gives a professional look to the document. To align or indent a paragraph, follow the steps given below:

1. Select the paragraph to be aligned or indented.
2. Use buttons on the Formatting toolbar to align or indent the paragraph. Some of the buttons used in aligning or indenting paragraph are given in Table 5.3.

Table 5.3 Paragraph Formatting

Command	Button	Description
Align Left		Left aligns the paragraph or selected text.
Center		Centre aligns the paragraph or selected text.
Align Right		Right aligns the paragraph or the selected text.
Justify		Justifies the paragraph or selected text.
Decrease Indent		Decreases the indentation of the selected paragraph.
Increase Indent		Increases the indentation of the selected paragraph.

Column Formatting

You can format the text in newsletter-style columns flowing from one column to the next on the same page. To do this, follow the steps given below:

1. Switch to the **Print Layout** view.
2. Select the text you want to format in columns. You can select the entire document or a part of the document.
3. Choose **Columns** from the **Format** menu to display the Columns dialog box (Figure 5.2).
4. Select the desired option under **Presets** section or specify a value in the **Number of columns** box indicating the number of columns you want to split the text.
5. Select the **Line between** checkbox if you want the columns to be separated by lines.
6. By default, all the columns are of equal width and have equal spacing in between. If you want the columns with different widths and spacing, clear the **Equal column width** checkbox and specify the desired values.

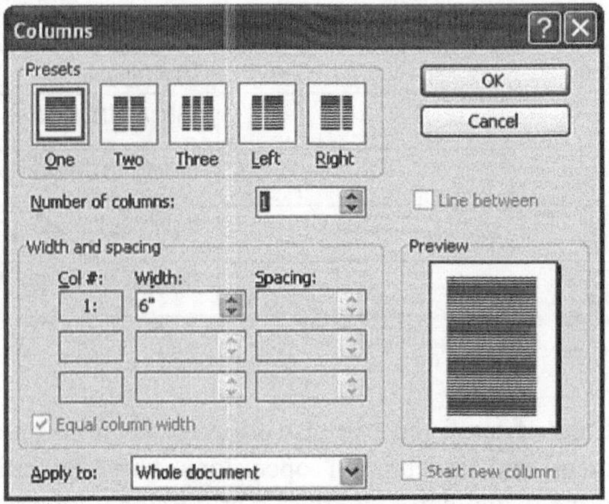

Figure 5.2 Columns Dialog Box

7. Select the **Whole document** option from the **Apply to** drop-down list box if you want to apply the changes to the entire document. In case you want to apply changes from the current cursor position onwards, select **This point forward** option.
8. Click the **OK** button to apply the changes and close the Columns dialog box.

8. What do you mean by a spreadsheet? What are its features?

Ans: 'Spreadsheet' is computer-based program that provides a better alternation of increasing accuracy and (saving time) to manual way of carrying out mathematical calculations and keeping records. The records may be of different types such as related to accounting information, daily expenses and salary sheet. Before the advent of spreadsheet, such records and calculations were implemented in notebooks and registers and it was very much time-consuming. However, with the advancement of computer into our daily lives, spreadsheets became the popular form of maintaining records by replacing the manual method.

A spreadsheet is used to organize information in a rectangular grid that consists of columns (designated by letters) and rows (designated by numbers). This enables users to organize and examine data in much efficient way. Apart from this, spreadsheet has got many other features. Some of these features are as follows:

- **Ease of use:** The spreadsheet programs are easy to learn and use. To learn spreadsheet, formal training is not required.
- **Time-saving:** There are many inbuilt functions and formulae in spreadsheet, which save our time in performing calculations.
- **Error-free:** Most of the calculations are performed by the computer, so there is less possibility of error unless we enter wrong data.
- **Help option:** The spreadsheet programs come with the built-in help option that can be queried to find any functions or any other feature.
- **Sorting:** Spreadsheet provides the option of sorting data that enable users to sort data in both ascending and descending orders.
- **Table and graphics:** The spreadsheet programs support the use of tables and graphics, which helps in better understanding of the text.
- **Password protected:** The work done in spreadsheet programs can be made password protected. This feature increases the security of the data.

- **What-if analysis:** This feature of spreadsheet allows automatic recalculation of operation when some data are modified.
- **Easy formatting:** This feature allows formatting the text by changing the font, font style, etc. and increasing the visual clarity of the text.

9. What is MS Excel? Explain the components of Excel window. What are various uses of MS Excel?

Ans: 'Microsoft Excel' (MS Excel) is a spreadsheet application that allows a user to perform various calculations, estimations and formulations with data. It also provides various facilities such as inserting charts, creating graphs and analysing situations and helps in decision making. It is one of the best management tools. Excel provides flexibility to the user to manipulate the data without worrying about the size of the data for general applications. Excel 2003 permits a wide selection of options to be used in the creation of worksheets and allows user to create an impressive spreadsheet presentation.

MS Excel Window

Whenever MS Excel is opened, the main screen of the application appears. This main window contains many parts, which are described as follows (Figure 5.3):

- **Title bar:** It is located at the top of the application window, which displays the name of the application and the active workbook.
- **Menu bar:** The Menu Bar is present below the Title Bar, which contains different menus that have all the options, functions and commands for the entire MS Excel application. By default, Microsoft Office Excel 2003 contains nine menus, each of which has an associated pull-down menu. For example, the **File** menu contains commands to open, create and print a workbook.
- **Toolbar:** It is positioned just below the Menu Bar. Toolbar contains buttons and menus or the combination of both, which allows you to perform many tasks in a single-click. By default, Standard and Formatting toolbars are displayed in the Excel environment. Additional toolbars such as Formula Auditing and Chart toolbars can be added by right-clicking on the Menu Bar and selecting the desired toolbar(s) from the Pop-up menu that appear.
- **Name box and formula bar:** Generally, the Name Box and Formula Bar are located below the Toolbars. The Name Box displays the name of the active cell or selected range and can be used to name a range of cells. The drop-down menu next to the **Name Box** is used to locate previously named regions. The **Formula Bar** displays the contents of the selected cell in the worksheet. It includes text, numbers, formulae and functions. One can also edit the contents of a cell from the formula bar.
- **Worksheet tabs and scrolling buttons:** Worksheet tabs appear at the bottom of the Excel window. Each tab represents a single sheet. Worksheet tabs allow moving from one worksheet to another within the same workbook. The scrolling buttons that appear to the left of the worksheet tab allow a user to scroll more quickly and easily through the sheets. A user can rename a sheet by right-clicking on the worksheet and selecting Rename from the Pop-up menu that appears.
- **Status bar:** The Status bar is located at the bottom of the Excel window and displays information about a selected command or an operation in progress. When a command is selected, the left side of the status bar briefly describes the command. It also indicates operations in progress, such as opening or saving a file, copying cells or recording a macro. The right side of the status bar shows whether keys such as CAPS LOCK, SCROLL LOCK or NUM LOCK are turned on.

- **Worksheet and workbook:** Worksheet is the area on a spreadsheet in which all the work is done. A 'worksheet' is made up of horizontal rows and vertical columns. An Excel worksheet contains 65,536 rows and 256 columns and each intersection of a column and a row forms a cell. Individual worksheets are linked to form a 'workbook'. Fundamentally, a workbook can be related to a very sophisticated ledger. It allows the user to work and store various kinds of related data within a single Excel file. By default, each workbook contains three worksheets (Sheet1, Sheet2 and Sheet3) that can be accessed by sheet tabs. If user needs more than three worksheets, choose **Worksheet** from the **Insert** menu and to delete any worksheet, choose **Delete Sheet** from the **Edit** menu.
- **Columns and rows:** In MS Excel, 'column' is defined as the vertical space from top to the bottom of the window. There are 256 columns in a single worksheet, which are labelled in alphabetical order (A, B, C…Z, AA, AB, AC…IV). The maximum number of characters that can be inserted in a column is 255. A 'row' is defined as the horizontal space across the window. The rows are labelled in a numbered order (1, 2, 3, …, 65536). The maximum limit of the height of a row is 409 points (547 pixels).
- **Cells:** The basic unit in spreadsheet is a 'cell'. A cell is formed by the intersection of a row and a column. This intersection gives the cell a unique address known as 'cell address' through which a cell can be referenced through its 'column name' or 'column letter' followed by its 'row number'. For example, the intersection of row 8 and column E gives cell E8. The cell that denotes the current position of the insertion point is known as 'active cell' and has a dark border around it. Data written in a cell includes text, decimal numbers, date and time, currency, percentage and scientific notation.

Uses of MS Excel

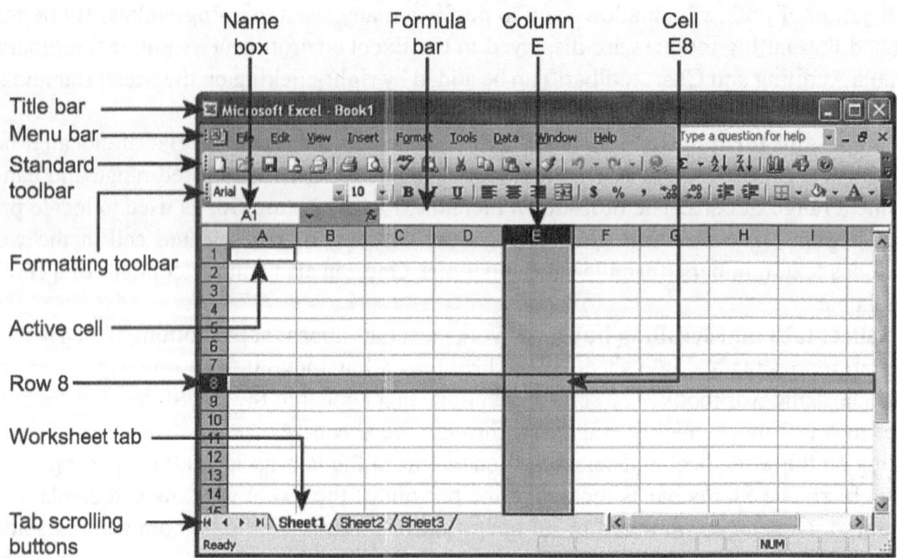

Figure 5.3 MS Excel Window

MS Excel is used for a variety of office tasks. Some of the popular uses of Excel are as follows:

- It allows users to create professional spreadsheets and charts.
- It performs numerous functions and formulas to assist in projects.
- It is useful in performing various mathematical calculations.
- It is used for transforming information into organized tables. This information is then analysed and operated according to our needs.

10. Define cell range. How would you name a range of cells?

Ans: A 'cell range' (also called 'block of cells') is a group of adjacent cells forming a rectangular area. A colon ':' called 'range indicator' is used for indicating range in Excel. For example, range from 'D4' to 'L28' is written as 'D4:L8' in the Excel program. Here, alphabets D and L represent columns, whereas numbers 4 and 8 represent rows.

A range of cells is formed by selecting a group of adjacent cells in a worksheet. Naming a cell or range of cells adds clarity and speeds up productivity especially when dealing with a very large spreadsheet. To name a range of cells in MS Office Excel 2003, follow the steps given below:

1. Select the cell or range of cells.
2. Click inside the **Name Box** to highlight the existing name of the cell.
3. Type in the name for the selected cell or range of cells and press the **Enter** key (Figure 5.4).

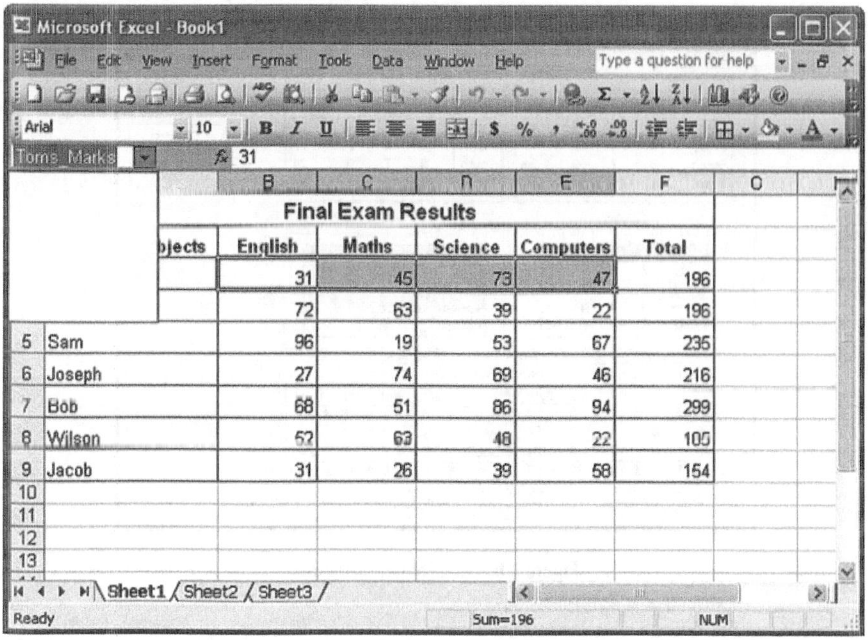

Figure 5.4 Naming a Range

11. Explain the types of data that can be entered into a cell of spreadsheet.

Ans: In MS Excel, there are three types of data that can be entered in a cell. These types are discussed as follows:

(i) **Text:** This type of data includes textual data and cannot be used to perform calculations. For example, 'Monday', 'hello' etc. Note that the textual data always appears on the left side of the cell.

(ii) **Values:** This type of data is used for calculations and includes *numbers* and *data and time.* Numbers include the numerical characters 0–9 and special characters such as +, –, (,), /, E, e, $ and %. The numerical values always appear on the right side of the cell. Date and time can be displayed in various built-in formats. For example, 3/14/06, 21-May-2006 etc. Note that when dates are entered in a dot format (such as 1.1.2006), Excel considers it (dates) as text rather than numbers. As a result, it is difficult to perform any calculation on the date.

(iii) **Formulas:** This type of data is used to perform calculations on the values stored in a cell or a range of cells. A 'formula' consists of an equal to sign (=), values, cell references and operators (addition, subtraction, multiplication etc.).

12. Describe the AutoFormat feature of MS Excel. Write the steps to use AutoFormat.

Ans: MS Excel provides a feature known as 'AutoFormat' that enables you to apply pre-defined layouts to selected tables in the worksheet. These layouts do not alter the position of your data but apply colour backgrounds and rearrange borders with some attractive effects. To AutoFormat tables in MS Office Excel 2003, select a range of the cells and follow the steps given below:

1. Select **AutoFormat** from the **Format** menu to display the AutoFormat dialog box (Figure 5.5).

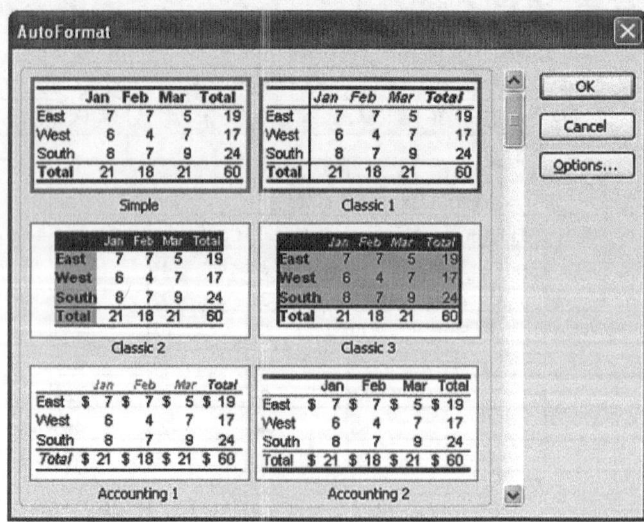

Figure 5.5 AutoFormat Dialog Box

2. From this dialog box, choose the appropriate option and click the **OK** button to format the table accordingly.

Note that if you want to revert to the original appearance of the cells, select Undo **AutoFormat** from the **Edit** menu.

13. Explain some library functions of MS Excel.

Ans: MS Excel contains many pre-defined or built-in formulas, which are known as 'functions'. These can be used to perform simple or complex calculations. They perform calculations by using specific values, called 'arguments' in a specific order. In Excel, functions have three parts, which are as follows:

1. '=' sign, which tells Excel that a formula or function follows.
2. Function name, such as SUM for addition or AVERAGE for determining the average of a series of numbers.
3. Arguments on which the particular function operate. The argument contains cell references to let the function know which data to calculate. In Excel, a function can accept a maximum of 30 arguments. The argument must also be enclosed by parentheses.

Some of the categories of library functions available in MS Excel are discussed as follows:

Math and Trig Functions

A user can perform simple calculations, such as rounding off a number or calculating the total value for a range of cells, with the help of mathematical and trigonometric functions. Various mathematical functions are listed in Table 5.4.

Table 5.4 Mathematical Functions

Formula	Description	Example
SUM(number1, number2,...)	Adds all the numbers in a range of cells.	SUM(10,20,30) Output: 60
ROUND(number, num_digits)	Rounds off a number to specified places of digits.	ROUND(3.628, 2) Output: 3.63
SQRT(number)	Returns a positive square root of a given number. If number is negative, SQRT returns the #NUM! error value.	SQRT(25) Output: 5
ABS(number)	Returns the absolute value of a number.	ABS(−100) Output: 100
TRUNC(number, num_digits)	Truncates a number to an integer by removing the fractional part of the number.	TRUNC(8.99,1) Output: 8.9
COUNT(value 1, value 2, ...)	Counts the number of cells that contain numbers and also numbers within the list of arguments.	COUNT (A4-A6) Output: 2

Logical Functions

Excel has a number of functions that allow the user to evaluate values and make decisions based on the result of the evaluation. These functions are known as 'logical functions'. The logical function returns either true or false value depending on the condition. Various logical functions are listed in Table 5.5.

Table 5.5 Logical Functions

Formula	Description	Example
AND(logical1, logical2, ...)	Returns value TRUE, if all its arguments are true and returns FALSE, if one or more arguments are false.	AND(1+2=3, 2−2=0, AND(1+2=3, 2−2=1)) Output: False
NOT(logical)	Reverses the value of its argument.	NOT(1+1=2) Output: False NOT(1+1=1) Output: True
OR(logical1, logical2,...)	Returns TRUE, if any argument is TRUE and returns FALSE only when all arguments are FALSE.	OR(1+2=3, 2−2=1) Output: True OR(1+2=2, 2−2=1) Output: False

Statistical Functions

In addition to mathematical functions, Excel provides a great deal of assistance to compute statistical data. All the functions are simple and take only a set of observations as arguments. Various statistical functions are listed in Table 5.6.

Table 5.6 Statistical Functions

Formula	Description	Example
MAX (number1, number2,...)	Returns the largest value in a given set of values.	MAX(60, 25, 5) Output: 60
MIN (number1, number2,...)	Returns the smallest value in a given set of values.	MIN(60, 25, 5) Output: 5
AVERAGE (number1, number2,...)	Calculates the arithmetic mean of all values in the list.	AVERAGE(60, 25, 5) Output: 30

Text Functions

In Excel, text functions are used not only to convert a value to text but also to join several text strings into one text string. Many functions are available that enable you to manipulate text strings, convert numeric entries into text strings and convert numeric text entries into numbers. Various text functions are listed in Table 5.7.

Table 5.7 Text Functions

Formula	Description	Example
CONCATENATE (text1, text2,...)	Joins several text strings into one text string.	CONCATENATE('Grand', ' ', 'Total') Output: Grand Total
LEN(text)	Returns the number of characters in a text string.	LEN('INDIA') Output: 5

(Continued)

Table 5.7 (Continued)

Formula	Description	Example
LOWER(text)	Converts all upper case letters in a text string to lower case.	LOWER('INDIA') Output: india
PROPER(text)	Capitalizes the first letter in each word of a text.	PROPER('INDIA') Output: India
UPPER(text)	Converts a text string to upper case.	UPPER('india') Output: INDIA
TRIM(text)	Removes all spaces from a text string except for single spaces between words.	TRIM(' INDIA ') Output: INDIA

Date and Time Functions

The date and time functions are used for working with date and time. Excel uses serial numbers to store date, giving each day of each year a unique number. Two of the date and time functions are listed in Table 5.8.

Table 5.8 Date and Time Functions

Formula	Description	Example
DATE(year, month, day)	Returns the number that represents the date in Excel date-time code.	DATE(1979,9,6) Output: 9/06/79
TIME(hour, minute, second)	Returns the number that represents a particular time.	TIME(19,23,7) Output: 7:23 PM
NOW()	Returns the current date and time.	NOW() Output: 4/30/10 8:39

14. Tabulate various types of errors along with their descriptions that are seen in Excel.

Ans: An error may occur in Excel while working with formulas when the intended task is not carried out in a proper way. For example, if you intend to add cells (A1:A4) and one of the cells say, A3 contains text, then the correct output will not be shown in the selected cell and an error state is said to have occurred. The errors may also occur due to some other reasons. Some of the common errors are listed in Table 5.9.

Table 5.9 Error Values

Type of Error	Description
######	This is not exactly a kind of error; it just specifies that the result is too long to fit in the selected cell. This error can be corrected by making the column wider.
#DIV/0!	This type of error occurs when a number is divided by zero. The error can be corrected by making sure that the divisor is not zero.
#NAME?	This type of error occurs when there is a name in the formula that Excel cannot recognize. This error can be avoided by selecting a name from the 'Name Box' instead of typing it. If you type a function, check the spelling and verify that the function exists or if users perform operations on text, enclose it in double quotation marks.
#REF!	This type of error occurs when cell reference is invalid. For example, when user deletes cells referred to in a formula or cells are pasted and moved elsewhere. This error can be corrected by entering the formula again.
#VALUE!	This type of error occurs when wrong operands or arguments are used within a formula. This error can be corrected by checking the passed arguments again and if wrong then passing them again.

15. What is presentation software? Describe its features.

Ans: 'Presentation software' is a computer software package that is used to display information in an attractive and illustrative manner. The information is displayed in the form of slide shows. Generally, the presentation software consists of three elements. First, they have editors for inserting and formatting text. Second, they support graphics, that is, one can insert and edit graphics. Finally, they have the slide-show system that is used to display the content. One of the commonly used presentation software is Microsoft PowerPoint.

Presentation software has various features that make it a powerful tool to design presentation. Some of these features are as follows:

- **Easy to learn:** It is easy to learn and use. No formal training is required to work with such software.
- **Different views:** It offers different views that enable the users to effectively use various features of the software.
- **Different types of output:** It has provision for different outputs. The outputs can be colour or black-and-white overheads, colour or black-and-white handouts, speaker's notes, on-screen electronic presentations etc.
- **Custom shows:** It allows you to create mini-presentations within a single file that are meant for a diverse audience.
- **Easy formatting:** It helps you to format style, font, paragraph etc. to enhance the visual appearance and increase the readability of the text.
- **Table and graphics:** It supports the use of tables, charts and graphics, which tend to increase the visual clarity of the text.

16. What is the purpose of Microsoft PowerPoint software?

Ans: 'Microsoft PowerPoint' (MS PowerPoint) is a powerful, yet easy-to-use presentation package, which is a part of Microsoft Office Suite of products. Its primary purpose is to help you design professional-style presentations quickly and easily. PowerPoint offers the tools to create a basic presentation and to enhance and customize it to meet its goal. For example, the tri-pane feature of PowerPoint 2003 allows you to view the slides, outline and notes simultaneously, so that you can easily organize the information to present in the slides.

Multiple-choice Questions

1. Office package is also known as ________.

   (a) Office product (b) Office collection
   (c) Office suite (d) All of the above

2. MS Office 2003 was released on ________.

   (a) 21 October 2003 (b) 22 October 2003
   (c) 20 October 2003 (d) 23 October 2003

3. Which of the following is not a feature of word processor?

   (a) Easy to learn (b) Compilation
   (c) Spelling and grammar check (d) Linking and embedding

4. ________ provides a quick way of copying formatting from one piece of text to another.

   (a) Copy command (b) Paste command
   (c) Format painter (d) All of these

5. Workbook is a collection of ________.
   (a) Page setup
   (b) Characters
   (c) Worksheets
   (d) Cells
6. A ________ is made up of horizontal rows and vertical columns.
   (a) Cell
   (b) Worksheet
   (c) Excel file
   (d) Workbook
7. How are cells in a spreadsheet addressed?
   (a) Column letter and row number
   (b) Row name and column name
   (c) Column number and row number
   (d) None of the above
8. ________ enables one to apply pre-defined layouts to selected tables in the worksheet.
   (a) AutoFormat
   (b) AutoPrint
   (c) Undo and redo
   (d) None of the above
9. MS Excel contains many pre-defined or built-in formulas, which are known as ________.
   (a) Arguments
   (b) Cells
   (c) Functions
   (d) AutoSum
10. ________ helps to design professional-style presentations quickly and easily.
   (a) MS PowerPoint
   (b) MS Excel
   (c) MS Word
   (d) All of the above

Answers

1. (c) 2. (a) 3. (b) 4. (c) 5. (c) 6. (b) 7. (a) 8. (a) 9. (c) 10. (a)

6

Networking and Internet

1. What is a computer network? Give its advantages.

Ans: A 'computer network' refers to a collection of two or more computers (nodes) that are connected together to share information and resources. Nodes are connected if they are capable of exchanging information with each other. Today, computer networks are being used in every facet of life, as it provides the following advantages:

- **Sharing information:** This is one of the most important advantages of a computer network. In the absence of a network, transferring information from one computer to another requires use of a compact disk, floppy disk, printer, etc. However, if the communicating systems are geographically apart, sharing information becomes even harder. Computer networks solve this problem, as computers connected to a network can share information whether they are in the same building or when they are located geographically apart. For example, when we connect to the Internet, we can open any website on our computer and can access information that is not stored in our own computers.
- **Sharing hardware resources:** A network facilitates sharing of hardware resources in an effective and user-friendly manner. When computers are connected to a network, they can share peripherals such as printer and hard disk drives with any other computer. For example, in an office having five to ten computers and one printer, in the absence of network, only the computer that is connected to the printer can be used to print data. If others have to access the printer, then they would first need to transfer their data to the computer connected to the printer. Contrastive to this, in a networked environment, the printer can be shared on the network and every computer on the network can easily access the printer without having the need to transfer data.
- **Sharing software resources:** Software resources are the programs or applications that are used by computers to perform any useful function or to carry out daily basis task. In an environment where networking is not available, users will have to install and configure any applications that they need individually. However, if the computers are connected via a network, the required software or application can be installed and configured centrally on a server and shared by all. This saves the valuable time and disk space.
- **Preserve information:** In addition to sharing information, a networked environment helps to preserve information as well. It is difficult to maintain regular backups of data on a number of stand-

alone computers and without backup, important data can be lost in case of some accident or failure of computer. However, in a networked environment, a copy of the important data can be kept on the server as well as on other connected computers on the network. In this case, failure of one computer will not result in loss of information, as the data can still be accessed from other computers whenever required.

- **Communication:** Computer networks have revolutionized the way people communicate. Rather than exchanging memos and directives on paper, which involves a lot of printing costs and delays, network users can instantly send messages to others and even check whether their messages have been received.

2. What do you understand by the term network topology? Discuss different network topologies.

Ans: The term 'topology' refers to the way a network is laid out, either physically or logically. A topology can be considered as the network's shape. It is the geometric representation of the relationship of all the links. There are five basic topologies: *bus*, *ring*, *star*, *tree* and *mesh*.

Bus Topology

Bus topology uses a common bus or backbone (a single cable) to connect all devices with terminators at both ends. The backbone acts as a shared communication medium and each node (file server, workstations and peripherals) is attached to it with an interface connector. Whenever a message is to be transmitted on the network, it is passed back and forth along the cable, past the stations (computers) and between the two terminators, from one end of the network to the other. As the message passes each station, the station checks the message's destination address. If the address in the message matches the station's address, the station receives the message. If the addresses do not match, the bus carries the message to the next station and so on. Figure 6.1 illustrates how devices such as file servers, workstations and printers are connected to the linear cable or the backbone.

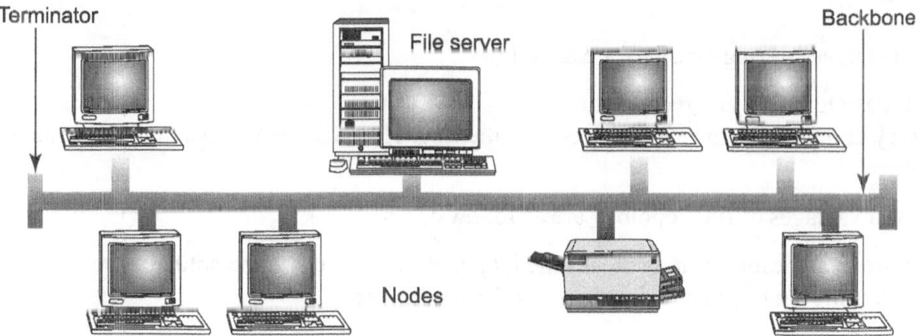

Figure 6.1 Bus Topology

The advantages of bus topology are as follows:

- It is easy to install and reconfigure. Connecting a computer or peripheral to a linear bus is easy.
- It requires least amount of cabling; thus, it is less expensive than other cabling arrangements.

The disadvantages of bus topology are as follows:

- A failure in backbone (cable) may cause the entire network to shut down.
- Heavy traffic can slow down a bus because computers on such networks do not co-ordinate with each other to reserve time to transmit.

Ring Topology

In this topology, computers are placed on a circle of cable without any terminated ends since there are no unconnected ends (Figure 6.2). Every node has exactly two neighbours for communication purposes. All messages travel through a ring in the same direction (clockwise or counter-clockwise) until it reaches its destination. Each node in the ring incorporates a repeater. When a node receives a signal intended for another device, its repeater regenerates the bits and passes them along the wire.

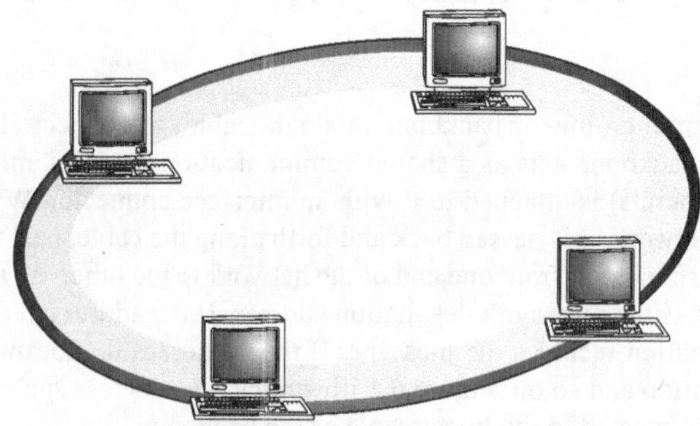

Figure 6.2 Ring Topology

The advantages of ring topology are as follows:

- It is easy to install and reconfigure.
- Every computer is given equal access to the ring. Hence, no single computer can monopolize the network.

The disadvantages of ring topology are as follows:

- Failure in any cable or node breaks the loop and can take down the entire network.
- Maximum ring length and number of nodes are limited.

Star Topology

In this topology, the devices are not directly linked to each other but they are connected via a centralized network component known as 'hub' or 'concentrator' (Figure 6.3). The hub acts as a central controller and if a node wants to send data to another node, it boosts up the message and sends the message to the intended node. This topology commonly uses twisted pair cable; however, coaxial cable or fiber-optic cable can also be used.

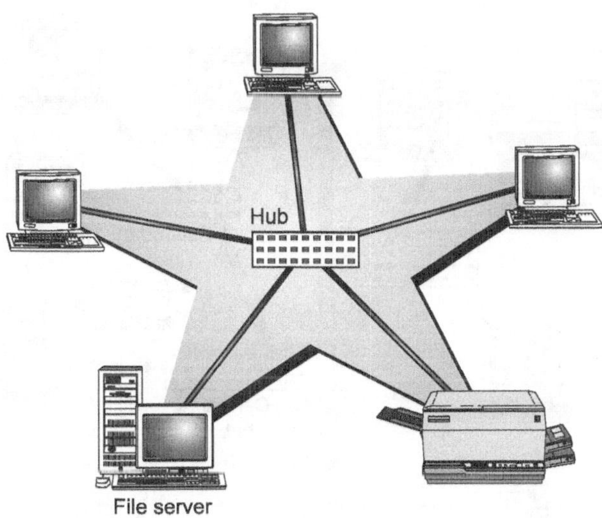

Figure 6.3 Star Topology

The advantages of star topology are as follows:

- It is easy to install and wire.
- The network is not disrupted even if a node fails or is removed from the network.
- Fault detection and removal of faulty parts are easier in star topology.

The disadvantages of star topology are as follows:

- It requires a longer length of cable.
- If the hub fails, nodes attached to it are disabled.
- The cost of the hub makes the network expensive as compared to bus and ring topologies.

Tree Topology

The tree topology combines characteristics of linear bus and star topologies. It consists of groups of star-configured workstations connected to a bus backbone cable (Figure 6.4). Not every node plugs directly to the central hub. The majority of nodes connect to a secondary hub that, in turn, is connected to the central hub. Each secondary hub in this topology functions as the originating point of a branch to which other nodes connect. A tree topology is best suited when the network is widely spread and partitioned into many branches.

The advantages of tree topology are as follows:

- The distance to which a signal can travel increases as the signal passes through a chain of hubs.
- It allows isolating and prioritizing communications from different nodes.
- It allows for easy expansion of an existing network, which enables organizations to configure a network to meet their needs.

The disadvantages of tree topology are as follows:

- If the backbone line breaks, the entire segment goes down.
- It is more difficult to configure and wire than other topologies.

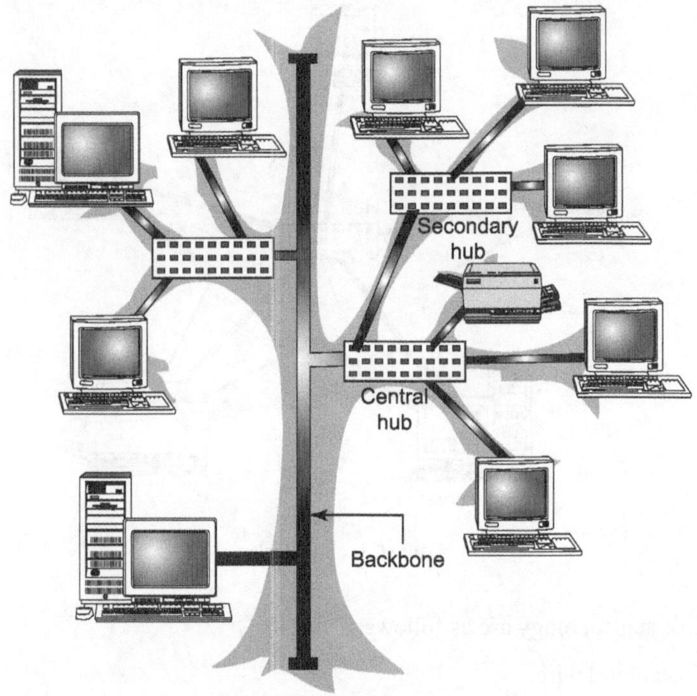

Figure 6.4 Tree Topology

Mesh Topology

In a mesh topology, every node has a dedicated point-to-point link to every other node (Figure 6.5). Messages sent on a mesh network can take any of several possible paths from source to destination. A fully connected mesh network has $n(n-1)/2$ physical links to link n devices. For example, if an organization has five nodes and wants to implement a mesh topology, then $5(5-1)/2$, that is, 10 links are required. In addition, to accommodate those links, every device on the network must have $n-1$ communication (input/output) ports.

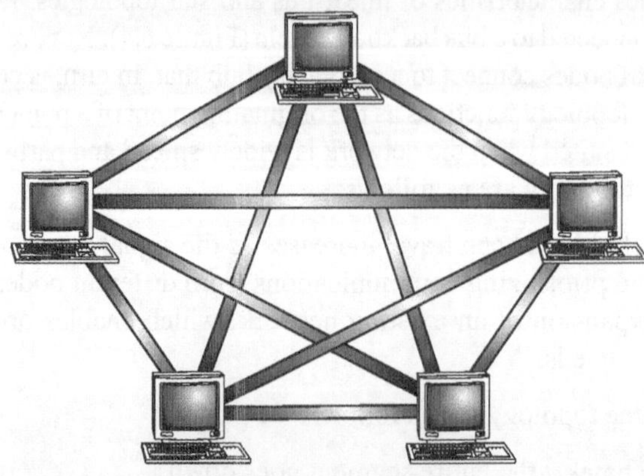

Figure 6.5 Mesh Topology

The advantages of mesh topology are as follows:

- If one link becomes unusable, the entire system does not get disabled.
- The use of large number of links eliminates network congestion.

The disadvantages of mesh topology are as follows:

- The amount of cabling required is very large.
- As every node is connected to the other, installation and reconfiguration are very difficult.
- The amount of hardware required in this type of topology makes it expensive to implement.

3. Write a short note on LAN, MAN and WAN.

Ans: A network can be as few as several personal computers on a small network or as large as the Internet, a worldwide network of computers. Today, when talking about networks, we are generally referring to three primary categories: Local Area Network (LAN), Metropolitan Area Network (MAN) and Wide Area Network (WAN).

Local Area Network (LAN)

A LAN is a computer network that covers only a small geographical area (usually within a square mile or less) such as an office, home or building (Figure 6.6). In a local area network, connected computers have a network operating system installed onto them. One computer is designated as the 'file server', which stores all the software that controls the network. It also stores the software that can be shared by the computers attached to the network. Other computers connected to the file server are called 'workstations'. The workstations can be less powerful than the file server and they may have additional software on their hard drives. On most LANs, cables are used to connect the computers. Generally, LAN offers a bandwidth of 10–100 Mbps.

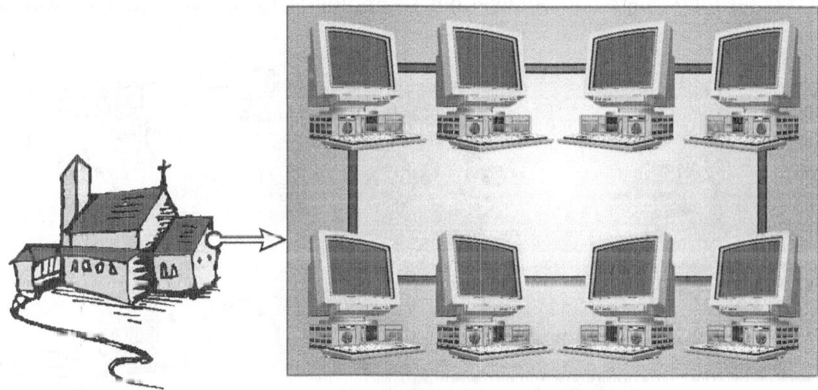

Figure 6.6 Local Area Network

Metropolitan Area Network (MAN)

A MAN is a network of computers spread over a 'metropolitan' area such as a city and its suburbs. As the name suggests, this sort of network is usually reserved for metropolitan areas where the city bridges its local area networks with a series of backbones, making one large network for the entire city (Figure 6.7).

It may be a single network such as a cable television network or it may be a means of connecting a number of LANs. Note that MAN may be operated by one organization (a corporate with several offices in one city) or be shared and used by several organizations in the same city.

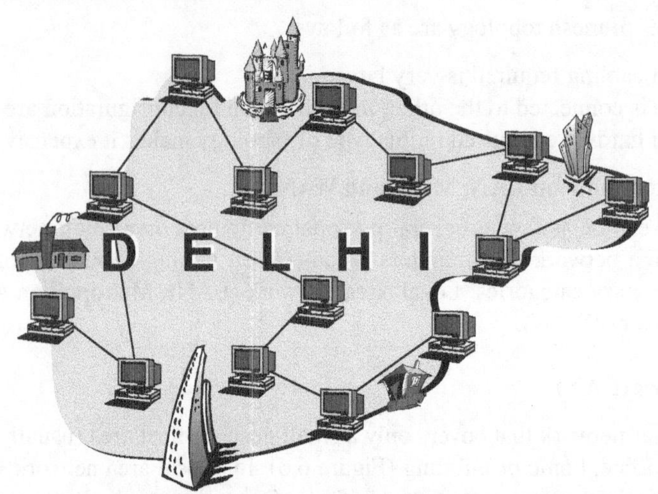

Figure 6.7 Metropolitan Area Network

Wide Area Network (WAN)

A WAN is a system of interconnecting many computers over a large geographical area such as cities, states, countries or even the whole world (Figure 6.8). These kinds of networks use telephone lines, satellite links and other long-range communications technologies to connect. Such networks are designed

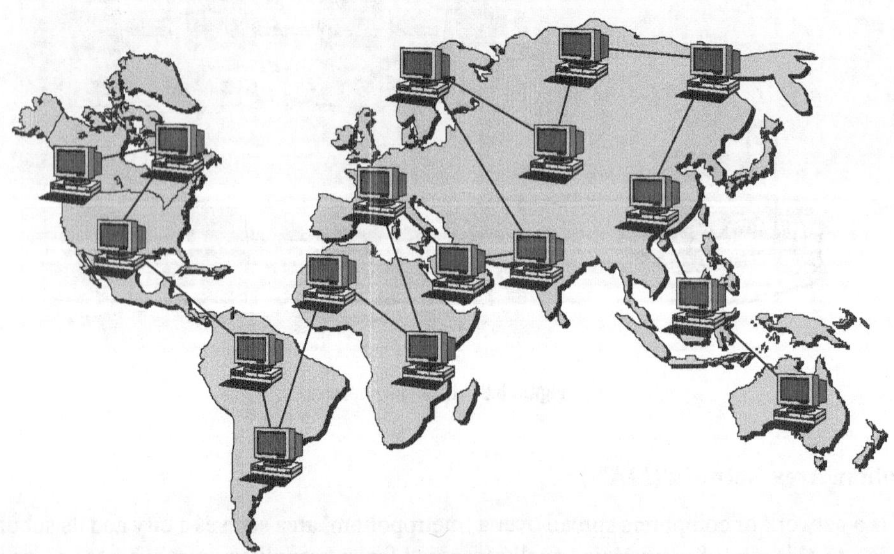

Figure 6.8 Wide Area Network

to serve an area of hundreds or thousands of miles such as public and private packet switching networks and national telephone networks. For example, a company with offices in New Delhi, Chennai and Mumbai may connect the LANs for each of those locations to each other through a WAN. Although a WAN may be owned or rented by private business, it is usually a public network designed to connect small- and intermediate-sized networks together. The largest WAN in existence is the Internet.

4. List any four advantages offered by WAN.

Ans: WAN offers many advantages to the business organizations. Some of these advantages are as follows:

- It offers flexibility of location because not all the people needing to use the same data have to work at the same site.
- Communication between branch offices can be improved using e-mail and file sharing.
- It facilitates a centralized company-wide data backup system.
- Companies located in a number of small, interrelated offices can store files centrally and access each other's information.

5. Explain various hardware devices used in computer network. Also give their functions.

Ans: Networks are becoming more complicated and more pervasive every day. Therefore, to reduce the complexity, various network devices have been developed. 'Network devices' (or 'hardware devices') are those devices that help nodes to get connected in a network for efficient communication. Network devices include *network interface card (NIC)*, *repeater*, *hub*, *bridge*, *switch*, *router* and *gateway*.

Network Interface Card (NIC)

It is a hardware device that connects clients, servers and peripherals to the network through a port. Most network interfaces come as small circuit board that can be inserted onto one of the computer motherboard's slots. Alternatively, modern computers sometimes include the network interface as part of their main circuit boards (motherboards). Each network interface is associated with a unique address called its 'media access control' (MAC) address. The MAC address helps in sending information to the intended destination. Network interface cards are the major factor in determining the speed and performance of a network. It is a good idea to use the fastest network card available for the type of workstation one is using.

Repeater

It is the most basic device on a network. Signals that carry information within a network can travel a fixed distance before attenuation endangers the integrity of the data. A repeater installed on the link receives signal, regenerates it and sends the refreshed copy back to the link. Doing this means that the new signal is clean, free from any background noise introduced while travelling down the wire. Repeaters are most commonly used to extend a network. All network cable standards have maximum cable length specification. If the distance between two network devices is longer than this specification, a repeater is needed to regenerate the signal. Without the repeater, the signal will be too weak for the computers on each end to reliably understand. A good example of the use of repeaters would be in a LAN using a star topology with unshielded twisted pair cabling. The length limit for unshielded twisted pair cable is 100 metres. The repeater amplifies all the signals that pass through it allowing for the total length of cable on the network to exceed the 100 metres limit. Nonetheless, repeaters have no in-built intelligence and they do not look at the contents of the packet while regenerating the signal. Thus, there is no processing overhead in sending a packet through a repeater. However, a repeater will repeat any errors in the original signal.

Hub

It is a small box that connects individual devices on a network, so that they can communicate with one another. The hub operates by gathering the signals from individual network devices, optionally amplifying the signals and then sending them onto all other connected devices. Amplification of the signal ensures that devices on the network receive reliable information. A hub can be thought of as the centre of a bicycle wheel, where the spokes (individual computers) meet.

Nowadays, the terms repeater and hub are used synonymously, but actually they are not same. Although at its very basic level, a hub can be thought of as a multi-port repeater. Typically, hubs have anywhere from 4 to over 400 ports. When a signal is received on one port of the hub, it is regenerated out to all the other ports. It is most commonly used to connect multiple machines to the same LAN. Administrators connect a computer to each port on the hub, leaving one port free to connect to another hub or to a higher-level device such as a bridge or a router.

Bridge

This device allows the division of a large network into two or more smaller and efficient networks. It monitors the information traffic on the both sides of the network, so that it can pass packets of information to the correct location. Most bridges can 'listen' to the network and automatically figure out the address of each computer on both sides of the bridge. A bridge examines each packet as it enters though one of the ports. It first looks at the MAC address of the sender and creates a mapping between the port and the sender's MAC address. It then looks at the address of the recipient, comparing the MAC address to the list of all learned MAC addresses. If the address is in the list, the bridge looks up the port number and forwards the packet to the port where it thinks the recipient is connected. If the recipient's MAC address is not in the list, the bridge then does a flood; it sends the signal to all the ports except the one from where it was received. As a result, a bridge reduces the amount of traffic on a LAN by dividing it into two segments. It inspects incoming traffic and decides whether to forward or discard it.

Bridges can be used to connect networks with different types of cabling or physical topologies. They must, however, be used between networks employing the same protocol. Since a bridge examines the packet to record the sender and lookups the recipient, there is overhead in sending a packet through a bridge. On a modern bridge, this overhead is miniscule and does not affect network performance.

Switch

It is a multi-port bridge. It connects individual devices on a network, so that they can communicate with one another. The behaviour of a switch is same as that of a bridge. It is capable of inspecting the data packets as they are received, determining the source and destination device of that packet and forwarding that packet appropriately. The difference is that most switches implement these functions in hardware using a dedicated processor. This makes them much faster than traditional software-based bridges.

Router

It is an essential network device for interconnecting two or more networks. The router's sole aim is to trace the best route for information to travel. As network traffic changes during the day, routers can redirect information to take less congested routes. A router creates and/or maintains a table, called a routing table, which stores the best routes to certain network destinations. While bridges know the addresses of all computers on each side of the network, routers know the addresses of computers, bridges and other routers on the network. Routers can even 'listen' to the entire network to determine which sections are the busiest. They can then redirect data around those sections until they clear up. Routers are generally expensive and difficult to configure and maintain. They are critical components of a network and if they fail, the network services will be significantly impaired. Most routers operate by examining incoming or outgoing signals for information at the network layer. In addition, they can permit or deny network communications with a particular network.

Gateway

It is an internetworking device, which joins networks operating on different protocols together. It is also known as 'protocol converter'. A gateway accepts the packet formatted for one protocol and converts the formatted packet into another protocol. For example, a gateway can receive e-mail message in one format and convert it into another format. A gateway can be implemented completely in software, hardware or as a combination of both. One can connect systems with different protocols, languages and architecture using a gateway.

6. Define Internet. Write a brief history of Internet.

Ans: The word 'Internet' is derived from two words: *Interconnection* and *Networks*. Also referred to as 'the Net', Internet is a worldwide system of computer networks, that is, a network of networks, which allows the participants (users) to share information. It consists of thousands of separately administered networks of various sizes and types. Each of these networks comprises tens of thousands of computers. Moreover, the total number of users of the Internet is known to be in millions. This high level of connectivity encourages an unparalleled degree of communication, resource sharing and information access.

The Internet traces its origin back to the 1960s, when it grew out of an experiment conducted by the US Department of Defense. They wanted to create a computer network that could continue to function in the event of a disaster, such as a nuclear war. Even if a part of the network was damaged or destroyed, the rest of the system would continue to work. That network was known as 'ARPANET' (Advanced Research Projects Agency Network), which linked US scientific and academic researchers. It is the forerunner of today's Internet.

By the 1970s, ARPA (Advanced Research Projects Agency) helped in the development of a new protocol known as TCP/IP (Transmission Control Protocol/Internet Protocol) for transferring data between the networks. The TCP/IP is the core of the Internet. Internet really took off in the 1980s when National Science Foundation (NSF) used ARPANET to link its five regional super computer centres at major universities, so that many users could share their work. Later on, NSF created 'NSFNET' (National Science Foundation Network) a series of networks for research and education and communication. Initially, NSFNET allowed only academic research. Over the time, this network expanded to include sites for business, universities, government etc. and finally becoming a network consisting of millions of computers, now known as the Internet.

In the 1980s, Usenet newsgroups and Electronic Mail (e-mail) came into picture. To keep track of the information on the Internet, indices such as Archie and the Wide Area Information Server (WAIS) were also created in this decade. To give users an easy-to-use interface to work with, the University of

Minnesota created Gopher, a simple menu-driven system for accessing files. Internet really became popular in the 1990s after the development of the World Wide Web (WWW). Before that, it was open for a handful of sites only. It is amazing that as recently as June 1993, there were only 130 websites, but now there are millions.

With the growth of Internet, the quality, quantity and variety of information also grew. The Internet today is a repository of every type of information. Nowadays, an Internet user can get all sorts of information ranging from how to add to the design of a functional spaceship to choosing a product for personal use.

7. Discuss the basic Internet terminologies used.

Ans: The basic Internet-related terminologies are discussed as follows:

World Wide Web (WWW)

The World Wide Web (abbreviated as Web or WWW) is a collection of linked documents or pages, stored on millions of computers and distributed across the world. The concept of the Web began at CERN (the European Center for Nuclear Research) Geneva, Switzerland in the year 1989. Since then, WWW is the most popularly used Internet sub-network. One of the main reasons that led to its popularity is that it provides information in multimedia form, that is, in more than one medium such as text, graphics, video and audio. Further, it provides a simple and consistent way of accessing the information available on the Internet by using *hypertext* system. In hypertext system, the documents are connected to other related documents on the Internet through links. The Web uses a specific Internet protocol called 'HTTP' to support hypertext documents.

Web Page

The hypertext documents on the World Wide Web are known as 'web pages'. A web page is written in a language called 'HTML' (Hypertext Markup Language), which enables to embed hypertext links (discussed later in this section) in the document. Using these hyperlinks, user can jump from one web page to another.

Website

A website is a set of related web pages (linked through hypertext links), published by an organization or an individual. Typically, a website contains a home page along with other additional web pages. Each website is accessed by its own address known as URL (Uniform Resource Locator). All the websites on the Internet constitute the World Wide Web.

Home page

When you browse the World Wide Web, you will often see the term 'Home Page'. A 'home page' ('index page') is the starting point or a doorway to the website; it refers to the web page that identifies a website and contains the hyperlinks to other web pages in the website. It may contain links to other websites also. Like the table of contents of a book, the home page usually provides an overview of what could be found at the website. If there is not much information, the home page may be the only page of the website. However, usually you will find at least a few other pages.

Browser

A browser (short for 'web browser') is special software that enables users to read/view web pages and jump from one web page to another. It is the software that is needed to find, retrieve, view and send information over the Internet. The most popular browsers are Microsoft Internet Explorer and Netscape Navigator.

Uniform Resource Locator (URL)

Each web page has a unique address, called a 'Uniform Resource Locator' (URL) that identifies its location on the Internet. Usually, the format of an URL consists of four parts: protocol, name of the web server (or domain name), path and filename. Here is an example, *http://www.xyz.com/tutor/start/main.htm*. The structure of this URL is:

- **Protocol:** http
- **Web Server Name/Domain Name:** www.xyz.com
- **Path:** tutor/start/
- **File Name:** main.htm

Hypertext

The hypertext is a system that provides a simple and consistent way to organize large data (that includes text, images, pictures, videos, etc) available on the Internet. In hypertext systems, the documents contain links to other related documents on the Internet. These links are called 'hyperlinks', 'hotlink' or simply 'links'. A hyperlink is used to jump to another part of the same page or to load a different web page. Usually, hypertext links appear in a different colour (typically in blue and underlined) from the rest of the text.

Internet Service Provider (ISP)

ISP is an organization that connects its subscribers' computer using modem to the Internet. The connections can be provided by telephone lines, cable lines or wireless connections. In order to use the Internet connection, the user has to first log on to the host computer using the username and password provided by the ISP. Some of the well-known ISPs are America Online (AOL), Microsoft Network (MSN), Yahoo! etc.

Web Server

A server is a computer equipped with server software, which provides a specific kind of services to client software running on other computers. It can refer to a particular piece of software, for example, a web server or to a machine on which the server software is running. A 'web server' receives request from the clients, processes this request and sends the result back to the client. In other words, web server fulfils the client's (browser) requests.

Download and Upload

'Download' refers to the act of transmitting data from a remote computer on the Internet or other network to one's own computer. When the user downloads a file, he/she is actually copying a particular file from the remote computer and placing it on their hard drive. Downloading allows a user to save a file for later use, thereby reduces the time spent online and the corresponding charges.

Upload is just the opposite of download. 'Upload' refers to the act of transmitting data from local computer to any other computer on the Internet or network. For example, a software company may upload a demonstration of its new software onto the web, so that users can then download the software.

Online and Offline

The term 'online' is commonly referred to the state of being connected to the networked computer system or Internet. For example, if you are browsing the WWW, your computer is said to be online. Being online also refers to any peripheral device (such as printer) that is connected to the system and ready to use.

'Offline' is just the opposite of online; it refers to the state of not being connected to the remote computer or Internet. A printer or other peripheral that is not ready to use is also considered offline.

8. List some advantages of Internet.

Ans: Internet offers various advantages. Some of them are as follows:

- **Information retrieval:** The Internet serves as the biggest and a valuable resource of information. One can find any type of information on any subject with the help of the search engines such as Yahoo and Google.
- **Communication:** The primary goal of the Internet is communication. It has done extremely well in this field; however, the development process is still going on to make it more dependable and quick. By sending an e-mail, we can contact a person who is physically present thousand miles away within the fraction of a second's time.
- **Entertainment:** Internet functions as a popular medium of entertainment. A wide variety of entertainment including video games, music, movies, chat room, news and others can be accessed through the Internet.
- **E-commerce:** It is the idea that is implemented for any form of commercial strategy or business transactions that entails the transmission of data from one corner of the world to another. E-commerce has become a fantastic option through which one can shop anything.
- **Formation of communities**: Internet helps in the formation of communities or forums. Here, a number of people can participate in different types of debates and discussions, express their views and gather valuable knowledge.
- **Services**: A variety of services are offered via Internet, for example, job searching, online banking, buying movie tickets, hotel reservations, consultation services etc.

9. Explain the structure of URL.

Ans: Usually, the format of a URL consists of four parts: protocol, server (or domain), path and filename. For example, *http://www.xyz.com/tutor/start/main.htm*. The structure of this URL is described as follows:

- **Protocol:** http
- **World Wide Web:** www
- **Domain Name:** xyz
- **Domain Type:** com
- **Path:** tutor/start/
- **File Name:** main.htm

The first part of the address, the part before the colon, is the 'protocol'. Most of the time when you see *http* (hypertext transfer protocol), you are accessing a web page. Apart from http, you could also find other protocols such as *ftp* (file transfer protocol), *news* (news server), *mailto* (mail server, used for accessing an e-mail server) and *telnet* (for accessing remote computers). The protocol is separated by colons and slashes. After the slashes, the 'World Wide Web' is indicated by *www*. Note that it is not necessary that all the addresses should contain *www*. Although most Internet addresses include a *www*, a web page can reside on the part of the Internet that is not found on the World Wide Web. Next is the 'domain name' where the information is located. A domain name is unique and case sensitive human-readable name for a host on the Internet. After the domain name, the domain type is displayed such as *com*. A 'domain type' represents the type of organization or country to which the host belongs. A dozens of domain types have been assigned to identify and locate files stored on host computers in countries around the world.

These are referred to as two-letter Internet country codes and have been standardized by the International Standards Organization (ISO). For example, *uk* for the United Kingdom, *de* for Germany, *au* for Australia and *in* for India. The last part of a URL consists of the path and the file name. 'Path name' specifies the hierarchic location of the said file on the computer. For instance, in *http://www.xyz.com/tutor/start/main.htm*, the 'file' *main.htm* is located in start, which is a sub-directory of tutor.

10. Explain how Internet connection can be established?

Ans: The Internet is a bunch of computers linked together through a network, so that computer users in different locations can have access to the same information. The basic requirements for getting connected to Internet are described as follows:

A TCP/IP-enabled computer

The computer must have at least 386-microprocessor chip with a minimum of 16 MB of RAM. For a good browsing experience, use a faster chip (Pentium III/Pentium IV) with more RAM (128/256 MB). In addition, a colour monitor, with at least 640 × 480 resolution and a capability of displaying a minimum of 256 colours, is also vital. The system should also possess a hard disk, with at least 200 MB of free space, to store Internet software and temporary Internet files. Since the web is a multimedia medium, you can also enjoy sound on your system with a sound card and a pair of speakers.

Modem

Apart from the previously mentioned configuration, a computer system must have a device called modem, which enables a computer to transmit data over telephone lines. A 'modem' (acronym for modulator-demodulator) is a hardware, which converts digital data into analogue signals (i.e., modulation) that can be sent over an analogue telephone line and convert the analogue signal back into digital data (that is, demodulation). Thus, when the modem receives the data from a web server via phone system, it reconstitutes the analogue signal into digital form, so that the computer can understand it. The most critical aspect of the modem is its speed of operation. The speed of modem is measured in Kilobits per second (Kbps). Modern modem supports 28-Kbps to 56-Kbps speeds. Modems are of two types:

(i) **Internal Modem:** It is a card, which is fitted inside the computer with a lead running directly from the computer to the phone socket.

(ii) **External Modem:** It is a small external box wired between the computer and the phone socket.

Internet Connection

Before connecting to the Internet, you need to buy an Internet connection from an authorized Internet Service Provider (ISP). The speed of accessing the Internet entirely depends upon the type of connection you bought from the ISP. Some of connections available for the users these days are discussed in the next question.

11. Explain various types of Internet access or connections.

Ans: Some of the common types of Internet access, available for the users these days, are as follows:

- **Dial-up:** A dial-up connection is the access method that uses telephone lines to connect to the Internet. It is the most common way for individuals who use home computers to connect to the Internet. To connect to the Internet by using dial up, the user needs to specify a username, a password and a telephone number. After the connection is established, the user can start browsing sites on the Internet.
- **ISDN:** It stands for Integrated Services Digital Network and is more common in business and commercial uses. It was the first high-speed alternative to regular analog phone modems. ISDN involves the digitization of telephone network, so that voice, graphics, text and other data can be provided to users from a single terminal over existing telephone wiring. Digital connections have fewer errors in transmission, which means speed of downloading graphics, web pages, sound and so on is increased to four times faster than with dial-up modems.
- **Cable Modem:** A cable modem connects the user to the Internet through a cable television line. Nowadays, many cable companies offer Internet along with television accessibility. A cable modem will typically have two connections, one to the television outlet and the other to the computer. Cable modems provide not only a faster Internet access (10 to 100 times as fast as the dial-up modem), but also interactivity to the television.
- **Leased Line:** This facility provides reliable and high-speed Internet access ranging from 2.4 Kbps to 45 Mbps. A leased line connection is an affordable way to link two or more sites for a fixed monthly charge. Usually, leased lines facility can be provided via a fibre-optic or copper line. Leased line service provides a consistent amount of bandwidth and is an excellent way to provide data, voice and video links between sites.
- **DSL:** DSL or Digital Subscriber Line service is provided through an existing phone line, but it works differently than regular analog modem dial-up access. DSL operates over normal telephone lines and it can be used simultaneously with the telephone. DSL can increase the connection speed by as much as ten-fold from a standard dial-up modem.
- **Broadband:** This type of access is good for remote locations, where ISDN, cable or DSL are not available. It gives a decent download speed, but to upload data, the user still needs a regular analog modem to dial in, via a phone line. Satellite connection can be either a two-way service or a one-way service. In case of two-way satellite service, the data is transmitted via satellite to a dish antenna at the user's house. In one-way system, the user needs a conventional modem and telephone link to an ISP. Satellite connection is expensive but sometimes is the only fast option for people who are beyond the service area of cable and DSL providers.

12. Briefly explain any three Internet applications or services.

Ans: The Internet has grown from a small project to today's biggest network of computers. Due to this colossal growth, the Internet has become the biggest domain of information. Nowadays, an Internet user has access to a wide variety of services such as electronic mail, file transfer, vast information resources, interest group membership, interactive collaboration, multimedia displays, real-time broadcasting, shopping opportunities and much more. Some of the important services provided by the Internet are as follows:

Electronic Mail (e-mail)

E-mail, is a fast, easy and inexpensive way to communicate with other Internet users around the world. It is one of the basic and earliest services of the Internet and the most used application on the Internet too. E-mail overcomes most of the problems and delays of getting a physical document from one person to another. Rather, it has the dual advantage of not only being faster but cheaper to use as well.

Each user of e-mail has a mailbox address to which messages are sent and the mailbox can be accessed from anywhere and at anytime. It does not matter what type of connectivity the user is having, they will always be able to use this service. One can receive and send e-mails from all systems whether it is a Windows PC or a UNIX machine. Not only this, e-mail can also be used to send documents, images, audio, video and so on as an attachment along with the mail.

File Transfer Protocol (FTP)

FTP is a set of rules that enables a user to log on to another computer and transfer information between it and his/her computer. It was the first service developed for the Internet, so that government and educational institutions could easily exchange files. FTP allows the user to get access to the files stored in the directory of a remote computer that is connected to the Internet. Using FTP, one can upload and download files from the remote computer (known as 'FTP servers'), if they have access permission on the remote machine. Though files can be transferred using e-mail, this is not a good choice if the file size is large or when there are many files. FTP sites can consist of hundreds to thousands of files with information on books, music, software, games, images, sounds, multimedia, course ware etc. FTP can be done using the command prompt, browsers and various GUI-based FTP software programs such as CuteFTP and WS_FTP.

Internet Relay Chat (IRC)

IRC is a service on the Internet that allows people to communicate in real-time and carry on conversations via the computer with one or more people. It provides the user with the facility to engage in simultaneous (synchronous) online 'conversations' with other users from anywhere in the world. Unlike other forms of group communication on the Internet, chat is instant communication. However, both parties must be connected to the Internet and that too at the same time, running the right software and actively participating in order to chat.

Generally, the user runs a program (called 'client') to connect to an IRC server. The server relays information to and from other servers on the same net. Popular IRC client applications are mIRC, Virc and LeafChat. Once connected to an IRC server on an IRC network, the user will usually join one or more 'channels' (also known as 'chat rooms') and converse with others there. Each channel is devoted to a different topic. Conversations may be public (where everyone in a channel can see what the user types) or private (messages between only two people, who may or may not be on the same channel).

13. Define the following terms:

(a) IP address

(b) HTTP

Ans: (a) Each system (computer or router) that connects to the Internet is assigned a specific Internet address. This Internet address, referred to as 'IP address', uniquely identifies the connection of the system to the Internet. Here, uniquely means that no two systems can be assigned the same IP address at the same time. Moreover, IP addresses are universal that means each system wishing to connect to Internet must accept the addressing system.

(b) HTTP (stands for 'hypertext transfer protocol') is the most common protocol that is used to access information from the WWW. It manages the transfer of data between the client and the server. The older version of HTTP was 1.0, in which TCP connection was released only after serving a single request. This was not adequate as every time a new connection had to be established. This led to the development of HTTP version 1.1 which supports 'persistent connection', that is, it is meant for multiple request-response operations. HTTP is a stateless protocol and all the transactions between the server and client are carried out in form of messages. The client sends a 'request message' to the server and the server replies with a 'response message'.

14. What is e-mail? Give its architecture.

(or)

With the help of an example, illustrate how e-mails are sent and received?

Ans: E-mail is the process of exchanging messages electronically via a communications network using the computer. It allows users to communicate with each other in less time and at nominal cost as compared to traditional phone or mail services. Apart from the textual message, e-mails can also consist of other data formats such as pictures, sound and video. E-mails can be sent anywhere in the world using the computer and a modem. Its delivery is almost instant and is very economical to use. One may send many messages at a time or just one to a designated location.

The architecture of e-mail includes three components, namely, the *user agent (UA)*, *message transfer agent (MTA)* and *message access agent (MAA)*. 'UA' is a program that helps the user in reading, writing, replying and forwarding message. It also handles the user's mailboxes. 'MTA' is a client/server program where the MTA client can push messages to the MTA server. 'MAA' is a client/server program where the MAA client pulls (retrieves) messages from the MAA server.

To understand how e-mail system works, consider two users *A* and *B* on two different systems. Further assume that both *A* and *B* are connected to their respective mail servers by LAN or WAN. When *A* wishes to send a message to *B*, it executes UA program to prepare the message. Now, as the message is to be sent to *A*'s mail server through LAN/WAN, a pair of MTAs (MTA client and MTA server) is used. The UA after preparing the message sends it to MTA client, which then sets up a connection with MTA server on the mail server. At *A*'s mail server, the message waiting to be sent is kept in a queue maintained by the mail server. Then, the mail server calls its MTA client to send the message to MTA server at *B*'s mail server connected via Internet. At *B*'s mail server, the received message for *B* is kept in his/her mailbox. To retrieve the message from mailbox at mail server, *B* calls the MAA client, which then establishes a connection with MAA server at the mail server. This way *B* can receive the message sent by *A*. Figure 6.9 depicts the whole mechanism.

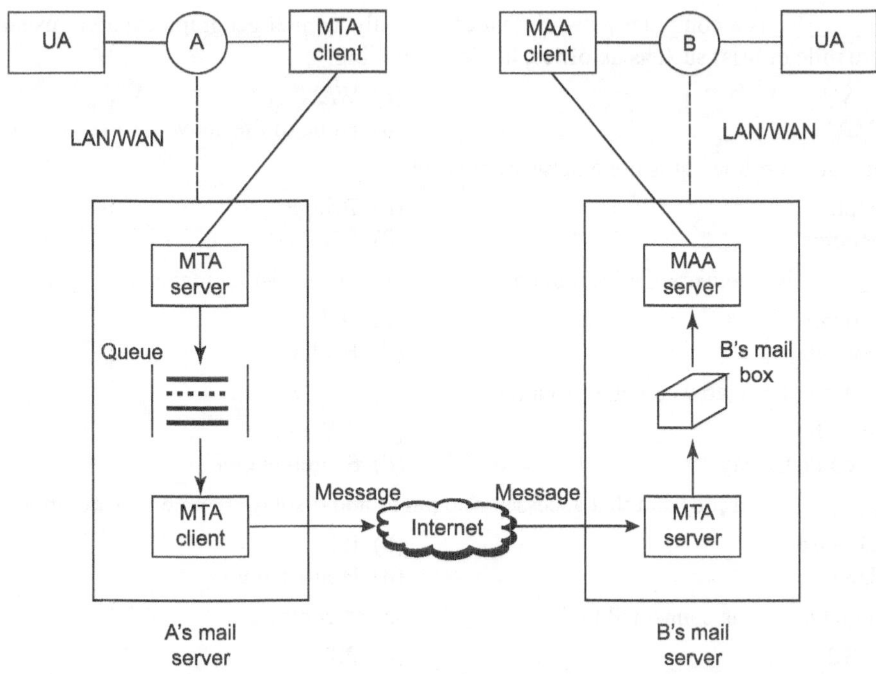

Figure 6.9 Mechanism of e-mail Transfer

15. Give some disadvantages of e-mail.

Ans: Though e-mail is quite popular and efficient, but it has got some disadvantages. These are as follows:

- Although e-mail is delivered instantly, the recipient may or may not read their mail on time. That defeats the quickness of electronic mailing.
- The slightest error in the address or a failure in one of the links between sender and receiver is enough to prevent a delivery.
- Most webmails either display advertisements during use or append them to mails sent. It results in increased size of the original mail, which brings a significant decrease in the speed of use.
- Since e-mail passes through network, it may be intercepted in between. Moreover, viruses can enter the system while downloading the e-mails.

Multiple-choice Questions

1. Which of the following is not a valid topology?

   (a) Bus　　(b) Ring
   (c) Grid　　(d) Tree

2. In a __________ network, all devices are connected to a device called hub and communicate through it.

   (a) Bus　　(b) Ring
   (c) Star　　(d) Mesh

3. A ________ is a computer network that covers only a small geographical area (usually within a square mile or less) such as an office, home or building.
   (a) LAN (b) WAN
   (c) MAN (d) None of the above
4. Which of the following is not a network device?
   (a) Hub (b) Bridge
   (c) Router (d) USB
5. ________ is a network device that connects two LANs or two segments of the same LAN.
   (a) Router (b) Hub
   (c) Switch (d) Bridge
6. Collection of related web pages is called ________.
   (a) Web book (b) Website
   (c) Web dictionary (d) Search engine
7. A ________ is a program that accesses web pages and displays them on the computer screen.
   (a) Browser (b) ISP
   (c) URL (d) Home page
8. A telephone line is connected to the ________ on the computer.
   (a) USB (b) PS2
   (c) Ethernet (d) Modem
9. Which of the following are the types of Internet access?
   (a) Dial-up (b) Broadband
   (c) DSL (d) All of the above
10. E-mail is the system for exchanging messages through ________.
    (a) Client (b) Network
    (c) Program (d) Backbone

Answers

1. (c) 2. (c) 3. (a) 4. (d) 5. (c) 6. (b) 7. (a) 8. (d) 9. (d) 10. (b)

PART II

Programming Concepts

1

Basics and Introduction to C

1. Why are computers used? Brief their benefits.

Ans: Computers play a vital role in the socioeconomic progress of a country. Every nation is paying great importance to computer literacy. Progress of individuals, surrounding region, nation and the world is ensured only with the introduction and use of computers. In every occupation, computers are being used increasingly. In every part of the world, computers are inducted to increase the overall productivity. Moreover, the quality of the products due to the application of computers is substantially improved. The impact of computers is very high on mass education, entertainment and productivity in all fields. The use of computers reduces drastically the cost of production, saves a lot of time and ensures the best quality.

In addition, the use of computer with some know-how (for the common users) and a lot of technical innovations (by the developers), numerical problems, business transactions and scientific applications can be computed in almost no time. A computer does various tasks based on the programs installed in it. Intellectual computer is certainly a powerful gadget, but human intellectual capability is much higher than that of a computer. Thus, computer does not have its own brain. Brainpower of computer is limited. Thus, human intellectual power is further reinforced by the use of computers frequently in the day-to-day life. By learning computer-programming languages, developing software packages and understanding and developing hardware of computers, one can make life and the nation economically prosperous.

2. Illustrate the functions of various parts of a computer.

Ans: Computer is a programmable electronic machine that accepts instructions and data through input devices, manipulating data according to instructions and providing finally result to the output device. The result can be stored in memory or sent to the output device. Figure 1.1 shows the block diagram of a conventional computer.

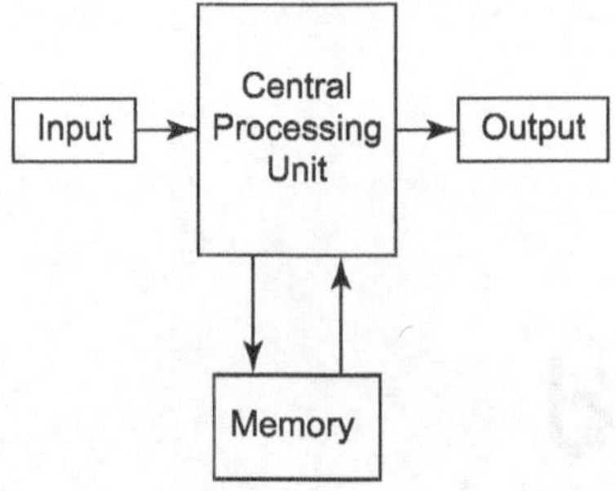

Figure 1.1 Block Diagram of a Conventional Computer

Figure 1.2 shows a computer system containing a monitor, a keyboard and a rectangular box comprising Central Processing Unit on the motherboard.

Figure 1.2 Computer System

A computer consists of the following main parts:

Input devices: They are used to accept the data and instructions into the computer. The various input devices that can be used in a computer are keyboard, mouse, analog-to-digital converters, light pen, track ball, optical character reader, scanner, etc.

Output devices: They are used to display the results on the screen or send the data to an output device. The processed data is ultimately sent to the output device by the computer. The various output devices that can be used in a computer are monitor, printer, LED, seven-segment display, D to A converter, plotter, etc.

Memory: Memory is used to store the program. The memory is categorized into the following types:

1. primary memory and
2. secondary memory.

Primary memory: It is made from semiconductors. Further, there are two types of semiconductor memories. They are:

1. RAM (random access memory) and
2. ROM (read-only memory).

Semiconductor memory is used for storing the instructions and data in the form of ones and zeros. It can be called user's memory or read–write memory. The processor first reads the instructions and data from the primary memory (semiconductor memory). Then, it executes the instructions.

One more memory device used by a computer is called read-only memory (ROM). This contains a fixed software program for providing certain operations. This is non-volatile memory. Its contents cannot be eliminated when power supply goes off. The basic input–output system (BIOS) is a software used to control various peripheral devices such as a keyboard, a monitor, a printer, a mouse and ports including serial and parallel ports. In fact, this is an operating system. It is possible to access the users' written programs, i.e., by loading a file, saving it and doing modifications to it in the later stage. As soon as a personal computer is switched on, the software is booted from ROM. Thus, various functions are assigned to all supporting peripherals of a central processing unit (CPU) and easy interactions are provided to the user by BIOS while booting the system.

Secondary memory: For storing a huge volume of data, secondary storage devices can be used. They are optical disc, magnetic disc, tapes, etc.

Central processor unit: The heart of a computer system is a CPU. It comprises arithmetic and logical unit, registers and control unit. The arithmetic and logical unit performs operations based on instructions. The control unit generates the timing and control signals for carrying out operations within the processor. Registers are used for storing the results temporarily.

3. What is ANSI C standard?

Ans: For many years, there was no standard version of C language and the definition provided in the reference manual was followed. Due to this reason, the portability feature of C language was not provided from one computer to another. To overcome this discrepancy, a committee was set up in the summer of 1983 to create a standard C version, which is popularly known as *American National Standards Institute* (ANSI) standard. This committee had defined finally a standard C language. The standardization process took about six years for defining the C language. The ANSI C standard was adopted in 1989 and its first copy of C language was introduced in the market in 1990. Thus, ANSI C is internationally recognized as a standard C language. The purpose of this standard is to enhance the portability and efficient execution of C language programs on different computers.

4. Explain the machine and assembly language concepts.

Ans: Machine language is a computer's natural language, which can be directly understood by the system. This language is machine dependent, i.e., it is not portable. A program written in 1s and 0s is called a machine language. A binary code is used in a machine language for a specific operation. A set of instructions in binary pattern is associated with each computer. It is difficult to communicate with a computer in terms of 1s and 0s. Hence, writing a program with a machine language is very difficult.

Instead of using a string of binary bits in a machine language, programmers started using English-like words as commands that can be easily interpreted by programmers. The program is in alphanumeric symbols instead of 1s and 0s. The designer chooses easy symbols that are to be remembered by the programmer, so that the programmer can easily develop the program in assembly language. The alphanumeric symbols are called mnemonics in the assembly language. The ADD, SUB, MUL, DIV, RLC and RAL are some symbols called mnemonics.

5. Why C language is called middle-level language?

Ans: The C language combines the features of a high-level language and functionality-like assembly languages. This language is designed for providing better programming efficiency (faster program development) as compared to machine-oriented and machine efficiency languages (faster program execution) and as compared to problem-oriented language. In C, one can develop a program fast and execute fast. It is neither a low-level language nor a high-level language. However, it is a combination of features of low- and high-level languages.

6. What is an algorithm? Explain in short.

Ans: An algorithm is a well-organized, pre-arranged and well-defined textual computational module that receives some value or set of values as input and provides a single value or a set of values as output.

These well-defined computational steps are arranged in a sequence, which processes the given input into an output. Writing precise description of the algorithm using an easy language is most essential for understanding the algorithm. An algorithm is said to be accurate and truthful only when it provides the exact required output. Lengthy procedure is sub-divided into small parts and thus steps are made easy to solve a given problem.

7. Mention and explain two types of algorithms.

Ans: Based on repetitive steps, an algorithm can further be classified into two types.

1. **Direct algorithm:** In this type of algorithm, the number of iterations is known in advance. For example, for displaying the numerical numbers from 1 to 10, the loop variable should be initialized from 1 to 10. The statement would be as follows:

```
for(j = 1; j < =10; j ++ )
```

   In the above statement, it is predicted that the loop will iterate 10 times.
2. **Indirect algorithm:** In this type of algorithm, steps are executed repetitively. Exactly how many repetitions are to be made is unknown. For example, the repetitive steps are as follows:
   (i) To find the first five Armstrong numbers from 1 to *n*, where *n* is a positive number. The *n* can be from 2 to any finite value say 100.
   (ii) To find the first three palindrome numbers from 1 to *n*, where *n* is a positive number. The *n* can be from 2 to any finite value say 1000.

8. What are the functions of a compiler and an interpreter?

Ans: Compilers are the translators, which translate all the instructions of the program into machine codes. The program, which is to be translated, is called the source program; after translation, the object code is generated. The source program is the input to the compiler. The object code is the output for the secondary storage device. The entire program will be read by the compiler first and generates the object code.

Interpreters also come in the group of translators. It helps the user to execute the source program with a few differences as compared to compilers. The source program is just like English words in both interpreters and compilers. The interpreter generates object codes for the source program. It reads the program line by line; however, in compiler, the compiler reads the entire program, which then generates the object codes. Interpreter directly executes the program from its source code. Due to this, every time the source code should be inputted to the interpreter. In other words, each line is converted into the object codes. It takes very less time for execution, because no intermediate object code is generated.

9. What is the difference between an interpreter and a compiler?

Ans: The interpreter executes the program line by line, whereas the compiler executes the complete program at a time; that is, it first creates intermediate codes, then executes it.

10. What is meant by compilation? Explain in detail.

Ans: The source program is the input to the compiler. The object code is the output for the secondary storage device. The entire program will be read by the compiler first and generates the object code. The compiler displays the list of errors and warnings for the statements violating the syntax rules of the language. Compilers may also have to link the subroutines of the program. The above procedure is called compilation.

11. Write the rules for writing a C program.

Ans: The rules for writing C programs are as follows:

1. Every program should have `main()` function as a starting point.
2. C statements should be terminated by a semicolon. The semicolon is used to mark the end of a statement.

   Example:
   ```
   printf("Hello!");
   ```
   It can also be used to separate the expressions in a `for` loop.

   Example:
   ```
   for(i = 0; i<=10; i++)
   ```
   The C programmer can also use the comma operator to separate the expressions.

   Example:
   ```
   int a,b;
   ```
3. An unessential semicolon if placed by the programmer is treated as an empty statement.
4. All statements should be written in the lowercase letters. Generally, the uppercase letters are used only for symbolic constants.
5. Blank spaces may be inserted between the words. This leads to improvement in the readability of the statements. However, this is not applicable while declaring a variable, keyword, constant and function.
6. It is not necessary to fix the position of statement in the program; i.e., a programmer can write the statement anywhere between the two braces following the declaration part. The user can also write one or more statements in one line separating them with a semicolon (;). Hence, it is often called a free-form language. The following statements are valid.

   $$a = b + c;$$
   $$d = b*c;$$
   or
   $$a = b + c; d = b*c;$$
7. The opening and closing braces should be balanced, i.e., if opening braces are four, closing braces should also be four.

12. Elaborate the different sections of a C program.

Ans: The sections in the C program are as follows:

Header files inclusion: In this section, all the header files that are needed are included using `#include` directive.

Global declaration: In this section, all the global variables are declared, which can be used from anywhere in the program.

`main()` function: This is the most important part of the program. The execution of every C program starts from the main function. It may contain function prototypes, local variable declaration, executable statements, comments, etc.

13. Explain the functions of a linker.

Ans: The linker puts together all other program files and functions that are required by the program. For example, if the programmer is using `pow()` function, then the object code of this function should be brought from math.h library of the system and linked to the `main()` program. After linking, the program is stored on the disc.

14. What is the role of curly braces ({}) in a C program?

Ans: The curly braces are used to define the block of statements. The statements inside the curly braces are having different scope than that of the statements outside the curly braces. The curly braces can be used to define the blocks for decision and loop statements.

15. What are the user-defined functions?

Ans: The user-defined functions are created by the user; the contents of the user-defined functions are completely known to the user and can be modified by the user.

16. Write details on header files `stdio.h` and `conio.h`.

`stdio.h`: Standard input and output file. All formatted and unformatted functions include file operation functions defined in this file. The most useful formatted `printf()` and `scanf()` are defined in this file. Most useful functions from this header files are `printf()`, `scanf()`, `getchar()`, `gets()`, `putc()` and `putchar()`.

`conio.h`: Console input and output file. This file contains input and output functions along with a few graphic-supporting functions. The `getch()`, `getche()` and `clrscr()` functions are defined in this file.

17. Which are the standard directories? Where are .h files kept?

Ans: The turbo-C has three standard directories; they are include, sys and lib. The sys is the sub-directory of include. The include directory contains all the header files and lib contains all the library files. The header files are stored in 'include' directory. The path could be c:/turboc2/include - if C is installed on 'drive C'.

18. Write any three advantages of the C language.

Ans: The advantages of the C language include the following:

1. It contains a powerful data definition. The data types supported are characters, alphanumeric, integers, `long` integer, floats and `double`. It also supports string manipulation in the form of character array.
2. It supports a powerful set of operators.
3. It also supports powerful graphics programming and directly operates with hardware. Execution of program is faster.
4. An assembly code is also inserted into C programs.

Multiple-choice Questions

1. Hard disc is a ________.

   (a) Input device (b) Output device
   (c) Both input as well as output (d) None of the above

2. Mouse is a ________.

   (a) Input device (b) Output device
   (c) Both input as well as output (d) None of the above

3. Brain of the computer system is _________.
   (a) Mouse
   (b) Printer
   (c) Keyboard
   (d) Central processing unit
4. ALU is a part of _________.
   (a) Input (b) Output (c) CPU (d) Memory
5. Laptop is a _________ device.
   (a) Non-portable (b) Portable (c) Desktop (d) Non-programmable
6. Monitor of computer system is _________.
   (a) Input (b) Output (c) Both input as well as output (d) None of the above
7. Random access memory is _________.
   (a) Non-volatile
   (b) Volatile
   (c) Both (a) and (b)
   (d) None of the above
8. Interpreter is a _________.
   (a) Hardware
   (b) Software
   (c) Both (a) and (b)
   (d) None of the above
9. Interpreter converts source code into _________.
   (a) Machine code
   (b) ASCII code
   (c) BCD code
   (d) Hamming code
10. The 'C' language has been developed by _________.
    (a) Patrick Naughton
    (b) Dennis Ritche
    (c) Ken Thompson
    (d) Martin Richards
11. The 'C' programming is a _________.
    (a) High-level language
    (b) Low-level language
    (c) Middle-level language
    (d) Assembly language
12. The 'C' programs are converted into machine language using _________.
    (a) An assembler
    (b) A compiler
    (c) An interpreter
    (d) An operating system
13. The 'C' language was developed in the year _________.
    (a) 1972
    (b) 1980
    (c) 1975
    (d) 1971
14. The 'C' language has been developed at _________
    (a) AT and T Bell Labs, USA
    (b) IBM, USA
    (c) Borland International, USA
    (d) Sun Microsystems
15. The 'C' program should be written only in _________.
    (a) Lower case
    (b) Upper case
    (c) Title case
    (d) Sentence case
16. The role of compiler is to translate source program statements to _________.
    (a) Object codes
    (b) Octal codes
    (c) Decimal codes
    (d) None of the above

17. The extension for ‘C’ program files by default is ________.
   (a) ‘.c’ (b) ‘.d’ (c) ‘.obj’ (d) ‘.exe’
18. The ‘C’ can be used with ________.
   (a) Only UNIX operating system (b) Only Linux operating system
   (c) Only MS-DOS operating system (d) All of the above
19. The ‘C’ language is closely associated with ________.
   (a) MS-DOS (b) Linux (c) UNIX (d) MS-Windows
20. The ‘C’ programs are highly portable means ________.
   (a) Same programs can be execute on different computers
   (b) Program executes only on the same computer
   (c) Program needs a lot of modification to run
   (d) None of the above
21. Each instruction in ‘C’ program is terminated by ________.
   (a) Dot (.) (b) Comma (,) (c) Semicolon (;) (d) Curly brace ({})
22. Which one of the following statements is incorrect?
   (a) A compiler compiles the source program.
   (b) An assembler takes an assembly program as input.
   (c) A compiler does the same type of function as interpreter.
   (d) None of the above.
23. ANSI committee was set up in the summer of ________.
   (a) 1983 (b) 1985 (c) 1990 (d) 1976
24. C is an offspring of the ________.
   (a) Basic combined programming language
   (b) Basic computer programming language
   (c) Basic programming language
   (d) None of the above
25. An interpreter reads the source code of a program ________.
   (a) One line at a time (b) Two lines at a time
   (c) Complete program in one stroke (d) None of the above
26. A compiler reads the source code of a program ________.
   (a) Complete program in one stroke (b) One line at a time
   (c) Two lines at a time (d) None of the above
27. ‘C’ keywords are reserved words by ________.
   (a) A compiler (b) An interpreter (c) Header file (d) (b) and (c)
28. The declaration of ‘C’ variable can be done ________.
   (a) Anywhere in the program (b) In the declaration part
   (c) In the executable part (d) At the end of the program
29. Variables must begin with character without spaces but C language permits ________.
   (a) Underscore symbol (_) (b) Asterisk symbol (*)
   (c) Ampersand symbol (&) (d) None of the above

30. In C, the statements following `main()` are enclosed within _________.
    (a) { }
    (b) ( )
    (c) < >
    (d) None of the above
31. Keys used for compiling the source program in C _________.
    (a) Alt-C (b) Alt-R (c) Alt-F (d) Alt-G
32. Keys used for running the source program in C _________.
    (a) Alt-C (b) Alt-R (c) Alt-F (d) Alt-T
33. Keys used for closing the C editor _________.
    (a) Alt-C (b) Alt-X (c) Alt-F (d) Alt-F3
34. Computer is a _________ electronic machine.
    (a) Programmable
    (b) Non-programmable
    (c) Unpopular
    (d) None of the above
35. Scanner is an _________ device.
    (a) Output (b) Input (c) Input and output (d) None of the above
36. Floppy is an _________ device.
    (a) Output (b) Input (c) Input and output (d) None of the above
37. Hard disc is a _________ device.
    (a) Semiconductor
    (b) Magnetic
    (c) Conductor
    (d) None of the above
38. Program execution takes place in _________.
    (a) CD (b) Tape (c) RAM (d) CPU
39. Header files appear in the C program _________.
    (a) After the `main()`
    (b) Before the `main()`
    (c) At the middle of the program
    (d) Nowhere
40. Comments in C are written within _________.
    (a) /* */ (b) [ ] (c) ( ) (d) < >
41. _________ is CPU dependent.
    (a) Compiler (b) Assembler (c) Interpreter (d) None of the above
42. C is a _________ language.
    (a) Portable
    (b) Non-portable
    (c) Both (a) and (b)
    (d) None of the above
43. Opening and closing braces in C should be _________.
    (a) Unbalanced
    (b) Balanced
    (c) Uncontrolled
    (d) None of the above
44. _________ are predefined in the compiler.
    (a) ASCII
    (b) Keywords
    (c) User defined functions
    (d) None of the above
45. _________ processes instructions and data.
    (a) Keys (b) CPU (c) Hard disc (d) Memory

Answers

1. (c)	2. (a)	3. (d)	4. (c)	5. (b)	6. (b)	7. (b)	8. (b)	9. (a)	10. (b)
11. (c)	12. (b)	13. (a)	14. (a)	15. (a)	16. (a)	17. (a)	18. (d)	19. (c)	20. (a)
21. (c)	22. (d)	23. (a)	24. (a)	25. (a)	26. (a)	27. (a)	28. (b)	29. (a)	30. (a)
31. (a)	32. (b)	33. (b)	34. (a)	35. (b)	36. (c)	37. (b)	38. (d)	39. (b)	40. (a)
41. (b)	42. (a)	43. (b)	44. (b)	45. (b)					

True or False

1. C language was developed by Ken Thompson.
2. C language was developed in 1972.
3. C language is closely associated with Linux.
4. C programs are not portable.
5. The ANSI C standard was developed in December 1989.
6. C programs are translated into object code by compiler.
7. An interpreter reads one line at a time.
8. Every `'C'` program should have `main()` function.
9. In C, all the statements should be written in small letters only.
10. After compilation, object file of source program is created.
11. It is not possible to create .exe file in C.
12. Compiler executes the program even when the program contains warning messages.
13. In Turbo C editor, Alt+C is used to execute the program.
14. A comment can be split in more than one line.
15. The source code for the UNIX operating system is in C.
16. The assembly language program is in alphanumeric symbols.
17. Linking software is used to bring together the source program and library code.

Answers

1. False 2. True 3. False 4. False 5. True 6. True 7. True 8. True 9. True 10. True 11. False
12. True 13. False 14. True 15. True 16. True 17. True

2

The C Declarations

1. What are the different data types?

Ans: C data type is classified as follows:

1. Basic data type: Basic data types are (a) integer (`int`), (b) character (`char`), (c) floating point (`float`) and (d) double floating point (`double`).
2. Derived data type: Derived data types are pointers, functions and arrays.
3. User-defined type: User-defined data types are `struct`, `union`, `enum` and `typedef`.
4. The `void` data type: It is an empty data set. This data type can be followed from the chapter on Functions.

2. What are the differences between `signed` and `unsigned` data types?

Ans: When a variable is declared as `unsigned`, the negative range of the data type is transferred to positive, i.e., doubles the largest size of the possible value. This is due to declaring `unsigned int`; the 16th bit is free and is not used to store the sign of the number.

Some differences between `signed` and `unsigned` data types are shown in the following table.

`signed int`	`unsigned int`
Range: −32,768 to 32,767	Range: 0 to 65535
Format `%d` or `%i` prints `signed` integers	Format `%u` prints `unsigned` integers
For `long signed int`, range is −2147483648 to 2147483647	For `long unsigned int`, range is 0 to 4294967295
Format `%ld` prints `long signed` integers	Format `%lu` prints `unsigned` integers

3. What do we mean by a variable and a constant?

Ans: A 'variable' is a data name used for storing a data value. Its value may be changed during the program execution. It has memory location and it can store a single value at a time. The 'constants' in C are applicable to the values, which do not change during the execution of a program.

4. Explain different types of constants in C.

Ans: Constants in C are as follows:

1. Numerical Constants
   (a) Integer constants: These are a sequence of numbers from 0 to 9 without decimal points or fractional part or any other symbols. It requires minimum 2 bytes and maximum 4 bytes of memory. Integer constant could be either positive or negative or may be zero.

   Example: `-10, 20, +30, -15.`

   Besides, representing the integers/real constants in decimal number system, they also can be represented in octal or hexadecimal number system based on the requirement.

   (b) Real Constants: Real constants are floating-point constants.

   Example: `2.5, 5.521, 3.14.`

2. Character Constant
   (a) Single character constants: A character constant is a single character (length = 1). It can also be represented with single digit or a single special symbol or white space enclosed within a pair of single quote marks.

   Example: `'a', '8', '-'.`

   (b) String constants: String constants are a sequence of characters enclosed within double quotation marks.

   Example: `"Hello", "India", "444", "a".`

5. How the octal and hexadecimal numbers represented in C?

Ans: Numbers or constants can be represented in octal or hexadecimal based on the requirement/applications.

Octal has base 8 and hexadecimal has base 16. The octal numbers are 0, 1, 2, 3, 4, 5, 6, 7 and hexadecimal numbers are 0, 1, 2, 3, 4, 5, 6, 7, 8, 9, A, B, C, D, E, F.

The representation of octal numbers in C would be done with leading digit 0 and for hex representation with leading 0X.

Following are a few examples of octal and hexadecimal numbers.

027, 037, 072 – Octal numbers

0X9, 0Xab, 0X4 – Hexadecimal

6. What are the C keywords? Elaborate them.

Ans: The C keywords are reserved words by the compiler having fixed meaning. They cannot be used as a variable name. The 32 C keywords provided in ANSI C are listed in the following table.

auto	double	int	struct
break	else	long	switch
case	enum	register	typedef
char	extern	return	union
const	float	unsigned	short
continue	for	signed	void

default	goto	sizeof	volatile
do	if	static	while

Additional keywords for Borland C:

asm	cdecl	far	huge
interrupt	near	pascal	

7. List the rules for declaring a variable.

Ans:

1. A variable must begin with a character without spaces but an underscore is permitted. The underscore is treated as one type of character.
2. The length of the variable varies from compiler to compiler. Generally, most of the compilers support eight characters. However, the ANSI standard recognizes the maximum length of a variable up to 31 characters.

   For external names, the variable names should be of six characters and in single case.
3. The variable should not be a C keyword.
4. The variable names may be a combination of uppercase and lowercase characters. For example, suM and sum are not the same. The traditional practice is to use lowercase letterers for variable names and upper case letters for symbolic constants.
5. The variable name should not start with a digit.
6. Blanks and commas are not permitted within a variable name.

8. What are the identifiers?

Ans: Identifier is a symbolic name used to refer to a variable, constant, function, structure, `union` etc. In other words, identifiers are the names of variables, functions, arrays etc.

Identifiers refer to variety of entities such as structures, unions, enumeration, constants, `typedef` names, functions and objects.

Identifiers are user-defined names. Identifiers are generally defined in lower case letters. However, the upper case letters are also permitted. The (_) underscore symbol can be used as an identifier. In general, underscore is used to link between two words for the `long` identifiers.

9. Explain the methods for initialization of variables.

Ans: Variables declared can be assigned or initialized using assignment operator '='. The declaration and initialization can also be done in the same line.

Syntax:

```
variable_name = constant;
or
data_type varaible_name= constant;
```

Example: `x = 5;` where x is an integer variable.

Example: `int y = 4;`

10. Explain constants and `volatile` variables.

Ans:

1. Constant variable

   If the value of a certain variable to remain the same or unchanged during the program execution, it can be done by declaring the variable as a constant. The keyword `const` is then prefixed before the declaration. It tells the compiler that the variable is a constant. Thus, constant declared variables are protected from modification.

   Example: `const int m=10;`

2. `Volatile` variable

   The `volatile` variables are those variables that can be changed at any time by other external program or the same program. The syntax is as follows:

   `volatile int d;`

11. Write a program on constant and `volatile` variables.

Ans:

```
void main()
{
const int a=11;
volatile num=12;
clrscr();
num=num-1;
printf("%d %d",num,a);
getche();
}
```

OUTPUT:

```
11 11
```

Explanation: `Volatile` variable can be changed, but constants cannot be changed. Hence, the results shown are based on the theory.

12. Write about space requirement for variables of different data types.

Ans: Following chart gives the space requirement for different data types.

Data Type	Space Requirement (Bytes)
`char`	1
`unsigned char`	1
`short` or `int`	2
`unsigned int`	2
`long`	4
`unsigned long`	4
`float`	4
`double`	8
`long double`	10

13. What are the delimiters? Explain their uses.

Ans: The language pattern of C uses special kind of symbols, which are called delimiters. They are:

Delimiters	Symbols	Use
Colon	:	Useful for label
Semicolon	;	Terminates statements
Parentheses	( )	Used in expression and function
Square brackets	[ ]	Used for array declaration
Curly braces	{ }	Scope of statement
Hash	#	Preprocessor directive
Comma	,	Variable separator

14. Is 'main' a keyword? Explain.

Ans: 'main' is not a keyword. The `void main()` function is a user-defined function. We can use the word main as an identifier to create variables.

15. List any three keywords with their use.

Ans:

1. `break:`
   It can be used to forcefully break an executing loop.
   For example,

```
int i;
for(i=0;i<5;i++)
{
    if(i==3) break;
}
```

2. `goto:`
   It can be used to transfer the control to a specified location in the program using 'label'.
   For example,

```
int i;
 scanf("%d",&i);
 if(i==0)
 goto ONE;
 else goto TWO;
ONE: printf("Demo");
TWO: exit(0);
/*SOME PROGRAM CODE*/
```

3. `return:`
   It can be used to `return` a definite value as per the `return` type of a function.
   For example, 'main' returns an integer

```
int main()
{
printf("Demo of return keyword");
return 0; /* '0' implies successful execution of program*/
}
```

16. What is the difference between %f and %g control strings? Whether both can be used for representing float numbers?

Ans: The format string `%f` or `%g` is used to represent floating point number or real number in the form of fraction, i.e., decimal notation. Precise results are obtained by `%f`. The precision indicates the number of significant digits. In case precision is missing, i.e. for zero precision, fractional part appears with six digits.

With `%g` the real number or floating point number appears up to two decimal digits after decimal point. Depending upon the applications we, therefore, can use one of them to represent the floats.

17. What do you mean by type conversion? Why is it necessary?

Ans: Type conversion converts one type of data into another type.

1. Assigning incompatible data types.

   Example:

   `int x= 3.5;`

   Here, the fraction part will not be assigned to integer variable and the part will be lost. The integer is 2-byte length data type without fractional part and `float` is 4-byte length data type with fractional part. We can use `'float'` instead.
2. Assigning out of range value.
   For example, suppose that you assign 35425 to `int x`; you will not get expected result, because 35425 is larger than short integer range.
   We may use '`long`' instead.
3. Sometimes a programmer needs the result in a certain data type; for example, division of 5 with 2 should `return float` value. Practically, the compiler always returns integer values because both the arguments are of integer data type.

To correct it, we use (`float`)5/2 in the program.

18. What is wrapping around?

Ans: When the value of variable goes beyond its limit, the compiler would not flag any error message. It just wraps around the value of a variable. For example, the range of `unsigned` integer is 0 to 65535. In this type, negative values and values greater than 65535 are compatible.

```
unsigned int x = 65536;
```

The value assigned is greater by 1 than the range. Here, the compiler starts again from beginning after reaching the end of the range and the value 1 is assigned to *x*.

19. List the name of type modifiers.

Ans: The keywords `signed`, `unsigned`, `short` and `long` are type modifiers. A type modifier changes the meaning of basic data type and produces a new data type. Each of these type modifiers is applicable to the basic data type int. The modifiers signed and unsigned are also applicable to the type char. The long type modifier can be applicable to double type.

Example:

```
long l; /*int data type is applied*/
int s; /*signed is default*/
unsigned long int x; /*int keyword is optional*/
```

20. What is dynamic initialization?

Ans: The initialization of variable at run time is called dynamic initialization. Dynamic refers to the process during execution. In C, initialization can be done at any place in the program; however, the declaration should be done at the declaration part only.

21. Write a program that supports dynamic initialization.

Ans:

```
void main()
{
int r=2;
float perimeter=2*3.14*r;
float area=3.14*r*r;
clrscr();
printf(" Perimeter=%g \nArea=%g ",perimeter,area);
getche();
}

OUTPUT:
Perimeter =12.56
Area =12.56
```

Explanation: Variables are initialized at run time.

Multiple-choice Questions

1. A character variable can store only _________.
   (a) 1 character (b) 20 characters (c) 254 characters (d) None of the above
2. A 'C' variable should not start with _________.
   (a) A number (b) An alphabet (c) A character (d) None of the above
3. A short integer variable occupies memory _________.
   (a) 2 byes (b) 4 bytes (c) 1 byte (d) 8 bytes
4. 'C' keywords are reserved words by _________.
   (a) A compiler (b) An interpreter (c) Header file (d) Both (b) and (c)
5. The declaration of 'C' variable can be done _________.
   (a) Anywhere in the program (b) In declaration part
   (c) In executable part (d) At the end of program

6. In 'C' one statement can declare _________.
   (a) Only one variables
   (b) Two variables
   (c) Ten variables
   (d) Any number of variables
7. The word 'int' is a _________.
   (a) Keyword
   (b) Password
   (c) Header file
   (d) None of the above
8. The variables are initialized using _________.
   (a) Greater than (>)
   (b) Equal to (=)
   (c) Twice equal to (==)
   (d) An increment operator (++)
9. An unsigned integer variable contains values _________.
   (a) Greater or equal to zero
   (b) Less than zero
   (c) Only zeros
   (d) Both (a) and (b)
10. The keyword 'const' keeps the value of a variable _________.
   (a) Constant
   (b) Mutable
   (c) Variant
   (d) None of the above
11. Identifiers are _________.
   (a) User-defined names
   (b) Reserved keywords
   (c) 'C' statements
   (d) None of the above
12. In 'C', every variable has _________.
   (a) A type
   (b) A name
   (c) A value
   (d) A size
   (e) All of the above
13. The range of character data type is _________.
   (a) –128 to 127
   (b) 0 to 255
   (c) 0 to 32767
   (d) None of the above
14. An unsigned integer variable occupies memory _________.
   (a) 2 byes
   (b) 4 bytes
   (c) 1 byte
   (d) 8 bytes
15. In 'C', double variable needs memory of size _________.
   (a) 4 bytes
   (b) 2 bytes
   (c) 10 bytes
   (d) All of the above
16. 'C', main() is a _________.
   (a) User-defined function
   (b) Library function
   (c) String function
   (d) Any number of variables
17. The word 'continue' is a _________.
   (a) Keyword
   (b) Password
   (c) Header file
   (d) None of the above
18. The volatile variables are those variables that remain/can be _________.
   (a) Constant
   (b) Changed at any time
   (c) Both of the above
   (d) None of the above

19. In C, the statements following `main()` are enclosed within _________.

(a) { } (b) ( ) (c) < > (d) None of the above

20. In 'C', the maximum value of `unsigned` character is _________.

(a) 255 (b) 127
(c) 65535 (d) None of the above

21. The range of `long signed` integer is _________.

(a) –2147483648 to 2147483647 (b) 0 to 255
(c) 0 to 4294967295 (d) None of the above

22. In C, '`sizeof`' is a/an _________.

(a) Variable (b) Operator
(c) Keyword (d) None of the above

23. Which is the incorrect variable name _________?

(a) `else` (b) name (c) age (d) `cha_r`

24. How many keywords are there in ANSI C _________?

(a) 32 (b) 33 (c) 42 (d) 15

25. Integer constants in C can be _________.

(a) Positive (b) Negative
(c) Positive or negative (d) None of the above

26. Which of the following statement is wrong?

(a) 5+5 = a; (b) ss = 12.25; (c) st = 'm' * 'b'; (d) is ='A'+10;

27. In C, the first letter of the variable should be _________.

(a) Integer (b) An alphabet or underscore
(c) Floating number (d) None of the above

28. What is the output of the following program?

```
#include <stdio.h>
#include <conio.h>
   void main()
   {
   unsigned long v=-1;
   clrscr();
   printf("\n %lu",v);
   }
```

(a) 4294967295 (b) 0
(c) –1 (d) None of the above

29. What would be the values of variables c and u?

```
#include <stdio.h>
#include <conio.h>
   void main()
```

```
{
char c=-127;
unsigned char u=-127;
clrscr();
printf("\n c=%d u= %d",c,u);
}
```

(a) $c = 127$ $u = 127$
(b) $c = -127$ $u = 127$
(c) $c = 127$ $u = 128$
(d) None of the above

30. The error message 'Cannot modify a constant object' is displayed when user ________.
    (a) Attempts to modify the constant variable
    (b) Attempts to use the variable in expressions
    (c) Attempts assign value of constant variable to another variable
31. The following program will display the warning message ________.

```
int x=2,y=2;
printf("x=%d",x);
```

    (a) 'y' is assigned a value which is never used in function `main()`
    (b) Expression syntax in main
    (c) Possible use of 'y' before definition in function main
32. The following program will display the warning message ________.

```
int x,y;
printf("x=%d",x);
```

    (a) 'y' is assigned a value which is never used in function `main()`
    (b) Expression syntax in main
    (c) Possible use of 'x' before definition in function main
33. Each header files extension in C program is done with ________.
    (a) `.h`
    (b) `.p`
    (c) `.c`
    (d) None of the above three
34. The format string for char data type is ________.
    (a) `%c`
    (b) `%d`
    (c) `%u`
    (d) `%f`
35. The format string for int is ________.
    (a) `%c`
    (b) `%d`
    (c) `%u`
    (d) `%f`
36. The format string for `long float` is ________.
    (a) `%c`
    (b) `%d`
    (c) `%u`
    (d) `%lf`
37. The format string for `float` data type ________.
    (a) `%f`
    (b) `%d`
    (c) `%u`
    (d) `%lf`

38. The word '`default`' is a _________.
    (a) Keyword
    (b) Password
    (c) Header file
    (d) None of the above
39. The identifiers are defined by _________.
    (a) Compiler
    (b) User
    (c) Function
    (d) None of the above
40. Variables must begin with character without spaces but it permits _________.
    (a) Underscore symbol (_)
    (b) Asterisk symbol (*)
    (c) Ampersand symbol (&)
    (d) None of the above

Answers

1. (a)	2. (a)	3. (a)	4. (a)	5. (b)	6. (d)	7. (a)	8. (b)	9. (a)	10. (a)
11. (a)	12. (b)	13. (a)	14. (a)	15. (a)	16. (a)	17. (a)	18. (b)	19. (a)	20. (a)
21. (a)	22. (c)	23. (a)	24. (a)	25. (c)	26. (a)	27. (b)	28. (a)	29. (d)	30. (a)
31. (a)	32. (c)	33. (a)	34. (a)	35. (b)	36. (d)	37. (a)	38. (a)	39. (b)	40. (a)

True or False

1. Data means combination of letters, digits, symbols, etc.
2. In C A to Z and a to z are treated as the same.
3. The **`signed`** is a `'C'` keyword.
4. The **new** is a C keyword.
5. 10.120 is a integer constant.
6. Identifiers are name of variables, arrays, functions, etc.
7. The constant in C is applicable to values which do not change during program execution.
8. 'A' is a character constant.
9. "India" is a string constant.
10. A variable is a data name used for storing data values.
11. The value of a variable can be changed during program execution.
12. A variable name can start with digit.
13. The C keyword can act as variable name.
14. In C the variable name sum and Sum are same.
15. short `int` and `int` are different from each other.
16. `int`, short `int` and `long int` belong to one category with different size and range of values.
17. `int` occupies 4 bytes in memory.
18. `const int` a=10; value of a will not be changed during program execution.
19. abc is a valid variable name.

Answers

1. True 2. False 3. True 4. False 5. False 6. True 7. True 8. True 9. True 10. True 11. True 12. False 13. False 14. False 15. False 16. True 17. False 18. True 19. True

Additional Questions

What will be the output of the following programs?

Character constants

1. Program to print a character.

```
void main()
{
char c=65;
clrscr();
printf("%c",c);
}

OUTPUT:
A
```

2. Program to print characters.

```
void main()
{
clrscr();
printf("%c %c",74+32,80+32);
}

OUTPUT:
j p
```

Character constants with ASCII values

3.

```
void main()
{
unsigned char c=65;
clrscr();
printf("%d  %c %d ",c,c,c);
}

OUTPUT:
65 A 65
```

4.

```
void main()
{
signed char c=80;
c+10;
c+26;
c=++c;
clrscr();
printf("%d %c %d",c,c,c);
}

OUTPUT:
65 A 65
```

5.

```
void main()
void main()
{
int a=12,b=78;
char c=a+b;
clrscr();
printf("\n c=%c c=%d",c,c);
}

OUTPUT:
c =Z c =90
```

Integers, `Float`, Long integers etc

6.

```
void main()
{
unsigned u=65536  ;
clrscr();
printf("%u",u);
}

OUTPUT:
0
```

7.

```
void main()
{
int x=5;
clrscr();
printf("%g",x/2.);
}

OUTPUT:
2.5
```

8.

```
void main()
{
int x=2.5;
float f=2.800000;
char c='s';
clrscr();
printf("x=%d f=%g c=%c",x,f,c-32) ;
}

OUTPUT:
x =2 f =2.8 c =S
```

9.

```
void main()
{
char c=78.5;
float f='C';
int k=2.5;
clrscr();
printf("%c  %g  %d" ,c,f,k);
}

OUTPUT:
N  67  2
```

10.

```
void main()
{
char r=127,q=130;
int x=r+q;
clrscr();
printf("\n x=%d",x);
}

OUTPUT:
x =1
```

11.

```
void main()
{
int sum, Keyword,a=21,b=29;
clrscr();
sum=a+b;
Keyword=a-b;
printf("\n %d %d ",Keyword,sum);

}

OUTPUT:
-8 50
```

12.

```
void main()
{
int  r=33000,q=-2000;
int x=r+q;
clrscr();
printf("\n x=%d",x);
}

OUTPUT:
31000
```

13.

```
void main()
{
unsigned u=2147483647;
long     l=2147483647;
clrscr();
printf("\n u=%u  l=%ld",u,l);
}

OUTPUT:
u = 65535  l = 2147483647
```

Integers with exponentiation

14.

```
void main()
{
  int x,a=3e1,b=2e2;
  clrscr();
  x=a+b;
  printf("x=%d",x);
}

OUTPUT:
x = 230
```

15.

```
void main()
{
  int x,a=1e1, b=0;
  clrscr();
  b+=1e1;
  printf("a= %d b=%d",a,b);
}

OUTPUT:
a = 10 b = 10
```

16.
```
void main()
{
  float a=3e2,b=2e4;
  clrscr();
  printf("a=%g b=%g",a,b);
}

OUTPUT:
a =300 b =20000
```

Float numbers

17.
```
void main()
{
  float a=3e2,b=2e4;
  clrscr();
  printf("a=%g b=%g",a,b);
}

OUTPUT:
a =300 b =20000
```

18.
```
void main()
{
  float   a=1e3, b=2e4,c;
  clrscr();
  c=(a*b)/(a+b);
  printf("\n %f  ",c);
  getche();
}

OUTPUT:
952.380981
```

String display and operation on it

19.

```
void main()
{
char arry[10]="PEARSON";
int i=0;
clrscr();
arry[i]=arry[i++];
printf("%s",arry);
}

OUTPUT:
PEARSON
```

20.

```
void main()
{
clrscr();
printf("HELLO!");
printf("\r\rC Programming");
}

OUTPUT:
C Programming
```

21.

```
void main()
{
  clrscr();
  printf("\t\a1b\bt\t2");
  printf("\\\\\\");
}

OUTPUT:
1t      2\\\
```

22.
```
void main()
{
 char name[]={'I','N','D','I','A','\0'};
 char name1[]={'I','N','D','I','A','\0'};
 clrscr();
 printf(name);
 printf(name1);
}

OUTPUT:
INDIAINDIA
```

Dynamic initialisation

23.
```
void main()
{
 int r=2;
 float perimeter=2*3.14*r;
 float area=3.14*r*r;
 clrscr();
 printf(" Perimeter=%g \nArea=%g ",perimeter,area);
 getche();
}

OUTPUT:
Perimeter =12.56
Area =12.56
```

Type conversion

24.

```
void main()
{
 clrscr();
 printf("\n%d",10/3);
 printf("\n%g",10.8/2);
 printf("\n%g",(float)11/2);
 getche();
}

OUTPUT:
3
5.4
5.5
```

25.

```
void main()
{
 int a=50,b=2,c;
 clrscr();
 c=(a*b)/(a+b);
 printf("\n %d  ",c);
 getche();
 }

OUTPUT:
1
```

Constant and `volatile` variables

26.

```
void main()
{
 const int a=11;
 volatile  num=12;
 clrscr();
 num=num-1;
 printf("%d  %d",num,a);
 getche();
}

OUTPUT:
11  11
```

Find the bug/s in the following program/s.

Characters, integers, `long`, `unsigned` etc

1.
```
void main()
{
unsigned int   d=65535;
unsigned char  p=65;
clrscr();
printf("%c %c",d,p);
getche();
}
```

Bug: No Bug. However, first `%c` is to be replaced by `%u` and then answer will be 65535 A

2.
```
void main()
{
char x=-127;
unsigned char p=-127;
clrscr();
printf("\n%d %d"x,p);
getche();
}
```

Bug: Missing, (comma) in `printf()`. Answer would be -127 129

3.
```
void main()
{
int x=2,
printf("%d",x);
}
```

Bug: Statement terminated by comma. Answer after correction will be 2.

4.

```
void main()
{
int 2x=2;
printf("%d",2x);
}
```

Bug: 2x is a invalid variable. Declaration error. x and p.

5.

```
void main()
{
int abcdefghijklmnopqrstuvwxyz=100;
printf("%d",++abcdefghijklmnopqrstuvwxyz);
}
```

Bug: No bug. Answer will be 101

6.

```
void main()
{
 int case=8;
 printf("%d",case);
}
```

Bug: `case` is a keyword. Keyword is not permitted. Answer with permitted variable name would be 8.

7.

```
void main()
{
int x,y;
x=8;
y=9;
z=x+y;
printf("%d",z);
}
```

Bug: Variable z is not declared in the program following `main()`.

8.

```
void main()
{
int x=-32769;
unsigned int p=-65534;
clrscr();
printf("\n%d %d", x p);
getche();
}
```

Bug: Missing , (comma) in the printf() statement. Unsigned must be +ve. Answer after correction 32767 2

9.

```
void main()
{
int x=-32768;
unsigned int  p=65535;
clrscr();
printf("\n%d %d", x  p);
getche();
}
```

Bug: Mistakes in printf(). Second %d replace with %u and put , (comma) in between x and p. Answer after correction -32768 65535

10.

```
void main()
{
int x=5,y=2;
printf("%f",x/y);
}
```

Bug: Format string %f is not suitable. Replace %f by %d. Answer will be 2.

11.

```
void main()
{
unsigned  x=-5;
clrscr();
printf("%u",x);
}
```

Bug: unsigned integer should not contain negative values

12.

```
void main()
{
clrscr();
int x=5;
x++;
printf("%d",x);
}
```

Bug: `clrscr()` is not allowed in declaration part

13.

```
void main()
{
long x=500000;
x++;
clrscr();
printf
("%ld",x);
}
```

Bug: Data type in capital letters are not permitted

14.

```
void main()
{
int x,y=5;
x+=y;
clrscr();
printf("%d",x);
}
```

Bug: Variable x should be analyzed. Assign value to x.

Integers with macros

15.

```
#define N= 90
void main()
{
int x=10,p;
clrscr();
p=x*N;
printf("\n%d ",  p);
getche();
}
```

Bug: Syntax error in first line `#define`. Remove = . Answer will be 900

16.

```
#define N >90
#define M >100
void main()
{
int x=10,p;
clrscr();
p=x*N;
p=p+M;
printf("\n%d ",  p);
getche();
}
```

Bug: Expression syntax in first two lines. Answer after removing > from them will be 1000

17.

```
#define N 2
#define M 3
void main()
{
 int x=10,p;
 clrscr();
 p=x*n;
 p=p*m;
 printf("\n%d ",  p);
 getche();
}
```

Bug: Undefined symbols n and m. Replace them with N and M. Answer will be 60

Float and double floats

18.

```
void main()
{
 float f=2.5;
 clrscr();
 printf("%d %f",f);
}
```

Bug: No bug. However, `%d` is unnecessarily written

19.

```
void main()
{
 float f=5/2;
 clrscr();
 printf("\n %f",f);
}
```

`Bug`: No bug. However, to get the desired output as 2.5, either 5 or 2 should be `float` or explicit type casting is required.

20.

```
void main()
{
 float   d=65535.43;
 double  p=65789.987654;
 clrscr();
 printf("%d %d",d,p);
 getche();
}
```

`Bug`: No bug. However, to get the desired output format provided is wrong. `%f` and `%lf` are needed. Answer would be
65535.429688 65789.987654

21.

```
void main()
{
 float d=1234567.43;
 double p=987654321.1234567;
 clrscr();
 printf("\n%f %lf",d,p);
 printf("\n%d %d",size of(d),size of(p));
 getche();
}
```

`Bug`: Space between size and of should be removed. The answer will be
1234567.375000 987654321.123457
4 8

Typecasting

22.

```
void main()
{
clrscr();
printf("\n %d", 7/2);
printf("\n%g",7.0/2);
printf("\n%g", float7/2);
getche();

}
```

Bug: `float` must be enclosed within bracket then answer will be 3

```
3.5
3.5
```

`volatile` and constants

23.

```
void main()
{
volatile  d=15;
const  p=25;
clrscr();
printf("%d %d"d+10,p+1);
getche();
}
```

Bug: Missing , (comma) in the `printf()`.

Answer after correction

```
25 26
```

24.

```
void main()
{
const   x=5;
clrscr();
x++;
printf("%d",x);
}
```

Bug: constant variable can be modified

3

Operators and Expressions

1. What is the role of operator?

Ans: An operator performs different operations on operands and produces result. An expression is to be created with the help of operator and operands, i.e., expression is build with operator and operands. For example, the following expression contains two operands and one operator.

$$a*b,$$

where *a* and *b* are operands and * is the operator.

Similarly, by using different operators' expressions can be built. Operator operates on single operand or more than one operand.

2. Explain different types of operators supported by C.

Ans: The C language supports different exhaustive operators. All of them are not elaborated. C provides the following four types of basic operators.

1. Arithmetic,
2. Relational,
3. Logical and
4. Bitwise.

Besides these four basic operators, 'C' also supports additional operators such as increment, decrement, conditional and assignment. Basic operators and others along with their symbolic representation are shown in Table 3.1.

Table 3.1 Types of Operators

Type of Operator	Symbolic Representation
Arithmetic Operators	+, −, *, / and %
Relational Operators	>, <, = =, >=.<= and !=
Logical Operators	&&, || and !
Increment and Decrement Operator	++ and − −
Assignment Operator	=, +=, −=, *=, /=, %=

(Continued)

Table 3.1 (Continued)

Type of Operator	Symbolic Representation
Bitwise Operators	&, |, ^, >>, << and ~
Comma Operator	,
Conditional Operator	?:

Arithmetic operators: They are used to perform arithmetic operations such as addition, subtraction, multiplication and division between integers/floating numbers.

Relational operators: These operators provide relationship between two expressions. If the relation is true then it returns a value 1 otherwise 0 for false. They are used to perform relational operations such as finding the greater or smaller of the operands, checking the equality of the operands etc.

Logical operators: Logical relationship between the two expressions is tested with logical operators. Each relational operator takes two expressions as operands and results either the integer value 1(**true**) or the integer value 0(False). The operands could be constants, variables, and expressions.

Bitwise operators: 'C' supports a set of bitwise operators for bit manipulation as listed in the Table 3.1. 'C' supports six-bit operators. These operators can operate only on integer operands such as `int`, `char`, `short`, `long` etc.

Assignment operator: Assigning a value to a variable is done with assignment operator. For example `int` $x = 5$; here 5 is assigned to x and this is carried out by the operator =. The equal (=) operator is used for assignment and hence the name assignment operator. We can associate assignment operator with other binary operators. Such a type of association of operators is called compound assignment operators.

Unary Operators: Unary operator performs operation on an operand. Unary operators are increment operator (++), decrement (−−), minus (−) etc.

Besides there are some other operators in C, which are not covered in this question.

3. What are the uses of comma (,) and conditional (?) operators?

Ans: The 'comma operator' is used to separate two or more expressions.
It is not essential to enclose the expressions with comma operators within the parentheses. We need to use comma operator in variable declaration, `printf`, `scanf` functions, in function prototypes etc.

For example, comma operators are used in the following expressions.

```
int a, b, c;
printf("%d %d", a, b);
```

The 'conditional operator' contains condition followed by two statements or values. The condition operator is also called the ternary operator. If the condition is true, the first statement is executed; otherwise, the second statement is executed. The condition operator is used when there are two different values to be used based on some condition.

An example on conditional operator is as follows:

Expr 1? Expr 2: Expr 3;

Expr 1 is evaluated first and if it is true, then Expr 2 is evaluated and its value is the result. If Expr 1 is false, then Expr 3 is evaluated and its value becomes the final answer.

```
(x>y)?printf("%d", x): printf("%d", y):
```

In the above example in case x is greater than y, then first `printf` gets evaluated and if is false, then second `printf` statement gets evaluated.

4. What are unary operators? Describe their uses.

Unary operators operate on only one operand. Examples of unary operators are increment, decrement, unary minus and & operator. Out of these, the increment operator increases the value of operand by one (++a), the decrement operand decrements the value of operand by one (—a), the unary minus operator is used to invert the sign of the operand (−a) and the & operator is used to dereference the operator.

Unary operators and their meanings are given in the Table 3.2.

Table 3.2 Unary Arithmetic Operators

Operator	Meaning or Action
−	Minus
++	Increment
−−	Decrement
&	Address operator
`sizeof()`	Gives the size of operator

5. Describe logical operators with their `return` values.

Ans: Logical operators perform the logical operations on the operands. Logical AND, OR, NOT etc. are the examples of logical operators. The value returned by the logical operators is either zero or one. When more than one condition is to be checked at a time, then logical operators are to be used. Result of operation is 1 if condition is true, `else` 0.

For example, on logical operators

(a && b), where && is logical AND

(a || b), where || is logical OR

! a, where ! is logical NOT

Table 3.3 describes the three logical operators together with examples and their `return` values.

Table 3.3 Logical Operators

<table>
<tr><th>Operator</th><th>Description or Action</th><th>Example</th><th>Return Value</th></tr>
<tr><td>&&</td><td>Logical AND</td><td>5>3 && 5<10</td><td>1</td></tr>
<tr><td>||</td><td>Logical OR</td><td>8>5 || 8<2</td><td>1</td></tr>
<tr><td>!</td><td>Logical NOT</td><td>8!=8</td><td>0</td></tr>
</table>

6. List the bitwise logical or binary operators supported by C.

Ans: C supports a set of bitwise operators for bit manipulation as listed in Table 3.4. These operators operate only on integer operands.

Table 3.4 Bitwise Operators

<table>
<tr><th>Operator</th><th>Meaning</th></tr>
<tr><td>>></td><td>Right Shift</td></tr>
<tr><td><<</td><td>Left Shift</td></tr>
<tr><td>^</td><td>Bitwise XOR (Exclusive OR)</td></tr>
<tr><td>~</td><td>One's Complement</td></tr>
<tr><td>&</td><td>Bitwise AND</td></tr>
<tr><td>|</td><td>Bitwise OR</td></tr>
</table>

7. Distinguish between logical and bitwise operators.

Ans: The logical operators perform the operations such as AND and OR with a single result that is either zero or non-zero, whereas bitwise operators operate on the bit stream obtained from the binary equivalent of the operand.

8. What are the relational operators?

Ans: Relational operators are used to perform comparison between two operands such as less than, greater than, equality and inequality. These operators are used to check the conditions. In case condition is true, the result returned would be 1 otherwise 0.

Assume that $a = 5$ and $b = 2$.

Result of the following expressions would as follows:

$(a > b)$ result of this expression is 1.
$(a < b)$ result of this expression is 0.

One can use different relational operators as listed below and see the results.

>,<,>=,<=,!=

The relational operators together with their descriptions, examples and their `return` values are given in Table 3.5.

Table 3.5 Relational Operators

Operator	Description or Action	Example	`Return` Value
>	Greater than	5>4	1
<	Less than	10<9	0
<=	Less than or equal to	10<=10	1
>=	Greater than equal to	11>=5	1
= =	Equal to	2==3	0
!=	Not equal to	3!=3	0

9. What is the difference between '=' and '= ='?

Ans: The operator '=' is the assignment operator used to assign the value. The operator '==' is equality operator use for comparing the values of the two operands / expressions. These two operators are completely different.

10. What are the symbols used for (a) OR, (b) AND, (c) XOR and (d) NOT operations?

Ans:

Bitwise OR uses | operator.
Bitwise AND uses & operator.
Bitwise NOT uses ! operator.
Bitwise XOR uses ^ operator.

11. What is the order of precedence of arithmetic operators such as *, /, +, and – etc ?

Ans: Precedence refers to the priority allotted to the different operators for processing. When an expression contains many operators then the high priority operators are evaluated first before lower priority operators.

Among arithmetic operators, the operators such as multiplication (*), division (/) and modulus (%) have highest priority and similar precedence. The operator + and – are having lowest precedence.

Example: 8 + 9 * 2 – 10

The operator * is highest priority. Hence multiplication operation is performed first.

The evaluation of expression is = 8 + 18 – 10

In the above expression + and – are having same priority. In such situation, associativity rule for operators to be followed i.e. left to right. The left most operation is evaluated first.

Further the evaluation of expression is = 26 – 10 and at last the result is 16.

In case expressions are within the bracket then they are evaluated first. In case same precedence operates appear in the expression and that too inside the parenthesis, then the associativity rule is followed for evaluation.

The result of the following expression is 1. Because evaluation starts from left to right.

$$((((2 + 3) - 4) * 5) - 4)$$

Following Table 3.6 shows the assessment of few arithmetic expressions by means of the precedence and associativity rule.

Table 3.6 Arithmetic Expressions Using Precedence and Associativity Rule

Expression	Corresponding expression	Result
3 + 5 – 4	(3 + 5) – 4	4
4 * 5 + 7	(4 * 5) + 7	27
2 * 10 + 10/2	(2 * 10) + (10/2)	25
2 + 3 – 2 + 6 * 5 + 5/2	((2 + 3) –2) + (6 * 5) + (5/2)	35

12. What are the differences between division and modulus division operations?

Ans: The division operator (/) returns the quotient of the division of two operands and the modulus division operator (%) returns the remainder of the division operation of the two operands.

Example: Assume that $x = 10$ and $y = 3$.

x/*y* operation gives result 3 and *x*%*y* gives result 1.

13. What are the limitations on modulus operator?

Ans: Modulus operator is to be applied only on integers, but not on floating numbers.

14. What are the ASCII codes? List the codes for digits 1 to 9, A to Z and a to z.

Ans: ASCII codes are the corresponding physical representation of all the characters used by C language; it has different values ranging from 0 to 255 for different characters. The ranges of the ASCII codes for the characters listed below are as follows:

1–9 ASCII value from 48 to 57.

A–Z ASCII value from 65 to 90.

a–z ASCII value from 97 to 122.

15. What is an assignment operator?

Ans: Assigning a constant value to a variable or value of one variable to another is done with assignment operator. For example, `int x=5;` here 5 is assigned to *x* and this is carried out by the operator =. The equal (=) is used for assignment and hence the name assignment operator.

16. List the assignment operators.

Ans: The list of assignment operators are given in Table 3.7.

Table 3.7 Assignment Operators

=	*=	/=	%=
+=	−=	<<=	>>=

17. What are compound assignment operators?

Ans: A compound assignment operator consists of a binary operator and assignment operator. They carry out binary operation and assign the result to the left operand.
Compound assignment operators and equivalent expressions are as follows:

a += *b* is equivalent to *a* = *a* + *b*

a −= *b* is equivalent to *a* = *a* − *b*

a *= *b* is equivalent to *a* = *a* * *b*

a /= *b* is equivalent to *a* = *a*/*b*

a %= *b* is equivalent to *a* = *a*%*b*

a <<= *b* is equivalent to *a* = *a* << *b*

a >>= *b* is equivalent to *a* = *a* >> *b*

a &= *b* is equivalent to *a* = *a*&*b*

a |= *b* is equivalent to *a* = *a*|*b*

a ^= *b* is equivalent to *a* = *a*^*b*

18. Explain precedence and associativity of operators.

Ans: Operators have the following properties:

1. Precedence: It refers to the priority given to the operator `while` evaluation of an expression. When an expression contains many operators, the operations are carried out according to the priority of the operators. The higher precedence operations are evaluated first.
2. Associativity: When an expression has operators with equal precedence, the associativity property decides which operation to be carried out first. Associativity means the direction of execution. It has two types.
   (a) Left to right: In this type, the expression evaluation starts from the left to the right direction.
   (b) Right to left: In this type, the expression evaluation starts from the right to the left direction.

19. What are the differences between precedence and associativity?

Ans: Precedence decides which operator to execute first when there are more than one different operators with different priorities. On the other hand, associativity decides which operator to execute first when there is more than one operator with same priority.

20. What is the difference between pre- and post-increments?

Ans: Consider the following pre- and post-increment operators:

1. Pre-increment example ++*a*;
2. Post-increment example *a*++;

In the first case, the variable *a*'s value is incremented first before being used and in the second case value of *a* is incremented after being used.

Programming example:

```
void main()
{
int a=2;
printf( "\n%d",++a);
printf( "\n%d",a++);
printf( "\n%d",a);
getche();
}

OUTPUT:
3
3
4
```

21. Comment on the execution speed of ++*a* and *a* +1.

Ans: ++*a* execution is faster than *a* +1. ++*a* needs single machine instruction and *a* +1 needs more instructions. In the latter case, the value of the variable is to be stored in the memory first and then it is be fetched by CPU and stored in some register and then 1 is added. After this process, result is assigned to *a*. Result of this operation is to be stored in the memory. Hence, CPU consumes more time. This procedure of execution needs more time. Hence, ++*a* is faster than *a* +1.
Note: Nowadays compilers are smarter, if it encounters *i* +1, then it replaces it by *i*++. Hence, it really does not matter for user since optimization is gained by compiler.

22. What are the rules for using unary ++ and – – operators?

Ans:

1. The operand should not be a constant but it should be a variable.
2. The ++ and — should not be applied on an expression.
3. The operator ++ and — may succeed or precede the operand.

23. What are the uses of masking?

Ans: A bit or desired bits of a binary number can be set to 0 with the help of masking. The AND operator is required for masking.

24. Which binary operator is suitable to check a bit is on or off?

Ans: & (AND) operator is suitable for checking whether a particular bit is on or off.
Following example can be referred for understanding the question.

```
void main()
{
int a=02,b=02;
printf("%d",a&b);
```

```
getche();
}

OUTPUT:
02
```

Due to ANDing between 02 and 02 answer returns 02. In case b = 00, the answer becomes 00.

25. Which binary operator is used for addition of two numbers?

Ans: EX-OR operator can be used for addition of two numbers.
One can verify from the following program.

```
void main()
{
int a=2,b=4;
printf("%d",a^b);
getche();
}

OUTPUT:
6
```

26. What is the `'sizeof()'` operator in C? Explain the use of `'sizeof()'`operator by using a `short` program?

Ans: The `'sizeof()'` operator is a unary operator. The `'sizeof()'` operator returns the size of data type/operand in bytes. The operand may be a variable or data type. Size of various data types are listed Table 3.8.

Table 3.8 Sizes of Various Data Types

Data Type	Size in Bytes
char	1
int	2
long int	4
float	4
double float	8
long double	10

Program by using `'sizeof()'` operator.

```
#include <stdio.h>
#include <conio.h>
void main()
{
 char a;
 printf("\n Sizeof(a) = %d bytes",sizeof(a));
```

```
 printf("\n Sizeof(int) = %d bytes",sizeof(int));
}

OUTPUT:
Sizeof(a) = 1 bytes
Sizeof(int) = 2 bytes
```

27. How can multiple assignments be written in C? Explain it with programming one example.

Ans: The syntax of multiple assignments is as follows: **identifier1=identifier2= identifier3=...............identifier N= value or expression.**

Note: The assignments are carried out from right to left.

Example:

```
#include <stdio.h>
#include <conio.h>
void main()
{
clrscr();
int x,y,z;
clrscr();
x=y=z=10;
printf("x = %d \ny = %d \nz = %d ",x,y,z);
getch();
}

OUTPUT:
x = 10
y = 10
z = 10
```

Explanation: In the above program, the expression $x = y = z = 10$ uses multiple assignment operator. The value 10 will be assigned to *x*, *y* and *z* from right to left, i.e., first assigns to *z*, then to *y* and at last to *x*.

28. Which type of operator is logical not? What is the associativity of logical NOT?

Ans: The not '!' is unary operator. Not operator negates the value of expression. The unary not operator is also known as logical not operator. The associativity of logical operator is from right to left.

29. What is type casting? Give an example.

Ans: It is a data type converter. For example, floating number can be converted to integers or result that produces integers can be converted to floating. The expected type of data is to be placed within the parentheses.

Programming example is as follows:

```
void main()
{
int a=12,b=5;
printf("%f",(float)a/b);
getche();
}

2.400000
void main()
{
float a=12.40;
printf("%d",(int)a);
}

OUTPUT:
12
```

30. Which binary shifting is equivalent to dividing an `unsigned` number by 2: right shifting by 1 or left sifting by 1?

Ans: Dividing an `unsigned` number by 2 is equivalent to right shifting an `unsigned` number by 1 is the correct option. This can be verified from the following example:

```
void main()
{
unsigned int a=8,b=1;
printf("%d",a>>b);
}

OUTPUT:
4
```

31. What is the difference between shift right (>>) and shift left (<<) operators?

Ans: The shift right >> operator shifts the bits of the variable/operand to right side. The shift left << operator is used to shift the bits of the variable/operand to left.

The syntax of shift right operator is as follows:

Variable >> number of bits to shift right.

The syntax of shift left operator is as follows:

Variable << number of bits to shift left.

The difference between shift right and shift left operator is as follows:

1. The shift right operator is used to divide the number by 2.
2. The shift left operator is used to multiply the number by 2.

Example:

Value of i	Execution of Each Statement	Final Value of i
i=4	00000100	4
I =i<<1	00001000	8
i=i>>1	00000010	2
i=i>>2	00000001	1

32. Which binary shifting is equivalent to multiplying an `unsigned` number by 2: right shifting by 1 or left sifting by 1?

Ans: Multiplying an `unsigned` number by 2 is equivalent to left shifting an `unsigned` number by 1 is the correct option. This can be verified from the following example:

```
void main()
{
unsigned int a=8,b=1;
printf("%d",a<<b);
}

OUTPUT:
16
```

33. What is the equivalent expression for x&3?

Ans: The equivalent expression for x&3 is x%4.

34. What is the result of expression (23*2) % (`int`) 5. 5?

Ans: 1

Explanation: As per precedence of operators multiplication of 23 and 2 is performed first, result of which is 46. Floating number 5.5 is converted to 5 due to type casting used in the expression. Ultimately, result of 46%5 is 1. Modulus operator provides remainder.

35. What is the result of 16>> 2?

Ans: 4

Explanation: Number 16 is shifted two bits right. This is as good as 16 is divided first by two and then result 8 is again divided by 2 whose result is 4.

36. What is the output of the following program?

```
void main()
{
int a=16,b=4;
clrscr();
printf("%d",a<<a/b-2;
}

OUTPUT:
64
```

Explanation: In the above program a/b – 2 works out to be 2. As per precedence of operators, division operator is performed first and then subtraction. Hence, a is shifted right two bits and, therefore, result is 64.

37. What is the result of 5&&2?

Ans: 1

Explanation: Logical ANDing between 5 and 2 is 1. Hence, the result is 1.

Multiple-choice Questions

Examples on Arithmetic Operators

1. What is the remainder of 9% 10 ________?

   (a) 5 (b) 2 (c) 1 (d) 9

2. What is the result of the expression ((10*2)*(10/5)%11)?

   (a) 7 (b) 10 (c) 8 (d) None of them

3. What is the result of expression (`float`)(12/4) * (`int`) 5. 3 ________?

   (a) 15.0000000 (b) 1 (c) 3 (d) None of them

4. What is the result of 4|2?

   (a) 1 (b) 6 (c) 2 (d) 0

5. Which of the following bracket is suitable for evaluation of arithmetic operations ________?

   (a) [ ] (b) { } (c) ( ) (d) None of the above

6. Multiplication (*) and division(/) operators have ________ priority than addition (+) operator.

   (a) Lower (b) Higher (c) Similar

Examples on Logical Operators

7. What is the result of 10&&4?

   (a) 0 (b) 1 (c) 2 (d) 5

8. The && operator is used to ________.

   (a) Compare two numeric value (b) Compare two `float` values
   (c) Compare two Boolean values (d) None of the above

Examples on Bitwise Operators

9. What is the result of 4 << 2?

(a) 8 (b) 16 (c) 2 (d) 0

10. The associativity of bitwise operators is ________.

(a) Right to left (b) Left to right (c) Both (a) and (b) (d) None of the above

Examples on Unary, Increment and Decrement Operator

11. The associatively of operators unary minus, increment and decrement is ________.

(a) Right to left (b) Left to right (c) Both (a) (b) (d) None of them

12. What is the result of the following program?

```
void main()
{
int a,x=15,y=10;
clrscr();
a=--x*y++;
printf("\n %d",a);
}
```

(a) 140 (b) 200 (c) 380 (d) 210

13. What will be the output of the following program?

```
#include <stdio.h>
#include <conio.h>
void main()
{
  int ans=2;
  int m=10;
  int k;
  k=!((ans<2) || (m>2));
   printf("\n %d",k);
}
```

(a) 1 (b) 0 (c) 2 (d) 4

14. What will be the output of the following program?

```
#include <stdio.h>
#include <conio.h>
void main()
{
  int m,j=3,k;
  m=2*j/2;
```

```
  k=2*(j/2);
  clrscr();
   printf("\n m=%d k=%d",m,k);
}
```

(a) $m=3$ $k=2$ (b) $m=3$ $k=3$ (c) $m=2$ $k=3$ (d) $m=2$ $k=2$

15. What will be the value of x, y and z after execution of the following program?

```
#include <stdio.h>
#include <conio.h>
void main()
{
int x,y,z;
y=2;
x=2;
x=2*(y++);
z=2*(++y);
printf("\n x=%d y=%d z=%d",x,y,z);
}
```

(a) $x=4$ $y=4$ $z=8$ (b) $x=6$ $y=4$ $z=8$ (c) $x=2$ $y=4$ $z=8$ (d) $x=4$ $y=4$ $z=4$

16. What will be the value of x after execution of the following program?

```
#include <stdio.h>
#include <conio.h>
void main()
{
   int x=!0*0;
}
```

(a) 0 (b) 1 (c) 10 (d) None of the above

17. What will be the value of k after execution of the following program?

```
void main()
{
int b,k=8;
b=(k++ - k++-k++,k++);
printf(" %d",k);
}
```

(a) 11 (b) 12 (c) 7 (d) 9

18. What will be the output of the following program?

```
void main()
{
int i=1,j=2,k=3;
clrscr();
printf("%d",!((j+k)>(i+5)));
}
```

(a) 0 (b) 1 (c) −1 (d) 2

19. What will be the value of *j* after execution?

```
void main()
{
float j=8,k=5; j*=k*+3.145;
clrscr();
printf("j=%g",j);
}
```

(a) 125.8 (b) 124.9 (c) 124.8 (d) 0

20. What will be the value of *y*?

```
(a) void main()
{
float y;
y=22/8*(3.145+2)*8/5;
clrscr();
printf("y=%g",y);
}
```

(a) 16.464 (b) 16.064
(c) 16 (d) 0

21. In C language, the compound statement $a* = a + 2$; means _________.

(a) a = a*(a + 2); (b) a = a*a + 2; (c) a = a + a*2; (d) a = a + 2*a;

22. In C language, the compound statement a%=5; means _________.

(a) a = a%5; (b) a = 5%a; (c) a = a*a%5; (d) a = a%5/5;

23. In C language, the statement *a*|*b*; means _________.

(a) AND operation between *a* and *b*
(b) OR operation between *a* and *b*
(c) NOT operation between *a* and *b*
(d) EXOR operation between *a* and *b*

24. In C language, the notation for 'not equal to' is _________.

(a) =! (b) != (c) ~! (d) ^!

25. Which of the following operator/s in C have the highest precedence?

(a) Comma operator (b) Arithmetic operators
(c) Logical operators (d) Bitwise operators

26. Which of the following operator in C has the highest precedence?

(a) * (b) + (c) <= (d) ~

27. Which of the following increment and decrement operators respectively in C are valid?

(a) + and – (b) ++ and – – (c) =+ and =– (d) += and –=

28. Which of the following operator requires three operands?

(a) Right shift (>>) (b) Comma (,)
(c) Ternary operator (?:) (d) Logical AND (&&)

29. Compile time operator is _________.

(a) Comma (b) Modulus (c) Right shift (d) `sizeof()`

30. Which data type is required for modules operator?

(a) Floating (b) Character (c) Integer (d) Long floating

31. What is the result of the following statement?

```
printf("%f",(float)14/3);
```

(a) 2.3 (b) 3.2 (c) 3.00 (d) 4.66

32. Which of the following is not a formatted function?

(a) `scanf()` (b) `printf()` (c) `gets()` (d) None of the above

33. What is the output of `sizeof (float)`?

(a) 2 (b) 1 (c) 4 (d) 8

34. p% q means

(a) (p – (p/q)*q) (b) (p + (p/q)*q) (c) (p*(p/q)*q) (d) None of the above

35. Bit wise ^ (EX_OR) operator is used for _________.

(a) Addition of numbers (b) Subtraction of numbers
(c) Multiplication of numbers (d) Compliment the bits

36. Which of the following is Boolean operator for logical OR?

(a) & (b) | (c) ! (d) &&

37. Which of the following is Boolean operator for logical EXOR?

(a) & (b) | (c) ^ (d) ||

38. Which of the following is Boolean operator for logical NOT (inverter)?

(a) ~ (b) | (c) ^

Answers

1. (d) 2. (a) 3. (a) 4. (b) 5. (c) 6. (b) 7. (b) 8. (c) 9. (b) 10. (b)
11. (a) 12. (a) 13. (b) 14. (a) 15. (a) 16. (a) 17. (b) 18. (b) 19. (a) 20. (a)
21. (a) 22. (a) 23. (a) 24. (b) 25. (b) 26. (a) 27. (b) 28. (c) 29. (d) 30. (c)
31. (d) 32. (c) 33. (c) 34. (c) 35. (d) 36. (b) 37. (c) 38. (a)

True or False

1. + is symbolic representation of increment operator.
2. In C, x=x–1 can be written as x– –.
3. Number of bytes needed to store a variable is indicated by `sizeof()` operator.
4. The '&' operator prints address of the variable.
5. >> is the relational operator.
6. >= is the binary operator.
7. != is the relational operator.
8. The logical AND (&&) operator provides true result when both expressions are true.
9. The logical NOT operator (!) provides 0 if the condition is true otherwise 1.
10. The logical OR (||) operator provides false result when one of the expressions is true.
11. Bitwise EX-OR operation is performed by the operator &.
12. One's complement is performed by operator ~.
13. Bitwise OR is performed by the operator |.

Answers

1. False 2. True 3. True 4. True 5. False 6. False 7. True 8. True 9. False 10. False 11. False
12. True 13. True

Additional Questions

What are the outputs of the following programs?

Questions on arithmetic operators

1. Enter basic salary of an employee as Rs 20000 and compute the output of the following program

```
void main()
{
float bas=20000,tot;
clrscr();
```

```
tot=bas+0.30*bas+0.18*bas;
printf("Total salary = %10.2f\n",tot);
getche();
}

OUTPUT:
Total salary = 29600.00
```

2. Program on some arithmetic operators

```
void main()
{
int a=32763, b=5,c;
unsigned int p=65535,q=1,r;
clrscr();
c=a+b,
r=p+q;
printf("\n c= %d",c);
printf("\n r= %u",r);
getche();
}

OUTPUT:
c = -32768
r = 0
```

3. Enter the principal amount, year and rate of interest as 5000 3 2 respectively. Find the output?

```
void main()
{
int prin=2000,year=2;
float rate=5,simple;
clrscr();
simple=prin*rate*year/100;
printf("\n %5.2f \n",simple);
getche();
}

OUTPUT:
200.00
```

4. Enter the radius and compute the area of the circle?

```
void main()
{
float area,radius=3.5;
const float pi=3.1413;
clrscr();
area=pi*radius*radius;
printf("\nArea of a circle =%2.2f",area);
getche();
}

OUTPUT:
Area of a circle =38.48
```

5. Program to convert decimal 10 in to Binary

```
void main()
{
     int n=10,i,x=7,y=3;
     clrscr();
     printf("Binary equivalent of decimal numer 10 is");
     while(n!=0)
     {
     i=n%2;
     n=n/2;
     gotoxy(x,y);
     printf("%d",i);
     x--;
     }
     getch();
}

OUTPUT:
Binary equivalent of 10 is 1010
```

6. Program on arithmetic operators.

```
#include <stdio.h>
#include <conio.h>
void main()
{
  clrscr();
  printf("%d",1000%5);
```

```
  printf("%d",1010%10);
  printf("%d",11010%15);
  printf("%d",0101110%20);
  getche();
}

OUTPUT:
00012
```

Examples on relational operators

7. Program on relational operators.

```
void main()
{
int x=40,y=80;
clrscr();
x<<=1,y>>=2;
printf("%d %d ",x,y);
getche();
}

OUTPUT:
80 20
```

8. Program on simple problem

```
void main()
{
clrscr();
printf("\n %d",15==15);
printf("  %d",11>=15);
printf(" %d",7<8);
printf("  %d", 'C'=='c');

getche();
}

OUTPUT:
1010
```

Examples on logical operators

9. Program on simple logical problem

```
void main()
{
int a=4,b=2,m,n,o;
clrscr();
m=a&&b;
n=a||b;
o=a==b;
printf("\n%d",m);
printf("\n%d",n);
printf("\n%d",o);
getche();
}

OUTPUT:
1
1
0
```

Examples on relational and logical operators

10. Program on simple logical problem

```
void main()
{
int  x=2,y=0,z=8,p;
clrscr();
z=x>y&&y;
p=x||z;
printf("\n%d\n%d",z,p);
getch();
}

OUTPUT:
0
1
```

11. Program on logical problem

```
void main()
{
int  x=2000,y=1000,z=20,p;
clrscr();
p=(x>z && y<z);
printf("\n%d",p);
getch();
}

OUTPUT:
0
```

12. Program on logical operation

```
#include <stdio.h>
#include <conio.h>

void main()
{
clrscr();
printf("\nCondition     : Return Values\n" );
printf("\n5>3 && 5<10   : %5d",5>3 && 5<10);
printf("\n 8>5 || 8<2   : %5d",8>5 || 8<2);
printf("\n !(8==8)      : %5d",!(8==8));
}

OUTPUT:
Condition : Return Values
5>3 && 5<10 : 1
8>5 || 8<2  : 1
!(8==8)     : 0
```

Examples are given on (+) unary operator

13. Program on unary operator

```
void main()
{
float  a=+15.4,c=-4.6;
clrscr();
c+=a;
```

```
printf("%10.2f",c);
getche();
}

OUTPUT:
10.80
```

14. Program on unary operator

```
void main()
{
int x=40,y=50,z=10;
clrscr();
x+=y;
z+=x;
printf("%d\n%d ",x,z );
getch();
}

OUTPUT:
90
100
```

Examples on `sizeof()` and & operators

15. Find the size of bytes for integer, character and `long` integers.

```
void main()
{
clrscr();
printf("\n size of int =%d",sizeof(int));
printf("\n size of char =%d",sizeof(char));
printf("\n size of long =%d",sizeof(long));
getche();
}

OUTPUT:
size of int =2
size of char =1
size of long =4
```

16. Find the size of bytes for integer, character and long integers.

```
#include <stdio.h>
#include <conio.h>

void main()
{
char x='a';
int y=2;
long int z=23456;
float p=2.345;
double q=12e10;
clrscr();
printf("\n size of a character(x)=%d byte",sizeof(x));
printf("\n size of an integer(y)=%d bytes",sizeof(y));
printf("\n size of long integer(z)=%d bytes",sizeof(z));
printf("\n size of float(p)=%d bytes",sizeof(p));
printf("\n size of double float (q)=%d bytes",sizeof(q));
printf("\n Address of x=%u y=%u z=%u p=%u q=%u",&x,&y,&z,&p,&q);
getche();
}

OUTPUT:
size of a character(x)=1 byte
size of an integer(y)=2 bytes
size of long integer(z)=4 bytes
size of float(p)=4 bytes
size of double float (q)=8 bytes
Address of x =65479 y =65480 z =65482 p =65486 q =65490
```

Examples on bitwise operators.

17. Left and right shift

```
void main()
{
int x=2,y=16,z;
clrscr();
x<<=2,y>>=1;
x&=y;
z=y|x;
printf("%d %d ",x,z);
getche();
}

OUTPUT:
8 8
```

18. Complement and ORing operation

```
void main()
{
int p=2,x=8,y=5,z;
clrscr();
x=~x;
z=y|p;
printf("%d %d",x,z);
getche();
}

OUTPUT:
-9 7
```

Find the bug/s in the following program/s.

Arithmetic operators

1.

```
void main()
{
int x=2,y=2,z=4;
clrscr();
z=((x+y)*z/2);
printf("%f",z);
}
```

Bug: `%f` is not expected in `printf()`. With `%d` the answer would be 8

2.

```
void main()
{
int x=10,y=20,z=30;
clrscr();
z=((x+y)*z/2);
z=z%4;
print("%d",z);
}
```

Bug: `printf()` is needed instead of print
Answer with correction would be 4

3.

```
void main()
{
int x=2,y=3,z;
x+y=z;
printf("z=%d",z);
}
```

Bug: Variable must be at left side

4.

```
void main()
{
clrscr();
printf("%d %d",+2,2+);
}
```

Bug: 2+ is not allowed

Relational operators

5.

```
void main()
{
clrsr();
printf("\n %d",20==15);
printf("  %d",10>=15);
printf(" %d",9<8);
printf("  %d", 'A'=='a');
}
```

Bug: Replace `clrsr` with `clrscr()` and answer of all conditional statements would be 0

6.

```
void main()
{
char a=4,b=16,m,n,o;
clrscr();
m=a<2;
n=b>3;
o=a!=b;
```

```
printf("\n%c",m);
printf("\n%c",n);
printf("\n%c",o);
getche();
}
```

Bug: Replace c by d in all `printf()` statements. Answer will be

```
0
1
1
```

7.

```
void main()
{
int x=2,z;
clrscr();
z=x=>2;
printf("%d",z);
}
```

Bug: => operator is invalid

Logical operators and conditional operator

8.

```
void main()
{
char p=90;
int a;
clrscr();
a=(p>=65 && p<=90 ? 1 : 0);
printf("Y :%c",a);
getche();
}
```

Bug: Replace `%c` with `%d` in `printf()` and answer would be Y:1

9.

```
void main()
{
int a,b,c;
clrscr();
a=4;
b=2;
c=(a<<b && b>>1 );
printf("\n c=%c",c);
getche();
}
```

Bug: Replace `%c` by `%d` in `printf()` and answer would be c = 1

4

Input and Output in C

1. What are the formatted and unformatted functions?

Ans: The formatted input and output functions supported by C are `scanf()` and `printf()` respectively. The `scanf()` reads the data into a variable from the keyboard and `printf()` prints/writes the formatted data on the monitor screen. The letter `f` in the `printf` and `scanf` stands for formatted. As per requirement, input and output data provided can be arranged in meticulous formatted.

It is essential for a programmer to provide proper conversion symbol/control string in the input and output functions to identify the data type. The control string in the input and output functions create formatted results. The `return` values are equal to the number of variables/arguments specified in the function and it must match with the fields of format specified in the control string of input/output functions.

The syntax of formatted input function `scanf()` is as follows:

```
scanf(control_string, argument1, argument2,---------, argument n);
```

Example: `scanf("%d",&x);`

Where `%d` is the control string that specifies the field format in which the data is to be entered. The other part is the variable x and a sign & (ampersand) must precede to x. The &x is the address location of the variable x.

Similarly, the syntax of formatted output function `printf()` is as follows:

```
printf(control_string, argument1, argument2,---------, argument n);
```

Example: `printf("%d %f %c",x,y,z);`

Here the control string is `%d %f %c` (type of values) and arguments are `x y z` are the identifiers whose data is to be printed.

Unformatted functions: The unformatted input/output functions work only with character data type. They do not require format conversion symbol for the formatting of data types, because they work only with character data type. There is no need to convert data.

In case values of other data types are passed to these functions, they are treated as character data.

A few examples of unformatted functions supported by C are as follows:

`getche()`, `getch()`, `gets()`, `getchar()`, `puts()` etc.

`getch()` accepts a character from a keyboard and can be stored in a variable.

`getche()` is similar to `getch()`. It also accepts a character from a keyboard and can be stored in a variable. However, unlike `getch()`, `getche()` displays the character on the screen.

2. What is the difference between character I/O and string I/O?

Ans: Character I/O: These functions work with single character at a time, e.g., `getc()`, `putc()`, etc.

String I/O: These functions work with set of characters (i.e., strings) at a time, e.g., `gets()`, `puts()`, etc.

3. What is the escape sequence? List and indicate the functions of escape sequences.

Ans: The `printf()` and `scanf()` statements follow the combination of characters called escape sequences. In order to come out, computers from routine sequence escape sequences are used. These are nothing but special characters starting with '\'. It is a combination of back slash(\) followed by a letter or combination of digits. Escape sequence in 'C' is viewed as single character and, therefore, it is a legitimate character constant. Following table gives escape sequence and their representations.

Escape Sequence	Meaning
\n	New line
\b	Backspace
\f	Form feed
\'	Single quote
\\	Backslash
\0	Null
\t	Horizontal tab
\r	Carriage `return`
\a	Alert
\"	Double quote
\v	Vertical tab
\?	Question mark
\ooo	Octal notation
\X hh	Hexadecimal notation

4. List any three escape sequences with their uses.

Ans:

1. \t: It is used for displaying a tab.
2. \n: It is used for displaying a new line.
3. \b: It is used for a backspace.

5. What is the difference between `puts()` and `putch()`?

Ans:

`puts()`: This function prints the string or character array.

`putch()`: This function prints any alphanumeric character (single character) taken by the standard input device.

6. What is the difference between `getch()` and `getche()`?

Ans: These functions are used to read the character from the standard input device. The `getch()` function gets the character from the console with no echo. Whereas `getche()` function gets the character from the console with echo.

7. Which are the character-oriented functions?

Ans:

1. `putchar();`
2. `getchar();`

8. Which header file is used for using i/o library functions?

Ans: `#include <stdio.h>` header file is supporting to any i/o library function. Hence, this header file is needed.

9. What is the use of & in the `scanf()` function?

Ans: The operator & is used to obtain an address of a variable. It is associated with the argument in the `scanf()` function. It is to be preceded to a variable.

10. Give the syntax of `getchar()`.

Ans:

```
Variable = getchar();
```

Example:

```
x=getchar();
```

Note: Value entered through the keyboard is stored in the variable x.

11. Give the syntax of `putchar()`.

Ans:

```
putchar(variable);
```

Example:

```
x=getchar();
putchar(x);
```

Note: Value entered through the keyboard is stored in the variable *x*. The stored value in *x* is displayed on the screen with the help of **`putchar()`**.

12. Write a program to read any one character or digit integer through keyboard by using `getchar()` and display it by using `putchar()`.

Ans:

```
#include<stdio.h>
#include<conio.h>
void main()
{
int x;
clrscr();
```

```
printf("Enter any alphanumeric: ");
x=getchar();
/* read char or number through keyboard */
putchar(x);
/* print on the screen */
getche();
}

OUTPUT:
Enter any alphanumeric: k
k
```

13. How `cgets()` is different from `gets()`?

Ans:

`gets()`: This function is used for accepting any string through stdin (keyboard) until enter key is pressed.

`cgets()`: This function reads string from the console. The syntax is as follows:

`char *cgets(char *st);`

It requires character pointer as an argument. The string begins from st[2].

14. How will you execute a DOS command through C program?

Ans: The `system()` function is helpful in executing different DOS commands. It returns 0 on success and –1 on failure.

The syntax is as follows:

Syntax:

```
system ("COMMAND");
```

The command should be enclosed within double quotation marks.

15. What is the use of the `exit()` function?

Ans: This function terminates the program. It is defined in process.h header file.

16. What is a stream?

Ans: Stream is a sequence of characters, e.g. “ABCDE”, “as 9” etc.

17. What are the tips to design the output?

Ans:

1. Give space between numbers.
2. Provide suitable and problem-related variable names and headings.
3. Provide user prompt, so that the user can understand what to do.
4. Provide a gap between two lines, so that the text should be readable.
5. Alert the user about what to do and what not to do.
6. Use formatted inputs and outputs for precisely inputting the data and outputting results.
7. It is recommended to use escape sequence characters such as \t, \b and \n.

Multiple-choice Questions

1. Which of the following is not character constant?

   (a) ‘a’ (b) ‘\’
   (c) ‘\n’ (d) ‘’’’

2. Which of the following is character constant?

   (a) ‘k (b) \’
   (c) ‘/’ (d) ‘\’

3. Which of the following is a valid string constant?

   (a) “pearson,” “ \”Education” (b) “pearson” , \“education”
   (c) “pearson” \”Education” (d) “person””

4. Which of the following is not a string constant?

   (a) “Pearson” (b) “**&&^”
   (c) “pearson,” “\”Education” (d) “pearson” \”Education”

5. What will be the output of the following program?

```
void main()
{
 printf("\n %d%d%d%d",'A','B','C','D');
}
```

   (a) 65666768 (b) ABCD
   (c) 91929394 (d) None of the above

6. What will be the values of *a* and *b* after execution of the following program?

```
#include <stdio.h>
#include <conio.h>
void main()
{
int a,b;
a=65*66;
b='A' *'B';
clrscr();
printf("a=%d b=%d",a,b);
}
```

   (a) a = 4290 b = 4290 (b) a = 4290 b = AB
   (c) a = 4290 b = 0 (d) None of the above

7. What function is appropriate for accepting a string?

   (a) `gets()` (b) `getch()`
   (c) `getche()` (d) `scanf()`

8. What is the ASCII range for 0 to 9 digits?

   (a) 48 to 57 (b) 65 to 90
   (c) 97 to 122 (d) None of the above

9. What is the ASCII range for A to Z letters?
   (a) 48 to 57
   (b) 65 to 90
   (c) 97 to 122
   (d) None of the above
10. The escape sequence '\t' is a ________.
   (a) Tab
   (b) Next line
   (c) Backspace
   (d) None of the above
11. What would be the value of *x* on execution of the following program?

```
#include <stdio.h>
#include <conio.h>
void main()
{
float x=2.3;
clrscr();
printf("%g",x);
}
```

   (a) 2.3
   (b) 4.3
   (c) 4
   (d) None of the above
12. Which is the correct statement for finding the cube of 2?
   (a) `pow(2,3);`
   (b) `pow(3,2);`
   (c) `pow(3);`
   (d) None of the above
13. The `abs()` function displays ________.
   (a) Absolute value
   (b) Negative value
   (c) Zero value
   (d) None of the above
14. What will be the output of the following program?

```
void main()
{
 printf("\n %d%d%d%d",'a','b','c','d');
}
```

   (a) 979899100
   (b) 87888990
   (c) 90919293
   (d) None of the above
15. What is the output of the following program?

```
#include <stdio.h>
#include <conio.h>
void main()
{
int a;
printf("\nAmit%n",&a);
printf(" %d",a);
}
```

(a) Amit (b) 4 Amit
(c) Amit 4 (d) Syntax error

16. Which of the following format specifier is used to read hexadecimal number?
(a) `%hex` (b) `%h`
(c) `%x` (d) `%hd`

17. Which of the option is used to print the value of `long` `float` $a = 12345.6789;$?
(a) `printf("%Lf",a);` (b) `printf("%fL",a);`
(c) `printf("%LF",a);` (d) `printf("%lf",a);`

18. Which of the following function every C Program must contain?
(a) `main()` (b) `begin()` (c) `start()`

19. What special character (symbol) is to be used to end the expression in C?
(a) : (b) ; (c) .

20. Which of the following is used to read the single character through keyboard?
(a) `getchar()` (b) `putchar()`
(c) `print()` (d) `puts()`

Answers

1. (b)	2. (c)	3. (a)	4. (d)	5. (a)	6. (a)	7. (a)	8. (a)	9. (b)	10. (a)
11. (a)	12. (a)	13. (a)	14. (a)	15. (c)	16. (c)	17. (d)	18. (a)	19. (b)	20. (a)

True or False

1. Formatted functions require format string to format the data.
2. The function `gets()` is unformatted function.
3. The `'\n` escape sequence inserts a tab.
4. Formatted functions `return` values.
5. The function `gets()` is defined in `<string.h>`.
6. Any signed data type can have negative as well as positive values.
7. The functions `cgets()` and `cputs()` work with character pointer as argument.
8. `While` inputting values through `scanf()`, `&` is required before variable name.
9. The `getche()` is used to read data character.
10. The `char` requires one byte space in the memory.
11. The `'\a'` is escape sequence is for alert bell.
12. The format string `%g` is used for `float` type.
13. The `%s` is used to format the string.
14. The format string `%P` is used to display hexadecimal in lower case.
15. The `%lf` is used for `long` integer.

Answers

1. True 2. True 3. False 4. True 5. False 6. True 7. True 8. True 9. True 10. True 11. True 12. True 13. True 14. False 15. False

Additional Questions

What is/are the output/s of the following program/s?

1.

```
void main()
{
clrscr();
printf("\n %o  %hx %p",45,65,65);
}

OUTPUT:
55  37  0041
```

2.

```
void main()
{
int x=67,y=68,z=69;
clrscr();
printf("\n%c %c  %c ",x,y,z);
getche();
}

OUTPUT:
C  D  E
```

3.

```
void main()
{
char str="C Programming";
clrscr();
puts(str);
getche();
}

OUTPUT:
No output
```

4.

```
#include <stdio.h>
#include <conio.h>
void main()
{
   int k='A';
   clrscr();
   while(k<='K') putch(k++);
}

OUTPUT:
ABCDEFGHIJK
```

Find the bug/s in the following program/s.

1.

```
void main()
{
int x=2;
char y='A';
float f=2.05;
clrscr();
printf("%d %c %f",f,y,x);
getche();
}
```

Bug: Formatted data cannot be displayed through unformatted functions. After putting them in sequence output will be 2 A 2.050000

2.

```
void main()
{
int x;
clrscr();
printf("Enter a Number :");
scanf("%d",x);
printf("%d",x);}
```

Bug: In scanf() & is not prefixed before variable name

3.

```
void main()
{
char x,d;
clrscr();
printf("%f",x);

}
```

Bug: Possible use of x. Value of x is not initialized.

5

Decision Statements

1. Why decision-making statements are used in the program?

Ans: In the programming languages, many times we need to change the sequence of execution of statements. Based on the condition, some option is to be selected. Decision-making statements are used to control the flow and execution of statements. Execution order of statements changes using decision-making statements.

2. What kinds of operators are used in the decision-making statements?

Ans: In the decision-making statements, logical, arithmetic, relational or conditional operators are used.

3. List the decision-making statements supported by C.

Ans: C supports the following decision-making statements.
The `if` statement.
The `if-else` statement.
The `switch case` statement.
The ternary or conditional operator.

4. Why C uses the keyword `if`?

Ans: C uses the keyword `if` to control the flow of execution of statements. When the logical condition is true, one set of statements get executed, i.e., statement(s) is/are executed only when the logical condition is true. It has only one option.

5. Write the syntax of `if` statement.

Ans: Syntax for the simplest `if` statement:

```
if(condition ) /* no semicolon */
 {Statement ;}
Next statement
```

6. Explain in brief the working of `if` statement.

Ans: Working of `if` statement is depicted in Figure 5.1 and its explanation is followed to it.

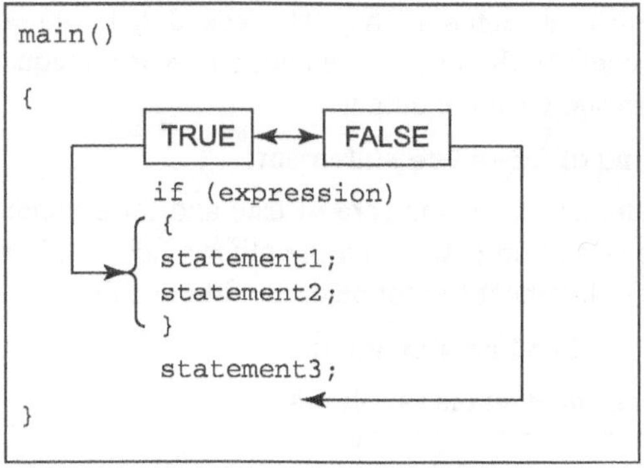

Figure 5.1 The `if` Statement

The `if` statement contains an expression. The expression is evaluated. If the expression is true, it returns 1 otherwise 0. The statement is executed when the condition is true. In case the condition is false, compiler skips the lines within the `if` block and the control goes to the next statement. In case the condition is true, two statements in the above figure are executed, otherwise statement 3 is executed.

7. Briefly explain the rules for using decision-making statements using C.

Ans: The conditional statement is always enclosed within a pair of parentheses.
The conditional statements should not be terminated with semicolons (;).
The statements following the `if` statement are normally enclosed within curly braces.
The curly braces indicate the scope of the `if` statement.
The `default` scope is one statement.
However, it is good practice to use curly braces even with a single statement is used following the `if` condition.

8. Write a program to check equivalence of two numbers using `if` statement.

Ans:

```
#include <stdio.h>
#include <conio.h>
void main()
{
int m,n;
clrscr();
printf("\n Enter Two Numbers :");
scanf("%d %d",&m,&n);

if(m-n==0)
printf("\n Two numbers are equal.");
getche();
    }

OUTPUT:
Enter Two Numbers : 5 5
Two numbers are equal.
```

Explanation: The two numbers are entered. They are checked by `if` statement whether their subtraction is 0 or not. If yes, one can confirm that they are equal, otherwise unequal. If the numbers are equal, a message will be displayed as shown at the output.

9. Explain the working of `if-else` statement.

Ans: The `if-else` statement takes the care of true and false conditions. It has two blocks. One block is executed when the condition is true and the other block is `else` and it is executed when the condition is false. The `else` statement cannot be used without `if`.

10. Give the syntax of `if-else` statement.

Ans: Syntax of `if-else` statement is as follows.

```
if(the condition is true)
execute the Statement1;
else
execute the Statement2;
```

OR

Syntax of `if-else` statement can be given as follows.

```
if(expression is true)
 {
 statement 1;            →        'if block'
 statement 2;
 }
else
 {
 statement 3;            →        'else block'
 statement 4;
 }
```

11. Give the flowchart for `if-else` statement.

Ans: Figure 5.2 illustrates the flowchart of `if-else` statement.

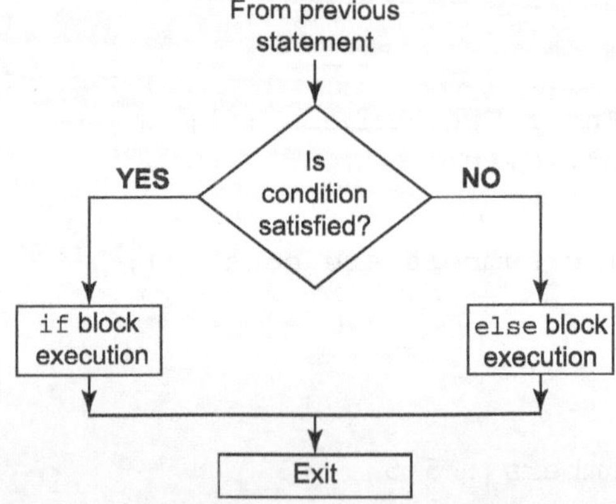

Figure 5.2 Flowchart for if-else statement

12. Read the values of a, b, c through the keyboard. Add them and after addition check if it is in the range of 100 and 200 or not. Print separate message for each.

Ans:

```
void main()
{
int a,b,c,d;
clrscr();
printf("Enter Three Numbers a b c :");
scanf("%d %d %d", &a,&b,&c);
printf("a=%d b=%d c=%d ",a,b,c);
d=a+b+c;
if(d<=200 & d>=100)
printf("\nSum is %d which is in between 100 & 200",d);
else
printf("\nSum is %d which is out of range ",d);
getche();
}

OUTPUT:
Enter three numbers a b c : 50 52 54
A=50 b=52 c=54
Sum is 156 which is in between 100 and 200.
```

Explanation: In the above program, three numbers are entered and their sum is assigned to *d*. The value of *d* is checked by the `if` statement. If the value of *d* is greater than 200 and less than 100, `if` block is executed, otherwise `else` block is executed.

13. Give the syntax and explain the nested `if-else` statements.

Ans: Syntax of nested `if-else` statements is as follows.

```
if(test condition 1)
{
if(test condition 2)
statement 1;
else
statement 2
 }
else
{
 if(test condition 3)
 statement 3;
 else
 statement 4;
 }
```

When conditional statements are placed within another conditional statement, such a structure is called nested. The `if-else` conditional statements can be placed within the `if` and `else` block.

14. Draw the flowchart for nested `if-else` statement?

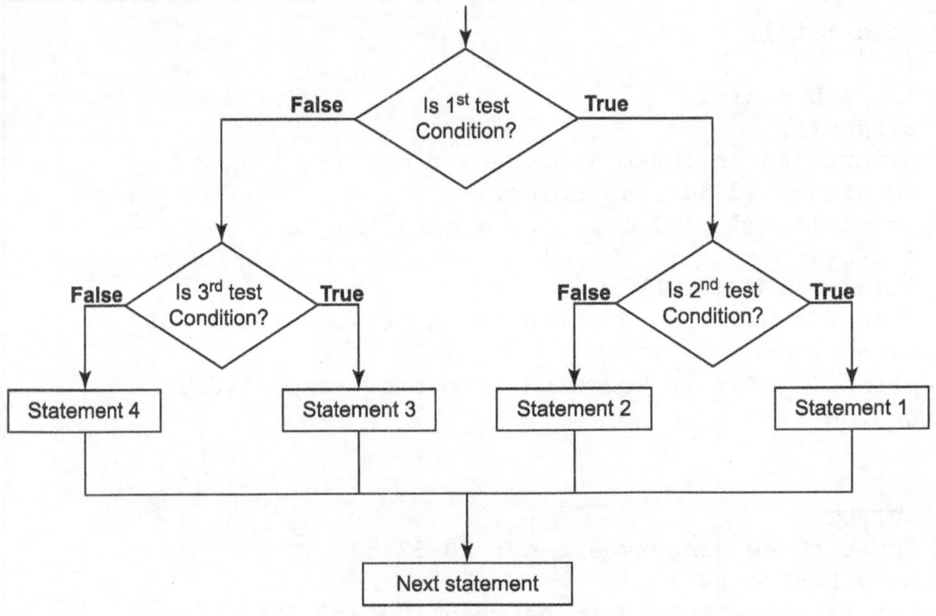

Figure 5.3 Flowchart for Nested `If-Else`

15. Demonstrate the use of nested `if-else` program by writing a program to find the largest number out of three numbers. Read the numbers through the keyboard.

Ans:

```
void main()
{
int x,y,z;
clrscr();
printf("\nEnter Three Numbers x, y, z :");
scanf("%d %d %d", &x,&y,&z);
printf("\nLargest out of Three Numbers is :");
if(x>y)
{
 if(x>z)
 printf("x=%d\n",x);
 else
 printf("z=%d\n",z);
}
else
{
```

```
  if(z>y)
  printf("z=%d\n",z);
  else
  printf("y=%d\n",y);
 }
 }

OUTPUT:
Enter three numbers x, y, z : 10 20 30
The largest out of three numbers is :z=30
```

Explanation: This is also an example of nested `if`s. When the `if` statement satisfies the condition, control passes to another `if` statement block. Three numbers are entered through keyboard. The first `if` statement compares the first number with the second number. If the condition is true, the block following the first `if` **statement** executes. Inside the block, `if` statement checks whether the first number is larger than the third number. If yes, then, the largest number is the first one and the same is displayed. Else the third number is the largest and the same is printed. In case, the first `if` statement fails for satisfying the condition the `else` block with nested `if` would be executed. The third number is compared with the second number. If it is true, the third number is the largest; otherwise, the second number is the largest.

16. Is it possible to use multiple `else` statements with `if` statement?

Ans: Any `if` statement can be paired with one and only one `else` statement; therefore, it is not possible to link an `if` statement with more than one `else` statement. In such case, we can use nested `if-else` statement or `if-else-if` ladder to solve the problem.

17. Is it possible to use multiple `default` statements in `switch` statement?

Ans: We cannot use multiple `default` statements in a single-`switch` statement, because `default` statement is executed when the `switch` variable does not match with any of the cases; therefore, it is meaningless to include more than one `default` statement in a single-`switch` statement.

There can be more than one `default` statements in a single-`switch` statement if it is a nested `switch` statement and all the `default` statements will be at different level of nesting.

18. Write the use of `else` and `default` statements in `if-else` and `switch` statements, respectively.

Ans: The `else` statement is used with `if` statement. There are some statements that we want to execute on the failure of some condition. All such statements are enclosed in the block followed by `else` statement.

The `default` statement is used with the `switch` statement. The `default` is used when the case variable mismatches with any of the cases present in the `switch` statement. In such a case, all statements are written under the `default` statement.

19. Why `goto` statement is avoided?

Ans: Using `goto` statement control of execution of the program is passed to the label that can be placed anywhere in the program. As the labels can be spread anywhere in the program, it is very difficult to monitor the flow of control in the program, which may lead to logical errors.

20. What is the use of the keyword `break`?

Ans: The keyword `break` allows the programmers to terminate the loop. The `break` skips from the loop or block in which it is defined. The control then automatically goes to the first statement after the loop or block. The `break` can be associated with all conditional statements.

We can also use `break` statements in the nested loops. If we use `break` statement in the innermost loop, then the control of the program is terminated only from the innermost loop.

21. Why the `break` statement is essential in the `switch` statement?

Ans: In `switch` statement, we find a number of cases written one after another. When the `case` variable matches with any of the cases, the control passes to that `case` and execution begins from the statement following to that `case`. If we do not write the `break` statement after each `case`, the control starts executing all the cases written after the `case` that has been matched; therefore, to avoid this situation, we have to write `break` statement after each `case`.

22. Is it permissible to use `break` statement outside the loop?

Ans: One should not use `break` statement outside the loop. It is used only exiting from the loop. Therefore, question does not arises to use outside the loop.

23. Which other functions or keywords can be used in place of the `break` statement?

Ans: The `break` statement is used to pass the control out of the loop. We can use the `goto` statement to pass the control outside the loop by writing a label at the end of the loop statement.

24. Is it possible to use the `else` statement in place of a `default` statement or vice versa?

Ans: The `else` statement can be used with only the `if` statement; therefore, we cannot use it at the place of a `default` statement.

Moreover, the `if` statement cannot be paired with any statement other than the `else` statement; therefore, we cannot use a `default` statement in place of the `else` statement.

25. Can we put `default` statement anywhere in the `switch case` structure?

Ans: Yes, we can put `default` statement anywhere in the `switch` statement, because in `switch` statement the sequence of cases does not matter in the execution of the statement.

26. What are the limitations of the `switch case` statement?

Ans: The `switch case` statement can check only for equality; we cannot have any logical expression in `case` statement, also we can use only integer or character value, the floating-point values are avoided in `case` statements.

27. What is a sequential execution?

Ans: When the control is passed line by line, one statement after another in the sequence without any jump, or looping without skipping any of the statements in the sequence, such an execution is called sequential execution.

28. What is the transfer of control?

Ans: The transfer of control means changing the statement that is going to execute next in the sequence.

29. Write short note on `goto` statement?

Ans: This statement does not require any condition. This is unconditional control jump. This statement passes control anywhere in the program, i.e., control is transferred to another part of the program without testing any condition. User has to define `goto` statement as follows:

`goto` ***label;***

where the label name must start with any character.

30. Write a program to detect whether the entered number is even or odd. Use `goto` statement.

Ans:

```
#include <stdio.h>
#include <conio.h>
#include <stdlib.h>
void main()
{
int x;
clrscr();
printf("Enter a Number :");
scanf("%d",&x);
if(x%2==0)
goto even;
else
goto odd;
even:
printf("\n %d is Even Number.");
return;
odd:
printf("\n %d is Odd Number.");
}

OUTPUT:
Enter a Number : 5
5 is Odd Number.
```

Explanation: In the above program, a number is entered. The number is checked for even or odd with modules division operator. When the number is even, the `goto` statement transfers the control to the label ***even***. Similarly, when the number is odd, the `goto` statement transfers the control to the label ***odd*** and respective message will be displayed.

31. Why `continue` statement is used in the program?

Ans: Loop interruption statement is done with `continue`. The `continue` statement is used within the loop control statements such as `while` or `do while`. It skips all the statements following the `continue` and transfers the control to the start of the loop.

32. What is the difference between `break` and `continue`?

break	**continue**
It is used to exit from current block or loop.	It is used to skip the current loop iteration and `return` the control to the next loop statement /iteration.
Terminates the loop.	Never terminates the loop/program.
Control passes at the beginning of loop.	Control passes to the next statement.

33. What is the difference between `break` and `exit()`?

Ans:

S.No.	`break`	`exit()`
1	It is a keyword.	It is a function.
2	No header file is needed.	Header file process.h must be included.
3	It stops the execution of the loop.	It terminates the program.
4	It does not require the header file process.h.	It requires header file process.h.

34. What is the difference between `switch case` and nested `if`s?

Ans:

`switch case`	nested `ifs`
The `switch` can only test for equality, i.e., only constant values are applicable.	The `if` can evaluate relational or logical expressions.
No two `case` statements have identical constants in the same `switch`.	Same conditions may be repeated for number of times.
Character constants are automatically converted to integers.	Character constants are automatically converted to integers.
In `switch case` statement nested `if` can be used.	In nested `if` statement `switch case` can be used.

35. When to use `switch` statement?

Ans: `Switch` statement can be used instead of multiple `if-else/if` conditions. The `switch` statement is used when there are more than one conditional expression based on single variable of integer or character type.

36. Explain in brief the syntax of `switch case` ?

Ans: The syntax of the `switch case` statement is as given below.

```
switch(variable or expression)
{
case constant A :
statement;
break;
case constant B :
statement;
break;
default :
statement ;
}
```

(a) ***The `switch` expression:***
In the block, the variable or expression can be a character or an integer. The integer expression following the keyword `switch` will yield an integer value only. The integer may be any value 1, 2, 3 etc. In case if a character is constant, the values may be with alphabetic such as '*x*', '*y*' and '*z*'.

(b) ***The `switch` organization:***
The `switch` expression should be terminated neither with (;) semicolon nor with any other symbol. The entire `case` structure following `switch` should be enclosed with curly braces. The keyword `case` is followed by a constant. Every constant terminates with a colon (:). Each `case` statement must contain different constant values. Any number of `case` statements can be provided. If the `case`

structure contains multiple statements, they need not be enclosed with curly braces. Here, the keyword **case & break** performs the job of opening and closing curly braces, respectively.

(c) ***The* switch *execution:***
When one of the **cases** satisfies, the statements following it are executed. In case there is no match, the **default** case is executed. The **default** can be put anywhere in the switch expression. The switch statement can also be written without **default** statement. The **break** statement used in switch passed control outside the switch block. By mistake if no **break** statements are given all the **cases** following it are executed.

37. Draw the flowchart for switch case?

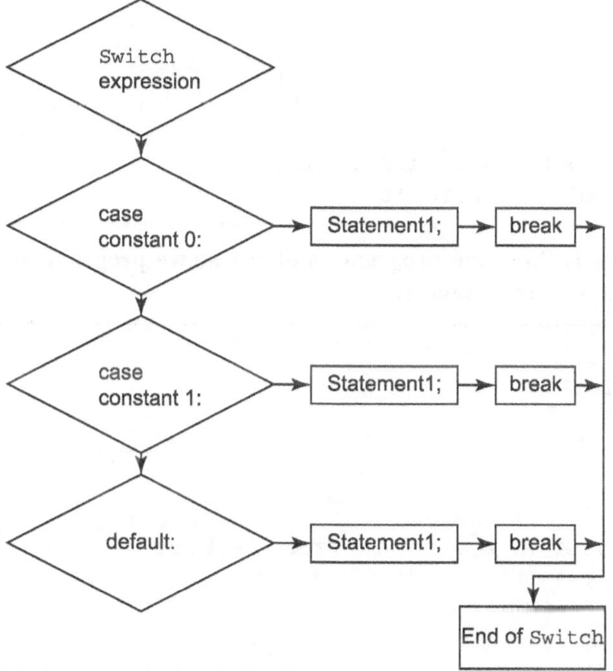

Figure 5.4 Flowchart for switch statement

38. Write a program using multiple if-else conditions and convert the same program using switch statements.

Ans: Program using multiple if conditions.

```
#include <stdio.h>
#include <conio.h>
void main()
{
  char x;
  clrscr();
  printf("\nEnter any alphabet from (a,b,c)");
```

```
   scanf(" %c",&x);
       if(x=='a')
        printf("\nYou have pressed Alphabet 'a'");
       else if(x=='b')
        printf("\nYou have pressed Alphabet 'b'");
       else if(x=='c')
        printf("\nYpu have pressed Alphabet 'c'");
        else
         printf("\nSorry  You  have  pressed  Alphabet  other  than
 (a,b,c):");
    getch();
    }

OUTPUT:
Enter any alphabet from (a,b,c):b
You have pressed Alphabet 'b'
```

Below given program is the same program as of the above program using `switch` statement instead of multiple `if-else` statement.

```
#include <stdio.h>
#include <conio.h>
void main()
{
   char x;
   clrscr();
   printf("\nEnter any alhabet from (a,b,c)");
   scanf(" %c",&x);
   switch(x)
   {
    case 'a':printf("\nYou have pressed Alphabet 'a'");
              break;
    case 'b':printf("\nYou have pressed Alphabet 'b'");
              break;
    case 'c':printf("\nYpu have pressed Alphabet 'c'");
              break;
  default:printf("\nSorry  You  have  pressed  Alphabet  other  than
  (a,b,c)");
   }
getch();
}

OUTPUT:
Enter any alphabet from (a,b,c)b
You have pressed alphabet 'b'
```

39. Is it necessary to use `default` case in `switch` statement? Justify your answer by using suitable program.

Ans: No, it is not necessary to use `default` case in `switch` statement. The `default` label is optional. Therefore, we can skip the `default` case in the `switch` statement. If there is no `default` label in your program and the expression of the `switch` statement does not match with any one of the `case` constant, then none of the statements within the body of `switch` statements is executed. In this case, the flow of program continues within the body of `switch`. However, using the `default` case in `switch` statement makes the programmer better to understand. The use of `default` case in the `switch` statement also helps the programmer for logic or error purpose.

Consider the successful execution of following program without making use of `default` case in `switch` statement.

```
#include <stdio.h>
#include <conio.h>
void main()
{
   char x;
   clrscr();
   printf("Enter one of the Alphabet from (a b c):");
   scanf(" %c",&x);
   switch(x)
   {
        case 'a':printf("\nUser has pressed a");
                    break;
        case 'b':printf("\nUser has pressed b");
                    break;
        case 'c':printf("\nUser has pressed c");
               break;
   }
getch();
}
```

OUTPUT:

```
Enter one of the alphabet from (a b c):g
```

Output: In the above program, there is no `default` case used in the program. The program does not print anything `if` programmer presses character other than (a, b, c).

Multiple-choice Questions

1. The statement `if(0)` is ________.

   (a) False (b) True (c) Invalid

2. The statement `if(-1)` is ________.

   (a) False (b) True (c) Invalid

3. The test condition given within the `if`, i.e., `if(condition)` is true, then ________.
   (a) `if` block executed
   (b) `else` block executed
   (c) Both blocks are executed
4. The scope of `if()` can be defined with ________.
   (a) { } (b) [] (c) ()
5. The keyword `else` is used with ________.
   (a) `if` *statement* (b) `switch` statement
   (c) `do..while()` statement (d) None of the above
6. The following keyword/statement is used to terminate from the innermost loop ________.
   (a) `default` (b) `break` (c) `case`
7. The following keyword is used for unconditional jump to a labelled statement ________.
   (a) `Go` (b) `goto` (c) `jump`
8. The value specified in the parentheses followed to `switch` is ________.
   (a) Real (b) Double floating-point number (c) Integer
9. Which warning message will be flagged by the compiler for the following program?
   `void main() { if(0) printf("1");}`
   (a) Unreachable code in function main
   (a) Constant expression required
   (b) Statement missing
10. The `if-else` and `switch` statements belong to ________.
    (a) Repetitive structure (b) Sequential structure
    (c) Selective structure (d) None of the above
11. The `default` is a ________.
    (a) Keyword in c (b) Function
    (c) Pointer (d) None of the above
12. The keyword `switch` is followed by ________.
    (a) `Switch` variable (b) `Constant`
    (c) `Float` variable (d) `goto`
13. The `default` statement can appear ________.
    (a) Anywhere within the `switch`
    (b) At the end of each `case`
    (c) At the end of `switch case`
14. By mistake if no `break` statements are given in each `case` statement, then ________.
    (a) All the cases following it are executed
    (b) Statements following to one `case` executes
    (c) None of the above
15. The `switch` statement is used to ________.
    (a) Switch between functions in a program
    (b) Switch from one variable to another variable

(c) Choose from multiple possibilities that may arise due to different values of a single variable
(d) Use switching variables

16. The `default` statement is executed when _________.
    (a) All the `case` statements are false
    (b) One of the `case` is true
    (c) One of the `case` is false
    (d) None of the above

17. Use of `default` in program is _________.
    (a) Optional
    (b) Compulsory
    (c) Both a and b
    (d) None of the above

18. `exit()` requires which of the following header file?
    (a) `process.h`
    (b) `dos.h`
    (c) `system.h`
    (d) `grahpics.h`

19. Each `case` statement in `switch` is separated by _________.
    (a) `break`
    (b) `continue`
    (c) `exit()`
    (d) `goto`

20. What will be the output of the following program?

```
#include <stdio.h>
#include <conio.h>
void main()
{
   char x='H';
      clrscr();
   switch(x)
{
case 'H': printf("%c",'H');
case 'E': printf("%c",'E');
case 'L': printf("%c",'L');
case 'l': printf("%c",'L');
case 'O': printf("%c",'O');
}
```

    (a) HELLO
    (b) HE
    (c) H
    (d) None of the above

21. The `case` constant cannot be _________.
    (a) `int`
    (b) `float`
    (c) `char`
    (d) All of the above

22. What will be the output of the following program?

```
void main()
{
 char x='G';
 switch(x)
 {
```

```
   if( x=='B')
  {
   case 'd': printf("%",'o');
   case 'B': printf("%s","Bad");
  }
   else
   case 'G': printf("%s","Good");
   default : printf("%s",  " Boy");
  }
}
```

(a) Good Boy (b) Bad Boy
(c) Boy (d) None of the above

23. What will be the output of the following program?

```
void main()
{
 char x='d';
 clrscr();
 switch(x)
 {
 case 'b':
 puts( "0 1 001");
 break;
 default :
 puts("1 2 3");
 break;
 case 'R' :
 puts("I II III");
 }
}
```

(a) 1 2 3 (b) 0 1 001
(c) I II III (d) None of the above

24. What will be the output of the following program?

```
void main()
{
 char y='p';
 clrscr();
 switch(y)
 {
 if( y=='p')
 {
```

```
 case 'p': printf("%s","Pleasant");
 case 'B': printf("%s","mood");
 }
 else
 case 'G': printf("%s","moo");
 default : printf("%s", " ");
 }
}
```

(a) pleasantmood (b) moo
(c) mood (d) None of the above

25. What will be the output of the following program?

```
void main()
{
 char x='H';
 clrscr();
 switch(x)
 {
 case 'H': printf("%c",'H');
 case 'E': printf("%c",'a');
 case 'L': printf("%c",'i');
 case 'l': printf("%c",'!');break;
 case 'O': printf("%c",'O');
 }
}
```

(a) Hai! (b) Hao
(c) oHai (d) None of the above

26. What will be the output of the following program?

```
void main()
{
char x=0;
clrscr();
switch(x)
{
 case 0 : printf("%c",'C'); break;
 case 0 : printf("%c",'d'); break;
 default :;
}
}
```

(a) cd (b) Program error (c) C

27. Which of the following is not a keyword in C

(a) `if` (b) then (c) `else`

28. The correct syntax of `'if'` statement is

(a)
```
if(condition)
statement;
```
(b)
```
if(condition)
{ statements; }
```
(c)
```
if(condition)
statement;
```
(d) all of these

29. Which of the following `'if'` statement(s) is/are unnecessary

(a) `if(1) statement;` (b) `if(0) statement;` (c) `if(27); statement;`

30. Which `'if'` statement will follow stmt17

(a) `if(1<0) stmt17;` (b) `if(78>79) stmt17;` (c) `if('a'>'A') stmt17;`

31. The correct syntax of '`if-else`' statement is/are

(a) `if(condition) statement; else(condition) statement;`
(b) `if(condition) statement; else { statements; }`
(c) `if(condition) { statements; }else(1) statement;`

32. The incorrect syntax of `'if-else if-else'` statement is/are

(a)
```
if(condition) statement else if(condition) statement;
else statement;
```
(b)
```
if(condition) statement;   else if { statements; }
else statement;
```
(c)
```
if(condition) { statements; }
 else if(2) statement;
 else if(1) statement;
 else statement;
```

33. What is the O/P?

```
void main()
{
 clrscr();
 if(1<0)
 printf("One");
 else if(0)
 printf("Two");
 getch();
}
```

(a) One (b) Two (c) Nothing

34.

```
void main()
{
 clrscr();
 if(condition1)
 if(condition1)
 if(!condition1)
```

```
      printf("A");
      getch();
    }
```

(a) always prints A (b) sometimes prints A depends on condition1 (c) never prints A

35. What is the O/P?

```
void main()
{clrscr();
 if(1)
 printf("One ");
 if(0)
 printf("Zero ");
 else if(2)
 printf("Two ");
 if(0>1)
 printf("Three ");
 else
 printf("else");
 getch();}
```

(a) One Zero Three (b) One Two else (c) Zero Three (d) Syntax Error

36. The `switch` can only test for _________.

    (a) Equality (b) non-equality (c) none of them

37. Only _________ values are applicable in `switch` structure

    (a) constants (b) variables (c) objects

38. No two `case` statements have _________ in the same `switch`.

    (a) identical constants (b) different constants (c) variables

39. In `switch`, character constants are automatically converted to _________

    (a) floats (b) integers (c) bool values

Answers

1. (a)	2. (b)	3. (a)	4. (a)	5. (a)	6. (b)	7. (b)	8. (c)	9. (a)	10. (c)
11. (a)	12. (a)	13. (a)	14. (a)	15. (c)	16. (a)	17. (a)	18. (a)	19. (a)	20. (a)
21. (b)	22. (a)	23. (a)	24. (a)	25. (a)	26. (c)	27. (b)	28. (d)	29. (c)	30. (c)
31. (b)	32. (b)	33. (c)	34. (c)	35. (b)	36. (a)	37. (a)	38. (a)	39. (b)	

True or False

1. The `else` is associated with `if`.
2. The `else` block is executed when condition is false.

3. The `if` statement can have multiple `else` statements.
4. The statement `if(1)` executes `if` block.
5. One `switch` statement can have multiple `case` statements but only one `default` statement.
6. The `default` statement can be written anywhere in the `switch` block.
7. The `break` statement is used to separate two `case` statements.
8. The `case` statement is always terminated by semi-colon.
9. The `switch` statement accepts only constant as an argument.
10. Like `if-else` the `switch` statement can be nested.
11. The `default` statement is compulsory for `switch` statement.
12. The `switch` statement testes for equality only.
13. The `if` statement can evaluate relational and logical expressions.
14. The `if` statement works with expression as well as constants.
15. The `default` statement if placed at the end of `switch`, at least one have statement in block.
16. The `default` statement can be placed at the beginning of `switch`, without any statement in its block.
17. The `switch` block should be terminated by semi-colon.

Answers

1. True 2. True 3. False 4. True 5. True 6. True 7. True 8. False 9. True 10. True 11. True 12. True 13. True 14. True 15. True 16. True 17. False

Additional Questions

What is/are the output/s of the following program/s?

1.

```
void main()
{
int number=7;
clrscr();
if(number %2==0)
      printf("\n The entered number %d is even",number);
      else
      printf("\n The Entered number %d is odd",number);
      getche();
}

OUTPUT:
The Entered number 7 is odd
```

2.

```
void main()
{
int b=4,a=1,c=2;
float x1,x2;
clrscr();
if(b*b>4*a*c)
{
x1=-b+sqrt(b*b-4*a*c)/2*a;
x2=-b-sqrt(b*b-4*a*c)/2*a;
printf("\n x1=%.1f x2=%.1f",x1,x2);
}
else
printf("\n Roots are Imaginary");
getch();
}

OUTPUT:
x1 = -2.0 x2 = -6.0
```

3.

```
void main()
 {
 float bs,hra,da,cv,incentive,bonus,sale=110000,ts;
 clrscr();
 if(sale> = 100000)
 {
 bs=3000;
 hra=20 * bs/100;
 da= 110 * bs/100;
 cv=500;
 incentive=sale*10/100;
 bonus=500;
 }
 else
 {
 bs=3000;hra=20 * bs/100;
 da= 110 * bs/100;
 cv=500;
 incentive=sale*5/100;
 }
```

```
 ts=bs+hra+da+cv+incentive+bonus;
 printf("\n %.2f",ts);
 getch();
 }

OUTPUT:
18900.00
```

4.

```
void main()
{
int x=6,y=5,z=10;
clrscr();
printf("\nAnswer is :");
if(x>y)
{
if(x>z)
printf("%d\n",x);
else
printf("%d\n",z);
}
else {if(z>y)
printf("%d\n",z);
else
printf("%d\n",y);
getche();
}

OUTPUT:
Answer is:10
```

5.

```
void main()
{
int initial=1000,final=1300,consumed;
float total;
clrscr();
consumed = final-initial;
if(consumed>=200)
total=consumed * 2.50;
```

```
else
total=consumed * 1.50;
printf("Total bill for %d units is Rs
%.2f",consumed,total);
getche();
}

OUTPUT:
Total bill for 300 units is Rs 750.00
```

6.

```
void main()
{
int a=2,b=4,c=1,temp;
clrscr();
if
(a<b)
{
if(a<c)
temp=a;
else
temp=c;
}
else
{
if(b<c)
temp =b;
else
temp =c;
}
printf("Answer out of three numbers (%d %d %d) is %d
\n", a,b,c, temp );
getche();
}

OUTPUT:
Answer out of three numbers (2 4 1) is 1
```

Find the bug/s in the following program/s?

1.

```
#include <stdio.h>
#include <conio.h>

void main()
{
int cet ;
clrscr();
printf("\n Enter marks obtained in CET examination : ");
scanf("%d",&cet);
if(cit>120)
printf("\n Eligible for admission in autonomous
Institute.");
getch();
}
```

Bug: Replace cet instead of cit in `if` statement.

2.

```
void main()
{
clrscr();
if(0)
printf("False");
else
printf("True");
}
```

Bug: `If(0)` use always false statement

3.

```
void main()
void main()
{
clrscr();
if(3>2)
printf("2 is smaller than 3");
printf(" and ");
else
printf("3 is greater");
}
```

Bug: scope of `if()` block is not defined

4.

```
void main()
{
clrscr();
if(3>2)
printf("2 is smaller than 3");
else
printf(" Numbers are equal");
else
printf("3 is greater");
}
```

Bug: `if` should not have multiple `else`

6

Loop Control Statements

1. What is a loop or iterative structure? Why it is necessary in a program?

Ans: Loop or iterative structure is the execution of statements repeatedly until a particular condition is true. It is necessary in the programming to include loop statements when we want to execute the set of statements a number of times until some condition is true.

2. Name the two types of loops.

Ans: The loops are of two types as follows.

1. Counter-controlled repetition and
2. Sentinel-controlled repetition.

3. What do you mean by counter-controlled loops?

Ans: This is also called definite repetition actions, because in advance, the number of iterations to be performed is fixed and defined in the program itself before entering the loop.

4. Give the format and a programming example of counter-controlled loop.

Ans: Format of counter-controlled loop is as follows:

1. Set initially counter with some initial value say 0 or 1.
2. Use `'while'` loop to test the count value up to certain value.
3. Execute loop body statements.
4. Update counter.
5. End.

Programming example:

```
int a=0;          /* Initial count value of a to 0 */
while(a<=5)       /* Test condition */
{
printf("\n Loop statement");      /* Body statement */
a++;                              /* Update the count */
}
```

5. Explain the steps for performing counter-controlled repetition.

Ans: Steps in counter-controlled loop are as follows:

1. **Loop variable:** It is a variable used in the loop.
2. **Initialization:** It is the first step in which starting/final value is assigned to the loop variable. Each time the updated value is checked by the loop itself.
3. **Incrimination/Decrementation:** It is the numerical value added or subtracted to the variable in each round of the loop. The updated value is compared with the final value and if it is found less than final value, the steps in the loop are executed.

6. What do you mean by Sentinel-controlled repetition?

Ans: This is also called 'indefinite repetition'; one cannot estimate how many iterations would be required. In this type loop, termination happens based on certain condition using decision-making statement.

7. Give a programming example that supports Sentinel-controlled loop. Example is to find total odd and even numbers until 0 is pressed using `'while'` loop.

Ans:

```
#include<stdio.h>
#include<conio.h>
void main()
{
int x,even=0,odd=0;
clrscr();
printf("Enter the number: ");
scanf("%d",&x);
while(x!=0)
{
if(x%2==0)
{
even++;
printf("\nEntered number %d is even ",x);
}
else
{
odd++;
printf("\n Entered number %d is odd ",x);
}
printf("\n\n Enter the number:");
scanf("%d",&x);
}
printf("\n %d %d',even,odd);
getche();
}
```

```
Enter the number: 3
Entered number 3 is odd
Enter the number: 5
Entered number 5 is odd
Enter the number: 4
Entered number 4 is even
Enter the number: 8
Entered number 8 is even
Enter the number: 0
2 2
```

8. List the different types of loop control statement supported by C language.

Ans: C language supports three different types of loop control statements.

1. `'for'` loop,
2. `'while'` loop and
3. `'do-while'` loop.

9. Can we use the words `for`, `do` and `while` as variables in the program?

Ans: No, we cannot use the variable names such as `for`, `do` and `while`, because they are keywords. Language does not permit to use keywords as variable.

10. Is it required to terminate the loop control statements by a punctuation mark semicolon (;)?

Ans: No, loop control statements except `'do-while'` loop are terminated by a mark semicolon.

11. What is the syntax of `'for'` loop?

Ans: The `'for'` loop allows to execute a set of instructions until a certain condition is satisfied. Condition may be predefined or open-ended. The general syntax of the `'for'` loop will be as given in Table 6.1.

```
for (initialize counter ;test condition ;re-evaluation parameter)
{
statement ;
statement ;
}
```

12. Explain the syntax of `'for'` loop in brief.

Ans: Syntax of `'for'` loop is as follows:

```
for (initialize counter ;test condition ;re-evaluation parameter)
{
statement ;
statement ;
}
```

Explanation: The `'for'` statement contains three expressions, which are separated by semicolons. Following actions are to be performed in three expressions.

1. The initialization counter sets a loop to an initial value. This statement is executed only once.
2. The test condition is a relational expression that determines the number of iterations desired or it determines when to exit from the loop. The `'for'` loop continues to execute as long as conditional test is satisfied. When the condition becomes false, the control of the program exits from the body of the `'for'` loop and executes next statement after the body of the loop.
3. The re-evaluation parameter decides how to make changes in the loop (quite often increment or decrement operations are to be used).

13. Write briefly about the body of the `'for'` loop.

Ans: The body of the loop may contain either a single statement or multiple statements. In case there is only one statement after the `'for'` loop, braces may not be necessary. In such a `case`, the only one statement is executed until the condition is satisfied. It is a good practice to use braces even for single statement following the `'for'` loop.

14. Draw the flowchart of the execution of `'for'` loop.

Ans: The three expressions of `'for'` loop are as follows:

`for` (initialize counter, i.e., expression 1; test condition, i.e., expression 2; re-evaluation parameter, i.e., expression 3)

```
{
statement ;
statement ;
}
```

Flowchart for the above `for` statement is as follows:

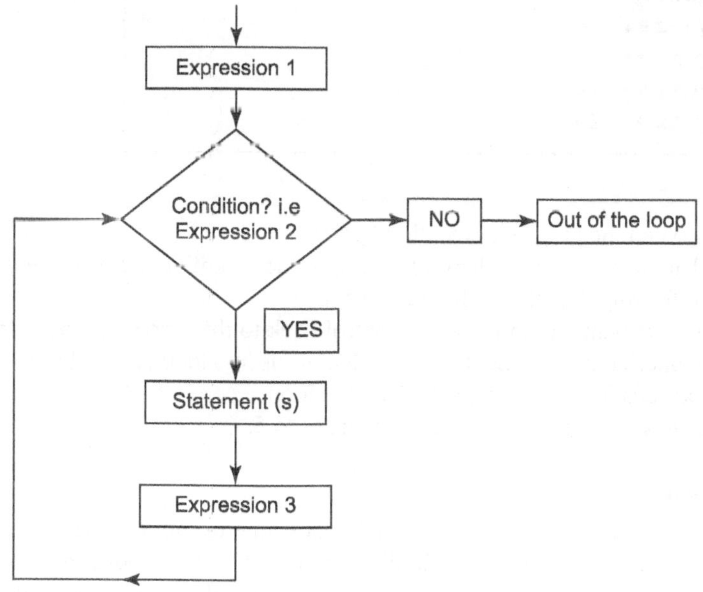

15. Explain the different ways of specifying the 'for' loop.

Ans: The 'for' loop can be used in different ways. Table 6.1 shows the different ways of using the for loop.

Table 6.1 Different ways to use the for loop

Syntax	Output	Remarks
(1) for(;;)	Infinite loop	No arguments
(2) for (a=0; a<=20;)	Infinite loop	'a' is neither incremented nor decremented.
(3) for (a=0; a<=10; a++) printf ("%d",a);	Displays value from 0 to 10	'a' is incremented from 0 to 10. Curly braces are not necessary. Default scope of 'for' loop is one statement after 'for' loop.
(4) for (a=10; a>=0; a--)	Displays value from 10 to 0	'a' is decremented from 10 to 0.

16. Write a program to display the square of first five numbers by using 'for' loop.

Ans:

```
void main()
{
int i;
clrscr();
for (i=1;i<=5;i++)
printf ("\number: %5d its square: %8d",i,i*i);
}

OUTPUT:
Number: 1 its square:  1
Number: 2 its square:  4
Number: 3 its square:  9
Number: 4 its square: 16
Number: 5 its square: 25
```

Explanation:

1. The value of *i* is initialized to 1 when the program execution begins.
2. The condition ***i*<=5** is specified and tested in each iteration. Initially, the condition is true since the value of *i* is 1. The statements following the 'for' loop executes.
3. Upon execution of printf() statement, compiler sends control back to the 'for' loop where the value of *i* is incremented by one. This is repeated till the value of *i* is less than or equal to 5.
4. The new updated value of *i* if exceeds 5, the control exits from the loop.
5. The printf() statement executes as long as the value of *i* reaches to 5.

17. What is nested 'for' loops?

Ans: Nested means loops within the loop. In 'nested for' loops, one or more 'for' statements are included in the body of the loop. In other words, **C** allows multiple 'for' loops in nested forms. The numbers of iterations in this type of structure will be equal to number of iteration in the outer loop multiply by number of iterations in the inner loop.

18. Write a program to illustrate an example of `'nested for'` loops.

Ans:

```
#include <stdio.h>
#include <conio.h>
void main()
{
int i,j;
clrscr();
for (i=1;i<=3;i++) /* outer loop */
{

for (j=1;j<=2;j++) /* inner loop */
printf ("\n i*j: %d",i*j);
}
}
```

OUTPUT:

```
i*j = 1
i*j = 2
i*j = 2
i*j = 4
i*j = 3
i*j = 6
```

Explanation: Here, in the above example, for each value of ***i***, the inner loop's *j* value varies from 1 to 2. Outer loop executes three times whereas the inner loop executes six times. The inner loops terminates when the value of $j = 2$ and the outer loop terminates when the value of $i = 3$. The total number of iterations = outer loop iterations (3) * inner loop iterations (2) = 6.

19. Is it possible to create `'for'` loop that never executes?

Ans: Yes, we can create `'for'` loop that never executes when initial condition itself is not true. In such a case, control will not be passed inside `'for'` loop even once.

20. What is the syntax of `'while'` loop?

Ans: The format of `'while'` loop is as follows:

Syntax:

```
while (test condition)
{
body of the loop
}
```

The test condition is indicated at the top and it tests the value of the expression before processing the body of the loop. The test condition may be any expression. The loop statements will be executed till the condition is true, i.e., the test condition is evaluated and if the condition is true, then the body of the loop is executed. When the condition becomes false, the execution will be out of the loop.

21. Is flowchart number correct?

Ans:

1. The test condition is evaluated and if it is true, the body of the loop is executed.
2. On execution of the body, test condition is repetitively checked and if it is true, the body is executed.
3. When the condition is false, the control is transferred out of the loop.

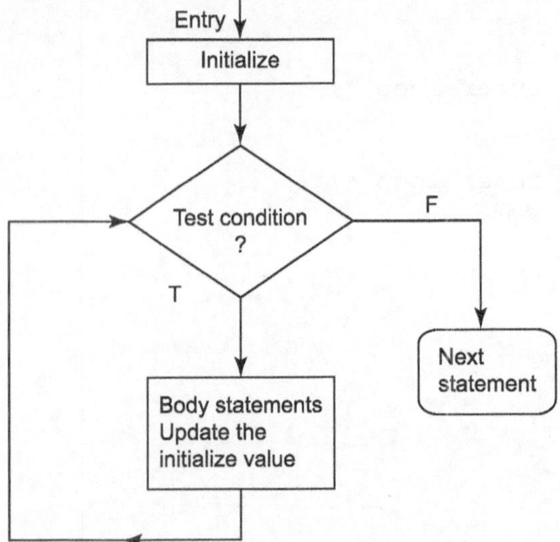

(a) Flowchart number 1

22. Write a program to print the string 'You have learnt C program' 9 times using 'while' loop.

```
void main()
{
int x=1;
while (x<10)
{
printf ("\n You have learnt C program");
x++;
}
}
```

```
OUTPUT:
You have learnt C program
You have learnt C program
You have learnt C program
You have learnt C program
You have learnt C program
You have learnt C program
You have learnt C program
You have learnt C program
You have learnt C program
```

Explanation: The parentheses after `'while'` contains a condition. As long as condition remains true, all the statements within the body of the loop get executed repeatedly. The variable *x* is initialized to 1. The compiler checks the condition and after satisfying it, the body of the loop is executed. The control then goes to the `'while'` loop. Next time, the value of *x* is incremented by 1. Now, *x* is 2 again it satisfies the condition and the body of the loop gets executed. This process is continued till the value of *x* reaches to 9. When the condition becomes false (after 9), the control passes to the first statement that follows the body of the `'while'` loop and the program is now terminated.

23. Write and explain the syntax of `'do-while'` loop.

Ans: Syntax of `'do-while'` loop is as follows:

```
do
{
statement/s;
}
while (condition);
```

In `'do-while'` loop, the condition is checked at the end of the loop. The `'do-while'` loop will execute at least one time even if the condition is false initially. The `'do-while'` loop executes as long as the condition becomes true.

24. What are characteristics of a 'do-while' loop?

Ans: In the `'do-while'` loop, the test condition is mentioned at the bottom of the `'do-while'` loop. The body statement(s) execute(s) once even when condition is false. Braces are essential even when a single statement exists.

25. Write a program to find the cubes of 1 to 10 numbers using `'do-while'` loop.

```
#include 'math.h'
void main()
{
int y,x=1;
clrscr();
printf ("\n Print the numbers and their cubes");
printf ("\n");
do
{
y=pow(x,3);
printf ("%4d %27d\n",x,y);
x++;

}
while (x<=10);
}
```

```
OUTPUT:
Print the numbers and their cubes
 1    1
 2    8
 3   27
 4   64
 5  125
 6  216
 7  343
 8  512
 9  729
10 1000
```

Explanation: Here, the mathematical function pow *(x, 3)* is used. Its meaning is to calculate the third power of x. With this function, we get the value of $y = x^3$. For use of the `pow ()` function, we have to include ***math.h*** header file.

26. What is the difference between `'while'` and `'do-while'` loops?

Ans:

S. No.	`'while'` loop	`'do-while'` loop
1	Condition is specified at the top.	Condition is mentioned at the bottom.
2	Body statement(s) is/are executed when condition is satisfied.	Body statement(s) execute(s) even when condition is false.
3	No brackets for a single statement.	Brackets are essential even when a single statement exits.
4	It is entry controlled loop.	It is exit controlled loop.

27. What happens if you create a loop that never ends?

Ans: If we create a loop that never ends, then the execution will not stop and may be the program will close automatically due to crashing of system stack.

28. Is it possible to nest `'while'` loop within `'for'` loops?

Ans: Yes, we can nest `'while'` loop within `'for'` loop, because there is no limitation on the statements that can be written inside the block of loop statement, we can write any statements enclosed in loop block.

29. How do you choose between `'while'` and `'for'` loops?

Ans: When we do not want to initialize any variables at the start of loop statement or we do not want to perform any repetitive operation after each execution of loop statement, the `'while'` statement is used; otherwise, we prefer to use `'for'` loop statement. Both of these statements can be used alternately with very less overhead.

30. What is the difference between (!0) and (!1)?

Ans: The (!0) condition is the condition that will never become false and (!1) is the condition that is always false, which is equivalent to Boolean values 1 and 0, respectively.

31. What are the values of NULL and !NULL?

Ans: The NULL value is used to check for the end of the string and !NULL can be used as condition that will be true until the end of the string does not occurs.

32. Is it possible to use multiple 'while' statements with 'do' statement?

Ans: We cannot use multiple 'while' statements with a single 'do' statement; every 'do' statement can be paired with one and only one 'while' statement in the 'do-while' loop.

33. What happens when the condition within the 'while' loop is not specified?

Ans: If the condition within the 'while' loop is not specified, the program will not execute. To execute it, the condition within the 'while' loop is must.

Proof:

```
#include <stdio.h>
#include <conio.h>
{
int i=10;
void main()
while()
{
printf("Hello");
}
getch();
}
```

When the above program is executed, it will not execute. It shows 'Expression syntax error'.

Multiple-choice Questions

1. In case 'for' loop, statement is terminated by semicolon __________.
   (a) The compiler will flag error message and program will not compiled
   (b) Program will be executed; however, scope of the 'for' loop will be NULL
   (c) The termination will not affect the performance of the 'for' loop
2. Which of the following loop statement uses two keywords?
   (a) for (b) do-while (c) while
3. Though the condition is false, which of the following loop statement executes once __________?
   (a) for (b) do-while (c) while
4. Entry-controlled loop is __________.
   (a) for (b) do-while (c) while
5. Exit-controlled loop is __________.
   (a) for (b) do-while (c) while
6. Which of the following loop statement is terminated by semicolon?
   (a) for (b) do-while (c) while

7. Which key you will use to terminate the infinite loop?

(a) Ctrl+Alt+Del (b) Ctrl+Break (c) Ctrl+Enter

8. Which of the following keyword you will apply to exit from the loop without increasing program code?

(a) `Continue` (b) `Break` (c) `Goto`

9. Which of the following is the infinite loop?

(a) `for(;;)` (b) `while` (condition) (c) None of the above

10. The role of `continue` with loop is, it takes ________.

(a) Next iteration (b) Reduced iteration (c) None of the above

11. What will be the value of x after the execution of the following program?

```
#include <stdio.h>
#include <conio.h>
void main()
{
int k;
float x=1;
clrscr();
for (k=0;k<4;k++)
x*=.2;
printf ("\nx=%g",x);
}
```

(a) $x = 0.0016$ (b) $x = 0.0008$ (c) $x = 1.6$ (d) None of the above

12. What will be the value of f after the execution of the following program?

```
#include <stdio.h>
#include <conio.h>
void main()
{
char k;
float f=5;
clrscr();
for (k=1;k<=10;k++)
{
f- =.1;
}
printf ("\nf=%g",f);
}
```

(a) $f = 4$ (b) $f = -65$ (c) $f = 66$ (d) None of the above

13. What will be the value of variable sqsum after the execution of the following program?

```
void main()
{
int i, sqsum=0;
clrscr();
for (i=1;i<=4;i++)
{
sqsum+=i*i;
}
printf ("\nThe Sum of Squares %d",sqsum);
}
```

(a) sqsum = 40 (b) sqsum = 30 (c) sqsum = 20

14. What will be the final value of *c* after the execution of the following program?

```
#include <stdio.h>
#include <conio.h>
void main()
{
int c=27,d=9;
clrscr();
while (d<=9)
{
d++;
printf ("\n %d",++c);
}
}
```

(a) 28 (b) 27 (c) 26 (d) 9

15. How many times the `printf()` statement will be executed?

```
void main()
{
int k;
k=11;
clrscr();
while(k<10)
{
```

```
printf("Hi");
--k;
}
}
```

(a) Not a single time (b) 11 times (c) Once (d) 1

16. What will be the value of variable sum?

```
void main()
{
int n=1245,k=1,sum=0;
clrscr();
while (n!=0)
{
k=n%10;
sum=sum+k;
k=n/10;
n=k;
}
printf ("Sum %d",sum);
}
```

(a) Sum =13 (b) Sum = 12 (c) Sum = 10

17. What will be the output of the following program?

```
void main()
{
int x=11,y=40;
clrscr();
while (x!=0)
{
gotoxy(y--,3);
printf ("%d",x%2);
x=x/2;
}
}
```

(a) 0011 (b) 1011 (c) 0010 (d) 0001

18. What will be the output of the following program?

```
void main()
{
char c=48;
clrscr();
while (c!='5')
{
while(1)
{
printf ("%c",c++);
break;
}
}
}
```

(a) 012345 (b) 01234 (c) 1

19. What will be the output of the following program?

```
void main()
{
char c=50;
clrscr();
while (c++!='5')
{
while(1)
{
printf ("%c",c++);
c+=2;
break;
}
c--;
printf ("%c",c);
break;
}
}
```

(a) 45 (b) 35 (c) 25 (d) 50

Problem on 'do-while' Loop

20. What would be the final value of x after execution of the following program?

```
#include <stdio.h>
#include <conio.h>
void main()
{
int x=1;
clrscr();
do
while (x<=7)
  {
  x++;
  } while (x<=5);
  printf ("\n x=%d",x);
}
```

(a) $x = 8$ (b) $x = 6$
(c) $x = 2$ (d) None of the above

21. What will be the final values of x and y?

```
#include <stdio.h>
#include <conio.h>
void main()
{
int x=1,y=1;
clrscr();
do
while (x<=8)
  {
  x++,y++;
  } while(y<=5);
  printf ("\n x=%d y=%d",x,y);
}
```

(a) $x = 9\ y = 9$ (b) $x = 8\ y = 6$
(c) $x = 6\ y = 6$ (d) None of the above

22. What is the output of the following program?

```
void main()
{
int nm=0;
do
{
--nm;
printf ("%d",nm);
nm++;
}
while(nm>=0);
}
```

(a) The loop will run infinitely. (b) The program will not be compiled.
(c) Loop will not be executed.

23. What will be the value of *s* after execution of the following program?

```
void main()
{
int i=5,a=1;
int s=0;
clrscr();
do
{s=s+a++;
} while (a<=i);
printf ("\b\bs=%d",s);
}
```

(a) $s = 15$ (b) $s = 36$ (c) $s = 40$

24. How many `'while'` statements are possible in `'do-while'` loop?

(a) 2 (b) 1 (c) 3 (d) None of the above

25. The `for` (; ;) is equivalent to __________.

(a) `while` (false) (b) `while` (true) (c) `while` (0) (d) None of the above

26. Which of the following is equivalent of executing `'for'` loop without its body?

(a) `for(; ;)` (b) `for(;)` (c) `for(; ;);` (d) `for()`

27. Which of the following loop is used in C language when programmer is not aware of number of iterations a loop will follow?

(a) `for` (b) `while` (c) `do-while`

28. The break statement exits __________.

(a) Only from the inner loop (b) From the innermost loop (c) Only from the inner `switch`

29. The correct syntax of `'for'` loop is

(a) `for(i=0;i<n;i++) {----}`
(b) `for(i=0,j=0;i<n && j<n; i++,j++) {-----}`

(c) `for(i=0;i++<n;){-----}`
(d) All of these

30. Which 'for' loop will terminate itself
(a) `for(i=1;i<10;i--) {----}`
(b) `for(i=1,j=1;i++>=1 && j++>=1;) {----}`
(c) `for(;;) {----}`
(d) `for(i=1,j=1;i||j;i++,j++) {----}`

31. The valid 'for' loop is
(a) `for(i=0;i<10)` (b) `for(i>4;i--)` (c) `for(i=3)` (d) `for(i=0;;)`

32. Which of the following prints 0 1 2 3.....9

(a)
```
void main()
{
    int i;
    clrscr();
 for(i=0;i<10;i++)
 printf("%d",i);
getch();
}
```

(b)
```
void main()
{
    int i,j;
    clrscr();
for(i=0,j=0;i<10;i++)
{
printf("%d",j);
j++;
}
 getch();
}
```

(c)
```
void main()
{
    int i,j;
for(i=0,j=0;j/2<10;i++,j=j+2)
printf("%d",i);
getch();
}
```

(d) All of the above

33.
```
void main()
{
int i;
clrscr();
for(i=0;++i<=10;)
printf("%d", i);
getch();
}
```

The output is
(a) 0 1 2,...9 (b) 1 2 3,...9 (c) 1 2 3,...10 (d) Error

34. Which is the correct o/p?

```
void main()
{
```

```
int i,j;
clrscr();
for(i=0;i<10;i++)
for(j=0;j<10;i++)
printf("%d",i*j++);
getch();
}
```

The output is

(a) 0 1 2.....99 (b) 0 1 2...9.....0 1 2...9
(c) 0 1 4 9 16.... 81 (d) 0 1 2 3... 9

Answers

1. (b)	2. (b)	3. (b)	4. (c)	5. (b)	6. (b)	7. (b)	8. (b)	9. (a)	10. (a)
11. (a)	12. (a)	13. (b)	14. (a)	15. (a)	16. (b)	17. (b)	18. (b)	19. (b)	20. (a)
21. (a)	22. (a)	23. (a)	24. (a)	25. (b)	26. (c)	27. (b)	28. (b)	29. (b)	30. (d)
31. (d)	32. (d)	33. (c)	34. (c)						

True or False

1. A loop repeatedly executes a block of statements for certain number of times.
2. The loop `for(; ;)` is a non-working loop.
3. The `for(; ;)` loop with no arguments can be executed.
4. The loop `for (a=1;a<20;a++)` will be executed for 20 times.
5. The `while(1)` is an infinite loop.
6. The loop cannot be nested.
7. Even if the condition is false the `do-while` loop executes once.
8. The `do while` loop must be terminated by semi-colon.
9. The `{ }` defines the block of the statement.
10. In case `{ }` is not defined after the loop statement, the `default` scope is one statement.

Answers

1. True 2. False 3. True 4. False 5. True 6. False 7. True 8. True 9. True 10. True

Additional Questions

Find the output/s of the following program/s.

1. Program to print numbers and their squares from 1 to 3 using `for` loop.

```
void main()
{
int i;
clrscr();
```

```
for (i=1;i<=3;i++)
{
printf ("\n %2d %3d",i,i*i);
}
}

OUTPUT:
1   1
2   4
3   9
```

2. Program to print numbers and their square roots from 1 to 4 using `for` loop.

```
#include <math.h>
void main()
{
int i;
float a;
clrscr();
for (i=1;i<=4;i++)
{
printf ("\n %d \t %.3f",i,a=sqrt(i));
}
getche();
}

OUTPUT:
1   1.000
2   1.414
3   1.732
4   2.000
```

3. Program to print factors of 10 using `for` and `if` loop.

```
void main()
{
int i,m=10;
clrscr();
for(i=1;i<=m;i++)
if(m%i==0)
printf("%d",i);
getche();
}

OUTPUT:
1  2  5  10
```

4. Program to print the numbers from 1 to 5 in ascending and descending order.

```
void main()
{
int i=0;
clrscr();
for (;++i<=5;)
printf ("%2d",i);
printf ("\n\n");
for (;--i>=1;)
printf ("%2d",i);
getche();
}

OUTPUT:
1 2 3 4 5

5 4 3 2 1
```

5. Program to print even numbers which lies between 1 to 9. Using `for` loop and nested `if..else` with `break` and `continue` keywords.

```
void main()
{
int i=1;
clrscr();
for ( ; ;)
          {
          if (i==9)
          break;
          else
          if (i%2==0)
          {
          printf ("%d\t",i);
          i++;
          continue;
          }
          else
          {
          i++;
          continue;
          }
          }
          getche();
}

OUTPUT:
2         4         6         8
```

6. Display ASCII values and corresponding characters

```
void main()
{
char x;
int i;
clrscr();
for(i=65;i<=68;i++)
        {
        printf("%d %c",i,i);
        }
getche();
}

OUTPUT:
65 A   66 B   67 C   68 D
```

7. Leap year program

```
void main()
{
int y,x=0;
clrscr();
for(y=2000;y<=2007;y++)
        {
        if(y%4==0 && y%100!=0 || y%400==0)
        {
        printf("%d",y);
        x++;
        }
        }
printf("\n\n%d",x);
getche();
}

OUTPUT:
2000  2004
2
```

8. Largest from an array

```
void main()
{
int x[5]={5,15,3,10,7};
int i;
clrscr();
for (i=0;i<5;i++)
```

```
{
        if(x[i]>x[i+1])
        x[i+1]=x[i];
}
printf ("%d\t",x[i]);
getche();
}

OUTPUT:
15
```

9. Identify exact square numbers up to 100

```
#include <math.h>
void main()
{
int i,x,count=0;
clrscr();
for(i=0;i<100;i++)
    {
    x=sqrt(i);
    if(i==x*x)
    {
            printf("%d",i);
            count+=1;
    }

    }
    getche();
}

OUTPUT:
0 1 4 9 16 25 36 49 64 81
```

10. Prime number program

```
void main()
{
int i=19,n;
clrscr();
    {
            for(n=2;n<i-1;n++)
            {
            if(i%n==0)
                    {
                    printf("\nThe number %d is not a prime",i);
```

```
                    getche();
                    exit();
                    }
            }
            printf("\nThe number %d is a prime",i);
            getche();
            }
    }

    OUTPUT:
    The number 19 is a prime
```

Programs on Nested for Loop

11. Some mathematical problem

```
void main()
{
int i,j=0;
clrscr();
for (i=48;i<=49;i++)
        {
        for (j=49;j<=50;j++)
        printf("%c%c",i,j);
        printf("\n");
        }
        getche();
}

OUTPUT:
01 02
11 12
```

12. Multiples of 1, 2 and 3

```
#include <math.h>
void main()
{
int i,x,j;
clrscr();
for(i=1;i<=4 ;i++)
        {
        for(j=1;j<=3;j++)
        printf("%d",i*j);
        printf("\n");
        printf("");
```

```
            }
             getche();
}

OUTPUT:
1 2 3
2 4 6
3 6 9
4 8 12
```

13. Prime number program

```
#include<math.h>
#include<stdio.h>
void main()
{
int i,n=0,j,x;
clrscr();
printf("\n\n Prime numbers from 1 to 15:-");
printf("");
for(i=1;i<=15;i++)
          {
          x=sqrt(i);
          for(j=2;j<=x;j++)
                   {
                   if(i%j==0)
                   goto end;
                   }
                   printf("%d",i);
                   n++;
                   end:;
          }
                   printf("\n\n Total prime numbers from
                   1 to 15:- %d\n",n);
   getche();
}

OUTPUT:
Prime numbers from 1 to 15: 1 2 3 5 7 11 13
Total prime numbers from 1 to 15: 7
```

14. Display stars in specific order.

```
#include <stdio.h>
void main()
{
```

```
    int x=3,i,j;
    clrscr();
    for (i=1;i<=x;i++)
            {
             for (j=1;j<=i;j++)
                     {
                      printf ("*");
                     }
             printf("\n");
            }
            getche();
    }

    OUTPUT:
    *
    *  *
    *  *  *
```

15. Display numbers in ascending order

```
    void main()
    {
    int x[5]={5,15,3,10,7};
    int i,j,temp;
    clrscr();

    for (i=0;i<5;i++)
        {
          for (j=i;j<4;j++)
          {
               if(x[i]>x[j+1])
               {
               temp=x[i];
               x[i]=x[j+1];
               x[j+1]=temp;
               }
          }
        }
    for (i=0;i<5;i++)
    printf ("%d\t",x[i]);
    getche();
    }

    OUTPUT:
    3       5       7       10      15
```

16. Program to display string.

```
void main()
{
int i=0;
char a[5]={'A','s','h','o','k'};
clrscr();
printf("\nTransmitted information is:-");

while(i<=4)
{
printf("%c",a[i]);
i++;
}
printf("\n Received information is:-");
i=0;
while (i<=4)
{
printf("%c",a[i]+3);
i++;
}
getche();
}

OUTPUT:
Transmitted information is:-  A  s  h  o  k
Received  information is:-    D  v  k  r  n
```

17. Program to display factorial of 6.

```
void main()
{
int a=6,b=1,fact=1;
clrscr();
do
{
    fact=fact*b;
    b=b+1;
}
while(b<=a);
printf("%d",fact);
getche();
}

OUTPUT:
720
```

18. Program to input binary number and find its decimal equivalent number.

```
void main()
{
int num=1111,rem,n,d,k=1,dec=0;
clrscr();
        n=num;
        do
        {
        rem=num%10;
        d=rem*k;
        dec=d+dec;
        k=2*k;
        num=num/10;
        }
        while(num>0);
printf("Binary number =%d& corresponding it's decimal
number=%d",n,dec);
}

OUTPUT:
Binary number = 1111 and its corresponding decimal
number = 15
```

Find the bug/s in the following program/s.

1.

```
void main()
{
float i;
clrscr();
for(i=20;i>=19;i=i-0.25)
     {
     printf("%2.2d",i);
     }
     getche();
}
```

Bug: `%f` is needed instead of `%d` in `printf` statement.

2.

```
void main()
{
int i;
clrscr();
for (i=1;i<5;)
```

```
  i++;
  printf ("\nnumber: %5d it's Square: %8d",i,i*i);
}
```

Bug: Statements following `i++` should be enclosed within curly braces `{}` as scope of `for` loop

3.

```
void main()
{
int i,j=1,n=4;
float sum=1.0;
clrscr();

       for(i=1;i<=n;i++)
       {
       j=j*i;
       sum=sum+i/j;
       }
       printf("\n %.2f",sum);
       getche();
}
```

Bug : `(float)i/j` is expected in sum statement.

4.

```
void main()
{
int  h,m,s;
clrscr();
for (h=1;h<=12;h++)
{
  clrscr();
  for (m=1;m<=59;m++)
{
  clrscr();
  for (s=1;s<=59;s++)
gotoxy(8,8);
printf ("hh  mm  ss");
gotoxy(8,9);
printf ("%d   %d   %d",h,m,s);
sleep(1);
}
}
}
```

Bug : Scope of `for` loop is not defined

7

Array

1. What is an array?

Ans:

1. An array is a linear data structure.
2. It is a finite collection of data elements.
3. An array permits homogeneous data. It means its each data element is of same type.
4. Similar data type elements are stored contiguously in the memory and that too under one variable name.

2. How elements of an array are stored?

Ans: Elements of array are stored in contiguous memory locations. One-dimensional or more than one-dimensional elements are stored contiguously. Figure 7.1 shows storage of elements of a one-dimensional array Num[5] contiguously.

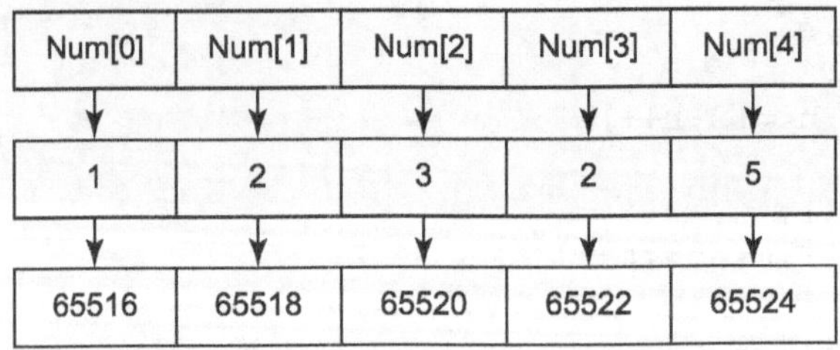

Figure 7.1 Storage of One-Dimensional Array

Where

```
Num[0] = 1 and its Address : 65516
Num[1] = 2 and its Address : 65518
Num[2] = 3 and its Address : 65520
Num[3] = 2 and its Address : 65522
Num[4] = 5 and its Address : 65524
```

3. Explain the syntax of a one-dimensional array.

Ans: Declaration of a one-dimensional array can be done with data type first, followed by it is variable name and, at last, the size is enclosed in square bracket.

The syntax of declaration of one-dimensional array is as follows:

```
Data-type var_name[Size];
```

Example:

int *a[5];*

It tells to the compiler that ***a*** is an integer type of array and can store five integers. The compiler reserves 2 bytes of memory for each integer array element, i.e., 10 bytes are reserved for storing five integers in the memory.

In the same way, array of different data types can be declared as follows:

```
char ch[10];
float real[10];
long num[5];
```

4. How are array elements accessed?

Ans: Individual elements of the array are accessed by specifying the subscript. Index is the other name of subscript. The subscript is enclosed in the square bracket. Subscript provides an easy way to address the individual elements of an array. Array elements are numbered starting from 0, i.e., subscript starts from 0. The first element of the array is num[0], second is num[1] and so on.

Subscript to the array specifies an exact element in the array.

For example,

```
num[0]=1; /* First element*/
num[1]=2;
num[2]=4;
num[3]=2;
num[4]=5;
```

5. How is one-dimensional array initialization done?

Ans: Assigning initial values to an array is nothing but initialization of an array. The array initialization can be done as under:

int *a [5]={1,2,3,4,5};*

where five elements are stored in an array ***a***. The array elements are stored sequentially in separate locations. Then, question arises how to call individually to each element from this bunch of integer elements. Reading of array elements begins from ***0***. By indicating the position of element, one can retrieve any element of an array. Array elements are called with array name followed by element numbers. Table 7.1 explains the same.

Table 7.1 Calling Array Elements

a[0] refers to 1st element i.e. 1
a[1] refers to 2nd element i.e. 2
a[2] refers to 3rd element i.e. 3
a[3] refers to 4th element i.e. 4
a[4] refers to 5th element i.e. 5

6. How the one-dimensional array elements are read from the keyboard and displayed on the screen?

Ans: Data in the array can be placed with the following C code:

```
int num[5];
int i=0;
while(i<5)
{
("Enter the elements of array:");
scanf("%d",&num[i]);
i++;
}
```

Array elements can be printed on the screen using `printf()` statement. Here, loop is to be used. For example,

```
for(i=0;i<5;i++)
{
printf("num[%d]=%d\n",i,num[i]);
}
```

7. What are the characteristics of array?

Ans:

1. The declaration **int** ***a[5]*** is nothing but creation of five variables of integer types in memory. Instead of declaring five variables for five values, the programmer can define them in an array.
2. All the elements of an array share the same name and they are distinguished from one another with the help of element number.
3. The element number in an array plays major role for calling each element.
4. Any particular element of an array can be modified separately without disturbing to other elements.

   int ***a[5]={1,2,3,4,8};***

   If programmer needs to replace 8 with 10, then it need not require changing all other numbers expect 8. To carry out this task, the statement ***a[4]=10;*** can be used. Here, other three elements are not disturbed.
5. Any element of an array ***a []*** can be assigned/equated to another ordinary variable or array variable of its type.

For example,

```
b = a[2];
a[2]=a[3];
```

(a) In the statement ***b*** = ***a[2]*** or vice versa, the value of ***a[2]*** is assigned to ***b***, where ***b*** is an integer.

(b) In the statement ***a[2]=a[3]*** or vice versa, the value of ***a[2]*** is assigned to ***a[3],*** where both the elements are of the same array.

(c) The array elements are stored contiguously in memory locations.

6. Once the array is declared, its lowest boundary cannot be changed but upper boundary can be expanded. The array name itself is constant pointer and we cannot modify it. Therefore, the lowest boundary of an array cannot be expanded. In other words, even if the boundary exceeds than specified, nothing happens. The compiler throws no errors.
7. We know that array name itself is pointer. Though it is a pointer, it does not need '*' operator. The brackets [] automatically denote that the variable is a pointer.

8. All the elements of an array share the same name and they are distinguished from one another with the help of the element number.
9. The amount of memory required for an array depends upon data type and number of elements. The total size in bytes for a one-dimensional array is computed as follows.

   Total bytes = sizeof(data type) X size of array

10. The operation such as insertion and deletion of an element can be done with list. List can be implemented with an array.
11. When an array is declared and not initialized, it contains garbage values. If we declared an array as **static**, all elements are initialized to zero. However, the values of `static` type data persist and remain in the memory as `long` as program executes. To overcome this problem, first, initialize the element of an array with zero or any number. All the remaining elements are automatically initialized to zero. Provided that the initialization should be done in the declaration statement of array.

8. Write a program to display one-dimensional array elements with their addresses.

Ans:

```
#include <stdio.h>
#include <conio.h>

int main()
{
int num[5]={1,2,3,2,5};
clrscr();

printf("\n num[0] = %d Address : %u",num[0],&num[0]);
printf("\n num[1] = %d Address : %u",num[1],&num[1]);
printf("\n num[2] = %d Address : %u",num[2],&num[2]);
printf("\n num[3] = %d Address : %u",num[3],&num[3]);
printf("\n num[4] = %d Address : %u",num[4],&num[4]);
return 0;
}

OUTPUT:
num[0] = 1 Address : 65516
num[1] = 2 Address : 65518
num[2] = 3 Address : 65520
num[3] = 2 Address : 65522
num[4] = 5 Address : 65524
```

Explanation: In the output of the program, elements and their addresses are displayed. Recall that integer requires two bytes in memory. Hence, the memory locations displayed at the output have a difference of two. From the above program, it is clear that array elements are stored in successive memory locations.

9. What are strings? How are they declared using an array?

Ans: In C language, the sequence of characters, digits and symbols that is enclosed within quotation marks is called string. The string is always declared as character array and its elements are stored in contiguous memory locations.

In other words, in C, a string is defined as an array of characters. To manipulate text such as words and sentences, normally strings are used. Every string is terminated with *'\0' (NULL)* character. The NULL character is a byte with all bits at logic zero. Hence, its decimal value is zero. A pointer can access the string. The value of the string is its base address, i.e., addresses of the first character. When a string is created, a few compilers place the string in the memory where it cannot be modified.
An example of a string is as follows:

char ***name[ ]={'I','N','D','I','A','\0'};***

10. Write a program to display character array with their addresses.

Ans:

```
#include<stdio.h>
#include <conio.h>
void main()
{
char name[10]={'A','R','R','A','Y'};
int i=0;
clrscr();
printf("\n Character Memory Location \n");
while(name[i]!='\0')
{
printf("\n [%c]\t\t [%u]",name[i],&name[i]);
i++;
}
}
```

OUTPUT:

```
Character Memory Location
[A]          4054
[R]          4055
[R]          4056
[A]          4057
[Y]          4058
```

Explanation: The elements of an array are stored in contiguous memory locations. In the above example, the elements of one-dimensional array 'A', 'R', 'R', 'A' and 'Y' are stored from location 4054 to 4058.

One-dimensional character array elements will be stored in memory as per Table 7.2.

Table 7.2 Character Array Elements and Their Locations

Array Element No	0	1	2	3	4
ELEMENTS	A	R	R	A	Y
MEMORY ADDRESSES	4054	4055	4056	4057	4058

11. What are the drawbacks of linear array?

Ans: Following are the drawbacks of linear array:

1. The number of elements, which are to be stored in an array, is to be known first.
2. When an array is declared, memory is allocated to it. If array is not filled completely, the vacant place occupies memory.
3. Once the array is declared, its dimension cannot be changed.
4. We cannot work with elements of dissimilar data type.
5. Insertion and deletion of an element is difficult in an array as elements are stored in contiguous memory locations.

12. Explain various operations that can be done on an array.

Ans: Besides deleting/inserting an element of an array, following additional operations can be performed on an array. In addition to insertion and deletion, as explained in Q 10 above, the following are some other operations on array.

1. Searching: An array element can be searched. The process of seeking specific elements in an array is called searching.
2. Merging: Merging of two arrays is an important operation with an array. The elements of two arrays are merged into a single one. The easier way of merging two arrays is first copy all elements of one array into third one and then copy all elements of the second array into the third one.

   One should take into account the following points.

   1. Elements of one array can be appended to end of the second array.
   2. Elements of two arrays can be merged in alternate order.
   3. The size of resulting array must be more than the size of the two arrays.

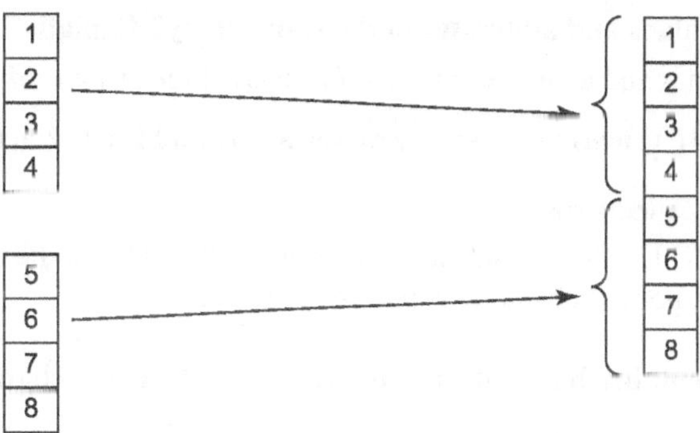

3. Sorting: Arranging elements in a specific order either in ascending or in descending order is known sorting.

13. Explain insertion and deletion of an element in array.

Ans:

1. Insertion: This operation is used to insert an element at a specified position in an array. Process of insertion requires three steps and they are shown in the following figure.

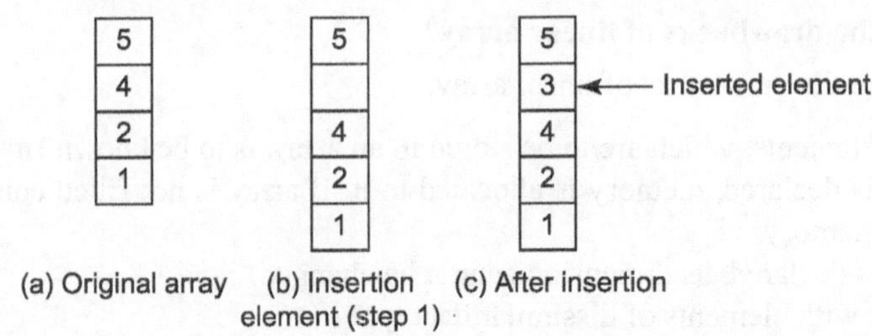

(a) Original array (b) Insertion element (step 1) (c) After insertion

2. Deletion: User specifies the element to be deleted. The specified element is then removed from an array. The memory location is the same; only its contents are changed as shown in the following figures.

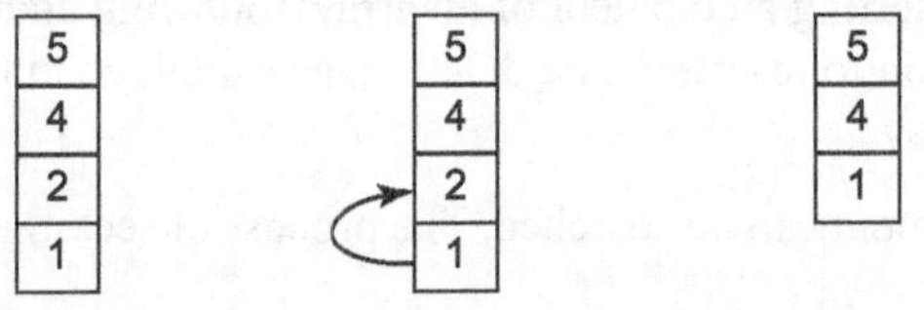

Original array Shifting one element up After deletion

14. What is the relation between array name and element number? How elements are referred using base address?

Ans: Array name contains base address of the array, i.e., address of the 0th element in the array. To refer element using array name, the following syntax is used.
array_name[index_of_element] or *(array_name + index_of_element+1)
where, index_of_element is the position of that element in the array.

15. Can we store values and addresses in the same array? Explain.

Ans: We can store values and addresses in the same array if the array is of `unsigned` integers.

16. Mention the differences between character array and integer array.

1. Character arrays are called strings.
2. In character array NULL ('\0'), a character is automatically added at the end, whereas in integer or other types of arrays, no null/character is placed at the end.

17. Array name contains base address of the array. Can we change the base address of the array?

Ans: The array name itself is a constant pointer and we cannot modify it.

18. Explain two-dimensional array.

Ans: Two-dimensional arrays can be thought of rectangular display of elements with rows and columns. Consider the following example:

```
int x[3][3];
```

```
        Column0 Column1 Column2
Row0 x[0][0] x[0][1] x[0][2]
Row1 x[1][0] x[1][1] x[1][2]
Row2 x[2][0] x[2][1] x[2][2]
```

Actually, the elements are stored in the contiguous memory locations. The two-dimensional array is a collection of two one-dimensional arrays. The meaning of the first argument is in *x* [3][3] means number of rows, i.e., the number of one-dimensional array and the second argument indicates the number of elements.

19. Explain the initialization procedure of two-dimensional array.

Ans: Two-dimensional array can be initialized as follows:

```
int empl[2][2] = {
                  {1,2},
                  {4,5}
                  };
```

Here, in this example, the elements of two rows and two columns are initialized. The internal pairs of braces are not obligatory. The same array can be initialized as follows:

```
int empl[2][2] = { 1,2,4,5};
```

We can also read the elements of the array through the keyboard with using nested loops.

20. Write a program to display the elements of two-dimensional array and their addresses.

Ans: The one-dimensional array can be accessed using a single loop.

```
#include <stdio.h>
#include <conio.h>

void main()

{

int i,j;
int a[3][3]={1,2,3,4,5,6,7,0,9};
clrscr();
printf("\n Array elements and address ");
printf("\n\t Col-0 Col-1 Col-2");
printf("\n\t ====== ====== ======");
printf("\nRow0");

for(i=0;i<3;i++)

{

for(j=0;j<3;j++)
printf(" %d[%u]",a[i][j],&a[i][j]);
printf("\nRow%d",i+1);

}

printf("\r ");

}
```

```
OUTPUT:
Array elements and address
        Col-0        Col-1       Col-2
   ====== ====== ======
   Row0 1 [65508] 2 [65510] 3 [65512]
   Row1 4 [65514] 5 [65516] 6 [65518]
   Row2 7 [65520] 8 [65522] 9 [65524]
```

Explanation: The one-dimensional array can be accessed using a single loop. From the above program's output, you can see that the memory address displayed is in sequence and it is true that elements of two-dimension array are stored in successive memory locations. However, for two-dimensional array, two loops are required for row and column. The inner loop helps to access the row-wise elements and outer loop changes the column number. Like, one-dimensional array base address of array can be stored in pointer.

21. Give the initialization of three-dimensional arrays.

Ans: Three-dimensional array can be initialized as follows:

```
int num[3][3][3] =
        {1,2,3,

         4,5,6,
         7,8,9,

         1,4,7,
         2,5,8,
         3,6,9,
         1,4,4,
         2,4,7,
         8,8,5};
```

Here, we can also read the elements of the array through the keyboard with using nested loops.

22. Is it possible to declare the size of an array at the run time?

Ans: No, it is not possible to declare the size of an array at the run time. Therefore, we can declare the size of an array at the compile time only.

23. Explain multi-dimensional array.

Ans: The C program allows array of two or multi dimensions. The compiler determines the restriction on it. The syntax of multi-dimensional array is follows:

```
arrayname[S1][S2][S3]...[Sn]
```

where S*i* is the size of the *i*th dimensions

For example, three-dimensional array can be initialized as follows:

```
int mat[3][3][3] =

{

1,2,3,
4,5,6,
7,8,9,
1,4,7,
```

```
2,5,8,
3,6,9,
1,4,4,
2,4,7,
8,8,5
};
```

Multiple-choice Questions

1. One-dimensional array needs only _________ subscript(s).
   (a) One
   (b) Two
   (c) Both of the above
2. An array is a collection of elements of _________ data type.
   (a) Dissimilar
   (b) Similar
   (c) None of the above
3. An array stores elements _________ in memory.
   (a) Randomly
   (b) Non sequentially
   (c) Contiguously
4. Each array element is stored in separate _________.
   (a) Memory locations
   (b) Value
   (c) Data type
5. `int` *x*[5]; this array can hold values between _________ and _________.
   (a) −32768; 32767
   (b) 0; 255
   (c) −32768; 32768
6. `int` *x*[5] = {2,3,4,5,6}; the base address is 65564 then the location of element 2 is _________.
   (a) 65564
   (b) 65566
   (c) 65568
7. `int` *x*[3] = {1,2,3}; then the *x*[2] is _________.
   (a) 1 (b) 3 (c) 2
8. What is the output of the following program?

```
void main()
{
int x[]={1,2.2,3},i;
```

```
clrscr();
printf("%f",x[1]);
}
```

(a) The program will not run.
(b) The program will run with warning messages.
(c) None of the above.
(d) 0th element (c) 1st element

9. The total memory occupied by the array `long` k[4] is ________.
   (a) 16
   (b) 8
   (c) 4
10. `int` *x*[2]={12,26}, then *x*[2] is ________.
   (a) 0
   (b) 15
   (c) Garbage value
11. `char` c[]="Hello" the H is stored at 65470, then the o is stored at ________.
   (a) 65474
   (b) 65475
   (c) 65480
12. In `int` *x*[10]; the number 10 specified in the square bracket represents the ________.
   (a) 10 addresses
   (b) 10 values
   (c) 10 lines
13. The first element according to C compiler physically is a ________.
   (a) 2nd element
   (b) 0th element
   (c) 1st element
14. What is the index number of last element of an array containing 10 elements?
   (a) 10
   (b) 11
   (c) 9
15. Which one of the following is correct declaration of an array?
   (a) arr[5];
   (b) `int` arr{5};
   (c) `int` arr[5];
16. Which one of the following is correct declaration of two-dimensional array?
   (a) arr arr[5];
   (b) `int` arr[5][5];
   (c) `int` arr[5]{5};

17. Array element of two dimensions is stored _________.
    (a) Contagious memory locations
    (b) Alternate memory locations
    (c) Any locations
18. A character array always ends with _________.
    (a) Null ('\0') character.
    (b) Question Mark (?).
    (c) Full Stop (.).
19. If you declare an array without static, the elements will be set to _________.
    (a) Null value.
    (b) Zero.
    (c) Garbage value.
20. Arrays cannot be initialized if they are _________.
    (a) Automatic
    (b) External
    (c) Static
    (d) None of the above
21. All the elements in the array must be _________.
    (a) Initialized
    (b) Defined
    (c) Both (a) and (b)
    (d) None of the above
22. What will happen if you assign values in a few locations of an array _________?
    (a) Rest of the elements will be set to 0.
    (b) Compiler error message will be displayed.
    (c) Possibly system will crash.
23. The array name itself is pointer to _________.
    (a) 0th element
    (b) 1st element
    (c) Last element
24. `int` *x*[3]; the base address of *x* is 65460, then all elements are stored at _________.
    (a) 65460, 65462, 65464
    (b) 65460, 65461, 65462
    (c) 65460, 65464, 65468
25. `int` j[4] the sizeof(j) and sizeof (`int`) will display the value _________.
    (a) 8, 2
    (b) 2, 8
    (c) 2, 2
26. Number of elements in an array between [ ] must be a (an) _________.
    (a) Integer expression
    (b) Character

(c) Float
(d) Double

27. How many rows and columns are there in int num[2][3]={ {1,2,3},{4,5,6} };?
(a) Two rows and three columns
(b) Three rows and two columns
(c) None of the above

28. What are the values of first row in int num[2][3]={ 1,2,3,4 };?
(a) 1, 2, 3,
(b) 2, 3, 4
(c) 1, 2, 4

29. What are the values of second row in int num[2][3]={ 1,2,3,4 };?
(a) 1, 2, 3,
(b) 2, 3, 4
(c) 4, 0, 0

30. What is the output of int num[2][3]={ {1,2,3,4},{3,4,5,6} };?
(a) 1, 2, 3,
(b) 2, 3, 4
(c) Compilation error

31. What is the value of a[1] in static int [3];?
(a) 1
(b) 2
(c) 0

32. A character array always ends with ________.
(a) Null ('\0') character
(b) Question Mark (?)
(c) Full Stop (.)

33. If you declare array without static, the elements will be set to ________.
(a) Null value
(b) Zero
(c) Garbage value

34. Assume name of the array is arr and its size is 10. What will be the address of first element of that array arr?
(a) &arr[1];
(b) arr;
(c) &arr[-1];.

35. What will be the output of the following program?

```
#include <stdio.h>
#include <conio.h>
void main()
{
```

```
int a1[5]={1};
int b=0,k=0;
clrscr();
for(b=0;b<=4;b++)
{
printf("%3d",++a1[0]);
}
}
```

(a) 2 3 4 5 6
(b) 1 2 3 4 5
(c) 1 1 1 1 1 1
(d) 1 2 2 2 2 2

36. What will be the output of the following program?

```
void main()
{
 int j[]={5,1,2,5,4,8};
 int m[]={1,5,8,4,5,9};
 int l[]={1,2,9,1,5,9},k;
 for(k=0;k<6;k++)
 l[k]=j[k]+m[k]-l[k];
 clrscr();
 for(k=0;k<6;k++)
 (" %d ", l[k]);
}
```

(a) 5 4 1 8 4 8
(b) 5 5 1 8 4 9
(c) 1 2 5 5 5 9

37. What is the output of the following program?

```
void main()
{
 int j[]={15,11,17,15,14,18};
 int m[]={1,5,8,4,5,9};
 int l[]={1,2,9,1,5,9},k;
 for(k=0;k<6;k++)
 l[k]=j[k]-m[k]/l[k];
 clrscr();
```

```
  for(k=0;k<6;k++)
  printf(" %d ", l[k]);
}
```

(a) 14 9 17 11 13 17
(b) 12 8 16 10 12 16
(c) 14 19 17 10 12 11

38. What is the output of the following program?

```
void main()
{
 char a[]={'A','B','C','D','E','F'};
 char b[]={'0','1','2','3','4','4'};
 char c[6],k;
 for(k=0;k<6;k++)
 c[k]=a[k]+b[k];
 clrscr();
 for(k=0;k<6;k++)
 printf(" %c ", c[k]);
 }
```

(a) q s u w y z
(b) Q S U W Y Z
(c) K J L M N O

39. If starting address of array `int arr[5] = {5,4,3,2,1};` is 1042 then value 1 is at location
(a) 1048
(b) 1050
(c) 1046
(d) Same as the array i.e. 1042

40. The valid 2D-array definition is
(a) `int b[][2] = {{1},{3,4}};`
(b) `int b[2][2] = {1,2,3,4};`
(c) `int b[][2] = {1,2,3};`
(d) All of these

41. The general syntax for any type of array is
(a) `data_type variable_name[size];`
(b) `data_type variable_name[];`
(c) `data_type variable_name[][] = initialization;`
(d) `data_type variable_name[size][];`

42. The correct syntax for integer array in C is
(a) `int b[3]; a[0]=1;a[1]=2;a[2]=3;`
(b) `int b[] = {1,2,3};`

(c) `int [3] = {1,2,3};`
(d) All the above

43. Choose the incorrect syntax
(a) `char c[]="India";`
(b) `char c[10]="India";`
(c) `char c[10]={"I","n","d","i","a"};`
(d) `char c[] = {'I','n','d','i','a'};`

44. `int a[2];` is integer array. Which of the following will correctly insert values into it?
(a) `a[1] = 1; a[2] = 2;`
(b) `for(i=1;i<=2;i++)a[i] = i;`
(c) `int a[0] = i; int a[1] = 2;`
(d) `for(i=0;i<2;i++)a[i] = i;`

45. `printf("%s",metro);` The metro will be correctly printed for
(a) `char metro [] = "Mumbai";`
(b) `char metro [6] = "Mumbai";`
(c) `char metro [6] = {'M','u','m','b','a','i'};`
(d) `char metro []; city = "Mumbai";`

46. `int a[] = {1,2,3,4,5};` to print the array the correct option is
(a) `printf("%d ",a);`
(b) `for(i=0;i<5;i++)`
(c) `printf("%d ",a++);`
(d) `for(i=0; i<5; printf("%d ", a[i++]));`
(e) `printf("%d %d %d %d %d ", a[1], a[2], a[3], a[4], a[5]);`

47. What is the o/p?

```
void main()
{
char name[] = "Neha",
int age[] = {21,22,23};
clrscr();
printf("%d %d %d %d ",sizeof(name),sizeof(age),
sizeof(*name),sizeof(*age));
getch();
}
```

The output is

(a) 1 2 2 2
(b) 5 6 1 2
(c) 6 2 2 2
(d) 1 6 2 2

48.

```
void main()
{
char c[] = "ABCDE"; /*The starting address is 2000.*/
int i;
```

```
clrscr();
for(i=0;i<sizeof(c);i++)
if(*(c+i) == 'c')
{
printf("C found");
break;
}
printf("%d",(c+i));
getch();
}
```

The output is
(a) 2000
(b) 2002
(c) 2006
(d) 2008

49. `char india[4][8] = {"India ","is ","my ","country"};`
The equivalent code for this is
(a) `char *india = "India is my country";`
(b) `char *india[] = {"India is my country"};`
(c) `char *india[] = {"India ","is ","my ","country"};`
(d) `char *india[] = "India is my country";`

50. `int arr[3][3]={{1,2},{3,4},{5,6}};`
The statement which prints 4 is
(a) `printf("%d ",*(*(arr+1)+1));`
(b) `printf("%d ",*(*a+4));`
(c) `printf("%d ",*(*(arr+2)-2));`
(d) All of these

Answers

1. (a)	2. (b)	3. (c)	4. (a)	5. (a)	6. (a)	7. (b)	8. (b)	9. (a)	10. (a)
11. (a)	12. (b)	13. (b)	14. (c)	15. (c)	16. (b)	17. (a)	18. (a)	19. (c)	20. (d)
21. (c)	22. (a)	23. (a)	24. (a)	25. (a)	26. (a)	27. (a)	28. (a)	29. (c)	30. (c)
31. (c)	32. (a)	33. (c)	34. (b)	35. (a)	36. (a)	37. (a)	38. (a)	39. (b)	40. (d)
41. (a)	42. (d)	43. (c)	44. (d)	45. (a)	46. (c)	47. (b)	48. (c)	49. (c)	50. (d)

True or False

1. An array is a collection of elements of similar data type.
2. There is no boundary checking in C for arrays.
3. When an array is declared memory is reserved for it.
4. Array can be defined of any data type but not of strut data type.

5. Array elements are stored in successive memory locations.
6. The array name itself is an address.
7. The `stdin()` is a predefined stream.
8. Character array always ends with NULL char.
9. Array cannot be declared as static.
10. Array can be declared as constant.
11. Matrix operations can be easily manipulated using arrays.
12. The `sscanf()` reads character from array.
13. If any array cannot be filled completely, the blank spaces turns to wastage of memory.
14. Array of pointers is collection of addresses.
15. Array of pointers cannot be addresses of array components.
16. Default initial component values of an array are zeros when declared with **`static`** keyword.

Answers

1. True 2. True 3. True 4. False 5. True 6. True 7. True 8. True 9. False 10. True 11. True 12. True 13. True 14. True 15. False 16. True

Additional Questions

What is/are the output/s of the following programs?

One Dimensional Array

1. Display few array elements

```
#include <math.h>
 void main()
 {
    int i,marks[5]={55,56,67,78,64};
    clrscr();
    for(i=2;i<=4;i++)
    printf("\n %d",marks[i]);
    getche();
 }

OUTPUT:
67
78
64
```

2. Display characters defined in the array

```
#include <math.h>
 void main()
 {
    char name []={'a','m','i','t'};
    int i;
    clrscr();
    for(i=0;i<=4;i++)
    printf(" %c",name[i]);
    getche();
 }

OUTPUT:
a m i t
```

3. Use of %s for displaying array elements

```
#include <math.h>
 void main()
 {
    char name []={'A','M','O','L'};
    int i;
    clrscr();
    for(i=0;i<=4;i++)
    printf(" %s",name);
    getche();
 }

OUTPUT:
AMOL AMOL AMOL AMOL AMOL
```

4. Display characters together with ASCII(Decimal) and ASCII HEX

```
void main()
{

char arr[6]={'H','e','l','l','o','!'};
int i;
clrscr();
      printf("Entered characters are:-");
      printf("\n Char ASCII ASCIIHEX ");
      printf("\n----------------------");
```

```
        for(i=0;i<6;i++)
        printf("\n %c \t%d \t%x",arr[i],arr[i],arr[i]);
        printf("\n----------------------");

        printf("\n");
        getche();
}
```

5. Sum of numbers from 1 to 10

```
#include <math.h>
 void main()
 {
    int i,sum=0,num[]={1,2,3,4,5,6,7,8,9,10};
    clrscr();
    for(i=0;i<=9;i++)
    sum=sum+num[i];
    printf(" %d",sum);
    getche();
 }

OUTPUT:
55
```

6. Multiplication table of 6

```
void main()
{
   int i,ans,num[5]={1,2,3,4,5};
   clrscr();
   for(i=0;i<=4;i++)
   {
   ans=num[i]*6;
   printf("\n %d*%d=%d",6,num[i],ans);
   }
}

OUTPUT:
6*1=6
6*2=12
6*3=18
6*4=24
6*5=30
```

7. Factorial of 5

```
void main()
 {
    int i,m=1,num[5]={1,2,3,4,5};
    clrscr();
    for(i=0;i<=4;i++)
    m=m*num[i];
    printf("Total is %d ",m);
    getche();
 }

OUTPUT:
120
```

8. Arrange numbers in ascending order

```
void main()
 {
    int i,k,temp,num[6]={4,6,8,3,2,10};
    clrscr();

    for(i=0;i<=5;i++)
    {
    for(k=i+1;k<5;k++)
          {
                if(num[i]>num[k])
                {
                      temp=num[i];
                      num[i]=num[k];
                      num[k]=temp;
          }
                }
   }
   for(i=0;i<6;i++)
   printf("\n %d",num[i]);
  getche();
 }

OUTPUT:
2
3
4
6
8
10
```

9. Reversing text and a number

```
void main()
{
   char name[7]={'M','A','L','A','L','A','M'};
   int i,rev[]={4,5,6};

   clrscr();
   for(i=6;i>=0;i--)
   {
   printf("%c",name[i]);
   }
   printf("\n");
   for(i=2;i>=0;i--)
   {
   printf("%d",rev[i]);
}

   getche();
}

OUTPUT:
MALALAM
```

10. Display array elements with pointer

```
void main()
{
   int j[4]={2,3,4,5};
   int i;
   clrscr();
   for(i=0;i<=3;i++)
   printf(" %d",*(j+i));
   getche();
}

OUTPUT:
2 3 4 5
```

Two Dimensional Array

11. Program to print array elements in reverse order.

```
void main()
 {
 int i,j;
 int a[3][3]={{9,8,7},{6,5,4},{3,2,1}};
 clrscr();
 printf("Elements of an array in reverse order.\n\n");
        for(i=2;i>=0;i--)
        {
        for(j=2;j>=0;j--)
        printf("%5d",a[i][j]);
        printf("\n");
        }
getche();
 }

OUTPUT:
Elements of an array in reverse order

    1     2     3
    4     5     6
    7     8     9
```

12. Display odd numbers using two **for** loops.

```
#include <stdio.h>
#include <conio.h>
void main()
{
  int j,k,x[4][2]={1,2,3,4,5,6,7,8};
  clrscr();
  for(j=0;j<4;j++)
  for(k=0;k<1;k++)
   printf(" %d",x[j][k]);
}

OUTPUT:
1 3 5 7
```

13. Display numbers in some sequence using two **for** loops

```
#include <stdio.h>
#include <conio.h>

void main()
{
  int j,k,x[4][2]={1,2,3,4,5,6,7,8};
  clrscr();
  for(j=0;j<3;j++)
  for(k=0;k<1;k++)
  printf(" %d",x[j][k]);
}

OUTPUT:
1 3 5
```

14. Display some numbers using an array

```
#include <stdio.h>
#include <conio.h>
void main()
{  int x[3][3]={4,5,6,7,8,9,10,11,12};
   int j,k;
   clrscr();
   for(j=0;j<3;j++)
   for(k=0;k<3;k++)
   printf(" %d ",x[k][j]);
}

OUTPUT:
4  7  10  5  8  11  6  9  12
```

More Than Two Dimensional Array

15. Display numbers using two for loops.

```
#include <stdio.h>
#include <conio.h>
void main()
{
  int array[2][2][2][2]={1,2,3,4,5,6,7,8};
  int a,b,c,d;
  clrscr();
 for(b=0;b<2;b++)
 for(a=0;a<2;a++)
  printf(" %d ",array[a][b][0][0]);
}

OUTPUT:
1  0  5  0
```

Find the bug/s in the following program/s.

1.
```
void main()
{

  int a[5]={5,2,3,1,4};
  int i,result=1;
clrscr();

      for(i=0;i<=5;i++)
      result=result*a[i];
      printf("\nresult of multiplication  =%d ",result);
      getche();
}

Bug: No bug
```

2.

```
void main()
{
int a[10]={5,6,7,8,9,3,4,5,4,6};
int i,sum=0;
float avg;
clrscr();
    for(i=0;i<=9;i++)
    {
    sum=sum+a[i];
    }
    avg=(float)sum/10;
    printf("\nSum of ten numbers =%d",&sum);
    printf("\nAverage of ten numbers=%.2f",&avg);
    getche();
}
```

`Bug:` `&` should be removed from the `printf` statements. Answer `Sum 57` `and average 5.7`

3.

```
#include <stdio.h>
#include <conio.h>
 void main()
{
  int i,num[]={24,34,12,44,56,17};
  int num1[]={12,24,35,78, 85,22};
  clrscr();
  printf("Array 1st - 2nd Array Addition\n");
  for(i=0;i<=5;i++)
  {
   num[i]=num1[i]+ ++num[i];
   printf("\n %d ",num[i]);
  }
}
```

`Bug: No bug.`

4.

```
#include <stdio.h>
#include <conio.h>
 void main()
{
  int i,num[]={24,34,12,44,56,17};
  clrscr();
  for(i=1;i<=5;i++)
  {
   printf(" %d ",num[i]);
  }
}


Bug: No bug.
```

5.

```
void main()
 {
   int i,j;
   int k[]={1,2,4,5,6,7,8,9};
   clrscr();
   clrscr();
   for(j=0;j<=8;j++)
   printf(" %u",*(k+j));
 }
```

Bug: Attempt to read more elements than declared in array

8

Strings and Standard Functions

1. What is a string? How it is declared?

Ans: A string is an array of characters. String can be declared with character array. It can also be declared with string pointer. To manipulate text such as words and sentences, normally strings are used. Every string is terminated with '\0' character or NULL. The NULL is a byte with all bits at logic zero. The value of the string is its base address, i.e., address of the first character. When a string is created, a few compilers place the string in the memory where it cannot be modified.

A string can be defined as follows:

```
char name[]={'I','N','D','I','A','\0'};
```

2. Which format specifier or control string is used in `printf()` to print a string?

Ans: The %s format specifier or control string is used in **`printf()`** to print the string.

3. Write a short program to read the string and display it using format specifier %s.

Ans:

```
#include <stdio.h>
#include <conio.h>
void main()
{
    char a[20];
    clrscr();
    printf("\nEnter the String:");
    scanf(" %s",a);
    printf("Entered string is: %s",a);
getch();
}
```

```
OUTPUT:
Enter the string: Amit
Entered string is: Amit
```

4. What precautions should be taken while entering the string using `scanf()`?

Ans: Following are the precautions to be taken while entering the string using `scanf()`.

1. The length of the string should not exceed the length of the array.

   Example: If the length of the array is 4, then the string length more than 4 is not acceptable.

2. The multi-word string is not acceptable by **`scanf()`**.

   Example: The multi-word string such as Amit Kamthane is not acceptable by **`scanf()`**. The string after space will not be read with `scanf()`. Refer to the programming example Q 6.

5. Is it possible to accept a multi-word string by `scanf()`? What is the solution to display a multi-word string?

Ans: The multi-word string is not acceptable by `scanf()`. This is one of the big disadvantages of **`scanf()`** function. The solution to accept the multi-word string is by using function **`gets()`**.

6. Prove using short program: How multi-word string is not accepted by function `scanf()`?

Ans:

```
#include <stdio.h>
#include <conio.h>
void main()
{
    char a[20];
    clrscr();
    printf("\nEnter the Multi-word String:");
    scanf(" %s",a);
    printf("Entered string is: %s",a);
getch();
}

OUTPUT:
Enter the String: Amit Kamthane
Entered string is: Amit
```

Explanation: In the above program, user enters the multi-word string **Amit Kamthane**. However, when we try to print the string using **`printf()`**, it displays only **Amit** and the rest of the part is ignored.

Therefore, by the above example, we can say that the function `scanf()` is incapable of accepting the multi-word string.

7. Write a short program to read the multi-word string using the function `gets()`?

Ans:

```
#include <stdio.h>
#include <conio.h>
void main()
{
   char a[20];
   clrscr();
   printf("\nEnter the Multi-word String:");
   gets(a);
printf("Entered string is: %s",a);
getch();
}

OUTPUT:
Enter the Multi-word String:Amit Kamthane
Entered string is:Amit Kamthane
```

Note: The multi-word string is acceptable by the function `gets()`.

8. Which format specifier is used in `scanf()` function other than %s to read the multi-word string?

Ans: The format specifier " **%[^\n]s**" is used to read the multi-word string.

9. Write a program to read the multi-word string using format specifier %[^\n]s.

Ans:

```
#include <stdio.h>
#include <conio.h>
void main()
{
   char a[20];
   clrscr();
   printf("\nEnter the Multi-word String:");
   scanf(" %[^\n]s",a);
printf("Entered string is: %s",a);
getch();
}

OUTPUT:
Enter the multi-word String: Amit Kamthane
Entered string is: Amit Kamthane
```

10. What is the NULL character? Why is it important?

Ans: The NULL character is a byte with all bits at logic zero. Hence, its decimal value is zero. Every string is terminated with '\0' (NULL) character.

11. Is it possible to initialize the NULL character in the string?

Ans: The last character in the string in C is always '\0'. It is not compulsory to write '\0' in string. The compiler automatically puts '\0' at the end of the character array or string. In addition, we can initialize the string with text containing null character, but part of the text after null character is not considered and string is terminated at null character.

12. Why is it necessary to count NULL characters while declaring a string?

Ans: In C, every string terminates with null character. Its ASCII value is zero; the memory required to store null character is one byte. If we do not count the null character while initialization of string, it will consider the garbage value at the next address inside memory until it finds null character.

13. Explain with different formats to display a string with different precisions.

Ans: The **`printf()`** function is used for displaying the various data types. The `printf()` function with *%s* format is to be used for displaying string on the screen. Various formats are shown in Table 8.1.

Table 8.1 Formatted `printf()` functions to display strings

S.No.	Statement	Output
1.	`printf("%s\n",text);`	PRABHAKAR
2.	`printf("%.5s\n",text);`	PRABHA
3.	`printf("%.8s\n",text);`	PRABHAKA
4.	`printf("%.15s\n",text);`	PRABHAKAR
5.	`Printf("%-10.4s\n",text);`	PRAB
6.	`Printf("%11s",text);`	PRABHAKAR

In the above table, the text is 'PRABHAKAR'.

1. The first statement displays the output ***PRABHAKAR***. The entire string can be displayed with the first statement.
2. We can also specify the precision with character string, which is to be displayed. The precision is (the number of characters to be displayed) provided after decimal point. For instance, in the second statement in Table 8.1, the first five characters are displayed. Here, the integer value 5 on the right side of the decimal point, which specifies the five characters to be displayed.
3. In third statement, first eight characters are displayed.
4. While the fourth statement displays the entire string.
5. The fifth statement with '–' sign (e.g. %-10.4s) displays the string with left justified.
6. When the field length is less than the length of the string, the entire string is printed. When it is greater than the length of the string, blank spaces are initially printed followed by the string. This effect can be seen in the sixth statement.

14. Write a program to display the string PRABHAKAR using various format specifications.

Ans:

Write a program to display the string 'PRABHAKAR' using various format specifications.

```
void main()
{
char text[15]="PRABHAKAR";
clrscr();
printf("%s\n",text);
printf("%.5s\n",text);
printf("%.8s\n",text);
printf("%.15s\n",text);
printf("%-10.4s",text);
printf("\n%11s",text);
}

OUTPUT:
PRABHAKAR
PRABH
PRABHAKA
PRABHAKAR
PRAB
  PRABHAKAR
```

15. Is it possible to display a string using %*c*?

Ans: No, it is not possible to display the whole string using %*c*. The control format %*c* is used to display the single character or number or symbol. Whereas %*s* is used to display the whole string.

16. Write a program to demonstrate difference between %*c* and %*s*.

Ans:

```
#include <stdio.h>
#include <conio.h>
void main()
{
char a[]= "Amit";
char b={'a'};
clrscr();
printf("\n %s",a);
printf("\n %c",b);
getch();
}

OUTPUT:
Amit
a
```

17. What is the difference between the functions `strcmp()` and `stricmp()`?

Ans: The `strcmp()` function compares the two strings. It is case sensitive, i.e., if we have given two strings 'hello' and 'Hello' as input to `strcmp()`, return value by `strcmp()` will not be zero, instead it will be 32. This is due to difference between the ASCII values of two characters (Lower case and upper case characters: example: Difference between ASCII values of a and A). Mismatch will be found between h and H.

On the other hand, `stricmp()` is also used to compare the two strings, but it is not case sensitive; therefore, the output given by `stricmp()` for above input will be zero, i.e., it will consider them as same strings.

18. Give the format and explain the `strlen()`.

Ans: The **`strlen()`** *function* counts the number of characters in a given string. The format of function is:

```
strlen(char *string);
```

19. What is the use of `strrev()` and `strlen()` functions?

Ans: The `strrev()` function is used to reverse the input string, for example, if we give the string 'apple' as input to function `strrev()`, it will convert the string to its reverse as 'elppa'.

The function `strlen()` is used to count the length of the string. The function `strlen()` will not consider the null symbol, for example, if we give the string 'Hello World!\0' as input to `strlen()`, the value returned will be 12.

20. What is the use of `strcpy()` and `strdup()` functions?

Ans: The `strcpy()` function copies the contents of one string into another.
The syntax of `strcpy()` is:

```
strcpy(char *s2, char *s1)
```

where *s*1 is the source string, *s*2 is the destination string and *s*1 is copied to *s*2.

The `strdup()` function is used for duplicating a given string at the allocated memory which is pointed by the pointer variable. The syntax of this function is:

```
char *strdup(char *)
```

21. What is the difference between `strcpy()` and `strncpy()` functions?

Ans: The function `strcpy()` is used to copy the source string into destination completely. The syntax of `strcpy()` function is:

```
strcpy(char *,char *)
```

On the other hand, `strncpy()` is used to copy the part of the source string into destination, the syntax of `strncpy()` function is:

```
strncpy(char *, char *, int)
```

The `strncpy()` function will behave same as that of `strcpy()`, when the parameter *n* is having the value same that of length of source string.

22. What is the difference between '\0' and '0'?

Ans: '\0' and '0' are not the same. The ASCII value of '0' is 48, whereas the ASCII value of '\0' is 0.

23. What is the task of `memcpy()` memory function?

Ans: The `memcpy()` function copies *n* number of characters from one string to another. The `memcopy()` function copies the contents of source string to destination directly from physical location.

24. Describe any three-string conversion functions.

Ans: The function `atof()` converts the given string to double, the syntax of function `at of()` is:

```
double atof(const char *string);
```

The function `atoi()` is used to converts the given string to int, the syntax of function `atoi()` is:

```
int atoi(const char *string);
```

The function `strtod()` separates char and float data from the given string.

25. What is the use of `atof()` function?

Ans: The function `atof()` is used to convert the given string into double. The syntax of function `atof()` is:

```
double atof(const char *string);
```

26. What is the use of `strlwr()` function? Give its syntax.

Ans: This function can be used to convert any string to a lower case. When you are passing any upper case string to this function, it converts it into lower case. The standard format of this function is as follows:

```
Char *strlwr(char *string);
```

27. What is the use of `strupr()` function? Give its syntax.

Ans: The `strupr()` function is the same as **`strlwr()`**, but the difference is that **`strupr()`** converts lower case strings into upper case. The format of this function is:

```
Char *strupr(char *string);
```

28. What is the use of `strcat()` function? Give its syntax.

Ans: The `strcat()` function appends the target string to the source string. Concatenation of the two strings can be done using this function. The format of this function is:

```
Char *strcat(char *des,char *src);
```

29. What is the use of `strlen()` function? Give its syntax.

Ans: The `strlen()` function counts the number of characters in a given string. The length of the string is calculated by this function. The format of function is:

```
size_t strlen(char *string);
```

30. What is the use of `strcpy()` function? Give its syntax.

Ans: The `strcpy()` function copies the contents of one string to another. The format of this function is:

```
char *strcpy(char *s2, const char *s1);
```

where *s*1 is source string, *s*2 is destination string and *s*1 is copied to *s*2.

31. What is the use of `strstr()` function? Give its syntax.

Ans: The `strstr()` function finds second string in the first string. It returns the pointer location from where the second string starts in the first string. In case the first occurrence in the string is not observed, the function returns a NULL character. The format of this function is:

```
char *strstr(char *string1,char *string2);
```

Multiple-choice Questions

1. A string in C is declared as _________.
   (a) Character array (b) String array
   (c) `long char` array
2. The string always ends with _________.
   (a) NULL `char` (b) `\ char` (c) `! char`
3. Which of the following function is appropriate to duplicate the string?
   (a) `strdup()` (b) `strupr()` (c) `strspn()`
4. Which function you will use for coping string from source to destination?
   (a) `strcpy()` (b) `strrev()` (c) `strlwr()`
5. All the string functions are defined in _________.
   (a) `string.h` (b) `math.h` (c) `iostream.h`
6. Which of the following one is not a string constant?
   (a) "String" (b) "C" (c) 'C'
7. Which of the following unformatted function is used to read string through keyboard?
   (a) `scanf()` (b) `gets()` (c) None of the above
8. The NULL `char` is useful for compiler to _________.
   (a) Detect the end of the string (b) Detect the beginning of the string
   (c) Search in the memory
9. c[] = 'CPLUSPLUS' in order to print the 'CPP' the statement will be _________.
   (a) `printf("%c %c %c",c[0],c[1],c[5]);`
   (b) `printf("%s %s %s",c[0],c[1],c[5]);`
   (c) `printf("%s %s %s",c[1],c[2],c[6]);`
10. Which of the following function is more appropriate for reading string with spaces?
    (a) `printf()` (b) `gets()` (c) `scanf()`

11. The `strlen()` function returns the length of the string including ________.
    (a) All characters, spaces and symbols, numbers excluding NULL `char`
    (b) All characters, spaces and symbols, numbers and NULL `char`
    (c) Characters, numbers and excluding spaces
12. `char x[] = "Program";` the `sizeof(x)` will return________.
    (a) 7 (b) 8 (c) 9
13. The string always ends with ________.
    (a) '\0' character (b) '\' character
    (c) '0\' character (d) None of the above
14. The ________ character also occupies memory space.
    (a) NULL char (b) '^' (c) ?
15. When a string is reversed, the NULL char will be at the ________.
    (a) Beginning of string (b) End of string (c) Inside the string
16. "B" is a ________ and 'B' is a ________.
    (a) *string constant; char constant* (b) char constant; string constant
    (c) string constant; string constant
17. The array char name[8] can hold maximum ________ characters excluding NULL.
    (a) 8 (b) 7 (c) 6
18. For the declaration such as `char x [ ] = "abcd"`, the size of array determined by ________.
    (a) Compiler (b) OS (c) Linker
19. The library function `strncpy()` requires ________ arguments.
    (a) 1 (b) 2 (c) 3
20. The `strlen()` function requires ________ arguments.
    (a) 1 (b) 2 (c) 3
21. The library function `strcpy()` requires ________ arguments.
    (a) 1 (b) 2 (c) 3
22. The `strlen()` function requires ________ arguments.
    (a) 1 (b) 2 (c) 3
23. The string function ________ compares characters of two strings up to the given length.
    (a) `strcmp()` (b) `strncmp()` (c) `strrcmp()`
24. The string function `strupr()` converts ________.
    (a) Converts lowercase characters of a string to uppercase
    (b) Converts lowercase characters of a string to title case
    (c) Converts lowercase characters of a string to sentence case
25. The string function `strncpy()` copies ________.
    (a) Copies all characters of a string to another string
    (b) Copies characters of a string to another string up to the specified length
    (c) None of the above

26. _________ function finds second string in the first string.

(a) `strstr()` (b) `strnstr()` (c) `strsearch()`

27. _________ function appends the target string to the source string. Concatenation of two strings would be done using this function.

(a) `strcat()` (b) `strncat()` (c) `strrcat()`

28. 'A' + _________ = 'a'.

(a) 33 (b) 32 (c) 12

29. The ASCII equivalent of 32 is _________.

(a) ? (b) – (c) Space

30. The statement `printf("%d",' ')` will print _________.

(a) 34 (b) 32 (c) 31

31. The `atoi(string)` converts a string of digits in to _________.

(a) Integers (b) Floating number (c) Characters

32. What will be the output of the program?

```
void main()
{
char nm[]={'A','N','S','I',0,'C','\0'}; int x=0;
clrscr();
while(nm[x]!='\0')
printf("%c",nm[x++]);
}
```

(a) ANSI (b) ANSI0C
(c) ANSIC (d) None of the above

33. What will be the size of character array?

```
void main()
{
char x[]={'s','a','\0'};
printf("\n %d", sizeof(x));
}
```

(a) 3 (b) 2
(c) 0 (d) None of the above

34. What will be the output of the following program?

```
#include <string.h>
void main()
{
```

```
char x[]="a1b2c3d4e5f6g7h8i9j0";
int t=0;
clrscr();
for(t=1;x[t]!=0 && t<=strlen(x);t+=2)
printf("%c",x[t]);
}
```

(a) 1234567890
(b) abcdefghij
(c) a1b2c3d4e5f6g7h8i9j0
(d) None of the above

35. What will be the output of the following program?

```
void main()
{
char txt[]="12345\0abcdef";
clrscr();
printf("%s",txt);
}
```

(a) 12345
(b) abcdef
(c) 12345\0abcdef
(d) None of the above

36. String contains _________.

(a) Characters
(b) Numbers
(c) Symbols
(d) All of these

37. Every string has a termination character called as null denoted by _________.

(a) '/0'
(b) '\0'
(c) '0/'
(d) '0\'

38. String is a _________.

(a) One D character array
(b) Two-D character array
(c) Three-D character array
(d) All of these

39. The size of string in bytes is _________.

(a) Equal to the length of string
(b) Equal to one more than length of string
(c) Equal to one less than length of string
(d) None of the above

40. One-D array of string is _________.

(a) One-D character array
(b) Two-D character array
(c) Three-D character array
(d) None of the above

41. The correct syntax of string is _________.

(a) `char c[] = "ABC";`
(b) `char c[] = {'A','B','C'};`
(c) `char c[5];`
(d) `c[0] = 'A'; c[1] = 'B'; c[2] = 'C';`
(e) All of the above

42. Choose incorrect one _________.

(a) `char c[] = {"A","B","C"};`
(b) `char c[] = "ABC";`
(c) `char c[] = {'A','B','C'};`
(d) `char c[5]; c = "ABC";`

43. Which of the following are string functions?
    (a) `strcat()` (b) `strstr()`
    (c) `strcpy()` (d) `strupr()`
    (e) All of these
44. Which of the following is not a string function?
    (a) `strchr()` (b) `strset()`
    (c) `strrev()` (d) `strvcat()`
    (e) `strcmpi()`
45. The characters in a string are
    (a) of 1 byte each (b) stored in contiguous memory locations
    (c) Both a and b (d) None

Answers

1. (a)	2. (a)	3. (a)	4. (a)	5. (a)	6. (c)	7. (b)	8. (a)	9. (a)	10. (b)
11. (a)	12. (b)	13. (a)	14. (a)	15. (b)	16. (a)	17. (b)	18. (a)	19. (c)	20. (a)
21. (b)	22. (a)	23. (b)	24. (a)	25. (b)	26. (a)	27. (a)	28. (b)	29. (c)	30. (b)
31. (a)	32. (a)	33. (a)	34. (a)	35. (a)	36. (d)	37. (b)	38. (a)	39. (b)	40. (b)
41. (d)	42. (d)	43. (e)	44. (d)	45. (c)					

True or False

1. A string is defined as an array of characters.
2. Every string ends with a `NULL` character.
3. The declaration `char name[ ] ="India";` is invalid.
4. The `strlen()` function returns the length of the given string.
5. The `strdup()` is used to copy the string.
6. The `sricmp()` and `strncmp()` are exactly same.
7. While reversing the string, address in memory also get changed.
8. If pre-existing string is replaced with new, memory addresses remain same.
9. If the string is reversed, the `NULL` character appears first.
10. The length of the string includes `NULL` character.
11. `"12345"` is a valid string.
12. `'A'` is a valid string.
13. If two strings are merged, the string contains two `NULL` characters.
14. The string is declared as character array.
15. The string is not stored in successive memory locations.
16. The char constant `'C'` ends with `NULL` character.

17. The format string `%c` is used to display string.
18. The `NULL` char and 0 are treated the same by a compiler.
19. `'A' > 'a'`.
20. The function `strstr()` finds second string in the first string.

Answers

1. True 2. True 3. False 4. True 5. True 6. False 7. False 8. True 9. False 10. False
11. True 12. False 13. False 14. True 15. False 16. False 17. False 18. True 19. False 20. True

Additional Questions

What are the outputs of the following programs?

Programs to display string and string operations.

1. Display a string “MAHARASHTRA”

```
#include <string.h>
void main()
{
char *a1[12]={"MAHARASHTRA"};
clrscr();
printf("%s  ",*a1);
getche();
}

OUTPUT:
MAHARASHTRA
```

2. Display a string "NAGPUR"

```
#include <string.h>
void main()
{
char a1[6]={"NAGPUR"};
int j;
clrscr();
for(j=0;j<6;j++)
printf("%c ",a1[j]);
++j;
getche();
}

OUTPUT:
N A G P U R
```

3. Display strings "MAHARASHTRA" & "MADHYAPRADESH" with and without pointer

```
#include <string.h>
void main()
{
char a1[12]="MAHARASHTRA";
char *a2[13]={"MADHYAPRADESH"};
clrscr();
printf("%s  ",a1);
printf("%s  ",*a2);
getche();
}

OUTPUT:
MAHARASHTRA  MADHYAPRADESH
```

4. Display strings "KOLHAPUR" & "NAGPUR" with and without pointer

```
#include <string.h>
void main()
{
char a1[7]={"NAGPUR"};
char *n="SOLAPUR";
clrscr();
n="KOLHAPUR",
printf("%s %s ",*&(n),a1);
getche();
}

OUTPUT:
KOLHAPUR NAGPUR
```

5. Display text with different formats

```
void main()
{
char text[15]="MOUNTAIN";
clrscr();
printf("%.5s\n",text);
printf("%.8s\n",text);
getche();
}

OUTPUT:
MOUNT
MOUNTAIN
```

6. Program on encryption of a string

```
void main()
{
char text[15]="MOUNTAIN";
int i;
clrscr();
for(i=0;i<=7;i++)
printf("%.8c ",text[i]+2);
getche();
}

OUTPUT:
O Q W P V C K P
```

7. Count the number of spaces in the sentence using `while` and `if` loop.

```
#include <stdio.h>
#include <conio.h>
void main()
{
char sentence[20]="Hello! How R U?";
int count=0,i=0;
clrscr();
printf("\n%s",sentence);
while(sentence[i++]!='\0')
if(sentence[i]==32 || sentence[i]=='\0')
count++;
printf("\n%d",count);
getche();
}

OUTPUT:
Hello! How R U?
4
```

8. Sorting the list of places without using string functions

```
#include <stdio.h>
#include <conio.h>
void main()
{
char place[5][20]={"Delhi","Chennai","Bangalore","Mumbai",
"Nanded"};
```

```
int  i,j;
clrscr();
printf("Sorted List of Cities.\n\n");
for(i=65;i<=122;i++)
{
for(j=0;j<5;j++)
{
if(place[j][0]==i)
printf("\n%s",place[j]);
}
}
getche();

}

OUTPUT:
Sorted list of cities.

Bangalore
Chennai
Delhi
Mumbai
Nanded
```

9. String copy and size of strings

```
#include <string.h>
void main()
{
char a[33]={"Software people are intelligent"};
char b[60]={"Highly knowledgeable people can design
hardware circuits"};
clrscr();
strcpy(a,b);
printf("\n%s  ",a);
printf("\n%d %d",sizeof(a),sizeof(b));
getche();
}

OUTPUT:
Highly knowledgeable people can design hardware circuits
33 60
```

10. Copying without `strcpy()`

```
void main()
{
char main[10]="abcd",dup[10];
int i;
clrscr();
for(i=0;i<10;i++)
dup[i]=main[i];
printf("Origional String : %s",main);
printf("\nDuplicate String : %s",dup);
getche();
}

OUTPUT:
Original string : abcd
Duplicate string : abcd
```

String copy up to certain length with `strncpy()` function

11. String copy up to certain length

```
void main()

{
char main[20]="Amit", photocopy[20];
int n =3;
clrscr();
strncpy(photocopy,main,n);
printf("Origional String : %s",main);
printf("\nDuplicate String : %s",photocopy);
getche();
}

OUTPUT:
Original string : Amit
Duplicate string : Ami
```

Programs on different string functions: `strcpy()`, `strlwr()`, `strupr`, etc

12. Use different string functions: `strcpy()`, `strlwr()`, `strupr`

```
#include <stdio.h>
#include <conio.h>
void main()
{
char a[50]={"Computer Education leads to Prosperity and fame"};
char b[50]; clrscr(); strcpy(b,a); printf("%s \n%s",a,b);
strupr(b);
printf("\n%s",b);
strlwr(b);
printf("\n%s",b);
strrev(b);
printf("\n%s",b);
getche();
}

OUTPUT:
Computer Education leads to Prosperity and fame
Computer Education leads to Prosperity and fame
COMPUTER EDUCATION LEADS TO PROSPERITY AND FAME
computer education leads to prosperity and fame
emaf dna ytirepsorp ot sdael noitacude retupmoc
```

String length with and without `strlen()` function

13. Program to find the length of the string.

```
void main()
{
char text[20];
int len;
clrscr();
printf("type text below.\n");
gets(text);
len=strlen(text);
printf("lenth of the strng is=%d",len);
}

OUTPUT:
My name is=Romali
Length of the string is=6
```

14. Length of a string without function

```
void main()
{
char group[15]={'I','n','d','i','a'};
int len=0,i;
clrscr();
for(i=0;group[i]!='\0';i++)
len++;
printf("Length of the string is=%d",len);
getch();
}

OUTPUT:
Length of the string is=5
```

15. Program to find the length of the strings without function

```
void main()
{
char str1[20]={'M','U','T','H','A'},
str2[20]={'M','U','L','H','A'};
int diff,i=0,j=0;
clrscr();
while(str1[i]!='\0')
i++;
printf("\n Length of the first string =%d",i);
while(str2[j]!='\0')
j++;
printf("\n Length of the second string =%d",j);

if(i==j)
printf("\n Length of the strings are same");
else
printf("\n Length of the strings are not same ");
getch();
}

OUTPUT:
Length of the first string =5
Length of the second string =5
Length of the strings are same
```

String comparison with and without `strcmp()` function

16. Program on comparison of two strings

```
void main()
{
char str1[20]={'C','o','m','p','u','t','e','r'},
str2[20]={'C','o','m','p','u','t','e','r'};
clrscr();
if( (strcmp(str1,str2))==0)
printf("Length of the strings are same \n");
else
printf("Length of the strings are not same \n");
getch();
}

OUTPUT:
Length of the strings are same
```

17. Program to compare the two strings

```
void main()
{
char str1[20]={'G','o','d','a','w','a','r','i'},
str2[20]={'S','a','r','a','s','w','a','t','i'};
int diff;
clrscr();
diff=(strcmp(str1,str2));
if(diff==0)
printf(" strings are same \n");
else
printf(" strings are not same \n");
getch();
}

OUTPUT:
strings are not same
```

18. Program on `stricmp()` function

```
#include <stdio.h>
#include <conio.h>
#include <process.h>
void main()
```

```
{
char ans[8];
int i;
clrscr();
for(i=1;i<=3;i++)
{
printf("\nWhat is the currency of India?");
scanf("%s",ans);
fflush(stdin);
if(stricmp(ans,"Rupees")==0)
{
printf("\nAnswer is Correct.");
exit(1);
}
else
if (i<3)
printf("\n Try Again !\n");
}
clrscr();
printf("\NCurrency of India  is Rupees.");
}

OUTPUT:
What is the currency of India?Rupee
Try Again !
What is the currency of India?Ruppea
Try Again !
What is the currency of India?Rupees
Answer is Correct.
```

19. Use of functions such as strcmp, strcat, and strlen

```
void main()
 {
 char str1[20]="C is", str2[20]="easy language";
 int x,y,z;
 clrscr();
 printf("\n Source String:-%s",str1);
 printf("\n Destination String:-%s",str2);
 y=strcmp(str2,str1);
 if(y==0)
 {
      z=strlen(str1)==strlen(str2);
      printf("\nLength of both the strings:- %d" ,z);
 }
```

```
 else
 {
      strcat(str1,str2);
      printf("\n Final string is :-%s",str1);
      x=strlen(str1);
      printf("\nLength of the final string:- %d" ,x);
 }
 getche();
 }

OUTPUT:
Source String:-C is
Destination String:-easy language
Final string is :-C is easy language
Length of the final string:- 16
```

Use of memcmp ( ) function

20. Find length of strings with memcmp ( ) function

```
#include <string.h>
#include <conio.h>
void main()
{
char text[30]="LATUR",text1[20]="UDGIR",chp;
clrscr();
 printf("\nFirst text  is:-%s",text);
 printf("\nSecond text is :-%s",text1);

 chp=memcmp(text,text1,5);
 if (chp!=0)
 printf("\nText length of first string is same as of
second");
 else
 printf("\nText length of the strings are not same ");
 getche();

}

OUTPUT:
First text  is:-LATUR
Second text is:-UDGIR
Text length of first string is same as of second
```

Find the bug/s in the following program/s.

String operations and display

1.

```
void main()
{
char name[6]={'S','A','N','J','A','Y'};  clrscr();
puts(name);
}
```

Bug: String is larger than the array capacity.

2.

```
void main()
{
char name[7]={'S','A','N','J','A','Y'};
clrscr();
printf("\n %.0s",name);
}
```

Bug: The zero before s restricts the output.

3.

```
#include <stdio.h>
void main()
{
char *name={"Have a Nice Day"},c;
clrscr();
for(c=0;c<15;c++)
printf("%s",name[c]);
}
```

Bug: Format string `%c` is required.

4.

```
#include <string.h>
void main()
{
char a1[]={"KOLKATTA"};
int i;
clrscr();
while(a1[i++]!='\0')
printf("%c ",a1[i]);
getche();
}
```

Bug: `'i'` is to be initialized with some value say `i=-1`.

5.

```
#include <string.h>
void main()
{
char a1[6]={'NAGPUR'};
clrscr();
printf("%c ",a1);
getche();
}
```

Bug: Array initialization is incorrect and `%s` is to used instead of `%c`.

6.

```
#include <string.h>
void main()
{
char *a[]="ROYAL";
clrscr();
printf("%s %u",*(a),&*a);
getche();
}
```

Bug: ROYAL must be enclosed within curly braces.

7.

```
#include <string.h>
void main()
{
char a1[6]={"CHENNAI"};
int i;
clrscr();
for(i=0;i<7;i++)
printf("%c ",a1[i]);
++i;
getche();
}
```

Bug: char array is to be initialized with 7 instead of 6.

8.

```
void main()
{
char text[15]="MOUNTAIN";
int i;
clrscr();
for(i=7;i>=0;i--)
printf("%.8d",text[i]);
getche();
}
```

Bug: Replace 'c' instead of 'd' in printf statement.

9.

```
#include <string.h>
void main()
{
char *a2[10]={"MADHYAPRADESH"};
clrscr();
printf("%s",*&(a2));
getche();
}
```

Bug: '&' operator to be deleted.

strcpy() Function

10.

```
void main()
{
char str1[15]='snowy', str2[15]='sunny';
clrscr();
printf("\n Source String-:%s",str1);
printf("\n Destination String-:%s",str2);
strncpy(str2,str1,3);
printf("\nDestination String -:%s",str2);
getche();
}
```

Bug: Double quotation mark is needed in char statement.

11.

```
#include <string.h>
void main()
{
char a[40]={"Software people are intelligent"};
char b[40];
clrscr();
strcpy (b,&a);
printf("%s \n %s",a,b);
getche();
}
```

Bug: `*&a` instead of `&a`.

`strchr()` Function

12.

```
#include <string.h>
#include <conio.h>
void main()
{
 char text[30]="SINGAPUR",cha,*chp;
 clrscr();
 printf("\nString is:-%s",text);
 printf("\nCharacter to find :");
 cha=getchar();
 chp=strchr(text[],cha);
 if(chp!=0)
 printf("Character %d found in text.",cha);
 else
 printf("Character %d not found in text.",cha);
}
```

Bug: `[]` is not needed in chp line and `%c` is to be placed in place of `%d` in `printf` statements.

`strset()` Function

13.

```
#include <string.h>
#include <conio.h>
 void main()
{
char text[20]="Great Sea";
char target='I';
clrscr();
printf("Before  strset() : %s\n", text);
```

```
getche();
}
```

Bug: Exchange target and text in `strset()`.

String Operations

14.

```
#include <string.h>
 void main()
{
char alpha='a';
int number=50;
char text1[20]="Happy";
clrscr();
alpha=a+25;
printf("\n%c %d",'calpha',alpha-1);
printf("\n%d %c", number*2,number*2);
printf("\n%s ", text1+1);
getche();
}
```

Bug: Character a should be enclosed with single quotation mark in alpha statement and instead of `'calpha'` it should be alpha in `printf()`.

15.

```
#include <stdio.h>
#include <conio.h>
void  main()
{
char text[30]={"Programming needs Patience"};
int count=0,i=0;
clrscr();
   do
   {
      if (text[i]==32 || text[i]=='\0')
      count++;
    }
      while (text[i++]!='\0')

   printf(" %d\n",count);
   getche();
}
```

Bug: ';' (Semicolon is missing in while statement).

16.

```
#include <string.h>
void main()
{
char a[]="C needs skills";
clrscr();
printf("%c %u",a,&a);
getche();
}
```

Bug: `%s` instead of `%c`.

`strcmp()` Function

17.

```
#include <string.h>
void main()
{
char a[40]={"Software people are intelligent"};
char b[60]={"Highly knowledgeable people can design
hardware circuits"};
clrscr();
printf("\n%s  ",a);
printf("\n%d",sizeof(a));
if(strcmp(b,a)==0);
printf("\n Lengths of Strings are identical ");
else
printf("\n Lengths of Strings are dissimilar ");
getche();
}
```

Bug: `if` statement never terminates with ; (Semicolon).

18.

```
#include <string.h>
void main()
{
char static a[10]="Smily";
char  static b[10]="Smily";
char  c[70];
int x;
clrscr();
printf("\n%s  ",a);
printf("\n%s  ",b);
```

```
x=strcmp(a,b);
if(x!=0);
{
printf("\nString lengths are dissimilar");
strcat(a,b);
printf("\n%s",a);
getche();

}
else
{
printf("\nString lengths are similar");
x=strlen(a);
printf("\n%d",x);
getche();
}
}
```

Bug: Remove the semicolon from the `if` statement.

String operations

19.

```
#include <string.h>
void main()
{
char a[5];
clrscr();
a[0]='v';
a[1]='i';
a[2]='j';
a[3]='a';
a[4]='y';
a[5]='\0';
printf("\n%s  ",a);
printf("\n%d %d",size of(a));
getche();
}
```

Bug: Place size of instead of size of in the `printf` statement.

20.

```
#include <stdio.h>
void main()
{char *am={"Amol"};
char *at={"Amit"};
char *st;
clrscr();
st=at;
at=am;
am=at;
printf("%s and  %s",at,am);
}
```

Bug: No error. However statement `am=st;`

9

Pointers

1. What are pointers?

Ans: Pointers refer to the memory lactation of another variable. It is possible to access and display the address of memory location of another variable using '&' operator. Pointer variable stores the memory address of any type of variable. The pointer variable and normal variable should be of the same type.

Memory space required for pointers of any data type is the same, whereas it is different for variables of different data types. This is due to the fact that pointers store address that is an unsigned integer.

2. What are the advantages of using pointers in C programming?

Ans: Following are the advantages of pointers in C programming.

1. The memory is accessed efficiently with the pointers. The pointer assigns the memory space and also it releases.
2. Pointers are used to allocate memory dynamically.
3. They are used with data structures. They are useful for representing one-dimensional and multi-dimensional arrays.
4. They are utilized in linked lists and call by reference functions.
5. They access the elements of any type of array irrespective if its subscript range.
6. They save the memory space.
7. Execution time with pointer is fast, because data is manipulated with the address, i.e., direct access to memory location.
8. Pointers are used in file handling.

3. How is a pointer declared?

Ans: Declaration of pointer variable is done with * operator. The * operator is also called indirection or dereferencing operator. It is to be placed before the variable and after the data type.

A few examples of declaration of pointers in C are as follows:

```
int *a;
char *b;
float *c;
```

4. Explain the use of (*) indirection operator.

Ans: Pointer variables are declared as follows:

Example:

```
int *x;
float *f;
char *y;
```

The indirection operator (*) is also called the dereferencing operator. When a pointer is dereferenced, the value at that address stored by the pointer is retrieved.

The indirection operator (*) is used in two distinct ways with pointers, declaration and dereference.

1. When a pointer is declared, a star (*) indicates that it is a pointer and not a normal variable.
2. When the pointer is dereferenced, the indirection operator indicates that the value at that memory location stored in the pointer is to be accessed rather than the address itself. For example, `printf('%d',*x);` will print the value of another variable stored in memory location *x*.

5. Write a program to display the value of a variable and its address using pointer.

Ans:

```
#include <stdio.h>
#include <conio.h>
void main()
{
int v=10,*p;
clrscr();
p=&v;
printf("\n Address of v = %u",p);
printf("\n Value of v = %d",*p);
printf("\n Address of p = %u",&p);
}

OUTPUT:
Address of v = 4060
Value of v = 10
Address of p = 4062
```

Explanation: In the above program, '*v*' is an integer variable and its value is 10. The variable '*p*' is declared as pointer variable. The statement ***p* = &*v*** assigns address of '*v*' to '*p*', i.e., '*p*' is the pointer to variable '*v*'. To access the address and value of '*v*', pointer '*p*' can be used. The value of '*p*' is nothing but address of variable '*v*'. To display the value stored at that location, ***p*** is used. The pointer variables also have an address and displayed using '&' operator. The statement used is **`printf("\n Address of p = %u", &p);`**. The above explanation is followed by Figure 9.1.

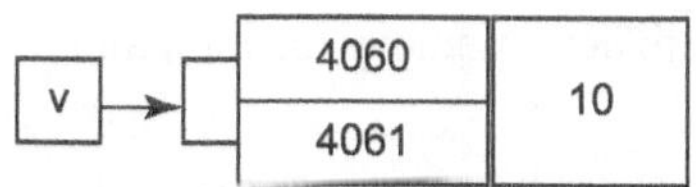

Figure 9.1 Variable Addresses and Value

The value of '*v*' is ***10*** and it is stored at location ***4060.*** Address of '*v*' ***4060*** is assigned to variable '***p***'. Address of pointer variable '***p***' is *4062*. Here, '*p*' is pointer type variable, which points to the variable '*v*'. Hence, it must be declared as **`int`** *v=10* and pointer variable as **`int`** **p;*.

6. Prove that pointer of any data type requires two bytes.

Ans: The float variable requires 4 bytes of memory for storage, but pointer to a float requires only 2 bytes, as it stores the address of a float variable, which is an unsigned integer.

Similarly, the integer variable requires 2 bytes of memory for storage, but integer pointer to a float requires only 2 bytes, as it stores the address of a float variable that is an unsigned integer.

Run the following program and verify the memory requirement to integer and float pointer.

```
void main()
{
float a;
float *p;
int b,*pa;
clrscr();
p=&a;
pa=&b;
printf("\n size of a=%d size of p=%d",sizeof(a), sizeof(p));
printf("\n Address of a=%u and with pointer address of a=%u",&a,
p);
printf("\n size of b=%d size of pa=%d",sizeof(b), sizeof(pa));
getche();
}

OUTPUT:
size of a=4    size of p=2
Address of a=65486 and with pointer address of a=65486
size of b=2    size of pa=2
```

Explanation: Memory required for floating and integer numbers are 4 and 2 bytes, respectively. However, memory required to pointers of any data type is 2 bytes.

7. Explain the effect of ++ and — operators with pointer of all data type.

Ans: Consider the following pointer declaration.

```
int *x;
```

++ and –– operators increment the normal variables, but when applied to a pointer of any data type they point to the immediate next and previous memory locations.

Hence, ++*x* will point to immediate next memory location and −−*x* will point to immediate previous memory location of *x*.

8. Apply post-increment operator on pointers in the program and show the effects.

Ans:

```
void main()
{
int b,*pa;
clrscr();
pa=&b;
printf("\n Address of b with pointer=%u", pa);
pa++;
pa++;
printf("\n Address of b after incrementing pointer for two times
= %u", pa);
getche();
}

OUTPUT:
Address of b with pointer=65492
Address of b after incrementing pointer for two times = 65496
```

Explanation: The integer pointer variable *pa* is post-incremented two times in the above program. Address of pointer after two post-incrementations is 65496. Initial address of pointer *pa* is 65492. Each integer pointer requires two bytes and hence after every incrementation of integer pointer, address gets incremented by two.

9. Apply post-decrement operator on pointers and show the effects.

Ans:

```
void main()
{
int b,*pa;
clrscr();
pa=&b;
printf("\n Address of b with pointer=%u", pa);
pa--;
pa--;
printf("\n Address of b after decrementing pointer for two
times= %u", pa);
getche();
}
```

```
OUTPUT:
Address of b with pointer = 65492
Address of b after decrementing pointer for two times = 65488
```

Explanation: Integer needs two bytes to store in the memory. Hence, after decrementing pointer, each time address gets reduced by two. Address of b after decrementing pointer for two times = 65488.

10. What do you mean by wild pointer?

Ans:

1. The wild pointer does not point either to a valid object or to a notable NULL value.
2. When pointer points to an unallocated memory location or to data value whose memory is de-allocated, such pointer are called 'wild pointer'.
3. The wild pointer generates garbage memory location and pendent reference.

11. Which are the reasons for pointer to become a wild pointer?

Ans: The pointer becomes wild due to following reasons:

1. Pointer declared but not initialized.
2. Pointer alternation.
3. Accessing destroyed data.

12. Write a program to show wild pointer and its output.

Ans:

```
#include <stdio.h>
#include <conio.h>
void main()
{
  int k,*x;
  clrscr();
  for(k=0;k<=3;k++)
  printf("%u",x[k]);
}

OUTPUT:
7272   24330   30559   27753
```

Explanation: In this program, pointer *x* is not initialized. The successive locations are displayed.

13. Write a short note on constant pointer.

Ans: The address of the constant pointer cannot be modified.

```
char * const str = "Constant";
```

In the above example, it is not possible to modify the address of the pointer str. The following operations will generate error messages.

```
/*   str = "san"; */ cannot modify a constant object
/* ++str *; / cannot modify a constant object
```

If pointer constant pointing to variable. We can change value of actual variable but not through the constant pointer. The following valid and invalid operations are given.

```
/* k=5; */ possible
/*   *pm=5; */ invalid
/* pm++; */ possible
/* *pm++;  */ invalid
/* *pm=5; */ invalid
```

14. Write a program to declare constant pointer and modify the value.

Ans:

```
#include <stdio.h>
#include <conio.h>
void main()
{
   int k=10;
   int const *pm=&k;
   clrscr();
   k=40;
   /*    *pm=50;    invalid operation */
   printf("k=%d",k);
}

OUTPUT:
K=40
```

Explanation: In the above program, variable *k* is an integer pointer and *pm is constant pointer of the same type. The value of *k* cannot be changed through the pointer *pm, because pm is a constant pointer. The value of variable can be changed only through itself. Any constant entity cannot permit any modification.

15. What is an array of pointer? How it is declared?

Ans: It is nothing but collection of addresses. Here, pointer points to the base address, i.e., first address of first item of array. Successive addresses of array items can be obtained by incrementing the pointer.

It is declared as:

```
data-type *array-name[size];
e.g., int *arrp[5];
```

where `arrp` is an array of 5 pointers.

16. Write a program for displaying the array items using pointer.

Ans:

```
void main()
{
int b[5]={1,2,3,4,5},*pa,i;
clrscr();
pa=b;
printf("\nElements of an array:");
for(i=0;i<5;i++)
{
printf("%d", *(pa+i));
}
printf("\nAnother way to get the elements of an array:");
for(i=0;i<5;i++)
{
printf("%d", *(pa));
pa++;
}
getche();
}

OUTPUT:
Elements of an array:  1  2  3  4  5
Another way to get the elements of an array:  1  2  3  4  5
```

17. Explain the relation between an array and a pointer.

Ans: Array name by itself is an address or pointer. It points to the address of the first element (0th element of an array). The elements of the array together with their addresses can be displayed by using array name itself, e.g., `arr[2]` displays third element of array `arr`. Array elements are always stored in contiguous memory locations.

18. Why addition of two pointers is impossible?

Ans: Pointers store addresses, which can be incremented/decremented, but two addresses are never added. Hence, the addition of two pointers is impossible.

19. Which are the possible arithmetic operations with pointers?

Ans:

1. Addition: A number can be added to a pointer or the addition of two variables through pointers can also be possible.
2. Subtraction: A number can be subtracted from a pointer. Subtraction of two variables through pointers can also be possible.
3. Multiplication of two variables through pointers can also be possible.
4. Similarly, division or modulus of two variables through pointers can also be possible.

20. WAP to perform addition, multiplication, subtraction, division and modulus operations between the values of variables using pointers.

Ans:

```
void main()
{
int b=3,*pa,i,a=6,*pb;
clrscr();
pa=&a;
pb=&b;
printf("\nAddition of values of a and b=  %d",
*pa+*pb);
printf("\nSubtraction between  a and b=  %d", *pa-
*pb);
printf("\nMultiplication of a and b=  %d",*pa**pb);
printf("\nDivision of a and b=  %d",(*pa)/(*pb));
printf("\nModulus   operation   on   a   with   b=
%d",(*pa)%(*pb));
getche();
}

OUTPUT:
Addition of values of a and b = 9
Subtraction between a and b = 3
Multiplication of a and b = 18
Division of a and b = 2
Modulus operation on a with b = 0
```

21. Explain comparison of two pointers.

Ans: The pointer variable should be of the same data type while a comparison is made. The comparison of pointers can test if either address is identical or not. For example, if pointers '*j*' and '*k*' are of integer data types and they point to the same integer variable '*a*', then they contain the same address and are equal.

22. How one pointer points to another pointer?

Ans: The pointer variable containing the address of another pointer variable is called the pointer to pointer.

```
e.g.,
int a,*p;
int **pp;
p=&a;
pp=&p;
```

23. How will you recognize pointer to pointer? What does the number of '*'s indicate?

Ans: The pointer variable containing the address of another pointer variable is called the pointer to pointer.

The number of '*'s indicates the level of pointer.

For example, *p indicates that *p* is a pointer to a variable (first-level pointer or single pointer), **pp indicates that *pp* is a pointer to a single pointer (second-level pointer or double pointer), and so on.

24. How strings are stored in pointer variables? Is it essential to declare length?

Ans:

```
char string[10],*ch;
ch = string;
```

Here, the address of the 0th element is assigned to character pointer ‘ch’. In other words, the base address of string is assigned to ‘ch’. The pointer ‘*ch’ points to the value stored at that memory location. To handle strings directly through pointer, we need not specify the length of string, as pointer stores only the base address. String of any length can be handled.

25. What is base address? How is it accessed differently for one- and two-dimensional arrays?

Ans: The base address is the address of first element of an array. To access the address of first element of one-dimensional array, we can directly use the array name, but to access the address of first element of two-dimensional array using a pointer, it is essential to have ‘&’ operator as prefix with an array name followed by element number; otherwise, the compiler shows an error.

26. Elaborate the address stored in the pointer and the value at that address.

Ans: ‘&’ is the address operator and it represents the address of the variable. Pointer stores the address of a variable.

For example, `int a,*p;`
`p=&a;` stores address of integer `'a'`.
To access the value of `a` via pointer, we use value at address operator (‘`*`’).
For example, `printf("%d",*p);`

27. Write a program to read and display a two-dimensional array of 5 by 2 numbers.

Ans:

```
void main()
{
int i,j;
int a[5][2];
clrscr();
printf("\nEnter elements of an array a[5][2]:");
for(i=0;i<5;i++)
{
      for(j=0;j<2;j++)
      {
       ("%d",&a[i][j]);
      }
}

printf("\nElements of an array with their addresses\n\n");
for(i=0;i<5;i++)
{
for(j=0;j<2;j++)
```

```
        {
        printf("\tElement %d and its address  %u",a[i][j],
&a[i][j]);
        }
        printf("\n");
    }
getch();
}

OUTPUT:
Enter elements of an array a[5][2]:1 2 3 4  5 6 7 8 9 0
Elements of an array with their addresses
Element 1 and its address 65480  Element 2 and its address
65482
Element 3 and its address 65484  Element 4 and its address
65486
Element 5 and its address 65488  Element 6 and its address
65490
Element 7 and its address 65492  Element 8 and its address
65494
Element 9 and its address 65496  Element 0 and its address
65498
```

28. Explain tiny and large memory models.

Ans:

1. Tiny memory model: All segment registers are initialized with the identical value and all addressing is accomplished using 16 bits. This means that the code, data and stack must all fit within the same 64-KB segment. Programs are executed quickly.
2. Large memory model: Both code and data are allowed to use multiple segments. All pointers are 32 bits in length. However, no single data item can exceed 64 KB. There is slower code execution.

29. What are the uses of `malloc()` and `free()` functions?

Ans:

1. `malloc()` function: It is used to allocate memory space in bytes to the variables of different data types. It reserves bytes of determined size and returns the base address to pointer variable. The prototypes are declared in `alloc.h` and `stdlib.h`. The format of the `malloc()` function is as follows:

   `pointer = (data type*) malloc(given size);`

   Here, from data type, compiler understands the pointer type and given size is the size to reserve in the memory.
   For example, `pnt = (int*) malloc (20);`

Here, in this declaration, 20 bytes are allocated to pointer variable `pnt` of type `int` and base address is returned to pointer `pnt`.

2. `free()` function: It is used to release the memory allocated by memory allocating functions. Thus, by using this function, the wastage of memory is prevented. The declaration of the function is as follows:

   ```
   free (pnt)
   ```

   In the above declaration, `pnt` is a pointer. The `free()` function releases the memory occupied by the pointer variable `pnt`.

30. Explain the concept of dynamic memory allocation.

Ans: There is a technique by which a program can obtain space in the main memory at run time that is called dynamic allocation. Dynamic allocation is a technique in which a program can acquire storage space in the main memory. In this method, the space for the program is allocated from the free space during the execution of the program. The free region of the memory is called the heap. Depending upon the memory model, the portions of the heap are allocated for memory requirement. Conceptually, the C programs are stored in the free space from the heap. The amount of memory requirement is decided by how the program is designed. For example, if a program is developed with many recursive functions, then this is implemented with stack.

31. Describe the various functions used for memory allocation.

Ans: The various functions that are used for memory allocation are `malloc, calloc, free, realloc` and `coreleft.`

For malloc and free functions, refer the answer to the question 19.

1. `calloc()` function: It is useful for allocating multiple blocks of memory. It is declared with two arguments. The prototypes are declared in `alloc.h` and `stdlib.h`. The format of the `calloc()` function is as follows:

   ```
   pnt = (int *) calloc (4,2);
   ```

   The above declaration allocates four blocks of memory; each block contains 2 bytes. The base address is stored in the integer pointer. This function is usually used for allocating memory for array and structure.

2. `realloc()` function: It reallocates main memory. The prototypes are declared in `alloc.h` and stdlib.h. Attempts are made to shrink or enlarge the previously allocated memory by `malloc()` or `calloc()` functions. It returns the address of the reallocated block, which can be different from the original address. If the block cannot be reallocated or size == 0, `realloc()` returns NULL. The syntax of the function is as follows:

   ```
   ptr = (type *) realloc (ptr, new size);
   ```

3. coreleft function: It returns a measure of unused memory. If the memory model selected is tiny, small or medium, then follow the function declaration as per statement (a). If the memory model selected is compact, large or huge, follow the declaration (b).

   (a) unsigned `coreleft(void);`

   (b) unsigned long `coreleft (void);`

Multiple-choice Questions

1. Which of the following one operation with addresses is not possible?
   (a) Addition of two addresses (pointers) (b) ++ (c) –
2. Which of the following one operation is possible with address holding (pointers)?
   (a) Multiplication of addresses or multiplication of address with a constant
   (b) Division of address with a constant
   (c) ++
   (d) None of the above
3. The declaration int `*arrp[3];` is nothing but ________.
   (a) Integer array (b) Integer pointer array (c) One of the above
4. Pointer to pointer can be denoted as ________.
   (a) **p (b) p** (c) *p
5. The following program will show the error message ________.
   `int p=2; char *c=&p;`
   (a) Expression syntax in function main
   (b) Non-portable assignment
   (c) Suspicious pointer conversion
   (d) None of the above
6. `int p=2,*k; int *c=&p; k=c;` we can say that ________.
   (a) Pointer c and k are pointing to p
   (b) Pointer k pointing to p and c
   (c) Only pointer c pointing to p
7. `int s,*j,**kk; j=&s; kk=&j;` we can say that ________.
   (a) kk is pointer of pointer (b) j is pointer of pointer (c) k is only pointer
8. A pointer is a memory variable that stores a ________.
   (a) memory address (b) value (c) None of the above
9. Pointer can have any name that is legal for other ________.
   (a) Variable (b) Keyword (c) Header file
10. Pointer is declared in the same fashion like other variable, but it is always denoted by ________ operator.
    (a) * (b) & (c) #
11. Pointers save the ________.
    (a) Memory space (b) Value (c) None of the above
12. Execution time with pointer is faster because ________.
    (a) Data is manipulated with the address (b) Data is manipulated (c) None of the above
13. Pointers are used with data structures. They are useful for representing ________ and multi-dimensional arrays.
    (a) Two-dimensional (b) Multi-dimensional (c) None of the above

14. In the statement int *x is a (an) ________.

(a) Integer pointer (b) Float pointer (c) Unsigned pointer

15. Declaration int *x; tells to the compiler that it holds the ________.

(a) Address of any integer variable
(b) Address of any float variable
(c) Address of any char variable

16. The indirection operator (*) is also called ________.

(a) Indirection or dereferencing operator (b) Declaration
(c) Deference (d) None of the above

17. When the pointer is dereferenced, the indirection operator indicates that the ________.

(a) Value at that address stored can be accessed
(b) Address of variable can be accessed
(c) None of the above

18. Fill the columns after ++ and — operations.

Data Type	Initial Address	Operation		Address After Operations	
Int i=2	4046	++	--	4048	4044
char c='x'	4053	++	--	4054	4052
float f=2.2	4058	++	--	4062	4054
Long l=2	4060	++	--	4064	4056

19. Array name by itself is an address or ________.

(a) Pointer (b) Value (c) Identifier

20. Array of pointers is nothing but ________.

(a) A collection of addresses (b) A collection of values (c) All of the above

21. The pointer variables also have an ________, which is stored in another pointer.

(a) Name (b) Address (c) Value

22. The pointer variable containing address of another pointer variables is called ________.

(a) Pointer to pointer (b) Pointer (c) Double pointer

23. The memory address of the variable is a (an) ________.

(a) Constant (b) Pointer constant (c) Integer

24. Which of the following statement is true after execution of following program?

```
void main()
{
int a[5]={2,3},*c;
clrscr();
c=a;
(*c)--;
printf("%d",a[0]);
}
```

(a) The value of a[0] will be 1.
(b) The value of a[0] will be 2.
(c) The value of a[1] will be 2.
(d) None of the above.

25. The fastest way to exchange two rows in a two-dimensional array is ________.
(a) Exchange the addresses of each element in the two rows.
(b) Exchange the elements of the two rows.
(c) Store the addresses of the rows in an array of pointers and exchange the pointers.
(d) None of the above.

26. Which is the correct way to declare a pointer?
(a) `int *ptr;`
(b) `* int ptr;`
(c) `int ptr*;`
(d) `int_ptr x;`

27. What will be the result of the following program?

```
void main()
{
int a=8,b=2,c,*p;
c=(a=a+b,b=a/b,a=a*b,b=a-b);
p=&c;
          clrscr();
    printf("\n %d",++*p);
}
```

(a) 45
(b) 46
(c) 47

28. What will be the resulting string after execution of following program?

```
#include <stdio.h>
#include <conio.h>
#include <string.h>
void main()
{
  char *str1, *str2, *str3;
  str1="The Capital of India is";
  str2="!!ihleD weN";
  str3="Bangalore";
  strncat(str1,strrev(str2),strlen(str3));
  clrscr();
  puts(str1);
}
```

(a) The Capital of India is New Delhi
(b) The Capital of India is New Delhi!!
(c) The Capital of India is Bangalore
(d) None of the above

29. What will be the values of variables ***a*** and ***b*** after execution?

```
#include <stdio.h>
#include <conio.h>
#include <string.h>
void main()
{
int a,*b=&a,**c=&b;
a=5;
**c=15;
*b= **c;
clrscr();
printf("A=%d, B=%d",a,*b);
}
```

(a) $A = 15, B = 15$ (b) $A = 15, B = 5$ (c) $A = 15, B = 16$ (d) None of the above

30. What will be the value of variable a1 and a2 after execution?

```
#include <stdio.h>
#include <conio.h>
void main()
{
int a1,a2,c=3,*pt;
clrscr();
pt=&c;
a1=3*(c+5);
a2=3*(*pt+5);
printf("\na1=%d a2=  %d",a1,a2);
}
```

(a) $a1 = 25, b1 = 24$ (b) $a1 = 24, b1 = 24$ (c) $a1 = 24, b1 = 26$ (d) None of the above

31. What will be the value of ***x*** after execution of the following program?

```
#include <stdio.h>
#include <conio.h>
void main()
{
int x,*p;
p=&x;
*p=2;
clrscr();
printf("\nValue of x=%d",x);
}
```

(a) $x = 2$ (b) $x = 0$ (c) $x = 65504$ (d) None of the above

32. The pointer can hold the address of
    (a) a variable
    (b) address of address of a variable and so on
    (c) points to a particular memory location
    (d) All of these
33. Which is incorrect
    (a) The pointer is variable and cannot be made constant
    (b) One type of pointer cannot hold the data with other data type
    (c) The value in one location cannot be copied to another location using pointer
    (d) All of these
34. Which segment is valid
    (a) `char *names[] = {"Rahul","Sachin"};`
    (b) `char *names = {"Rahul","Sachin"};`
    (c) `char **names = {"Rahul","Sachin"};`
    (d) All are valid
35. Choose the correct output.

```
void main()
    {
    int a[2][3][2] = {{{2,4},{7,8},{3,4}},{{2,2},{2,3},
    {3,4}}};
    clrscr();
    printf("%u %u %u %d \n",a,*a,**a,***a);
    getch();
    }
```

(Assume the starting address 2000)

The output is

(a) 2000 2000 2000 2
(b) 2000 2002 2002 2
(c) 2000 2002 2004 2
(d) 2000 2 2 2

36. Choose the correct output.

```
void main()
    {
    int a[2][3][2] = {{{2,4},{7,8},{3,4}},{{2,2},{2,3},{3,4}}
};
    clrscr();
    printf("%u %u %u %d \n",a+1,*a+1,**a+1,***a+1);
    getch();
    }
```

(Assume the starting address 2000)

The output is

(a) 2012 2004 2002 3
(b) 2024 2008 2002 2002
(c) 2024 2004 2002 3
(d) 2012 2008 2002 2002

Answers

1. (a)	2. (c)	3. (b)	4. (a)	5. (a)	6. (a)	7. (a)	8. (a)	9. (a)	10. (b)
11. (a)	12. (a)	13. (a)	14. (a)	15. (a)	16. (a)	17. (a)	18. –	19. (a)	20. (a)
21. (b)	22. (a)	23. (b)	24. (a)	25. (a)	26. (a)	27. (b)	28. (a)	29. (a)	30. (b)
31. (a)	32. (d)	33. (d)	34. (a)	35. (a)	36. (a)				

True or False

1. Memory space required for pointers of any data type is the same.
2. A pointer is a memory variable that stores memory address of another variable.
3. Pointers can be used to represent arrays.
4. The indirection operator (*) is used to identify the pointer variable.
5. The '&' is an address operator and represents the address of the variable.
6. The physical memory locations of the variable is system dependent.
7. The user can predict the address of the memory variable.
8. The pointer of any data type itself requires only four bytes.
9. A pointer cannot point to another pointer variable.
10. The address of an integer a is 4044 and after incrementing a's value by one, the address becomes 4046.
11. The pointer variable holding address of another pointer is pointer to pointer.
12. `p**` is pointer to pointer.
13. `*p` is a pointer.
14. `char **q` is pointer to pointer.

Answers

1. True	2. True	3. True	4. True	5. True	6. True	7. False	8. True	9. False
10. False	11. True	12. False	13. True	14. True				

Additional Questions

What is/are the output/s of the following programs?

1. Use pointer and display value and address of an integer element

```
#include <stdio.h>
#include <conio.h>
void main()
{
 int num=10,*p;
 p=&num;
 clrscr();
 printf("%d",*p);
 printf("%d",num);
 printf("%u",&num);
 printf("%u",p);
 getche();
}

OUTPUT:
10  10 65498 65498
```

2. Use pointer and display a number

```
#include <stdio.h>
#include <conio.h>
void main()
{
  int p=10;
  void *pt=&p;
  clrscr();
  *(int*)pt=12;
  printf("%d",p);
}

OUTPUT:
12
```

3. Use pointer and display number by different ways

```
void main()
{
int t=10,*p;
clrscr();
p=&t;
printf("\n t = %d t = %d t = %d",t,*(&t),*p);
}

OUTPUT:
t =10  t =10  t =10
```

4. Use pointers and display long integers and floating point numbers

```
#include <stdio.h>
#include <conio.h>
void main()
{
long int a,*pa;
float b,*pb;
clrscr();
printf("Enter Integer & float Value :");
scanf("%ld %f",&a,&b);
pa=&a;
pb=&b;
printf("\n Address of a=%u",pa);
printf("\n Value of a=%ld",a);
printf("\n Value of a=%ld",*(&a));
printf("\n Value of a=%ld",*pa);
printf("\n Address of b=%u",pb);
printf("\n Value of b=%.2f",b);
printf("\n Value of b=%.2f",*(&b));
printf("\n Value of b=%.2f",*pb);
}

OUTPUT:
Enter integer and float value :2345 2.345
Address of a = 65492
Value of a = 2345
Value of a = 2345
Value of a = 2345
Address of b = 65496
Value of b = 2.35
Value of b = 2.35
Value of b = 2.35
```

5. Display the memory requirement for character, integer and float number and their pointers.

```
#include <stdio.h>
#include <conio.h>
void main()
{
clrscr();
printf("char  %d byte & its pointer %d bytes\
n",sizeof(char),sizeof(char*));
printf("int   %d byte & its pointer %d bytes\
n",sizeof(int),sizeof(int*));
printf("float %d byte & its pointer %d
bytes\n",sizeof(float),sizeof(float*));
}

OUTPUT:
char  1 byte and its pointer 2 bytes
int   2 byte and its pointer 2 bytes
float 4 byte and its pointer 2 bytes
```

6. Program on display of a string using pointer

```
#include <stdio.h>
#include <conio.h>
void main()
{
 char c[]="India";
 char *p;
 p=c;
 clrscr();
 printf("%s",p);
}

OUTPUT:
India
```

7. Display two strings

```
#include <stdio.h>
#include <conio.h>
void main()
{
 #include <stdio.h>
 #include <conio.h>
```

```
void main()
{
 char *c="India";
 char *p ="Bharat";
 char *k;
 k=p;
 p=c;
 clrscr();
 printf("%s",p);
 printf(" %s",k);
}

OUTPUT:
India Bharat
```

Arithmetic operations with pointers

8. Use pointers and display addition of two numbers with and without pointers

```
#include <stdio.h>
#include <conio.h>
void main()
{
 int a=5,b=7,c,d,*ap,*bp;
 clrscr();
 ap=&a;
 bp=&b;
 c=a+b;
 d=*ap+*bp;
 printf("\n Sum of A & B : %d",c);
 printf("\n Sum of A & B : %d",d);
}

OUTPUT:
Sum of A and B : 12
Sum of A and B : 12
```

9. Use pointers and display addition, subtraction, multiplication and division of two numbers with pointers

```
#include <stdio.h>
#include <conio.h>
void main()
{
int a=25,b=10,*p,*j;
p=&a; j=&b;
clrscr();
printf(" %d  %d  %d  %d %d",*p+b,*p-b,*p * *j,*p /
*j,*p % *j);
}

OUTPUT:
35  15  250  2 5
```

10. Multiplication and addition of pointers

```
#include <stdio.h>
#include <conio.h>
void main()
{
 int num=10,*p;
p=&num;
 clrscr();
 num=*p**p+*p+*p;
 printf(" %d",num);
 getche();
}

OUTPUT:
120
```

11. Use pointer increment operation display characters

```
#include <stdio.h>
#include <conio.h>
void main()
{
 char name[15]="He",*ch;
```

```
 ch=name;
 clrscr();
 while(*ch!='\0')
 {
  printf("%c",(*ch)+1);
  ch++;
 }
}

OUTPUT:
If
```

12. Display elements of an array without pointer

```
#include <stdio.h>
#include <conio.h>
void main()
{
int x[]={1,2,3,4,5,6,7},k=1;
clrscr();
while(k<=5)
{
 printf("%2d",k[x-1]);
 k++;
}
}

OUTPUT:
1 2 3 4 5
```

13. Perform operation on array elements and display them

```
#include <stdio.h>
#include <conio.h>
void main()
{
 int a[]={15,20,40},b[3],j=0,k=2;
 clrscr();
 for(j=0;j<3;j++)
{
 b[j]=a[k];
  k--;
```

```
}
 j=0;
 while(j<3)
 printf(" %d ",b[j++]);
}

OUTPUT:
40  20  15
```

14. Three by three matrix and printout its numbers

```
#include <stdio.h>
#include <conio.h>
void main()
{
int i,j=1,*p;
int a[3][3]={{1,2,3},{4,5,6},{7,8,9}};
clrscr();
printf("\tElements of An Array with their addresses\n\n");
p=&a[0][0];
for(i=0;i<9;i++,j++)
{
printf("%5d [%5u ]",*(p),p);
p++;
if(j==3)
{
printf("\n");
j=0;
}
}
}

OUTPUT:
Elements of an array with their addresses
1 [65482 ]    2 [65484 ]    3 [65486 ]
4 [65488 ]    5 [65490 ]    6 [65492 ]
7 [65494 ]    8 [65496 ]    9 [65498 ]
```

15. Display original array and duplicate array elements

```
#include <stdio.h>
#include <conio.h>
void main()
{
int so[]={1,2,3,4,5},*pb,ds[5],i;
pb=so;
clrscr();
for(i=0;i<5;i++)
{
 ds[i]=*pb;
 pb++;
}
printf("Original Array  Duplicated Array");
for(i=0;i<5;i++)
printf("\n\t%d\t\t %d", so[i],ds[i]);
}

OUTPUT:
Original Array  Duplicated Array
        1                1
        2                2
        3                3
        4                4
        5                5
```

Pointer to Pointer

16. Use pointer to pointer and display values of element

```
#include <stdio.h>
#include <conio.h>
void main()
{
 int a=2,*p,**q;
 p=&a;
 q=&p;
clrscr();
 printf("%d  %d  %d",a,*p,**q);
}

OUTPUT:
2  2  2
```

17. Use pointers to pointers and display numbers

```
#include <stdio.h>
#include <stdio.h>
#include <conio.h>
void main()
{
int k;
int a[]={1,2,3};
int *b[3];
int **c[3];
int ***d[3];
int ****e[3];
int *****f[3];
clrscr();
for(k=0;k<3;k++)
{
        b[k]=a+k;
        c[k]=b+k;
        d[k]=c+k;
        e[k]=d+k;
        f[k]=e+k;
}
for(k=0;k<3;k++)
{
printf("%3d",*b[k]);
printf("%3d",**c[k]);
printf("%3d",***d[k]);
printf("%3d",****e[k]);
printf("%3d\n",*****f[k]);
}
}

OUTPUT:
1  1  1  1  1
2  2  2  2  2
3  3  3  3  3
```

Find the bug/s in the following programs.

1.

```
#include <stdio.h>
void main()
{
char  *c;
float  x=10;
c=&x;
printf("%d",*c);
}

Bug: Pointer and variable it pointing to should be
of same type
```

2.

```
#include <stdio.h>
void main()
{
float  x=10.25,*f;f=x;
clrscr();
printf("%g",*f);
}

Bug: & is missing in assignment statement
```

3.

```
#include <stdio.h>
void main()
{
float  x=10.25,*t,*f;
t=&x;
f=&t;
clrscr();
printf("%g",**f);
}

Bug: **f should be declared as pointer of pointer
```

4.

```
#include <stdio.h>
void main()
{
char sa[]="How are you ?";
char t,*f;f=&sa;
```

```
clrscr();
printf("%s",f);
}

Bug: & is not needed
```

5.

```
#include <stdio.h>
void main()
{int *t,x;t=&x;x=11;
*t++;
clrscr();
printf("%d",*t);
}

Bug: *t++; does not work. It must be ++*t;.
With this change this answer will be 12.
```

6.

```
#include <stdio.h>
void main()
{
int t[]={1,2,3,4,5};
 int *p,*q,*r;p=t;q=p[1];
 r=p[2];
 clrscr();
 printf("%d  %d  %d",*p,*q,*r);
}

Bug: & is required in q=p[1]; and r=p[2];
```

7.

```
#include <stdio.h>
void main()
{
int num[2][3]={1,2,3,4,5},*k;
k=&num;
clrscr();
printf("%d",*k);
}

Bug: k=&num;  should be k=&num[0][0];
```

8.

```
#include <stdio.h>
void main()
{
int x=5,y=8,z;
int *px,*py,*pz;px=&x;py=&y;pz=&z;pz=*px+*py;
clrscr();
printf("%d",z);
}

Bug: In the assignment statement *pz required
```

9.

```
#include <stdio.h>
void main()
{
int x=5;
int *px=&x,*py;
clrscr();
printf("%d",px);
}

Bug: %u is required for formatting address
```

10.

```
#include <stdio.h>
void main()
{
int x,*px;
*px=5;
px=&x;
clrscr();
printf("%d",x);
}

Bug: The statement  *px=5; should appear after px=&x;
```

11.

```
#include <stdio.h>
#include <conio.h>
void void main()
{
 int *p,*q,a=2;
 p=&a;
 q=p;
```

```
 clrscr();
 printf("%d  %d", p ,q);
}

Bug: * is missing (*p,*q)
```

10

Functions

1. What is a function?

Ans: A function is a self-contained block or a sub-program containing one or more statements that perform a particular task.

2. How a function is invoked?

Ans: The desired function is called from the `main()` function. The statement(s) of a called function are written outside the `main()` function.

3. List the types or classify the functions supported by the C language?

Ans: C language supports the following two types of functions:

1. Library functions and
2. User-defined functions.

4. What do you mean by library functions? Briefly explain it by giving its example.

Ans: The library functions are pre-defined set of functions. Their task is limited. User should not worry to understand the internal working of these functions. They can only use the functions but cannot change or modify them. Source code cannot be modified.

Example: ***sqrt (81)*** gives result ***9***. Here, the user need not worry about its source code, but the result is provided by the function.

5. List any five library functions and illustrate them with suitable examples.

Ans: There are a number of library functions are available such as `printf()`, which is used to display the message, `scanf()`, which is used to take the input from user, `clrscr()`, which is used to clear the output screen, `pow()` function, which is used to calculate power of the argument and `getch()`, which is used take a single character as input.

For example:

```
printf("Hello");
   prints message Hello on output screen.
```

```
scanf("%d",&n);
```
takes the integer input from user and stores it into variable n.
```
clrscr();
```
after execution, it will clear the screen.
```
pow(4,2);
```
will calculate square of the number 4; therefore, the value returned will be 16.
```
getch();
```
is used to take a character as input from user and returns it to the variable.

6. What do you mean by user-defined functions? Briefly explain it by giving its example.

Ans: The functions defined by the user according to their requirement are called as user-defined functions. The user can modify the function according to their requirement. They certainly understand the internal working of the function. They have full scope to implement their own ideas in the function. Thus, the set of such user-defined functions can be useful to another programmer. One should include the file in which the user-defined functions are stored to call the function in the program.

Example: Let the **`square(9)`** is a user-defined function that gives the result ***81***. Here, user knows the internal working of the **`square()`** function, as its source code is visible.

7. Is the `main()` a user-defined or library function?

Ans: Yes, the `main()` is a user-defined function. In the `main()`, required code is written. The code may be statements or functions.

8. Why to use functions?

Ans:

1. If we want to perform a task repetitively, then it is not necessary to re-write the particular block of the program repeatedly. Shift the particular block of statements in user-defined function. The function defined can be called any number of times to perform the task.
2. Using functions, large programs are reduced to smaller ones. It is easy to debug and find out the errors in it. It also increases readability.

9. How do functions help to reduce the program size?

Ans: By writing the functions, we can reduce the space required for the part of the program that is repeated a number of times, by including it into a function. On the function call instead of writing the whole code repeatedly, the control is transferred to the function.

10. Write the syntax of function definition.

Ans: Function definition begins as per format given below:

```
function-type function_name (argument/parameter list)
 {
   local variable declaration;
   Statement1;
   Statement2;
   return(value);
}
```

The function type indicates the return type of the value returned by the function. It may be `void()`, `int`, `float` etc. The function name is the name of the function.

11. What are the void functions?

Ans: The `void` functions are the functions that may or may not have arguments, but these functions do not return any value.

12. How to invoke a function from the main() function?

Ans: Table 10.1 describes how to invoke a function from a `main()` function. The `main()` is a user defined function and user can invoke a function called as abc(x,y,z).

Table 10.1 Invoking a function from a `main()` function

```
void main()
{
   ----------
   ----------
   ----------
abc(x,y,z);        ──────►    Function Call
    └────────────────────►    Actual argument

   ----------
   ----------
}

abc(data type 1, data type k, data type j) ──►Function definition
{   └─────────────────────►    Formal arguments
  ----------
   ----------
   return();        ──────►  return value
}
```

1. **Actual argument:** The arguments of calling functions are actual arguments. In Table 10.1, the variables *x*, *y* and *z* are actual arguments.
2. **Formal argument:** The arguments of called function are formal arguments. In Table 10.1, the variable *i*, *k* and *j* are formal arguments.
3. **Function name:** A function must follow the same rule as we follow for variable naming in C.

Example: `sum (int a, int b);`
Function call: A compiler executes a function when a semicolon (;) is followed by function name. A function can be called simply using its name like other 'C' statement, terminated by semicolon (;). Following example shows invoking a function from the `main()`.

```
int a,b;
sum (a, b);
```

where, `sum()` is a user-defined function and **'a'** and **'b'** are actual integer variable arguments. The function name must be ended by a semicolon (;).

4. **Argument/parameter list**
   The argument list means variable names enclosed within the parentheses. They must be separated by comma (,). These formal arguments (consignment) are to be received values from actual argument and for performing this, a communication between consignee and consignor functions is made.

13. Should we use the same variable names for actual and formal arguments?

Ans: No, we should not use the same variable names for actual and formal arguments .This is because the scope of actual and formal variables is different in different functions. Therefore, we should try to avoid using the same variable name for formal and actual arguments.

14. How does a function work?

1. Once a function is defined and called, it takes some data from the calling function and returns a value to the called function.
2. The detail of inner working of a function is unknown to the rest of the program. Whenever a function is called, the control passes to the called function and the working of calling function is paused. When the execution of called function is completed, the control returns back to the calling function and executes the next statement.
3. The values of actual arguments passed by the calling function are received by the formal arguments of called function. The number of actual and formal arguments should be same. Extra arguments are discarded if they are defined. If the formal arguments are more than the actual arguments, then the extra arguments appear as garbage. Any mismatch in the data type will produce the unexpected result.
4. The function operates on formal arguments and sends back the result to calling function. The **`return()`** statement performs this task.

15. What are the uses of the `return()` statements?

Ans: The return statement is used to return a value from the function to the invoking function. We can also use the return statement to transfer the control to the invoking function without any return value. Every function can return almost one value.

16. What does it mean if there is no return statement in the function?

Ans: If a function does not have return statement, then it means that the return type of the function is void, that is, the function processes the input and returns the control without any return value.

17. Explain the different formats of `return()` statements. How many values does a return statement return at each call?

Ans: The return statement may or may not return value; therefore, there are two formats of return statement:

```
return(argument);
```

In the above format, the return statement returns the value to the function from which the function is invoked.

```
return();
```

In this format, as the return statement does not have any argument, it will only return the control back to the invoking function.

A return statement can return only one value. We may include an expression within return statement. In that case, first, the expression is evaluated, then the value is returned.

18. What is a global pointer? Illustrate with a suitable example.

Ans: If we define a pointer above `main()` function, it will become a global pointer. The scope of this pointer is throughout the program. We can use this pointer in any part of the program.

19. Why is the return statement not necessary when a function is called by a reference?

Ans: When we pass the arguments by reference, any changes in formal arguments are reflected in actual arguments; therefore, we need not to return any value from the called function. The function can be called by reference by passing the address of the arguments to the function.

20. Distinguish between function prototype and function definition.

Ans: The function prototype informs the compiler about the function name, its argument and return type. The function prototype can be given globally or local to `main()`. However, the function prototype must precede function call if the function is not defined before the function call.

The function definition is the actual definition of the function; it also contains function prototype below which the function body is given.

21. Does the function prototype match with the function definition?

Ans: The function prototype is declared to inform the compiler about function. The function prototype and function definition may have different variable names, but their types must match with each other.

22. Can we define a user-defined function with the same library function name?

Ans: In C language, we cannot define the function with the same name as library function, because on doing so, we will get error due function redeclaration.

23. What is recursion? Explain its advantages.

Ans: When a function invokes itself from its own function body, it is called recursion. The recursions are of two types, which are direct recursion and indirect recursion. In the direct recursion, the same function calls itself from its own body. In indirect recursion, the function invokes some other function, which again invokes the function that has invoked it. That is, it creates a cycle of function calls. Recursion can be used to reduce the code length in some special types of problems. These problems become simpler when coded with recursion than iterative approach.

24. Explain the types of recursions.

Ans: The recursions are of two types, which are direct recursion and indirect recursion. In the direct recursion, the same function calls itself from its own body. In indirect recursion, the function invokes some other functions, which again invokes the function that has invoked it. That is, it creates a cycle of function calls.

25. Is it possible to call library function recursively?

Ans: As we know that we cannot edit the code of the library functions; the library function are not recursive previously, so we cannot call them recursively.

26. Explain call by value and call by address with programming example of each one.

Ans: When value is passed in a function, it is known as call by value. Value is changed only inside the function. The changed value is not reflected in the original value.

For example,

```
#include<stdio.h>
#include<conio.h>
void swap(int,int);
void main()
{
int a,b;
clrscr();
printf("enter two integer number\n");
scanf("%d%d",&a,&b);
printf(" before calling swap function \n");
printf("a=%d\t b=%d\n",a,b);
swap(a,b);
printf("after calling swap function");
printf("a=%d\tb=%d\n",a,b);
getch( );
}
void swap(int p,int q)
{
int t;
t=p;
p=q;
q=t;
}
```

Call by reference: In call by reference, in the following example, addresses of the variables/arguments *a* and *b* are supplied to the called function `swap()`.Whatever changes we perform inside the function through pointers *p* and *q*, the same are reflected back in the original actual parameters *a* and *b* in the calling function.

In call by reference, one can manipulate with physical address in the memory and can make changes as per requirement. The call by reference can be implemented by passing pointers to the variables as arguments to the function. Ultimately, these pointers are used by the called function to acees the argumentsvariables and make changes as per requirement. Thus, with this method whatever changes are made in the arguments in the called function through addresses, the same are reflected in the actual arguments even if control returns to the calling method.

```
#include<stdio.h>
#include<conio.h>
void swap(int*,int*);
void main()
{
int a,b;
```

```
clrscr();
printf("enter two integer number\n");
scanf("%d%d",&a,&b);
printf("before calling swap function \n");
printf("a=%d\t b=%d\n",a,b);
swap(&a, &b);
printf("after calling swap function");
printf("a=%d\tb=%d\n",a,b);
getch( );
}
void swap(int *p, int *q)
{
int t;
t=*p;
*p=*q;
*q=t;
}
```

27. Write a program to reverse a number using function.

```
#include<stdio.h>
#include<conio.h>
long int reverse(long int);
void main()
{
int n,rev;
clrscr();
printf("enter a number");
scanf("%d",&n);
rev=reverse(n);
printf("reverse number of %d is %d",n,rev);
getch();
}
long int reverse(long int a)
{
int r,rev=0;
while(a!=0)
{
r=a%10;
rev=rev*10+r;
a/=10;
}
return rev;
}
```

Multiple-choice Questions

1. The arguments of caller function are called by _________.
   (a) Actual arguments (b) Formal arguments (c) Memory variable
2. Which keyword is used for a function not returning any value?
   (a) `void` (b) `int` (c) `auto`
3. Function prototype is not compulsory when function definition given _________.
   (a) Before caller function (b) After caller function (c) At the end of program
4. The limitation of return statement _________.
   (a) Can return only one value (b) Is critical to use (c) Consumes more memory space
5. The recursion of the function can be stopped _________.
   (a) Using conditional statement (b) By pressing Ctrl + Break (c) Using keyword return
6. In C functions, return statement is not compulsory because return address is _________.
   (a) Stored on the stack
   (b) Stored into the pointer
   (c) Stored in register variable of the CPU
7. The use of return statement is to _________.
   (a) Return value
   (b) Inform compiler end of program
   (c) To push back the control of the program
8. When a user-defined function is invoked, values are passed _________.
   (a) On the stack (b) Into ROM (c) To memory variables
9. When a function returns value 0 (zero), it indicates _________.
   (a) Normal termination (b) Erroneous termination (c) None of the above
10. Arrays are passed to function by _________.
    (a) Value (b) Address (c) None of the above
11. It is necessary to declare void type in the function definition when a function does not return _________.
    (a) Any value (b) Integer (c) Float
12. By default function returns _________.
    (a) Integer (b) Float (c) Null
13. The main is a _________.
    (a) Keyword (b) User-defined function (c) Library function
14. Which is the correct statement for finding the cube of 5?
    (a) `pow(5,3);` (b) `pow(3,5);`
    (c) `pow(3);` (d) None of the above
15. The `floor()` function returns _________.
    (a) Round down value (b) Round up value
    (c) Absolute value (d) Zero value

16. Recursion is a process in which a function calls _________.
    (a) Itself
    (b) Another function
    (c) `main()` function
    (d) None of the above
17. The meaning of keyword void before function name means _________.
    (a) Function should not return any value
    (b) Function should return any value
    (c) No arguments are passed
    (d) None of the above
18. A global pointer can access variable of _________.
    (a) All user-defined functions
    (b) Only `main()` function
    (c) Only library functions
    (d) None of the above
19. The `if (fun())` transfers the control to _________.
    (a) The function `fun()`
    (b) The condition specified followed by `if(fun)` statements
    (c) The statements specified followed by `if(fun)`
    (d) None of the above
20. The arguments in a function are provided _________.
    (a) Within the parentheses
    (b) Within the braces
    (c) Within angle bracket angles
21. Global variables appear _________.
    (a) Outside the `main()`
    (b) Within the `main(_)`
    (c) Above the header file
    (d) None of the above
22. The library function _________ returns absolute value.
    (a) `pow()`
    (b) `abs()`
    (c) `sum()`
23. The header file _________ contains all the mathematical functions.
    (a) `stdio.h`
    (b) `math.h`
    (c) `conio.h`
24. The functions defined by user are _________.
    (a) User-defined functions
    (b) Standard functions
    (c) Library functions
25. The user cannot change the definition of _________.
    (a) User-defined functions
    (b) System functions
    (c) Library functions
26. When a function executes itself, the process is called _________.
    (a) Iteration
    (b) Recursion
    (c) Looping
27. The _________ function cannot be used for recursion.
    (a) User-defined functions
    (b) System functions
    (c) Library functions
28. While defining recursion function, a provision should be made to _________.
    (a) Store the value
    (b) Tracing the program
    (c) Stop the program
29. The result obtained by function is sent back to the calling function through the _________ statement.
    (a) Exit
    (b) Return
    (c) Array
30. Whenever a function is called, the _________ passes to the called function.
    (a) Arguments
    (b) Control
    (c) Data

31. void sum(void) means _________.
    (a) Function neither sends any argument nor returns any result
    (b) Function sends argument but not returns result
    (c) Function returns results but not required any input
32. float `sum()` means _________.
    (a) It returns float value (b) It returns int value (c) It is a void
33. int avg (float, float, float) means _________.
    (a) Returns float value and passes three float values
    (b) Returns int value and passes three float values
    (c) Returns long int value and passes three float values
34. int sum(int *) means _________.
    (a) Address is passed (b) Value is passed (c) No value is passed
35. In call by address call formal arguments are pointer to _________.
    (a) `main()` function (b) Actual arguments (c) Itself
36. A function can return more values by the method called _________.
    (a) Call by value (b) Call by address (c) Call by parameter
37. In _________, addresses of the array elements are passed to function.
    (a) Call by value (b) Call by reference (c) None of the above
38. Function by default returns _________ value
    (a) Integer (b) Float
    (c) Character (d) None
39. In main function when we write return(0) it refers to _________.
    (a) Compiler (b) Operating System (c) None of this
40. In function calling the values are _________.
    (a) passed from right to left
    (b) passed in the sequence in which they are returned
    (c) passed from left to right
41. The useful data structure in function calling is _________.
    (a) heap (b) queue
    (c) stack (d) link-list
42. The stack is _________.
    (a) FIFO data structure (b) LIFO data structure
    (c) Random data structure (d) Two way data structure
43. When a function is called _________.
    (a) the caller functions variables are pushed on to the stack
    (b) the function to be called is pushed on to the stack
    (c) control is transferred to that function
    (d) All of these

44. Choose correct o/p option.

```
int fun()
{
   printf("Hi ");
   return 0;
   printf("Hello ");
   return 23;
}
void main()
{
   int i;
   clrscr();
   i = fun();
   printf(" %d ",i) ;
   getch();
}
```

The output is

(a) Hi 0 Hello 23
(b) Hi Hello 0 23
(c) Hi 0
(d) Hi 23

Answers

1. (a)	2. (a)	3. (a)	4. (a)	5. (a)	6. (a)	7. (a)	8. (a)	9. (a)	10. (b)	11. (a)
12. (a)	13. (b)	14. (a)	15. (a)	16. (a)	17. (a)	18. (a)	19. (a)	20. (a)	21. (a)	22. (b)
23. (b)	24. (a)	25. (c)	26. (b)	27. (c)	28. (a)	29. (b)	30. (b)	31. (a)	32. (a)	33. (b)
34. (a)	35. (b)	36. (b)	37. (b)	38. (a)	39. (b)	40. (a)	41. (c)	42. (b)	43. (d)	44. (c)

True or False

1. Every 'C' program starts with function `main()`.
2. Library function can be defined by the user.
3. User-defined functions have serious limitations.
4. The `sum()` is a standard library function.
5. The `abs()` is a standard library function.
6. The `abs()` gives absolute value.
7. Mathematical library functions are defined in `math.h`.
8. Functions not returning any value are known as `void`.
9. The `return()` statement can return more than one value at a time.
10. The arguments of function which are invoked are called actual arguments.

11. A user-defined function cannot call another user-defined function.
12. A user-defined function cannot call a `main()` function.
13. The scope of local variables is limited to the block in which they are defined.
14. Actual and formal arguments can have same variable name.
15. In call by value, values are passed to formal arguments.
16. In call by address, formal arguments are pointer to actual arguments.
17. A change made in formal arguments can change the value of variable permanently.
18. A function prototype gives information in advance to the compiler.
19. A function can pass arguments to another function.
20. The data type before the function name indicates the type of value the function will return.
21. By default, function returns integer value.
22. When a function calls itself, the process is called recursion.
23. Like variable, functions also have address in the memory.
24. Functions can be invoked using pointers to function.
25. Function prototype is not necessary to match with actual function definition.

Answers

1. True	2. False	3. False	4. False	5. True	6. True	7. True	8. True	9. False
10. False	11. False	12. False	13. True	14. True	15. True	16. True	17. False	18. True
19. True	20. True	21. True	22. True	23. True	24. True	25. False		

What is/are the output/s of the following programs?

1.

```
void main()
{
clrscr();
printf("\n India is ");
sub();
getche();
}
sub()
{
printf(" my Country");
}

OUTPUT:
India is  my Country
```

2.

```
void main()
{
clrscr();
printf("\n India is ");
sub();
secondsub();
printf("\n I love my country");
getche();
}
   sub()
   {
   printf(" my Country");
   }
secondsub()
{
 printf( " ");
}

OUTPUT:
 India is  my Country
 I love my country
```

3.

```
void main()
{
clrscr();
sum();
getche();
]

sum()
    {
    int a=7,f=0,d;
    while(a>=1)
    {
    f=f+a;
    a=a-1;
    }
    printf("\n%d",f);
    }

OUTPUT:
28
```

4.

```
void main()
{
clrscr();
fact();
getche();
}

fact()
    {
    int a=5,f=1,d;
    while(a>=1)
    {
    f=f*a;
    a=a-1;
    }
    printf("\n%d",f);
    }

OUTPUT:
120
```

5.

```
void main()
{
int a=4,fac;
clrscr();
fac=fact(a);
printf("\n%d",fac);
getche();
}

fact(x)
int x;
    {
    int f=1,d;
    while(x>=1)
    {
    f=f*x;
    x=x-1;
    }
    return(f);
    }

OUTPUT:
24
```

6.

```
void main()
{
int a=3,b=4,c=5,d;
clrscr();
mul();
d=a+b+c;
printf("\n%d",d);
getche();
}

mul()
   {
   int a=2,b=3,c=4,d;
   d=a*b*c;
   printf("\n%d",d);
   }

OUTPUT:
24
12
```

7.

```
#include <stdio.h>
#include  <conio.h>
void main()
{
int result;
clrscr();
result=sq();
printf("\n Result of function
is= %.2d",result);
getche();
}

  sq()
  {
  int x=2,y=3;
  return(x*x+y*y);
  }

OUTPUT:
Result of function is = 13
```

8.

```
#include <stdio.h>
#include  <conio.h>
void main()
{
int  num=5,result;
clrscr();
result=cb(num);
printf("\n Result of function is=
%.2d",result);
getche();
}

  cb(int x)
  {
  float y;
  y=x*x*x;
  return(y);
  }

OUTPUT:
Result of function is = 125
```

Find the bug/s in the following program/s.

1.

```
#include <stdio.h>
#include <conio.h>
void main()
{
int sum( int j, k,l);
clrscr();
sum(1,2,3);
}

 sum (int j,int k, int l)
 {
   printf("%d  %d  %d",j,k,l);

 }
```

Bug: Function prototype error

2.

```
#include <stdio.h>
#include <conio.h>
void main()
{
void show (void);
clrscr();
show();
}
 show()
 {
  puts("Hello");
 }
```

Bug : In function definition void is not mentioned

3.

```
#include <stdio.h>
#include <conio.h>

void main()
{
float  ave (int,int,int);
float av;
clrscr();

av=ave (3,3,5);
printf("%g",av);

}

 float ave(int j,int k, int l)
 {
  float x= j+k+l/3.0;

 }
```

Bug : No bug. However, warning message appears.

4.

```
#include <stdio.h>
#include <conio.h>


void A( )
{
  clrscr();
  printf("\n in A");
}


void main()
{
   A('x','x');

}

Bug: No Bug
```

5.

```
#include <stdio.h>
#include <conio.h>

void main()
{

int B();
B(5.5);
}

B(float a)
{
clrscr();
printf(" %f",a);

}
```

Bug: Function prototype error

6.

```
#include <stdio.h>
#include <conio.h>
void main()
{

int B();
B();
}
C()
{
 printf("In C");
}

B( )
{
 printf("In B");
 C();
 B();

}

Bug:  infinite recursion
```

11

Storage Class

1. What are defined in the storage class?

Ans: The life time and scope of the variable or/and function in a program are defined in the storage class.

2. List the storage classes supported by C.

Ans: C supports the following storage classes and the corresponding C keywords associated with them are as follows:

Storage class	Keyword
1. Automatic	`auto`
2. External	`extern`
3. Static	`static`
4. Register	`register`

3. Give the importance of storage class.

Ans: The storage class of a variable tells the compiler:

1. The storage area or scope of the variable.
2. The initial value of variable if not initialized.
3. The scope of the variable.
4. Life of the variable, i.e., how long the variable would be active in the program.

4. What does scope of the variable mean?

Ans: Area or the scope, where the variable is to be accessed. Some variables are global and can be accessed anywhere in the program, whereas some variables scope is in the block where they are declared. This area is local for them.

5. What are the `auto` variables?

Ans: The variables that are available only to the current block or program are `auto` variables. The `auto` variables are stored in the main memory of the system. By default, the storage class of variables is `auto`.

6. What are the additional uniqueness of auto variables?

Ans:

1. The auto variables are defined inside a function. The keyword auto should only be used within the function.
2. The scope of the auto variables is local to the block in which they are defined. Once the executions of the function take place and return turns off the function, the contents and existence of the auto variables or local variable vanishes.
3. The auto variables are stored in the main memory. They are stored in the stack at run time.
4. The keyword 'auto' is used for declaration of automatic variables. By default, every variable pertains to auto storage class. The 'auto' is optional.

7. Write a program on auto variables.

```
void main()
{
auto int b=7;
int c=5;
clrscr();
printf("\n %d %d",b,c);
{
auto int  b=10;
printf("\n %d",b);
}
printf("\n %d",b);
getche();
}

OUTPUT:
7 5
10
7
```

Explanation: In the above program, declaration and initialization of *b* is made two times with different values. In the first block, the *b* value is 7 and in second block its value is 10. Before passing control to the second block, the value of *b* variable printed is 7 and after passing control to the second block, the value of *b* is changed to 10. By default, the storage class for *c* is auto.

8. What are the register variables?

Ans: The 'register' variables are stored in the registers of the CPU. Accessing variables through the register of the CPU is faster than the memory access.

9. Give the characteristics of register variables.

Ans:

1. Speed of execution of program is fast because variables are stored in CPU register. Accessing variables through the CPU register is faster than RAM. The keyword register tells the compiler that the variable list followed by it is kept on the CPU registers.

2. Maximum size of the variable is equal to the size of the `register`. Usually, it is one word.
3. The unary operator is not to be applied on `register` variables.

10. List the limitations of `register` variables.

Ans:

1. CPU registers are limited in number. Hence, we cannot declare more variables with `register` variables. Thus, compiler automatically converts `register` variables to non-register variables, once the limit is reached.
2. User cannot determine the success or failure of `register` variables.
3. We cannot use `register` class for all types of variables.
4. The data types float and double need more than 16 bits space. If we define variables of these data type with `register` class, no errors will be shown. The compiler treats them as a variable of `auto` class.

11. Write a program on `register` variable.

Ans:

```
void main()
{
register int m=0;
clrscr();
for(m=0;m<5;m++)
printf("\t%d",m);
getche();
}
```

OUTPUT:

0   1   2   3   4

Explanation: In the above program, the variable *m* is declared and initialized to 0. The 'for' loop displays values from 0 to 4. The `register` class variable is used as loop variable.

12. What are external variables? Give a few of its features.

Ans: The external variables are available to all the functions, i.e., entire program can access the `extern` variables. In other words, the scope of the `extern` variables is global. The variables are called external or global variables. External variables are declared outside the function body. In case in a program both external and `auto` variables are declared with the same name, the first priority is given to the `auto` variable. In this case, external variable is hidden.

13. Display the external variable in different blocks.

Ans:

```
int v=10;
void main()
{
clrscr();
call1();
call2();
printf("\n In main() V=%d",v);
}
call1()
{
printf("\n In Call1() V=%d",v);
}

 call2()
 {
 printf("\n In call2() V=%d",v);
 }

OUTPUT:
In Call1() V=10
In call2() V=10
In main() V=10
```

Explanation: In the above program, the variable *v* is declared outside the function body and initialized it to value 10. Every function can access the variable *v*, so no re-declaration or local variable is created. Every function in turn prints the value of *v*. The same value is printed by all the functions.

14. What is a `static` variable?

Ans: The `static` variable may be of an internal or external type, depending where it is declared. If it is declared outside the function body, it will be `static` global. In case declared in the body or block, it will be an `auto` variable. When a variable is declared as `static`, its garbage value is removed and initialized to zero. The scope of the `static` variables is local to the block in which they are declared. The contents stored in these variables remain constant throughout the program.

15. Give the characteristics of `static` storage class.

Ans: In a `static` storage class, a `static` variable is initialized only once; it is never reinitialized. The value of the `static` variable persists at each call and the last change made in the value of the `static` variable remains throughout the program execution. Using this property of the `static` variable, we can count how many times a function was called.

16. Write a program on `static` variable.

Ans:

```
void main()
{
clrscr();
for(;;)
print();
}
print()
{
int static m;
m++;
printf("\nm=%d",m);
if(m==3)
exit(0);
}

OUTPUT:
m=1
m=2
m=3
```

Explanation: In the above program, `print()` function is called. The variable *m* of `print()` function is `static` variable. It is increased and printed in each call. Its contents persist at every call. In the first call, its value is changed from 0 to 1, in second call 1 to 2 and in the third call 2 to 3.

17. Distinguish between `static` and `auto` variables.

Ans: In `static` storage class, the value of variable retains between function calls; however, in `auto` storage class, it does not.

a. First, program to verify the above point with `static` keyword:

Ans:

```
void func(void);
static c=4;
void main()
{
clrscr();
while(c--)
{
fun();
}
}
```

```
void func(void);
static c=4;
void main()
{
clrscr();
while(c--)
{
fun();
}
}

OUTPUT:
i is 1 and count is 3
i is 2 and count is 2
i is 3 and count is 1
i is 4 and count is 0
```

b. Program with auto keyword

```
void func(void);
int c=4;
void main()
{
clrscr();
while(c--)
{
fun();
}
}
fun( void )
{
auto  int i=0;
i++;
printf("i is %d and count is %d\n", i, c);
}

OUTPUT:

i is 1 and count is 3
i is 1 and count is 2
i is 1 and count is 1
i is 1 and count is 0
```

Explanation: Due to `auto` class, the value of variable does not retain between calling function; hence, the value of *i* remains 1 throughout the different calling functions.

18. Why `register` storage class does not support all data types?

Ans: The CPU registers 8086 in microcomputer are 16-bit registers. The data types float and double need more than 16 bits space. If we define variables of these data type with `register` class, no errors will be shown. The compiler treats them as a variable of `auto` class.

19. Can we declare a variable in different scopes with different data types? Answer in short.

Yes, we can declare the variable in different scopes with different data types except for some data types with `register` scope or storage class.

20. Explain lifetime and visibility of a variable.

Ans:

Lifetime of a variable: Every variable has its lifetime, i.e., its time duration during which its status is active in the program. We can also say that lifetime of a variable is the time gap between its declaration and cleanup. The lifetime depends upon the storage class. For example, `auto` variable gets destroyed immediately when the function execution is over, whereas `static` variable remains in the memory.

Visibility of a variable: It is another property. It defines its scope. The scope is of two types, i.e., local and global. Global is recognized throughout the program, whereas the local variable scope is limited to the declaration block.

Multiple-choice Questions

1. A `static` variable is one that ________.
   (a) Retains its value throughout the life of the program
   (b) Cannot be initialized
   (c) Is initialized once at the commencement of the execution and cannot be changed at the run time
   (d) Is the same as an automatic variable, but is placed at the head of the program
2. An external variable is one ________.
   (a) That is globally accessible by all functions
   (b) That is declared outside the body of any function
   (c) That resides in the memory till the end of the program
   (d) All of the above
3. If a storage class is not mentioned in the declaration, then default storage class is ________.
   (a) `auto` (b) `static` (c) `extern` (d) `register`
4. If the CPU fails to keep the variables in CPU registers, in that case the variables are assumed ________.
   (a) `auto` (b) `static` (c) `extern` (d) None of the above
5. What will be the value of variable *x* on execution of the following program?

```
int x;
void main()
{
clrscr();
x++;
printf("\n %d",x);
}
```

(a) $x = 1$ (b) I = 0 (c) Garbage value (d) None of the above

6. Which variables of following storage class are stored in RAM?

   (a) `auto` (b) `register` (c) None of the above

7. Which variables of the following storage class are stored in CPU registers?

   (a) `auto` (b) `register` (c) None of the above

8. Which of the following is not C keyword?

   (a) automatic (b) `register` (c) `static` (d) `extern`

9. Which of the following storage class is faster?

   (a) `auto` (b) `register` (c) `static` (d) `extern`

10. Which of the following storage class provides garbage value when variables are not initialized?

    (a) `auto` (b) `static` (c) `extern`

11. The basic task of storage class is to determine the variable's _________.

    (a) Scope (b) Default value (c) Storage (d) All of the above

12. What is the output of the following program?

```
static x=2;
void main()
{
printf("%d",++x);
}
```

    (a) 2 (b) 3
    (c) 1 (d) None of the above

13. What is the output of the following program?

```
void main()
{
extern x
printf("%d",++x);
}
```

    (a) 0 (b) Garbage value (c) Syntax error

14. What is the output of the following program?

```
int x;
void main()
{
extern x;
printf("%d",++x);
}
```

    (a) 1 (b) Garbage value (c) Syntax error

15. What is the output of the following program?

```
int x=5;
void main()
{
extern x;
printf("%d",x++);
}
```

(a) 1 (b) Garbage value
(c) 5 (d) None of the above

16. The scope of `static` variables is the same as that of _________.
(a) `auto` (b) `static`
(c) `extern` (d) None of the above

17. The scope of `extern` variables is _________.
(a) Local (b) Global
(c) Inside the function (d) None of the above

18. Even if not initialized, which of the following type of variable dose not hold garbage value?
(a) `Auto` variable (b) External variable (c) `Register` variable

19. The `auto` variable can be of _________.
(a) `Static` (b) External (c) Pointer

20. The storage class of the variable tells the compiler _________.
(a) Storage area of variable
(b) The scope of the variable
(c) Both (a) and (b)

21. If external and `auto` variables are declared with the same name, priority is given to _________.
(a) `Auto` variable (b) External variable (c) None of them

22. Which of the following keyword is not related to C storage classes?
(a) `static` (b) `auto` (c) case

Answers

1. (a) 2. (a) 3. (a) 4. (a) 5. (a) 6. (a) 7. (b) 8. (a) 9. (b) 10. (a)
11. (d) 12. (b) 13. (c) 14. (a) 15. (c) 16. (a) 17. (b) 18. (b) 19. (a) 20. (c)
21. (a) 22. (c)

True or False

1. `Auto` variables are defined inside the function.
2. `Auto` variable must be prefixed with keyword `auto`.
3. `Auto` functions are defined on the stack.
4. `Auto` variables are global variables.

5. The external variables are available to the entire program.
6. The external variables are global in access.
7. External variables are defined outside the function.
8. In case both external and `auto` variables are defined with same name, external variables get identified (assume only `main()` function exists).
9. `Static` variable can be of external and `auto` types.
10. The value of `static` variables persists.
11. A `static` variable must be initialized explicitly.
12. We can place value of variable in CPU register using the keyword `register`.
13. We can confirm if the values are placed or not in CPU register.
14. If `register` variables are not kept in the CPU register, they are treated as `auto` variables.

Answers

1. True 2. False 3. True 4. False 5. True 6. True 7. True 8. False 9. True 10. True 11. False 12. True 13. False 14. True

Additional Questions

What will be the output of the following programs?

1.

```
#include <stdio.h>
#include <conio.h>
void main()
{
    int v-5;
    clrscr();
{
    int v=4;
    printf(" %d ",v);
}
    printf(" %d ",v);
{
    int v=9;
    printf(" %d ",v);
}
    printf(" %d ",v);
}

OUTPUT:
4  5  9  5
```

2.

```
#include <stdio.h>
#include <conio.h>
void main()
{
  int x=11;
  clrscr();
  printf("\n x=%d",x);
{
  float x=2.5;
  printf("x=%g",x);
}
{
  char *x="Auto Storage Class";
  printf("x=%s",x);
}
}

OUTPUT:
x = 11 x = 2.5  x = Auto Storage Class
```

3.

```
#include <stdio.h>
#include <conio.h>
int v=10;
void main()
{
  clrscr();
  call1();
  call2();
  printf("In main()");
}
call1() { printf(" In call1()"); }
call2() { printf(" In call2()"); }

OUTPUT:
In call1() In call2() In main()
```

4.

```
#include <stdio.h>
#include <conio.h>
int v=10;

void main()
{
  clrscr();
  call1();
  call2();
  printf(" In main()");
}
call1() { printf("In call1() v-%d",v); }
call2() { printf("In call2() v=%d",v); }

OUTPUT:
In call1() v = 10 In call2() v = 10 In main()
```

5.

```
#include <stdio.h>
#include <conio.h>
int v=10;

void main()
{
 clrscr();
 for(;;)
 print();
}
 print()
{
  int static m;
  m++;
  printf(" %d",m);
  if(m==3) exit(0);
}

OUTPUT:
1 2 3
```

6.

```
#include <stdio.h>
#include <stdio.h>
#include <conio.h>

void main()
{
  auto int j=1;
  clrscr();
{
{
{ printf("%d",j);
}
  printf("%d",j);
}
  printf("%d",j);
}
}

OUTPUT:
1 1 1
```

7.

```
#include <stdio.h>
#include <stdio.h>
#include <conio.h>

void main()
{
  auto int j=1;
  clrscr();
{
  auto int j=2;
{
  auto int j=3;
  printf("%d",j);
}
  printf("%d",j);
}
  printf("%d",j);
}

OUTPUT:
321
```

8.

```
#include <stdio.h>
#include <stdio.h>
#include <conio.h>

void main()
{
 clrscr();
 increment();
 increment();
 increment();
}
 increment()
{
  static int j=1;
  printf("\n%d",j);
  j++;
}

OUTPUT:
1  2  3
```

Find the bug/s in the following programs.

1.

```
auto int x=20;
#include <stdio.h>
void main()
{
auto int x=10;
clrscr();
printf("\nx=%d",x);
}
```

Bug : Automatic variables cannot be defined outside functions

2.

```
#include <stdio.h>
void main()
{
register  x=10;
printf("\nx=%d",x);
}
```

Bug : No bug

3.

```
#include <stdio.h>
void main()
{
clrscr();
value();}
static value()
{
 printf("Hi");
}
```

Bug: No Bug

4.

```
#include <stdio.h>
void main()
{
   int x=25;
   clrscr();
   printf("%d\n",x);
   show();
}
show() { printf("%d",x); }
```

Bug: Compiler error

5.

```
#include <stdio.h>
void main()
{
int count =5;
printf("\n%d",count--);
if(count!=0)
main();
}
```

Bug: No bug. But, the count should be `static`

6.

```
#include <stdio.h>
float x=5.5;
void main()
{
 float y,f();
 clrscr();
 x*=4.0;
 y=f(x);
 printf("%g %g",x,y);
}
 float f(float a)
{
  a+=1.3;
   x-=4.5;
 return a+x;
 return 0;
}
```

Bug: Return 0 should be removed

7.

```
#include <stdio.h>
register int i;
void main()
{
clrscr();
for(i=3;i>0;i--)
printf("\ % d",i);
getche();
}
```

Bug: Incompatible storage class

12

Preprocessor Directives

1. What is a preprocessor directive?

Ans: One of the most important features of 'C' language is to offer preprocessor directives. They are not the program statements but directives to the preprocessor. The preprocessor directives are included at the beginning of the program before the `main()`. They can be placed anywhere but quite often it is included at the beginning before the `main()` or any particular function. They begin with the symbol # (hash) to be placed at the first column.

2. How to define preprocessor macro?

Ans: The preprocessor macro is defined as follows.

```
#define identifier substitute
```

The preprocessor replaces any occurrence of identifier in the program by substitute.
For example,

```
#define PI 3.14
```

This statement defines PI as macro template and 3.14 as macro substitute. During preprocessing, the preprocessor replaces every occurrence of PI (identifier) with 3.14 (substitute value). Here, PI is a macro template and 3.14 is its macro expansion. The macro templates are generally declared with capital letters for quick identification. One can also define macros with small letters. The macro templates and its expansions must be separated with at least one blank space. It is not necessary to provide space between # and **define**. It is optional to the programmer. To increase readability, the programmer should provide space. The macro definition should not be terminated with semicolon i.e. preprocessor directives are not terminated by semicolons.

3. Replace PI as 3.14 in the program and find the area of a circle.

Ans:

```
#define PI 3.14
void main()
{
float r,area;
clrscr();
```

```
printf("\n Enter radius of circle in cms :-");
scanf("%f",&r);
area=PI*r*r;
printf("Area of a Circle = %.2f cm^2",area);
getche();
}

OUTPUT:
Enter radius of circle in centimetres: 7
Area of a circle =153.86 cm^2
```

Explanation: In the above program, PI replaces with 3.14 during the program execution. In the program, instead of writing the value of PI as 3.14, we define directly the value of PI as 3.14. The term PI is replaced with 3.14 in the program. PI macro is used for calculating the area of a circle.

4. What is the #include directive? How does it help the programmer?

Ans: The #include directive loads specified file in the current program. The included programmers file executes along with the current program. The macros and functions of loaded file can be included in the current program. Both the included file and the current program are complied.

5. What is the syntax of #include directive? Elaborate it with examples.

Ans: Syntax of #include directive is as follows:

(a) **`#include "filename"`**

or

(b) **`#include <filename>`**

where **#** is a symbol used with directives.

(a) The file name is included in the double quotation marks indicating that the search for the file is made in the current directory and in the standard directories.

For example, **`#include "stdio.h"`**

(b) When the filename is enclosed within angle brackets without double quotation marks, the search for file is made only in the standard directories.

For examples, **`#include <stdio.h>`**
`#include "udf.h"`

6. Write a program on `include` directive.

Ans:

```
#include <stdio.h>
#include "abc.c"
#include <assert.h>
```

```
void main()
{
int x=4;
clrscr();
assert(x==4);
printf("%d",x);
printf("%d",a);
}

OUTPUT:
44
```

Explanation: In this program, the abc.c **file** is included. Its contents are simply int *a*=4; it is a user-defined function file. It is complied before the main program. The complete program along with the included file gets executed. The output of the program is as shown above.

7. What is the difference between functions and preprocessor directives?

Ans: The preprocessor directives are normally included at the beginning of the program or before the main() function in C. They alter the source code through macro expansion, produce precompiled files and finally pass it for compilation.

However, function is block of statement(s) that is to be invoked by the programmer from one function for carrying out task repeatedly if needed. The functions are called methods or subprograms. Calling subprogram from one function and executing the same subprogram requires more time than execution of preprocessor directives. Hence, preprocessor directive execution is fast.

8. What is the use of stringizing operator?

Ans: The stringizing operator converts macros arguments into strings. The stringizing operator # carries the operation. It is placed before the argument.

For example,

```
#define say(m) printf(#m)
void main()
{
clrscr();
say(Hello);
getche();
}

OUTPUT:
Hello
```

Explanation: In the above program, after conversion, the statement **say(Hello)** is treated as **printf("Hello")**. It is not essential to enclose the text with quotation marks in the stringizing operator. If # is removed from macro definition, the user has to enclose the text in double quotes.

9. Write a program to double and triple a given number using stringizing operator.

Ans:

```
#define DOUBLE(x) printf("Double of "#x" = %d\n",x*2)
#define TRIPLE(x) printf("Triple of "#x" = %d\n",x*3)
void main()
{
int m;
clrscr();
printf("Enter a number :");
scanf ("%d",&m);
DOUBLE(m);
TRIPLE(m);
getche();
}

OUTPUT:
Enter a number: 5
Double of m = 10
Triple of m = 15
```

Explanation: In the above program, the value of *m* is passed to **DOUBLE()** and **TRIPLE()** macros that is assigned to **x. #x** prints the name of the variable passed through the macros.

10. List predefined macros according to ANSI standard together with their uses.

Ans: Every predefined macro name is defined with two underscores as prefix and suffix. These macros are useful for finding system information such as date, time, file name and line number. Predefined macro functions together with their meaning are as follows:

_ _DATE_ _	Displays system date in string format
_ _TIME_ _	Displays system time in string format
_ _LINE	Displays line number as an integer
_ _FILE_ _	Displays current file name in string format
_ _STDC_ _	In ANSI 'C', the value returned will be non-zero.

11. Write a program on predefined macros.

Ans:

```
#include <stddef.h>
void main()
{
clrscr();
printf("\nDATE : %s",__DATE__);
printf("\nTIME : %s",__TIME__);
printf("\nFILE NAME : %s",__FILE__);
printf("\nLINE NO. : %d",__LINE__);
}

OUTPUT:
DATE : Jul 04 2011
TIME : 20:08:12
FILE NAME : POINTERE.C
LINE NO. : 9
```

Explanation: In the above program, five macros are used in the **`printf()`** statements. On its execution, the output of the program is displayed as shown above. The program displays **system date, time, program file name and total lines** in the program. The **STDC** indicates whether or not the **version of C compiler follows ANSI 'C' standard**. Here, the result is one. Hence, the compiler follows ANSI C standards. The programmer should set ANSI keyword on option by selecting option menu of the editor – **compiler-source – ANSI keywords only on.**

12. Elaborate on conditional compilation.

Ans: Quite often, one can use conditional compilation directives in the programs. The most frequently used conditional compilation directives are **#ifdef, #else, #endif** etc. These directives allow the programmer to include the portions of the codes based on the conditions. The compiler compiles selected portion of the source codes based on the conditions. The syntax of the **#ifdef** directive is as follows:

Syntax:

```
#ifdef identifier
{
statement1;
statement2;
}
#else
{
statement3;
statement4;
}
#endif
```

The **#ifdef** preprocessor tests whether the identifier has defined substitute text or not. If the identifier is defined, then **#if** block is compiled and executed. The compiler ignores **#else** block even if errors are intentionally made. Error messages will not be displayed. If identifier is not defined, then **#else** block is compiled and executed.

13. Write a program with conditional compilation statement.

Ans:

```
#define LINE 1
void main()
{
clrscr();
#ifdef LINE
printf("This is line number one.");
#else
printf("This is line number two.");
#endif
getche();
}

OUTPUT:
This is line number one.
```

Explanation: In the above program, **#ifdef** checks whether the **LINE** identifier is defined or not. If defined, the **#if** block is executed. On execution, the output of the program is **"This is line number one"**. In case the identifier is undefined, the **#else** block is executed and output is **"This is line number two"**.

14. What are # pragma DIRECTIVE?

Ans: These **#pragma** directives are defined with **#(hash)** and these are the preprocessor directives. These directives deal with formatting source listing and placing components in the object file generated by the compiler.

The **#pragma** directive sets/resets certain warning and errors during compilation of C program. When a program is compiled, the compiler throws errors and warnings. The programmer should see the errors rather than the warnings. After the removal of errors, the programmer can turn attention on warnings and take further steps for sorting warnings.

15. How you set different warnings on and off?

Ans: The syntax for warning on and off is as follows:

1. #pragma warn +xxx
2. #pragma warn –xxx

The first statement turns on the warning message. The second statement sets off the warning message.

16. Write a program to set off certain errors using #pragma directives.

Ans:

```
#pragma warn -aus
#pragma warn -def
#pragma warn -rvl
#pragma warn -use
int main()
{
int x=2,y,z;
printf("\n y= %d",y);
}
```

Explanation: The above program contains the following warnings:

1. Possible use of *y* before definition in function.
2. *z* declared but never used in function main.
3. *x* is assigned a value, which is never used in function.
4. Function should return a value in function main.

The display of these warning messages can be made on or off by setting the pragma options. In the above program, the four pragma options are set to off. Hence, after compilation, the above-listed lines will not be displayed. If the four pragma options are set to on, the compiler will display these warning messages.

17. Can we undefine a predefined macro?

Ans: Yes, we can undefine a predefined macro. A macro defined with `#define` directives can be undefined with **`#undef`** **directive.**

Syntax:

`#undef identifier_macro_template substitute`

It is useful when we do not want to allow the use of macros in any portion of the program.

18. Write a program to undefine a macro.

Ans:

```
#define wait getche()
void main()
{
int k;
#undef wait getche()
clrscr();
for(k=1;k<=5;k++)
printf("%d\t",k);
wait;
}
```

Explanation: In the above program, **wait** is defined in place of **`getche()`**. In the program, **`#undef`** **directive** undefines the same macro. Hence, the compiler flags an error message "**undefined symbol 'wait' in function main.**" In case one more statement "`#define` wait `getche()`" is written after

"# undef wait getche()", then the compiler does not show any error and the output displayed on the screen would be "1 2 3 4 5".

19. What is an assert() macro?

Ans: An assert macro is defined **assert.h** header file. This macro tests the value of an expression. If the expression contains false value, assert displays error message and executes the function abort() to abort the program execution.

20. Write a program on an assert() macro.

Ans:

```
#include <assert.h>
void main()
{
int x=4;
clrscr();
assert(x!=4);
printf("%d",x);
}

OUTPUT:
Assertion failed: x!=4, file AMIT\POINTERE.C, line 7
Abnormal program termination
```

Explanation: In this program, the value of *x* is 4. The assert() macro checks the value of *x*. If the condition is false, the macro executes abort() and the program is terminated.

Multiple-choice Questions

1. Consider the statement #define PI 3.14, it means _________
   (a) Every occurrence of PI (identifier) is replaced with 3.14 (substitute value)
   (b) Occurrence of PI only in expressions is replaced with 3.14
   (c) None of the above
2. A macro defined with # define directives can be undefined with _________.
   (a) #undef directive (b) #ifndef (c) #!def
3. The file name is included in the double quotations marks indicates that _________.
   (a) The search for the file is to be made in the current directory and in the standard directories
   (b) The search for the file is to be made in the current directory
   (c) The search for the file is to be made in the entire system
4. When the file name is included without double quotation marks and when program is executed, the message appears on the screen will be _________.
   (a) The search for file is made only in the standard directories
   (b) The search for file is made only in the current directory
   (c) The search for the file is to be made in the entire system
   (d) Bad file name format in include directory

5. Generally, the standard directories for header file and library files are ________.
   (a) include and lib (b) turboc2 and include (c) tc2 and lib
6. The standard directory called 'include' contains ________.
   (a) Header files (b) Library file (c) Program file
7. The standard directory called 'lib' contains ________.
   (a) Header files (b) Library file (c) Program file
8. The conditional compilation directives allow the programmer to ________.
   (a) Compile a part of program (b) Compile entire program
   (c) Compile program excluding header files
9. In the statement `#ifdef`, `#else`, `#endif`, the compiler ignores `#else` block ________.
   (a) When macro is not defined
   (b) When macro is defined
   (c) None of the above
10. Which of the following is not a preprocessor directive?
   (a) `#undef` (b) `#define` (c) `#2def`
11. Which of the following preprocessor directive works exactly opposite to #ifdef?
   (a) `#undef` (b) `#ifndef` (c) `#nodef`
12. Which of the following preprocessor directive displays user-defined error message?
   (a) `#undef` (b) `#error` (c) `#errordef`
13. What is the output of the following program?

```
#define SQUARE    X*X*X
void main()
{
int X=10;
printf("%d",SQUARE);
getche();
}
```

   (a) 100 (b) 1000 (c) 10

14. What is the output of the following program?

```
#define PI 3.14
void main()
{
float x;
clrscr();
for(x=PI*2;x<=7.28;x++)
printf("%g",x);
getche();
}
```

(a) 7.28 (b) 6.28
(c) 6.28 (d) 7.28

15. The program typed in the editor is the _________ to the preprocessor.
    (a) Source code (b) Object code (c) ASCII code
16. The preprocessor passes the source code to the C _________.
    (a) Compiler (b) Assembler (c) Interpreter
17. The preprocessor directives are always included at the _________.
    (a) Beginning of the program (b) Run time (c) Compile time
18. The preprocessor begins with the symbol _________.
    (a) // (b) # (c) $
19. A macro defined with _________ directives can be undefined with `#undef` directive.
    (a) `#define` (b) `#include` (c) `#ifdef`
20. In _________ operation, the macro argument is converted to string.
    (a) String concatenation (b) Stringizing operation (c) String coping
21. The _________ loads specified file in the current program.
    (a) `#include` (b) `#define` (c) `#ifndef`
22. The _________ is used to display user-defined message during compilation of the program.
    (a) `#error` (b) `#pragma` (c) `#stderr`
23. Inline directive reports the compiler that the source code has in line _________ statements.
    (a) bsm code (b) asm code (c) C++ code
24. What will be the value of *y* after the execution of the following program?

```
#include <stdio.h>
#include <conio.h>
#define plus(x)   x;
#define minus(x)  --x+ plus(x);
void main()
{
 int x=8,y;
 clrscr();
 y=minus(x)
 printf("\n y = %d",y);
}
```

(a) $y = 14$ (b) $y = 15$
(c) $y = 13$ (d) None of the above

25. What will be the values of variables *x* and *y* after execution of the following program?

```
#include <stdio.h>
#include <conio.h>
#define P   x++;
```

```
#define plus(x)   P
void main()
{
   int x=2,y;
   clrscr();
   y=plus(x)
   printf("\nx = %d y = %d",x,y);
}
```

(a) $x=3$ $y=2$
(b) $x=3$ $y=3$
(c) $x=2$ $y=2$
(d) None of the above

26. In the following example, whether macro is treated as ________.

```
#include <stdio.h>
#include <conio.h>
#define S "This Book Teaches C"
void main()
{
   printf("\n %s",S);
}
```

(a) Macro as well as array
(b) Only macro
(c) Only array
(d) None of the above

27. What will be the output after execution of the following program?

```
#include <stdio.h>
#include <conio.h>
#define S  "This Book Teaches C"
void main()
{
  clrscr();
  printf("\n %c",*(S+3));
}
```

(a) s
(b) h
(c) i
(d) T

28. What will be the value of variable *z* after the execution of the following program?

```
#include <stdio.h>
#include <conio.h>
#define ROW 2
#define COL 3
```

```
int a[ROW][COL]={8,6,4,2,0,-2};
void main()
{
  int x,y,z=0;
  clrscr();
  for(x=0;x<ROW;x++)
  for(y=0;y<COL;y++)
  if(a[x][y]>z)
  z=a[x][y];
  printf("\nz = %d",z);
}
```

(a) $z = 8$ (b) $z = -2$
(c) $z = 0$ (d) $z = 2$

29. What will be the value of variables ***k*** and ***m*** after the execution of the following program?

```
#include <stdio.h>
#include <conio.h>
#define product(k) k*k
void main()
{
int k=3,m;
m=product(k++);
clrscr();
printf("\t k=%d m=%d",k,m);
}
```

(a) $k = 5$ $m = 9$
(b) $k = 4$ $m = 16$
(c) $k = 5$ $m = 25$
(d) $k = 4$ $m = 9$

30. What will following program the display?

```
#include <stdio.h>
#include <conio.h>
#define P &x
void main()
{
int x=2;
clrscr();
printf("\t %u",P);
}
```

(a) Address (b) Value
(c) Error message (d) None of the above

31. What is the output of the following program?

```
#include <stdio.h>
#include <conio.h>
void main()
{
int x=2,*p=5;
p=&x;
#define P &p
clrscr();
printf("\t %d",**P);
}
```

(a) 2 (b) 5
(c) 65500 (d) None of the above

Answers

1. (a) 2. (a) 3. (a) 4. (d) 5. (a) 6. (a) 7. (b) 8. (a) 9. (b) 10. (c)
11. (b) 12. (b) 13. (b) 14. (b) 15. (a) 16. (a) 17. (a) 18. (b) 19. (a) 20. (b)
21. (a) 22. (a) 23. (b) 24. (d) 25. (a) 26 (a) 27. (a) 28. (a) 29. (a) 30. (a)
31. (a)

True or False

1. The pre-processor is executed before the actual compilation of program code begins.
2. The program typed in the editor is source code for the pre-processor.
3. The `#define` defines the macro templates.
4. The macro definition must be terminated by semi-colon.
5. The `define` is a keyword.
6. The `#undef` undefines the macro.
7. The `#include` loads the specified file.
8. `#include "stdio.h"` the compiler searches the file in entire system.
9. `#include <stdio.h>` the compiler searches the file in standard directory.
10. Conditional compilation means few statements can be skipped from compiler.
11. The `#ifdef` and `#ifndef` work exactly the same way.
12. The `#error` flags are user-defined messages.

13. The `#pragma` sets off/on warning and error messages.
14. The `#ninclude` closes the file loaded by `#include`.

Answers

1. True 2. True 3. True 4. False 5. False 6. True 7. True 8. False 9. True 10. True
11. False 12. True 13. True 14. False

Additional Questions

What is/are the output/s of the following programs?

1.

```
#include <stdio.h>
#include <conio.h>
#define PI 3.14
void main()
{
 float r=2.2,area;
 area=PI*r*r;
 clrscr();
 printf("Area of a Circle = %.2f  cm2",area);
}

OUTPUT:
Area of Circle =15.20 cm2
```

2.

```
#include <stdio.h>
#include <conio.h>
#include <stdio.h>
#include <conio.h>
#define N 5
#define say printf
void main()
{
int k;
clrscr();
for(k=1;k<=N;k++)
say (" %d ",k);
}

OUTPUT:
1 2 3 4 5
```

3.

```
#include <stdio.h>
#include <conio.h>
#define DOUBLE(a) a*2
void main()
{
int a=1;
clrscr();
for(;a<=5;a++)
printf(" %d",DOUBLE(a));
}

OUTPUT:
2 4 6 8 10
```

4.

```
#include <stdio.h>
#include <conio.h>
#define say(m) printf(#m)
void main()
{
  clrscr();
  say(C is portable );
}

OUTPUT:
C is portable
```

5.

```
#include <stdio.h>
#include <conio.h>
#define MAX(x,y) if(x>y) c=x; else c=y;
void main()
{
   int x=3,y=5,c;
   clrscr();
   MAX(x,y);
   printf("\n Largest of two numbers = %d",c);
}

OUTPUT:
Largest of two numbers = 5
```

Find the bug/s in the following programs.

1.

```
#include <stdio.h>
#define 3.14 PI
void main()
{
printf("%f",PI);
}
```

Bug : The statement defining macro should be # define PI 3.14

2.

```
#include <stdio.h>
#define DOUBLE(a)  a*2# define TRIPLE(a) a*3
void main()
{ int a=1;
clrscr();
  for(;a<=5;a++)
  printf("\n %d \t%d\t %d",a,double(a), TRIPLE(a));
}
```

Bug : The macro DOUBLE is typed as double

3.

```
#include <stdio.h>
#define wait getche()
void main()
{
int k;#undef wait()
getche();
clrscr();
for(k=1;k<5;k++)
printf(" %d ",k);wait;}
```

Bug : The macro wait is undefined

4.

```
#include <stdio.h>
#define say(m) printf(m)
#define show(m) printf(#m)
void main()
{
clrscr();
say(Hello);
show(Hello);
}
```

`Bug:` The text Hello should be enclosed in double quotes in say macro

5.

```
#include <stdio.h>
#define  T  8
void main()
{
clrscr();
#ifndef T
printf("\n Macro is not defined");
#else
printf("\n Macro is defined");
}
```

`Bug:` `#endif` is missing

13

Structure and Union

1. What is a structure in C?

Ans: A structure is a collection of same or different data types, grouped together under a single structure name. It is a derived data type arranged in a group of related data items of different data types.

2. How is a structure declared?

Ans: Structure is declared as follows:

```
struct struct_name
{
data type 1 variable1;
data type 2 variable2;
------------------
------------------
};
```

Explanation: Structure declaration always starts with `struct` keyword. Here, `struct_name` is known as **tag.** The `struct` declaration is enclosed with a pair of curly braces. Closing brace is terminated with a semicolon. After closing brace and before structure termination, we can provide object names as optional for accessing the structure elements. Using `struct` and `tag`, a user can declare structure elements such as `variable1` of `data type1, variable 2` of `data type 2,` etc. These are the structure members. They are declared in the structure within curly braces.

3. What is the use of the keyword `struct`?

Ans: The `struct` is a keyword in C. It is used to declare a structure of various data types/elements followed by a tag name of that structure.

4. How to declare structure variables?

Ans: The structure variables can be declared by including variable names between the closing brace and the terminating semicolon in the structure definition. This can be followed from the following example.

```
struct book
{
char titile[20];
int pages;
int cost;
}

bk1,bk2;
```

In the above example, the `bk1` and `bk2` are the variables of type `struct book.` Alternately, one can also declare the structure variables as per the following example.

```
struct book
{
char titile[20];
int pages;
int cost;
};
struct book bk1,bk2;
```

In the above example `bk1,bk2` are the structure variables of type `struct book`.

5. When is memory allocated to a structure members?

Ans: Memory is not allocated/reserved when the structure is defined. Structure definition describes the template. Memory is allocated only after declaration of variables of the corresponding type.

For example, in the following example, memory is not reserved when structure is declared.

```
struct book1
{
char book[30];
int pages ;
float price ;
};
```

After declaring, the variables of structure memory are allocated.

After writing the above code, one can write the following code:

```
struct book1 bk1;
```

The `bk1` is the variable and now memory is allocated to the members of structure `book1.`

6. Explain the use of the dot operator.

Ans: The dot (.) operator accesses the structure members.

For example, `structure_variable.member` or `bk1.book`

7. Write a program to access members of a structure using dot operator.

```
void main()
{
struct book1
{
char book[30];
int pages;
float price;
};
struct book1 bk1={"Programming in C",600,185};
clrscr();
printf("\n Book Name : %s",bk1.book);
printf("\n No. of Pages : %d",bk1.pages);
printf("\n Book Price : %.2f",bk1.price);
getche();
}

OUTPUT:
Book Name : Programming in C
No. of Pages : 600
Book Price : 185.00
```

Explanation: In the above program, the `struct book1` is defined with its member variables `char book [30]`, `int pages` and `float price`. The `bk1` is an object of the `struct book1`. The statement `struct book1 bk1={"Programming in C" 300,285};` defines object `bk1` and initializes the variables with the values enclosed in the curly braces, respectively. Using `printf()` statement and dot operators, members are accessed and they are displayed.

8. How are structure elements stored in memory? Give a programming example.

Ans: The structure elements are stored in contiguous memory locations.

```
void main()
{
struct student
{
int age;
float weight;
};
```

```
struct student amit={21,45.5};
clrscr();
printf("\n Age in years : %d",amit.age);
printf("\n Weight in kg : %f",amit.weight);
   printf("\n Memory location for weight (float) : %u",&(amit.
weight));
   printf("\n Memory location for Age(integer) : %u",&(amit.
age));
   getche();
}

OUTPUT:
Age in years : 21
Weight in kg : 45.500000
Memory location for weight (float): 65490
Memory location for Age(integer) : 65488
```

Explanation: Memory for `float` and `int` require 4 and 2 bytes, respectively. Program's output together with memory locations for storing elements is indicated at the output.

9. Explain nested structure. Draw a diagram to explain a nested structure.

Ans: We can also take objects of one structure as a member in another structure, to create complex data applications. The syntax of the nested structure is as follows:

```
struct time
{
int second;
int minute;
int hour;
};
struct t
{
int carno;
struct time st;
struct time et;
};
struct t player;
```

Following diagram depicts the view of nested structure.

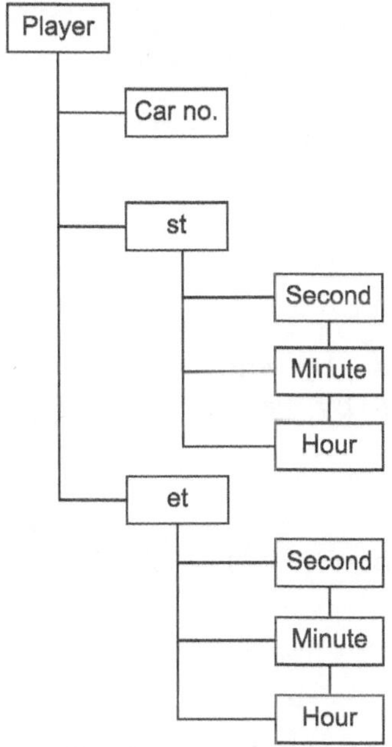

10. How are arrays of structure variables defined? How are they beneficial to the programmers?

Ans: As we know, an array is a collection of similar data types. In the same way, in array of structures, every element is of structure type. Array of structure can be declared as follow:

```
struct time
{
int second;
int minute;
int hour;
} t[3];
```

In the above example, `t[3]` is an array of three elements containing three objects of time structure. They are more useful for database applications where a large data is to be stored.

11. How are structure elements accessed using pointer? Which operator is used?

Ans: To access the structure elements using pointer, an arrow operator → (– and > together) is used instead of dot (.) operator. The syntax for using pointer(ptr) with member(data_member) is as follows:

```
ptr->data_member.
```

12. Is it possible to a pass structure variable to function? Explain in detail the possible ways.

Ans: Yes, structure variables can be passed to the function by value or address. The syntax of the same is as under.

```
struct book
{
char name[35];
char author[35];
int pages;
} b1;
void main()
{
------------
------------
show(&b1);   /* Pass  by address */
print(b1);   /* Pass by value   */
-------------
-------------
}
void show (struct book *b2)    /* Pass  by address */
{
------------
------------
}
void print (struct book b2)    /* Pass by value    */
{
------------
------------
}

OUTPUT:
```

Similarly, individual structure members can be passed to a function.

13. How are user-defined data types defined?

Ans: The statement `typedef` is to be used while defining the new user-defined data type. The syntax is as follows:

```
typedef type dataname;
```

where type is the datatype and dataname is the user-defined name for that type.
For example, `typedef int hours;`
where hours is another name for int and now we can use hours instead of `int` in the program as follows:

```
hours hrs;
```

14. Explain the importance of bit fields. How do bit fields save memory space?

Ans: Bit field provides exact amount of bits required for storage of values. If a variable value is 1 or 0, we need a single bit to store it. In the same way, if the variable is expressed between 0 and 3, then the two bits are sufficient for storing these values and so on.

The number of bits required for a variable is specified by non-negative integer followed by a colon. To hold the information, we use the variables. The variables occupy minimum one byte for `char` and two bytes for `int`. Instead of using complete integer if bits are used, the space of memory can be saved.

For example,

```
struct vehicle
{
unsigned type:  3; /* Three bits */
unsigned fuel:  2; /* Two bits   */
unsigned model: 3; /* Three bits */
};
```

15. Explain the enumerated data type.

Ans: The `enum` is a keyword. It is used for declaring enumeration types. The programmer can create their own data type and define what values the variables of these data types can hold. This enumeration data type helps in reading the program.

Consider the example of 12 months of a year.

```
enum month{Jan, Feb, Mar, Apr, May, Jun, Jul, Aug, Sep, Oct, Nov, Dec};
```

This statement creates a user-defined data type. The keyword `enum` is followed by the tag name month. The enumerators are the identifiers `Jan, Feb, Mar, Apr, May` and so on. Their values are constant unsigned integers and starts from 0. The identifier `Jan` refers to 0, `Feb` to 1 and so on.

16. What is a union in C? How is data stored using union?

Ans: Union is a variable, which is similar to the structure. Union contains a number of members, but it holds only one object at a time with a common memory location for all objects.

It allocates fixed specific bytes of memory for the access of data types irrespective of any data type. The union requires bytes that are equal to the number of bytes required for the largest members.

For example, if the union contains `char`, `integer` and `long integer`, then the number of bytes reserved in the memory for the union is 4 bytes.

17. What are the differences between union and structure?

Union	Structure
Holds one object at a time.	Holds many objects at a time.
Members have a common shared memory space.	Each member has its own memory location.
Size of union is equal to the maximum memory required by a member of a union.	Size of structure is equal to the total memory required for all its members.

18. Explain REGS and SREGS unions. List any five CPU registers of each union type.

Ans: The C language defines a union type called 'REGS' and structure type called 'SREGS' in the file 'DOS.H', which escort the C compiler. These data types are used to pass parameters to the CPU registers.

The union type 'REGS' defines AX, BX, CX, DX and SI registers. These registers are used for holding the data temporarily. The structure type 'REGS' defines AX, BX, CX, DX and SI registers. The structure type 'SREGS' defines the segment registers DS, ES, CS and SS. REGS and SREGS are used to invoke the DOS functions.

19. Explain `int86()` and `intdos()` functions. How they used to interact with hardware?

Ans: The `intdos()` is used for calling DOS interrupt. The `intdos()` invokes a DOS function by issuing software interrupt `INT 21H`.

The `int86()` stands for 8086 interrupt. The `int86()` functions invoke a BIOS functions by issuing a software interrupt. The `int86()` function can be invoked with the following three arguments.

Interrupt type number corresponding to ROM-BIOS service. Two arguments of UNION type REGS. They are 'x' and 'h'. The `int86()` function takes the values of input registers from one 'REGS' union and returns the output registers in another.

Multiple-choice Questions

1. Which of the following keywords C supports for storing variables of different data types under one name?
   (a) class
   (b) struct
   (c) enum
   (d) All of these
2. Structure is a _________.
   (a) Collection of different data types only
   (b) Collection of same data types only
   (c) Collection of similar as well as different data types
   (d) None of these
3. When we declare a structure, _________.
   (a) It defines form of structure only
   (b) It reserves space in memory only
   (c) It defines form of structure as well as reserves space in memory
   (d) None of these
4. The elements of structure _________.
   (a) Are stored in contiguous memory locations
   (b) Share some part of memory location
   (c) Have the same location as that of the largest data type
   (d) Are scattered in memory, but linked together
5. The valid syntax for structure is _________.
   (a)
   ```
   struct abc{
   ----
   ----
   };
   ```
   (b)
   ```
   struct abc{
   ----
   ----
   }a,b,c;
   ```
   (c)
   ```
   struct{
   ----
   ----
   }a,b,c;
   ```
   (d) All of these are valid
6. The structure elements are accessed using _________.
   (a) . (dot operator)
   (b) ->(arrow operator)
   (c) Both of the above
   (d) None of the above

7. What is the output of the following program?

```
void main()
{
struct abc
{
int x;
char y;
};
struct abc a1,a2;
clrscr();
a1.x = 65;
a2.y = 'B';
a1.y = a2.y;
a2.x = a1.x;
printf("%d %d %d %d",a1.x,a2.x,a1.y,a2.y);
getch();
}
```

(a) 65 65 66 66
(b) A A B B
(c) Compile error
(d) Runtime error

8. Which of the following are correct?
   (a) We can create array of structure variable.
   (b) We can make one structure variable an element of other structure.
   (c) We can declare pointer variable inside structure.
   (d) All of the above.

9. Union is the same as that of structure, because _________.
   (a) Both of them are used to collect same or different data types
   (b) In both cases, the elements are stored in contiguous memory locations but do not share memory
   (c) In both cases, the elements share memory
   (d) Both a and b
   (e) None of the above

10. The size of union is the size of _________.
   (a) The sum of sizes of total variables
   (b) The mean of largest variable and smallest variable
   (c) The largest variable
   (d) The difference of largest variable and smallest variable

11. What is the output of the following program?

```
void main(){
    union abc{
    int i;
    char c;
    };
    union abc a;
    clrscr();
    a.i = 256+48;
    printf("%d %c",a.i,a.c);
    getch();
}
```

(a) 256 48
(b) 256 0
(c) 304 48
(d) 304 0

12. The enum elements ________.

(a) Are constants
(b) Are variables
(c) Are always start with 1
(d) Cannot be changed inside enum

13. Convenience and readability of "enum" can also be achieved by using ________.

(a) Structure
(b) Union
(c) Macro
(d) None of the above

14. Various members of the structure are specified ________.

(a) Within the couple of curly braces separated by semicolons
(b) Unions that are like structures
(c) Unions that are less frequently used in the program
(d) Unions that are used for set operations

15. Memory is reserved when ________.

(a) Structure is defined
(b) Structure variables are declared
(c) Ampersand (&) operator is used

16. The members of structure are ________.

(a) Similar or dissimilar data types
(b) Signed data types
(c) Unsigned data types

17. The structure is a ________.

(a) User-defined data type
(b) System-defined variable
(c) Keyword

18. The typedef is a ________.

(a) Variable
(b) System-defined file
(c) Keyword

19. The size of structure is decided by ________.

(a) Its members
(b) One of its members
(c) None of the above

20. Number of bytes required for enumerated data type in memory is _________.
    (a) 2 bytes (b) 1 bytes (c) 3 byte
21. The int86( ) function invokes _________.
    (a) DOS function (b) BIOS function (c) User-defined function
22. The intdos() function invokes _________.
    (a) User-defined function (b) DOS function (c) Both (a) and (b)
23. Int 33 is a _________.
    (a) Software interrupt (b) Hardware interrupt
    (c) Both (a) and (b) (d) None of the above
24. The structure holds memory of _________.
    (a) One element at a time (b) Elements defined in structure
    (c) Both (a) and (b) (d) None of the above
25. Bit fields are used only with _________.
    (a) Unsigned int data type (b) float data type
    (c) char data type (d) int data type
26. Observe the following program neatly and choose the appropriate `printf()` statement from the options.

```
 struct company
 {
char *company ;
 };
void main()
{
struct company m={"Dorling"};
----
}
```

    (a) `printf("\n company : %s",m.company);`
    (b) `printf("\n company : %s",m->company);`
    (c) `printf("\n company : %s",m.*company);`
    (d) `printf("\n company : %s",*m.company);`
27. The union contains char, integer and double, then the number of bytes reserved in the memory for the union is _________ bytes.
    (a) 8 (b) 1 (c) 2
28. By using structures, we can make a group of variables, _________, pointers c.
    (a) Arrays (b) Classes (c) Functions
29. If objects b and c are structure data type, then the contents of b can be copied to c using _________.
    (a) = (b) == (c) Copying

30. The typedef _________.

    (a) Gives new name to existing new data type
    (b) Gives new definition to existing new data type
    (c) None of the above

31. Bit field provides exact amount of _________ required for storage of values.

    (a) Bits (b) Bytes (c) Words

32. The values of enumerated data types are _________.

    (a) Constant unsigned integers (b) Constant signed integers (c) Unsigned integers

33. We can access _________ and _________ services through C language.

    (a) BIOS & DOS (b) DOS and Windows (c) BIOS

34. The 8086 CPU registers are _________ bits in size.

    (a) 16 bits (b) 8 bits (c) 4 bits

35. We can also invoke BIOS services by using C functions such as _________.

    (a) int86() (b) intx() (c) intdos()

36. Union is a variable, which is similar to the structure. It contains a number of members such as structure, but _________.

    (a) It holds only one object at a time
    (b) It holds two objects at a time
    (c) It holds values exactly like structure

37. Union members _________.

    (a) Share the same memory locations
    (b) have different memory locations
    (c) None of the above

38. The union requires bytes that are equal to the number of bytes required for _________.

    (a) The largest data member (b) The smallest members (c) Size of object

39. Identify the most appropriate sentence to describe `union`.

    (a) **union** contains members of different data types that share the same storage area in memory
    (b) **union** is exactly same as structure
    (c) **union** is occasionally used in the program
    (d) **union** is used for set operations

40. The typedef statement is used for _________.

    (a) Declaring user-defined data types (b) Declaring variant variables
    (c) Typecasting of variables (d) None of the above

41. The service number is always initialized in the register

    (a) AH (b) AL
    (c) BH (d) AX

42. The intdos() function invokes interrupt number ________.
    (a) 0x21
    (b) 0x17
    (c) 0x18
    (d) No
43. When memory is allocated to union in C?
    (a) When union structure is declared.
    (b) When union structure and variables are declared.
    (c) None of the above.
44. Is it possible to nest union with structure?
    (a) No
    (b) Yes
45. For storing the data with more than one data types, C provides ________.
    (a) Class
    (b) Structure
    (c) Enum
    (d) All of these
46. When we declare structure, ________.
    (a) It defines form of structure only
    (b) It reserves space in memory only
    (c) It defines form of structure as well as reserves space in memory
    (d) None of the above
47. The elements of structure ________.
    (a) Are stored in contiguous memory locations
    (b) Share some part of memory location
    (c) Have the same location as that of the largest data type
    (d) Are scattered in memory but linked together
48. Which of the following is the valid syntax for structure?
    (a)
    ```
    struct abc{
     ----
     ----
     };
    ```
    (b)
    ```
    struct abc{
     ----
     ----
     }a,b,c;
    ```
    (c)
    ```
    struct{
     ----
     ----
     }a,b,c;
    ```
    (d) All of these are valid
49. The structure elements can be accessed using ________.
    (a) . (dot operator)
    (b) ◊ (arrow operator)
    (c) Both of the above
    (d) None of the above
50. What is the O/P of the following program?

```
void main()
{
   struct abc{
        int x;
        char y;
}
struct abc a1,a2;
clrscr();

a1.x = 65;
a2.y = 'B';
a1.y = a2.y;
a2.x = a1.x;
printf("%d %d %d %d",a1.x,a2.x,a1.y,a2.y);
getch();
}
```

The output is

(a) 65 65 66 66
(b) A A B B
(c) Compile error
(d) Runtime error

51. What is the O/P of the following program?

```
void main()
{
   struct abc{
        int x;
        char y;
};
 struct abc a1,a2;

clrscr();
a1.x = 65;
a1.y = 'B';
 a2 = a1;
printf("%c %c %c %c",a1.x,a2.x,a1.y,a2.y);
getch();
}
```

(a) 65 65 66 66
(b) A A B B
(c) 65 A 66 B
(d) Compile error

52. The data stored on the disk is in _________.

(a) Text format
(b) Binary format
(c) Encrypted format
(d) None of the above

Answers

1. (b)	2. (c)	3. (a)	4. (a)	5. (d)	6. (c)	7. (a)	8. (d)	9. (a)	10. (c)
11. (d)	12. (a)	13. (c)	14. (a)	15. (b)	16. (a)	17. (a)	18. (c)	19. (a)	20. (a)
21. (b)	22. (b)	23. (a)	24. (b)	25. (a)	26. (a)	27. (a)	28. (a)	29. (a)	30. (a)
31. (a)	32. (a)	33. (a)	34. (a)	35. (a)	36. (a)	37. (a)	38. (a)	39. (a)	40. (a)
41. (a)	42. (a)	43. (b)	44. (b)	45. (b)	46. (a)	47. (a)	48. (d)	49. (c)	50. (c)
51. (b)	52. (b)								

True or False

1. A structure is a set of different data type.
2. A **`struct`** is a keyword.
3. Structure elements can be accessed directly.
4. The dot operator can be used to access the **`struct`** variable.
5. The structure definition must be terminated by semi-colon.
6. The declaration and initialization of structure variable can be done at once.
7. Structure can be defined inside another structure(nested).
8. It is possible to pass structure elements to function.
9. The array structure elements cannot be declared.
10. The ptr is pointer to structure and it can access elements using -> operator.
11. Bit fields provide exact amount of bits required for storage.
12. Bit fields are always defined of **`signed`** type.
13. The **`enum`** keyword is used to define enumerated data type.
14. The value of enumerated data type starts from 1.
15. Structure elements are stored in the separate memory locations.
16. **`union`** elements are stored at random memory locations.
17. **`Union`** have common storage space for all its variable.
18. **`Union`** requires more space as compared to structure.

Answers

1.True	2. True	3. False	4. True	5. True	6. False	7. True	8. True
9. False	10. True	11. True	12. False	13. True	14. False	15. True	16. False
17. True	18. False						

Additional Questions

What are the outputs of the following programs?

Programs on declaration and initialization of structures

1. Program to display information of a student

```
#include <stdio.h>
#include<conio.h>

void main()
{
struct emp
{
char name[30];
int  age;
int sal ;
};
struct emp e={"Satish",28,20000};
clrscr();
printf("\n Name  : %s",e.name);
printf("\n Age : %d",e.age);
printf("\n Salary : %d",e.sal);
getche();
}

OUTPUT:
Name  : Satish
Age : 28
Salary : 20000
```

2. Program to display time

```
#include <stdio.h>
#include <conio.h>
void main()
{  struct time
   {
    int second;
    int minute;
    int hour;
   } t;
```

```
 t.second=45;
 t.minute=15;
 t.hour=11;
 clrscr();
 printf("%d:%d:%d",t.hour,t.minute,t.second);
}

OUTPUT:
11 : 15 : 45
```

3. Program to display information of a book

```
#include <stdio.h>
#include <conio.h>
 void main()
{
  struct book
  {
    char *book;
    int pages;
    float price;
  };
   struct book bk;
   bk.book="Programming in C";
   bk.pages=300;
   bk.price=250.00;
   clrscr();
   printf("\n Book : %s",bk.book);
   printf("\n Pages : %d",bk.pages);
   printf("\n Price : %g",bk.price);
}

OUTPUT:
Book : Programming in C
Pages : 300
Price : 250
```

4. Program to display total size of variables

```
#include <stdio.h>
#include<conio.h>
 void main()
 {
struct emp
{
char name[30];
int  age;
int sal ;
};
struct emp e={"Santosh",28,7000};
clrscr();
printf("\n SIZE OF e : %d",sizeof(e));
}

OUTPUT:
SIZE OF e : 34
```

5. Program to display numbers

```
#include <stdio.h>
#include<conio.h>
 void main()
 {
struct emp
{
int k;
int a;
int s;
};
struct emp e={1,2,4};
e.k++;
clrscr();
printf("%d  %d  %d",e.k,e.a,e.s);
}

OUTPUT:
2  2  4
```

6. Program to display author's information

```
#include <stdio.h>
#include<conio.h>

 void main()
 {
struct emp
{
char book_name[40];
char author[20];
int pages;
int cost;

};
struct emp e={"Programming with ANSI and Turbo
C","Ashok",594,195};
clrscr();
printf("\n Book Name : %s",e.book_name);
printf("\n Author's Name  : %s",e.author);
printf("\n Pages  : %d",e.pages);
printf("\n Cost   : %d",e.cost );

getche();
}
OUTPUT:

Book Name : Programming with ANSI and Turbo C
Author's Name  : Ashok
Pages  : 594
Cost   : 195
```

7. Some tricky problems.

```
#include <stdio.h>
#include<conio.h>
void main()
{
struct emp
{
int a;
int b;
int c;
};
```

```
struct emp e={10,20,40};
e.a++;
e.b++;
e.c=e.a+e.b;
clrscr();
printf("%d  %d  %d",e.a,e.b,e.c);
getche();
}

OUTPUT:
11  21  32
```

8. Program to display book information

```
#include <stdio.h>
#include <conio.h>
 void main()
{
  struct book
  {
    char *book;
    int pages;
    float price;
  };
   struct book bk,ck;
   bk.book="Data Structure through C";
   bk.pages=400;
   bk.price=215.00;
   ck=bk;
   clrscr();
   printf("\n Book : %s",ck.book);
   printf("\n Pages : %d",ck.pages);
   printf("\n Price : %g",ck.price);
}

OUTPUT:
Book : Data Structure through C
Pages : 400
Price : 215
```

Program on Structure within Structure

9. Program to display information of an officer and his date of joining

```
#include <stdio.h>
#include <conio.h>
void main()
{
struct name
{
char first[7];
char second[7];
};

struct j_date
{
int day;
int month;
int year;
};

struct data
{
struct name   nm;
struct j_date bt;
};
struct data r1={"Thomas","Rajesh",10,01,2005};

clrscr();

printf("Name        : %s %s \n",r1.nm.first,r1.nm.second);
printf("Joining Date : %d.%d.%d",r1.bt.day,r1.bt.month,r1.
bt.year);
getche();
}

OUTPUT:
Name           : Thomas Rajesh
Joining Date   : 10.1.2005
```

Programs on Pointer to Structure

10. Program to display numbers with pointers

```
#include <stdio.h>
#include <conio.h>

void main()
{
int *p;

    struct num
    {
    int a;
    int b;
    int c;
    };
struct num d;
d.a=2;
d.b=3;
d.c=4;

p=&d.a;

clrscr();

    printf("\n a=%d",*p);
    printf("\n b=%d",*(++p));
    printf("\n c=%d",*(++p));
}

OUTPUT:
a=2
b=3
c=4
```

11. Program to display time

```
#include <stdio.h>
#include <conio.h>
void main()
{
 struct time
```

```
  {
   int second;
   int minute;
   int hour;
  } ;
 struct time *t;
 t->second=50;
 t->minute=20;
 t->hour=12;
 clrscr();
 printf("%d:%d:%d",t->hour,t->minute,t->second);
}

OUTPUT:
12 : 20 : 50
```

Program on Union and Structure

12. Program to display numbers with structure and union

```
#include <stdio.h>
#include <conio.h>

void main()
{
struct x
{
float f;
char p[2];
};
union z
{
struct x set;
};
union z st;
st.set.f=5.9;
st.set.p[0]=67;
st.set.p[1]=69;
clrscr();
printf("\n %g",st.set.f);
printf("\n %c",st.set.p[0]);
```

```
printf("\n %c",st.set.p[1]);
}

OUTPUT:
5.9
C
E
```

Programs on Typedef

12.

```
#include <stdio.h>
#include <conio.h>
# define H 60
void main()
{
 typedef int hours;
 hours hrs=2;
 clrscr();
 printf("\n Minutes : %d",hrs*H);
 printf("\n Seconds : %d",hrs*H*H);
}

Minutes : 120
Seconds : 7200
```

13.

```
#include <stdio.h>
#include <conio.h>
void main()
{ typedef char string [20];
  string a="Hello";
  clrscr();
  printf("\n %s",a);}
}

OUTPUT:
Hello
```

14. Program to display information of an employee

```
#include <stdio.h>
#include <conio.h>

void main()
{
  typedef struct
  {
    char name[20];
    char sex[2];
    int acno;
  } info;
   info empo={"Sanjay","M",1452};
   clrscr();
 printf("\n %s  %s  %d", empo.name, empo.sex, empo.acno);
}

OUTPUT:
Sanjay  M  1452
```

Programs on Enumerated Data Type

15. Program to display the values of some months with enum data

```
#include <stdio.h>
#include <conio.h>
void main()
{
  enum  {Jan,Feb,March,Apr,May};
  clrscr();
 printf("Jan=%d",Jan);
 printf("\nFeb=%d",Feb);
}

OUTPUT:
Jan=0  Feb=1
```

Program on Union

16. Sizes of union and structure

```
void main()
{
union result
{
int  marks;
char grade;
};

struct res
{
char name[15];
int  age;
union result perf;
} data;
clrscr();
printf("Size of union : %d\n",sizeof(data.perf));
printf("Size of Structure : %d\n", sizeof(data));
}

OUTPUT:
Size of union :  2
Size of Structure : 19
```

Programs on Calling Bios and Dos Services

17. Use of REGS

```
#include <stdio.h>
#include <conio.h>
#include <dos.h>
void main()
{
 union REGS in,out;
 in.h.ah=02;
 in.h.dl=89;
 clrscr();
 intdos(&in,&out);
}

OUTPUT:
Y
```

Find the bug/s in the following programs.

1.

```
#include <stdio.h>
void main()
{
struct book
   {
    int pages;
    float price;
   } *b1;
  b1.pages=500;
  b1.price=255;
  clrscr();
  printf("\n Pages : %d",b1.pages);
  printf("\n Price : %g",b1.price);
}
```

Bug: `*b1` is a pointer and hence operator -> is to be used in place of `dot(.)`

2.

```
#include <stdio.h>
void main()
{
 struct book
 {
   int pages;
   float price;
 } b1
  b1.pages=450;
  b1.price=450.55;
  clrscr();
}
```

Bug: structure should be terminated by semi-colon

3.

```
#include <stdio.h>
void main()
{
 struct book
{   int pages;
 float price;
} b2,*b3;
```

```
b3=&b2;
b3->pages=400;
b2.price=700.00;
clrscr();
printf("\n Pages : %d", b2->pages);
printf("\n Price :%g", b3->price);
}
```

Bug: Variable b2 is not pointer and hence use of -> is invalid

4.

```
#include <stdio.h>
void main()
{
struct book
 {
   int pages;
   float price;
 } b2;
 b2.pages=400;
 b2.price=700.00;
 clrscr();
 show (b2);}
 show ( struct book b1)
{ printf("\n Pages : %d",b1.pages);
  printf("\n Price : %f",b1.price);
}
```

Bug: Structure should be defined outside all functions

5.

```
#include <stdio.h>
void main()
{
typedef hours int;
hours hrs;
hrs=120/60;
clrscr();
printf("\n 120 minutes=%d Hours",hrs);}
```

Bug: typede int hours

6.

```
#include <stdio.h>

void main()
{

struct vehicle
{
unsigned type : 3;
int  fuel :32;
}  ;

struct vehicle v;
  v.type=2;
  v.fuel=1;
  clrscr();

  printf("\n%d",v.type);
  printf("\n%d",v.fuel);
}
```

Bug: `int` type can hold 32 (4 bytes) data

14

Files

1. What is the difference between end of a file and end of a string?

Ans: The `feof()` function indicates the end of any file that may be binary or text file. It is used as indication to stop reading the characters from a character array and its ASCII value is 0. Whereas the end of a string is used to terminate the string and it is indicated by `NULL` character and can be written as `'\0'`. It is used as indication to stop reading the characters from file and its ASCII value is 0.

2. Distinguish between text mode and binary mode operations of a file.

Ans: Streams are categorized in to two types. They are text and binary.

Text file contains records or lines. Text or stream files compose characters. In text files, the end of file is detected with `feof()` function. A special character whose ASCII value is 26 is inserted after the last character of a file. As such a special character is absent in binary file.

Text files contain lines or records of text and each of its line has end of line marker at the end of line. Whereas binary files are not broken into lines or records. Hence, end of line marker is absent while writing in to binary files.

Binary files are a collection of bytes. Binary stream files would be used to read or write binary files such as reading graphics files.

In text mode of operation, every character is treated takes one byte memory space for storage, so when we want to store the numbers, e.g. 12345, it will take 5 bytes of memory.

To avoid this wastage of memory, binary files are used; in binary mode of operation, every value is stored in its binary form, so it will require only two bytes of storage to store a number.

3. What is the use of `fseek()`? Explain its syntax.

Ans: The `fseek()` function is used to set the position of read or write pointer to some particular byte location. The syntax of `fseek()` function is:

```
fseek(FILE *file_pointer, int offset, int position);
```

where offset indicates the number of bytes the pointer to be moved and position indicates the position from which the offset is to be counted; it can be current position, beginning of the file or the end of file.

The positions beginning, current and end are represented by the macros `SEEK_SET`, `SEEK _CUR`, `SEEK _END`, respectively.

4. Distinguish between the following functions.

(a) **`scanf()` and `fscanf()`**
(b) **`getc()` and `getchar()`**
(c) **`putc()` and `fputc()`**
(d) **`putw()` and `getw()`**
(e) **`ferror()` and `perror()`**
(f) **`feof()` and `eof()`**

(a) The function `scanf()` is formatted input function used to take input from user that is read the data from standard input, whereas the function `fscanf()` is the formatted input function used to read the data from file.
(b) The function `getc()` function takes the character as input from the file, whereas the function `getchar()` takes the character as input from the standard input that is from user.
(c) The function `putc()` writes the character to the file, whereas the function `putchar()` writes a character to the standard output.
(d) The function `getw()` takes an integer as input from the file, whereas the function `putw()` writes an integer to the file.
(e) The function `ferror()` reports the error occurred while read/write operations, whereas the function `perror()` prints compilers error messages along with user-defined messages.
(f) The function `eof()` checks for end of file and its syntax is `int eof(int handle);`, whereas the function `feof()` returns non-zero value if the end of file is reached at stream f and its syntax is int `feof(FILE *stream);`.

5. How does an append mode differ from a write mode?

Ans: In write mode, after opening the file, all the previous contents of the file are removed from the file and the write pointer is set to the beginning of the file, whereas in append mode, the contents of file are not erased on opening the file and the position of write pointer will be at the end of the file.

6. Why the header file stdio.h is frequently used in C language?

Ans: The header file `stdio.h` contains all the functions that are to be used for input and output operations from the input and output devices, respectively. The full form of the `stdio.h` is standard input output device, that is, this header file contains the functions for input from standard input device and it is used to display the output at standard output device.

7. Compare between `printf` and `fprintf` functions.

Ans: Both the functions `printf()` and `fprintf` are formatted output functions; out of which, the function `printf()` is used to produce the output at the standard output device; on the other hand, the function `fprintf()` is used to write the output to the file.

8. Distinguish between the following modes.

(a) **`w` and `w+`**
(b) **`r` and `r+`**
(c) **`rb` and `rb+`**
(d) **`a` and `a+`**

(a) The mode w truncates the contents of the file and the write pointer is set at the start of the file. If the file is not there, then a new file will be created. The w+ mode is also same as w, but it also allows user to read the contents.
(b) The `r` mode allows us to read the contents of the file; on the other hand, the `r+` mode allows both reading and writing to the file.
(c) The `rb` mode opens a binary file for reading only, whereas the `rb+` mode opens the binary file for both reading and writing.
(d) The a mode allows to only append the contents to the file; however, in a+ mode, we can append the content as well as we can update the contents of the file.

9. Explain low-level disk operations.

Ans: In the low-level disk I/O disk operation, data cannot be written as character-by-character or with sequence of characters, as it is carried in the high-level disk I/O functions. In the low-level disk I/O functions, buffers are used to carry the read and write operations. Buffer plays an important role in the low-level disk I/O program. The low-level disk I/O operations are more efficient and quick than the high-level disk I/O operations.

10. Explain command line arguments.

Ans: An executable program that performs a specific task for operating system is called a command. Some arguments are to be associated with the commands; hence, these arguments are called command line arguments. These associated arguments are passed to the program.

In C language, every program starts with a `main()` function and it marks the beginning of the program. The `main()` function can receive two arguments and they are: (1) `argc` and (2) `argv`. The information contained in the command line is passed on to the program through these arguments when the `main()` is called up by the system. The argument `argc` indicates the number of command line arguments and `argv`, which is an array of strings that receive the command line arguments in the form of strings.

11. Explain environment variables.

Ans: Environment variables provide different system settings/path related to operating system. These variables are available in both MS-DOS and UNIX operating systems. The output depends upon the operating system.

12. How is redirection of input and output done. Explain in brief.

Ans: Consider the DOS command `dir>abc;` execute it at the DOS prompt. Here, `dir` is the internal DOS command and `abc` is the name of the file. Here, the list of files and directories, instead of displaying on the screen, is redirected in a text file `abc`.
As the output of the command can be redirected to another file similarly using redirection, the output of the program instead of displaying on the screen can be stored on the disk in the form of a file.

By using this redirection concept, both read and write operations are possible. Following steps can be adopted to follow the concept of redirection:

1. Compile a program.
2. Get an executable file .exe.
3. Execute this .exe file on the DOS prompt with redirection.

For example, `read.exe>input.txt`

4. Input the data from keyboard.
5. See the typed data on DOS prompt by typing Type `input.txt`.

Multiple-choice Questions

1. Which one of the following file modes searches for file and if it is found, contents are destroyed?
   (a) w (b) w+ (c) r
2. What is the use of `putc()`?
   (a) Writes characters one by one to a file. (b) Reads characters one by one from a file.
   (c) Both (a) and (b) (d) None of the above
3. One of the jobs of `fopen()` is _________.
   (a) Opening the file (b) Closing the file (c) None of the above
4. A file opened in wb mode _________.
   (a) Opens a file in binary mode for writing
   (b) Opens a file in binary mode for reading
   (c) Opens a file in text mode for reading
5. Environment variables are available in _________.
   (a) C Editor (b) MS-DOS
   (c) Both (a) and (b) (d) None of the above
6. The current position of the file pointer can be checked with a function `fseek()` _________.
   (a) `unlink()` (b) `fseek()`
   (c) `remove()` (d) None of the above
7. Which of the following function is used to detect the end of file?
   (a) `feof()` (b) `ferror()`
   (c) `fputs()` (d) `fgetch()`
8. The EOF is equivalent to _________.
   (a) Non-zero (b) 0 (c) None of the above
9. The environment variables are used to display _________.
   (a) System setting (b) Compiler setting
   (c) Editor setting (d) None of the above
10. The argument `argc` _________.
    (a) Counts total number of arguments (b) Displays total arguments (c) None of the above
11. The argument `argv` is a pointer to an array of _________.
    (a) Character string (b) Integer array
    (c) Float array (d) None of the above
12. The size of the buffer can be set using the function _________.
    (a) `set( )` (b) `setbuf()` (c) `setsys()`

13. The file can be deleted from the disk using the function ________.
    (a) `remove()` (b) `delete()` (c) `erase()`
14. The file can be renamed by using the function ________.
    (a) `rename()` (b) `change()` (c) `alter()`
15. The file pointer can be set to the beginning of the file using ________.
    (a) `reverse()` (b) `rewind()` (c) `rev()`
16. The current position of the file pointer can be known by ________.
    (a) `ftell()` (b) `fprintf()` (c) `ftalf()`
17. The `fopen()` performs opens file with the help of ________.
    (a) file pointer (b) char pointer (c) None of the above
18. Which of the following type is associated with the file pointer?
    (a) FILE (b) file (c) POINTER
19. In sequential file, data is stored in ________.
    (a) Non-sequential (b) Sequential (c) Randomly
20. The file object contains ________.
    (a) Current pointer position (b) End of file
    (c) Pointer to any error (d) All of the above points
21. The `fscanf()` statements read data from the ________.
    (a) File (b) Keyboard
    (c) Both (a) and (b) (d) None of the above
22. When `fopen()` fails to open a file, it returns ________.
    (a) NULL (b) –1
    (c) 1 (d) None of the above
23. A file opened in w+ mode can be ________.
    (a) Read/ write (b) Only read
    (c) Only write (d) None of the above
24. Command line arguments are used to accept argument from ________.
    (a) Command prompt of operating system (b) Through `scanf()` statement
    (c) Both (a) and (b) (d) None of the above
25. The *redirection operator* '>' transfers any output to ________.
    (a) Text file (b) Console
    (c) Both (a) and (b) (d) None of the above
26. ________ function searches the disk for opening of the file.
    (a) `fopen()` (b) `fwind()` (c) `fread()`
27. Which of the following mode opens a new file on the disk for writing?
    (a) r (b) w (c) a

28. In low-level disk I/O operations, _________ is used to carry the read/write operations.
(a) Array (b) Buffer (c) Structure
29. In random access file, the data is read _________.
(a) Randomly (b) Sequentially (c) Circularly
30. In a+ mode, records are added _________.
(a) At the beginning of the file (b) At the end of the file (c) Nowhere
31. The `write()` function is used to write data into the file. This function is defined in the header file _________.
(a) `io.h` (b) `sys.h` (c) types
32. Whenever a file is opened, the pointer points to the _________.
(a) First character (b) Last character (c) Tenth character
33. The macro ______ is defined in the header file stdio.h.
(a) null (b) NULL (c) NUL
34. When the file opened by `fopen()` is huge, then file is loaded _________.
(a) At once (b) Part by part (c) Half
35. Using the file opening option 'r', the operation _________ can be performed.
(a) Write (b) Read/write (c) Deletion
36. In the _________ type of file, records can be read one after another.
(a) Random access file (b) Sequential file (c) Binary file
37. The file opening mode _________ can be used to perform read and write operations.
(a) r+ (b) r (c) w
38. The option wb opens a _________ file.
(a) Text (b) Binary (c) ASCII
39. All the files opened by `fopen()` can be closed by _________ at a time.
(a) `fclose()` (b) `fcloseall()` (c) `close()`
40. The `SEEK_SET` is equivalent to _________.
(a) 0 (b) 1 (c) 2
41. The `SEEK_CUR` is equivalent to _________.
(a) 0 (b) 1 (c) 2
42. The `SEEK_END` is equivalent to _________.
(a) 0 (b) 1 (c) 2
43. File is a _________.
(a) Set of records (b) Group of characters (c) Part of memory
44. Which of the following mode opens a pre-existing file for reading?
(a) w (b) r (c) a
45. Which of the following mode opens a pre-existing file for appending data?
(a) r (b) w (c) a

46. Which one of the following is true for *argc*?
    (a) Total number of arguments passed from command prompt
    (b) Total number of arguments passed by the user in the program
    (c) None of the above
47. Which arguments receive by `main()` function from command prompt?
    (a) argc and argv (b) apgc and apgv (c) None of the above
48. Which one of the following is correct way of declaration of `main()` when it receives commands from command prompt?
    (a) `int main( int argc, char *argv[])`
    (b) `int main(argc,argv)`
    (c) `main( int argc,int argv)`
49. What ***c*** stands in argc in the `int main(int argc, char *argv[])`?
    (a) Argument count (b) Integer count (c) Float count
50. What is the meaning of argv in the int `main( int argc, char *argv[])`?
    (a) It is a pointer to an array of character strings.
    (b) It is a pointer to an array of integers.
    (c) It is a pointer to an array of float numbers.
51. The different operations for files are ________.
    (a) Deletion of a file (b) Closing a file
    (c) Writing to a file (d) All of these
52. To perform operations on a file, we need to create a pointer variable of type ________.
    (a) file (b) File (c) FILE (d) None of these
53. The FILE is a ________.
    (a) Macro (b) Structure
    (c) Union (d) Function
54. The functions used in the file operation are in the header file ________.
    (a) `file.h` (b) `stdlib.h` (c) `stdio.h` (d) `conio.h`
55. The file can be opened in ________.
    (a) Append mode (b) Write mode
    (c) Read mode (d) All of these
56. To create a new file, we need to open it in ________.
    (a) Read mode (b) Write mode (c) Append mode (d) Both (b) and (c)
57. At the end of file, the character written has the ASCII value ________.
    (a) 0 (b) 26
    (c) 35 (d) 36
58. To read and write from a file, the functions used are ________.
    (a) `fgetc` and `fputc` (b) `fgets` and `fputs`
    (c) Both of these (d) None of these

59. The function used to read and write from a file are _________.

(a) `fscanf` and `fprintf` respectively (b) `fprintf` and `fscanf` respectively
(c) Both of the above (d) None of these

60. The 'EOF' is a _________.

(a) Constant (b) Structure
(c) Macro (d) None of these

61. What is the O/P of the following program?

```
/* //////// file.c ///////// */
void main()
{
    FILE *f;
    char c;
    clrscr();

    f = fopen("file.c","r");
    c = fgetc(f);
    printf("%c",c);

    if(c==EOF) printf("End");
    getch();
}
```

(a) The whole file content with end at last (b) v
(c) / (d) Compile error

62. For line-by-line input and output for a file, the functions used are _________.

(a) `fgetc` and `fputc` (b) `fgets` and `fputs`
(c) `fprintf` and `fscanf` (d) None of these

Answers

1. (b) 2. (a) 3. (a) 4. (a) 5. (b) 6. (b) 7. (a) 8. (a) 9. (a) 10. (a) 11. (a)
12. (b) 13. (a) 14. (a) 15. (b) 16. (a) 17. (a) 18. (a) 19. (b) 20. (d) 21. (a) 22. (a)
23. (a) 24. (a) 25. (a) 26. (a) 27. (a) 28. (b) 29. (a) 30. (b) 31. (a) 32. (a) 33. (b)
34. (b) 35. (b) 36. (a) 37. (a) 38. (b) 39. (b) 40. (a) 41. (b) 42. (c) 43. (a) 44. (b)
45. (c) 46. (a) 47. (a) 48. (a) 49. (a) 50. (a) 51. (d) 52. (c) 53. (b) 54. (c) 55. (d)
56. (d) 57. (b) 58. (c) 59. (a) 60. (a) 61. (c) 62. (b)

True or False

1. A file is a set of records.
2. The `FILE` pointer contains all information about file.
3. Without the file pointer, file can be operated in C.
4. In sequential file, data can be read directly.

5. In random file, the last record can be read first.
6. The fopen() is used to open file.
7. The statement FILE *p declares file pointer.
8. The “r” mode means file is opened for writing only.
9. The “w” mode opens a new file on the disk.
10. The function fputc() writes data to the file.
11. The fprintf() is similar to printf().
12. The function feof() finds the end of file.
13. The getw() is not associated with any file operation.
14. The SEEK_CUR indicates current position of the file pointer.
15. The ferror() reports error occurred during file read/write operation.
16. The function rewind() reverse the contents of file.
17. The “wb” creates a file in binary mode.
18. The O_APPEND is a low-level disk operation.
19. The argc and argv are not command line arguments.

Answers

1. True 2. True 3. False 4. False 5. True 6. True 7. True 8. False 9. True
10. True 11. False 12. True 13. False 14. True 15 .True 16. False 17. True 18. True
19. False

Additional Questions

What is/are the output/s of the following programs?

1.

```
#include <stdio.h>
#include <conio.h>
#include <process.h>
void main()
{
FILE *fp;
char c;
clrscr();

printf("Contents of file before appending :\n");
        fp=fopen("data.txt","w+");
        while(!feof(fp))
        {
```

```
        c=fgetc(fp);
        printf("%c",c);
        }
        fp=fopen("data.txt","a");
        if(fp==NULL)
        {
        printf("File can not appended");
        exit(1);
        }
printf("\n Enter string to append :");
        while(c!='.')
        {
        c=getche();
        fputc(c,fp);
        }
        fclose(fp);
printf("\n Contents of file After appending :\n");
        fp=fopen("data.txt","r");
        while(!feof(fp))
        {
        c=fgetc(fp);
        printf("%c",c);
        }
}

OUTPUT:
Contents of file before appending:
String is terminated with '\0'.
Enter string to append:
This character is called as NULL character.
Contents of file after appending:
String is terminated with '\0'.
This character is called as NULL character.
```

2.

```
#include <stdio.h>
#include <conio.h>
#include <process.h>
void main()
{
FILE *fp;
Char c=' ';
Clrscr();
```

```
fp=fopen("data.txt","w+");
if(fp==NULL)
{
printf("Can not open file");
exit(1);
}
printf("Write data & to stop press '.' :");
while(c!='.')
{
c=getche();
fputc(c,fp);
}
rewind(fp);
printf("\n Contents read :");
while(!feof(fp))
printf("%c",getc(fp));
}

OUTPUT:
Write data and to stop press '.': ABCDEFGHIJK.
Contents read : ABCDEFGHIJK.
```

3.

```
#include <stdio.h>
#include <conio.h>
#include <process.h>
void main()
{
FILE *fp;
char c=' ';
clrscr();
fp=fopen("data.txt","a+");
if(fp==NULL)
{
printf("Can not open file");
exit(1);
}
printf("Write data & to stop press '.' :");
while(c!='.')
{
c=getche();
fputc(c,fp);
}
```

```
printf("\n Contents read :");
rewind(fp);
while(!feof(fp))
printf("%c",getc(fp));
}

OUTPUT:
Write data and to stop press '.' : This is append and read
mode.
Contents read: This is append and read mode.
```

Find the bug/s in the following programs

1.

```
#include <stdio.h>
#include <conio.h>
#include <process.h>
void main()
{
FILE *fp;
char c=' ';
clrscr();
fp=fopen("data.txt","w");

if(fp==NULL)
{
 printf("Cannot read file");
 exit(0);
}
 printf("Write data  & to stop press . : ");
 while(c!='.')
 {
 c=getche();
 fputc(c,fp);
 }
 printf("\n Contents Read :");
 fp=fopen("data.txt","r");
 while(!feof(fp))
 printf("%c",getc(fp));
}
```

Bug: After writing data file should be closed

2.

```
#include <stdio.h>
#include <conio.h>
#include <process.h>
void main()
{
FILE *fp;
char c=' ';
clrscr();
fp=fopen("data.txt","w");

if(fp==NULL)
{
 printf("Cannot read file");
 exit(0);
}
 printf("Write data  & to stop press . : ");
 while(c!='.')
  {
  c=getche();
  fputc(c,fp);
  }
 printf("\n Contents Read :");
 fp=fopen ("data.txt","r");
 while(!feof(fp))
 printf("%c",getc(fp));
}
```

Bug: The file opening mode "w" is invalid

3.

```
#include <stdio.h>
#include <conio.h>

void main()
{
  FILE *fp;
char text[30];
clrscr();
fp=fopen("text.txt","w");
clrscr();
puts ("\n Enter Text Here ");
gets(text);
fprintf("%s",text);
}
```

Bug: The file pointer is missing in `fprintf()`

4.

```
#include <stdio.h>
#include <conio.h>
#include <process.h>

void main()
{
FILE *fp;
char c;
clrscr();
fp=fopen("text.txt","r");
if(fp==NULL)
{
 printf("\n cannot open file");
}
 while( (c=getc(fp)) !=EOF)
 printf("%c",c);
 fclose(fp);
}
```

`Bug:` In `if()` statement exit(0) statement is required

5.

```
#include <stdio.h>
#include <conio.h>
void main()
{
FILE *fr;
Char c,file[]="text.txt";
Fr=fopen(file,"w");
clrscr();
while(feof(fr))
{
c=fgetc(fr);
if(ferror(fr))
{
perror(file);
exit(0);
}
else
printf("%c",c);
}
fclose(fr);
}
```

`Bug:` while `(!eof(fr))` is correct condition

6.

```
#include <stdio.h>
#include <conio.h>

void main()
{
char buff[10];
clrscr();
setbuf(stdout,buff);
printf("This Book is very good");
fflush(stdout);
}
```

Bug: The size of the buffer is too small.

15

Graphics

1. What is a video display adapter?

Ans: Video display adapter is a card on motherboard of a computer. It is an expansion card on the motherboard. It consists of RAM, CPU etc. In short, it is used for processing graphics on monitor display. Nowadays, display adapter hardware is integrated in the motherboards of a computer.

2. Describe graphics display resolution of a monitor display.

Ans: It is the width and height dimensions of a computer monitor in pixels. A few standard sizes of VGA (video graphics array) are 640*480, 800*480, 800*600 etc. Extended graphics arrays with higher resolutions are available in the market. With higher resolution graphics adapter, the graphics processed will be sharper than VGA. Good quality pictures can be obtained with high-resolution adapters.

3. What are the functions of graphics.h header file?

Ans: The header file graphics.h is to be included at the beginning of the C program. This header file comprises the definitions and explanations of all the graphic functions, which we use in the C program.

```
graphics.h
initgraph()
gm, gm
```

4. Write the initialization procedure of graphics under C.

Ans: To switch over to the graphics mode, a function `initgraph()` must be invoked. It selects the best resolution and puts the corresponding number in gm, where gm is the graphics mode.

Prototype is defined in `"graphics.h"`. It is declared as follows:

```
void far initgraph(int far *gd, int far *gm, char far *pathtodriver);
```

where gd is graphics driver and gm is graph mode.

In real application, to detect graphics drives `DETECT` macro is used.

5. What are the functions of video display adapter?

Ans: The display adapter facilitates the programmer to show the various figures and text on the screen with different resolutions. Most of the adapters operate both in text and in graphic modes.

The clarity and quality of picture with VGA, SVGA, etc. are better than CGA and monochrome adapters. The display adapter transfers the information written by a processor to screen.

6. What are the display adapters available in the market?

Ans: VGA, XGA, SVGA, CGA and monochrome adapters.

7. What is the use of `line();` function. Give its declaration.

Ans: The function **`line()`** draws a line between two specified points. This function is declared as follows:

```
void far line(int x1, int y1, int x2, int y2);
```

Draws a line from ($x1$, $y1$) to ($x2$, $y2$) using the current colour, line style and thickness.

8. What is the use of `closegraph();` function. Give its declaration.

Ans: This `closegraph();` function shuts down the graphics system. The declaration is as follows. Prototype is defined in `"graphics.h"`.

```
void far closegraph(void);
```

9. What is the use of `restorecrtmode();` function. Give its declaration.

Ans: This function restores the screen mode to its pre-initgraph setting. Its prototype is defined in `"graphics.h"`. Its declaration is as follows:

```
void far restorecrtmode(void);
```

10. List a few graphics library functions and explain their details.

1. `circle();` – This function draws a circle at (x, y) of the given radius. It is declared as follows:
   ```
   void far bar(int left, int top, int right, int bottom);
   ```
2. `arc();` – This function draws an arc. It is declared as follows:
   ```
   void far outtextxy(int x, int y, char far *textstring);
   ```
   where (x, y) is the centre point. The variables sa and ea are the start and the end angles in degrees and variable *r* is the radius.
3. `ellipse();` – This function draws an elliptical arc. It is declared as follows:
   ```
   void far ellipse(int x, int y, int sa, int ea, int xr, int yr);
   ```
   where (x, y) is the centre point. The variables *sa* and *ea* are the start and end angles in degrees, respectively. The variables xr and yr are horizontal and vertical radii.
4. `bar();` – This function draws a bar using given co-ordinates. It can be declared as follows:
   ```
   void far bar(int left, int top, int right, int bottom);
   ```
5. `setcolor();` – This function sets the current drawing colour. It is declared as follows:
   ```
   void far setcolor(int color);
   ```
6. `outtextxy();` – This function displays a string at the specified location (graphics mode). It is declared as follows:
   ```
   void far outtextxy(int x, int y, char far *textstring);
   ```
7. `settextstyle();` – This function sets the current text attributes. It is declared as follows:
   ```
   void far settextstyle(int font, int direction, int fontsize);
   ```
8. `settextjustify();` – This function sets text justification for graphics mode. It is declared as follows:
   ```
   void far settextjustify(int horiz, int vert);
   ```
   It affects text output with `outtext()` function. Text is justified horizontally and vertically.
9. `getcolor();` – This function returns the current drawing colour. It is declared as follows:
   ```
   void far getcolor(void);
   ```

11. Write a program to draw the circle of the given radius.

Ans:

```
#include <stdio.h>
#include <conio.h>
#include <graphics.h>
void main()
{
    int gd =DETECT,gm,x,y;
    initgraph(&gd,&gm,"d:\turboc2\bgi");
setcolor(WHITE);
circle (160,260,35);
getch();
closegraph();
restorecrtmode();
}
```

Explanation: This program draws circle using given arguments.

12. Write a program to draw the line.

Ans:

```
#include <stdio.h>
#include <conio.h>
#include <graphics.h>
void main()
{
    int gd =DETECT,gm,x,y;
    initgraph(&gd,&gm,"d:\turboc2\bgi");
line (100,100,100,400);
getch();
closegraph();
restorecrtmode();
}
```

13. Write a program to draw ellipse.

Ans:

```
#include <stdio.h>
#include <conio.h>
#include <graphics.h>
void main()
```

```
{
    int gd =DETECT,gm,x,y;
    initgraph(&gd,&gm,"d:\turboc2\bgi");
    ellipse (100,100,100,300,300,200);
    getch();
    closegraph();
    restorecrtmode();
}
```

14. Using the loop, the drawn figure moves on the screen. Write a program to draw a circle and move it on the screen.

Ans:

```
#include <stdio.h>
#include <conio.h>
#include <graphics.h>
void main()
{
    int gd =DETECT,gm,x,y;
    initgraph(&gd,&gm,"d:\turboc2\bgi");
clrscr();
for (x=30;x<400;x+=10)
{
fillellipse (x,50,30,30);
sleep(1);
clrscr();
}
closegraph();
restorecrtmode();
}
```

Explanation: In this program, using `fillellipse()` function moon-like shape is drawn. Using the loop, the drawn figure moved on the screen. The `sleep()` function halts the execution for a second.

Multiple-choice Questions

1. Which of the following supports for displaying text and pictures?

   (a) DMA card (b) Video adapter card (c) Floppy controller card

2. High resolution of monitor provides _________.

   (a) Good quality of picture and text
   (b) Look wise monitor is elegant
   (c) More controls are provided to the monitor

3. Which of the following function should be invoked for graphics mode?
   (a) `initgraph()` (b) `restorecrtmode()` (c) `graphresult()`
4. Which of the following prototype is defined for using `closegraph()` function?
   (a) `graphics.h` (b) `stdio.h` (c) `conio.h`
5. How many arguments should be passed for drawing a bar in C using `bar()` function?
   (a) 3 (b) 4 (c) 5
6. The initialization of graphics under C is done with the function _________.
   (a) `loadgraph()` (b) `initgraph()` (c) `modegraph()`
7. Which of the following function is used to close the graphics mode in C?
   (a) `closeall()` (b) `closegraph()` (c) `cls()`
8. Video display unit is an _________ device of the computer system.
   (a) Input (b) Output (c) Input/output
9. Which of the following function returns maximum x screen coordinate?
   (a) `getmaxx()` (b) `getmayy()` (c) `getmaxy()`
10. Which of the following function returns an error code for the last failed graphics operation?
    (a) `graphresult()` (b) `error()` (c) `mistake()`
11. _________ returns maximum *y* screen coordinate.
    (a) `getmaxy()` (b) `getmaxx()` (c) `getmayy()`
12. Which of the following function displays a string at the specified location?
    (a) `outtextxy()` (b) `settextstyle()` (c) `setcolor()`
13. Which of the following function sets the current text attributes?
    (a) `settextstyle()` (b) `setcolor()` (c) `outtextxy()`
14. Which of the following function displays string at a specific location?
    (a) `settextstyle()` (b) `settextjustify()` (c) `outtextxy()`
15. Which of the following function should be used for filling a pattern with different colours?
    (a) `floodfill()` (b) `patfull()` (c) `patdif()`
16. Which of the following function checks whether the mouse drive is loaded?
    (a) `load()` (b) `initmouse()` (c) `start()`
17. Which of the following function defines the area in which mouse pointer can be pointer?
    (a) `areaload()` (b) `mousearea()` (c) `mouspoi()`

Answers

1. (b) 2. (a) 3. (a) 4. (a) 5. (b) 6. (a) 7. (b) 8. (b) 9. (a) 10. (a)
11. (a) 12. (a) 13. (a) 14. (c) 15. (a) 16. (b) 17. (b)

Index

D

E

F

N

O

P

R

S

T

U

V